Social History of Canada

H.V. Nelles, general editor

Peasant, Lord, and Merchant
Rural Society in Three Quebec Parishes, 1740–1840

Rural life in pre-industrial Quebec was essentially organized around
a feudal society. Allan Greer takes a close look at that society and
its economy in three parishes in the Lower Richelieu valley – Sorel,
St Ours, and St Denis – from 1740 to 1840. He finds a pronounced
pattern of household self-sufficiency; as in other peasant societies, the
habitants lived mainly from produce grown through their own
efforts on their own lands. How the family-based economy operated
and how the household was reproduced over the generations
through marriage, birth, inheritance, and colonization, together form
a major focus of this study.

The habitants were never entirely independent, however. Greer
shows that they were compelled to turn over part of what they grew
to support local seigneurs and priests. The 'feudal burden' of tithes,
rents, and other economic exactions, as well as the political domination that guaranteed them, was much more significant, according to
Greer, than earlier historians have allowed.

Into this world of aristocrats and self-sufficient peasants came mercantile capital, an intrusive force that was making its presence felt
over many parts of the globe at this time. Greer chronicles the activities of grain merchants and fur-traders in the Lower Richelieu and
finds them to be traditionalists who soon found a comfortable place
for themselves in the existing order. Growing commercial activity dissolved neither peasant self-sufficiency nor aristocratic ascendancy.
Instead, it created new lines of dependency through debt and often
hindered the emergence of a modern capitalist society. In stressing
the basic continuity of the structures of rural life prior to 1840, Greer
challenges two influential interpretations of Lower Canadian history,
both of which posit a fundamental break – either an agricultural
crisis or a rapid commercialization – around the turn of the nineteenth
century.

ALLAN GREER is a member of the Department of History at the
University of Toronto.

ALLAN GREER

Peasant, Lord, and Merchant: Rural Society in Three Quebec Parishes 1740–1840

UNIVERSITY OF TORONTO PRESS
Toronto Buffalo London

© University of Toronto Press 1985
Toronto Buffalo London
Printed in Canada

ISBN 0-8020-2559-5 (cloth)
ISBN 0-8020-6578-3 (paper)

COVER DRAWING
Habitants in their summer dress by John Lambert, from his *Travels through Lower Canada* ... (London 1810)
C1703 Public Archives Canada

Canadian Cataloguing in Publication Data

Greer, Allan
Peasant, lord, and merchant : rural society in three Quebec parishes, 1740–1840

INCLUDES BIBLIOGRAPHICAL REFERENCES AND INDEX
ISBN 0-8020-2559-5 (bound) – ISBN 0-8020-6578-3 (pbk.)

1. Quebec (Province) – Social conditions.   2. Quebec (Province) – Economic conditions – To 1867.   3. Richelieu River Valley (Richelieu, Quebec) – Social conditions.   4. Richelieu River Valley (Richelieu, Quebec) – Economic conditions.   5. Habitants – Quebec (Province) – Richelieu River Valley (Richelieu, Quebec).   I. Title.

HC117.Q4G74 1985   971.4'5102   C85–098751–2

Social History of Canada 39

This book has been published with the help of a grant from the Social Science Federation of Canada, using funds provided by the Social Sciences and Humanities Research Council of Canada, and a grant from the Andrew W. Mellon Foundation to the University of Toronto Press.

FOR BRENDA

Contents

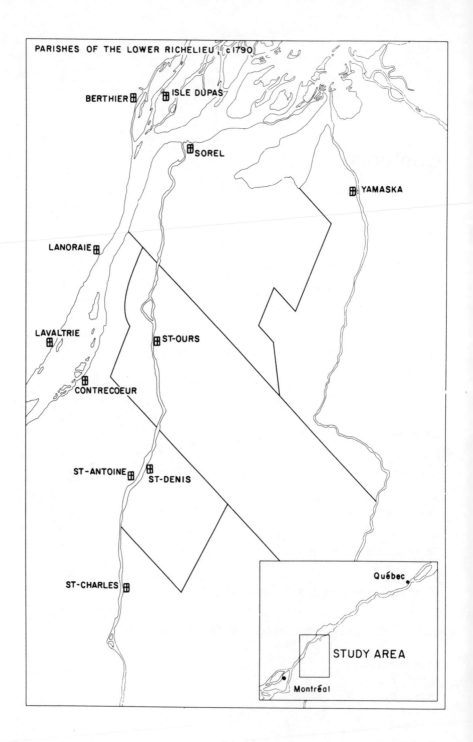

PARISHES OF THE LOWER RICHELIEU, c1790

BERTHIER
ISLE DUPAS
SOREL
YAMASKA
LANORAIE
LAVALTRIE
ST-OURS
CONTRECOEUR
ST-ANTOINE
ST-DENIS
ST-CHARLES

Québec
STUDY AREA
Montréal

Preface

Historians, sociologists, and anthropologists often speak of a 'traditional French-Canadian rural society' as if it were familiar and well known, and yet there are surprisingly few studies of the subject. Important work has been done or is under way on the Quebec countryside in the late nineteenth and twentieth centuries, when capitalism had transformed large sections of the peasantry into part-time wage-earners.[1] At the other end of the chronological scale, there is Louise Dechêne's magisterial volume on seventeenth-century Montreal.[2] Her monograph, dealing with a wide range of topics relating to the city and its environs, is primarily about the establishment of a colonial society. Between these two chronological extremes lies a long and relatively neglected epoch during which French civilization was firmly rooted in the soil of the St Lawrence valley, but before it had become a society of salaried workers and owners. This study of the Lower Richelieu region (Sorel, St Ours, and St Denis parishes) from 1740 to 1840 is situated in this pre-capitalist or 'traditional' period of Quebec's social evolution. It centres on one element of rural society, the habitants, settler-peasants who constituted the overwhelming majority of French Canada's population at that time.

The topic is certainly not a new one. The habitant has long suffered, not so much from historiographic neglect, as from superficial treatment. Every textbook has its paragraph or two about the sturdy, lazy, polite, brave, docile, extravagant, and independent habitant. But where do these characterizations originate? Invariably they are drawn from the writings of governors, intendants, bishops, or visiting gentlemen, and these upper-class observers had, in line with their own social perspective, particular expectations and reasons for being interested in the habitants. People of this sort naturally tended to view the peasantry, whether in Europe or in the wilds of Canada, as a *resource*. A military and an economic instrument, the peasantry was important mainly as a source of manpower and agricultural produce to support the aristocracy, the bourgeoisie, and their state. Thus, discussions of the habitants in letters, reports, and travel accounts generally revolve around questions of their martial valour, their agricultural productivity, and their disposition to obey or to rebel. Views changed somewhat over the years and from one observer to the next – writers of the French régime, for instance, were usually more interested in military potential, while British observers of the late eighteenth century had their eye on the capacity to grow grain surpluses – but always it is the peasants' usefulness to others that is at issue.

Using accounts of this sort, historians have put together portraits of the French-Canadian peasantry that emphasize various characteristics but retain the essential frame of reference provided by non-habitant sources. Were the habitants really indolent? Did they spend too much on fine clothes? Did they have too many horses? Were they bad farmers? The different schools of thought propose different answers, but too often the questions themselves have a built-in upper-class bias. Even quite recent work, using all the tools of modern 'scientific' scholarship, still retains much of the élitist perspective. For example, debates about the efficiency of habitant agriculture seldom take account of the purposes of husbandry for the habitants themselves. In a more subtle way, the peasants are relegated to the position of a resource when they, along with the sheep and oxen, are discussed under the heading 'Agriculture.'

It was in an attempt to get beyond this view from the manor and the counting house that I embarked on this study of habitant society and economy in pre-industrial Quebec. I wanted to find out more about country life 'from below' (to use the cliché of modern social history), that is, from the vantage point of the rural masses themselves. This led me, like other researchers of my generation, to explore previously neglected sources – abundant but often opaque – such as notarial contracts, parish registers, seigneurial estate records, and the correspondence of merchants and priests. It also led me to turn to the French social historians for methodological models. Finally, the literature from various countries and disciplines on 'peasant studies' was very helpful. Placing historical data on the Quebec peasantry into comparative perspective, I was able to test many widely held interpretations which have relied quite heavily on the supposedly unique features of French-Canadian society or on the special circumstances of the New World to explain developments in Quebec.

Were the habitants of pre-industrial French Canada truly peasants? That of course depends on what is understood by the term, and specialists are quite divided on the question of exactly what constitutes a peasantry. Are peasants to be recognized by their attitudes? their way of making a living? their wealth or lack of it? their power or powerlessness? their habitat? Are peasantries a 'cultural' type? a form of society? a class? Discussions continue about these issues but, for present purposes, I propose a definition distilled from the writings of several specialists who emphasize 'materialist' criteria.[3]

1 Peasants are small-scale agricultural producers who use simple equipment to grow crops and raise animals.

2 They generally work as a family.

3 Economically they are self-sufficient to a large degree, though not completely.

4 They possess the 'means of production,' particularly land, even if they do not own them. In other words, they manage their farms as they see fit – individually or collectively in a village community – but these may be subject to some form of domain that deprives the peasant of perfect ownership.

5 They are dominated and exploited, some of what they grow being appropriated to support privileged classes.

The habitants of the pre-industrial Lower Richelieu, as I hope to show, displayed all five of these traits and it is therefore proper to study them as a North American version of the peasant social type.

I shall argue further that these Canadian peasants were subject to a specific form of 'exploitation and domination' which I call 'feudal.' I have in mind a particular 'mode of production' found, inter alia, in western Europe from the Middle Ages until the time of the French Revolution. What could the Europe of the eleventh century have in common with Louis xv's France, never mind his North American colony? These societies, obviously different in so many respects, did stand upon fundamentally similar politico-economic bases. The hallmarks of the 'feudal mode of production' they shared are, in my view, a predominantly agrarian economy with self-sufficient peasant households as the primary productive unit, the ascendancy of a lay and clerical aristocracy, an overt and political system of redistribution which forced the peasantry to turn over some of its produce to the aristocracy and, finally, an ambiguous conception of land ownership that helped to legitimate this appropriation. In the pages that follow, I hope to flesh out this brief definition and show that it describes the eighteenth-century Lower Richelieu in its essentials.

Although my understanding of the term 'feudal' is in line with that of many European historians, mainly Marxists,[4] it may not be considered orthodox from the point of view of contemporary liberal historiography. The latter, following the lead of Marc Bloch and others, tends to see feudalism as a strictly medieval phenomenon. Emphasizing such characteristics as the fragmentation of state authority, the importance of personal ties of loyalty within the warrior class, the institution of serfdom, and the non-commercial 'natural economy,' this school would consider the peasant-aristocrat relations of eighteenth-century western Europe and its Canadian colony as, at the most, ghostly remnants of a feudal past.[5] All this demonstrates that words have different meanings for different writers. The Marxist conception of 'feudal' does seem to be truer than the Blochian definition to Early Modern usage (presumably the deputies of the National Assembly thought they were attacking something real when they 'abolished' feudalism on 4 August 1789).[6] In any case, it is surely futile to argue over the 'correct' definition of vocabulary. As long as it is clear what I mean by the word, readers who object to it may mentally substitute any term that seems more suitable where I have written 'feudal.' I myself am unable to think of a better way to describe a society, like that of the eighteenth-century Lower Richelieu, where the fundamental classes were self-sufficient peasants, on one side, and the priests and seigneurs they supported on the other.

Of course not everyone in the eighteenth-century Lower Richelieu belonged to one of the 'fundamental classes' of peasants and aristocrats. The region's social landscape also included a complement of artisans, 'professionals,' and merchants, but these groups played only an auxiliary role in the economy and, for a time at any rate, in the society. Businessmen in particular played an increasingly important role over the years. In fact, if there is a unique feature in the economic development of the Lower Richelieu (and, perhaps to a lesser extent, in rural Quebec generally), it lies in the rapidity with which this once commercially isolated area was brought into the world of buying, selling, and hiring. The intrusion of mercantile capital occurred mainly in the second half of the eighteenth century. Creightonian ideologies to the contrary, there was nothing very revolutionary, heroic, or even progressive about this thrust. The fur barons, the grain traders, and the local shopkeepers drew a profit from the feudal society they found in the Richelieu countryside and in certain respects they reinforced the existing exploitation and economic backwardness rather than challenging the dominion of the aristocrats. Their efforts certainly had an impact on local life, but there were few signs by the early nineteenth century of any developments in the direction of a genuinely capitalist order, that is, to 'a society producing commodities for exchange in the market, whose principal classes were capital-owning entrepreneurs and propertyless wage-earners.'[7]

The theme of this book then could best be summed up as the encounter of merchant capital with a feudal peasantry. The work is made up really of two parts; one of them, comprising the first five chapters, describes and analyses the 'original' feudal socio-economic structures of the eighteenth century. The second part, Chapters 6 to 8, deals with the intrusion of capital and its results. These two parts are conceptually distinct, but they do not coincide with neatly defined periods. Chronologically, centre stage tends to shift from the middle of the eighteenth century in the 'feudal' chapters to the turn of the nineteenth century in the second part, but it should be clear that there was always mercantile activity in the Lower Richelieu since the seventeenth century and that feudal structures had not disappeared by 1840, the terminal date for this study.

In the ideologically charged atmosphere of Quebec history, the characterization of the Richelieu as feudal could be misunderstood, for superficially similar interpretations have been used since the days of Parkman and Durham to justify the ascendancy of the English and the bourgeoisie in Canada. French-Canadian culture bears the imprint of a feudal past, so one school of thought maintains, and it is accordingly unprogressive and resistant to capitalism. The British Conquest offered liberation from the shackles of the past, but only the anglophone merchants grasped its promise and strove to attain within Quebec (Lower Canada) a supremacy that was right, proper, and natural, as well as beneficial to all sections of society. One problem with this position is that it adopts the point of view of the commercial bourgeoisie so completely as to regard *feudal* exactions as the only form of exploitation, *feudal* hierarchies as the only kind of inequality, and *feudal* stagnation as the only variety of economic backwardness.[8] My own insistence on the feudal aspects of rural society in early Canada, on the other hand, is not meant to identify any non-capitalist cultural legacy (what nation of European descent does not have a feudal past, after all?). Nor can it be construed, given the treatment of the mercantile element in the second half of this work, as an apology for the bourgeoisie.

This critical approach to the 'Montreal Merchants' suggests links with another powerful historiographical current, that of the middle-class nationalists of Quebec. It does lend support to the nationalist view that English capital gained a foothold in the country thanks to the defeat of France, and that the conquests of the British bourgeoisie spelled class and national oppression for the bulk of the canadiens. However, my conclusions about the feudal nature of early Canadian rural society are at odds with a central strand of most recent versions of the nationalist interpretation. In insisting on the leading role of the traders in New France before the British Conquest derailed the colony's 'normal' development, many nationalist historians play down the significance of seigneurial relations to the point of denying altogether the existence of any genuine feudal element. For these scholars, the habitant mass was made up of independent petty producers and, until the British took over, there was no real class antagonism, only rivalries within the colonial élite.[9] The implication almost seems to be that oppression was entirely an imported commodity in French Canada. A monograph on three rural parishes obviously cannot discuss all the issues involved in this position, but it can argue that exploitation, domination, and the clash of interests were characteristics of rural Canada since the early years of the French régime.

This study of the Lower Richelieu covers a variety of aspects of rural life, but there is certainly no pretense of providing a 'complete picture', an impossible achievement in any case. Economic matters receive the most attention, but, even in this area, more work needs to be done. Beyond the strictly material realm, there is no end to the subjects where a broadening or a deepening of the often rather sketchy analysis presented here seems desirable. Although there is a good deal in Chapter 3 about population patterns, inheritance, and migration, I am sure that a more specialized study making use of refined methods such as family reconstitution would provide much more precise and solid information on these topics. Undoubtedly, more could also be said about habitant 'cultural' life – religion, amusements, attitudes, and ideas – which are largely neglected here. Finally, I am most acutely aware of the need to know more about social tensions and overt struggles. Judicial records may some day tell us about confrontations between habitants and seigneurs, officials or merchants, but these sources do not lend themselves to a local study. Similarly, the parish monograph does not seem to be the best framework for a closer look at the habitant role in such dramatic events as the American invasion of 1775 or the rebellions of 1837–8. Indeed, the Lower Richelieu was a major centre of rural unrest on both these occasions, but, after attempting unsuccessfully to integrate them into this work, I concluded that both insurrections really need to be studied at the level of Quebec as a whole.

The local approach does indeed have drawbacks as a means of apprehending some phenomena, but it also has some clear advantages and it is hard to imagine a more practical way to study the structures of rural life and their mechanisms of change. I chose to study Sorel, St Ours, and St Denis for quite mundane reasons: they seemed to be exceptionally well documented. Furthermore, by covering three parishes instead of just one, I tripled my chances of finding source material on any given aspect of rural life; thus, I encountered easily accessible population records for Sorel, massive seigneurial archives for St Ours, and a rich collection of merchants' papers relating to St Denis.

There are always those who will ask of any community study, 'Is it representative?', usually without any clear idea of what a 'representative' parish would look like. Sorel, St Ours, and St Denis were certainly not typical in every respect of eighteenth-century Quebec, but of course no community was. On the other hand, travellers and government officials did not write of them as if they were particularly unusual. Every parish had its peculiarities and there were some interesting contrasts between Sorel and the other two localities that seem to reflect the importance of fur-trade labour in the former. Indeed, one of the advantages of the microscopic approach is that it makes possible this sort of analysis which would be impossible if data from heterogenous communities were always lumped together in aggregates. D.E.C. Eversley's remark about local population trends could equally be applied to other phenomena, such as economic fluctuations: 'National movements are the aggregates derived from these individual movements, but because they are averages of local experience, they may tend to hide the nature of the mechanism of change.'[10] Viewed from this angle, concern about the representativeness of local monographs could be turned around; we might well ask whether national or provincial data are 'representative' of the experience of any human communities. In other words, the problem of relating specific empirical research to broad theories and interpretations is in no sense peculiar to the community study. Whether they study national political campaigns, local death rates, or fluctuations in overseas trade, historians have to make judgments about how far the facts they uncover modify current views in the field.

A word about French words and phrases: in a book of this sort these are unavoidably numerous and it might be distracting to readers if they were all italicized. Most are therefore printed in ordinary type, the only exceptions being words, such as *engagement*, that occur in English with a different meaning.

ACKNOWLEDGMENTS

A great many individuals and institutions helped in the research and writing of this book and, although I cannot thank them all, I would like to mention a few. Archivists at the Public Archives of Canada and at various branches of the Archives nationales du Québec were most helpful and so were the people in charge of local Roman Catholic archives: Mgr J-C. Leclaire, curé, St-Pierre-de-Sorel; Mr R. Beauregard, curé, Immaculée-Conception-de-St-Ours; Mr D. Léveillé, curé, St-Denis-sur-Richelieu, and Mgr J-R. Choinière, chancelier, évêché de St-Hyacinthe. I am particularly grateful to these clergymen for it was hardly part of their job to open their records – and, in some cases, their homes – to visiting researchers. Funding for the research came from the Social Sciences and Humanities Research Council, the Queen Elizabeth Ontario Fellowship, and the University of Maine at Orono Summer Research Grants program.

Louise Dechêne, Brenda Gainer, Viv Nelles, Carmela Patrias, Wally Seccombe, and Arthur Silver were kind enough to read all or part of this book in draft form and, although I did not always follow their advice, I know their suggestions and comments greatly improved the argument and the style.

Like every work of scholarship, this one is partly the creation of the teachers who guided the author's intellectual apprenticeship. My graduate school mentors – J.F. Bosher, T.J.A. LeGoff, and Fernand Ouellet, in particular – therefore deserve recognition and thanks. I would also like to pay special tribute to the teachers, often forgotten on occasions of this sort, who succeeded in awakening an undergraduate's passion for history: E. J. Hundert, Daniel Klang, and Steven Straker, of the University of British Columbia, excellent historians and fine human beings.

Finally, let me offer warm thanks to my wife, Brenda. She gave me invaluable advice on statistics and computer work and helped in a thousand other ways.

PEASANT, LORD, AND MERCHANT

1

Introduction: seventeenth-century beginnings

THE ORIGINS OF RURAL CANADA

There is a sense in which French Canada is a creation of European merchant capital. Crossing the Atlantic on the first great wave of imperial expansion, Frenchmen established settlements on the St Lawrence in order to engage in the lucrative trade with the native Indians of the country. Tadoussac was founded and, in the early seventeenth century, Quebec and Trois-Rivières, to collect beaver pelts and other furs which commanded attractive prices in Europe. Although the French Crown set up chartered companies in an attempt to harness the fur trade to the imperialist ambitions of the state, and the Counter-Reformation Church did its best to attach a missionary enterprise to the commerce, business was still the main business of the colony. Moreover, furs remained Canada's principal export and the trade in pelts the economic life-blood of its cities for almost 200 years.

Rural Canada had a quite different origin however. It was the French monarchy, a centralizing administration standing at the top of a landed aristocracy, rather than the merchants of the Atlantic ports, that made New France into a settlement colony. Early efforts in this direction were frustrated. The government attempted at first to make a succession of chartered companies carry settlers to America as a condition of trading monopolies. Recent research shows that the Company of New France was not as negligent in this regard as had previously been supposed,[1] but the company nevertheless was unable to attach any sizeable French population to the little commercial colony. Most of the work of trapping animals, processing their skins, and transporting them to the coast was performed by self-supporting Indians. Therefore only a handful of Europeans was needed for this enterprise, and their food needs were limited. Accordingly, the fur 'staple trade' could give little encouragement to demographic growth or agricultural development. Under its auspices, Canada remained essentially a trading post, and a vulnerable one, attacked by Iroquois raiders and captured and held for a time by British free-booters. Only when young Louis xiv had secured control of his unruly kingdom and decided to take over direct rule of Canada in 1663 was a genuine 'New France,' with a sizeable European population, a rural and agrarian majority, and a social order resembling that of the mother coun-try, erected on the site staked out earlier by the fur traders.

This was indeed a revolution in the life of the St Lawrence colony. Within a decade, Louis' colonial minister Colbert reorganized Canada's administration, sent over a sizeable military contingent, vitalized colonial industry and agriculture, and saw to it that French immmigrants were established in unprecedented numbers. Fur-trade profits could scarcely have been the primary concern of the Crown, for these were quite paltry relative to the huge amounts France would have to spend on New France.[2] Trade was certainly one preoccupation of Colbert and his suc-cessors when they reinforced the North American colony, but so were territorial expansion, glory, and dynastic politics. Compared to the fabu-lously bountiful sugar islands of the West Indies, Canada emerged as a colony where, in the language of mercantilism, 'considerations of plenty' were less important than 'considerations of power.'

The rural Canada born of this royal intervention was the legitimate daughter of absolutist France; its social and economic structures were 'feudal' (in the post-medieval sense discussed in the preface) and es-sentially similar to those of the mother country. Of course there was still a place for the commercial element in New France after 1663, just as there was in Old France. Indeed the fur trade flourished and, despite some temporary setbacks, expanded for another century and a half. Most of the beaver and other pelts came from Indians living far to the west of the French settlements on the St Lawrence and consequently the commerce was scarcely affected by the growth of these settlements. Commercially, Montreal and Quebec remained what they had always been, stations in a trans-Atlantic trading system linking Europe with the Indian nations of the North American interior, and furs remained their major export. A small but active bourgeoisie inhabiting the towns de-voted itself to the accumulation of profits taken from these exchanges. Many ordinary settlers were also involved in the seventeenth century, as casual labourers or as independent traders on a small scale, but the role of the rural population tended to diminish in the late seventeenth century as the fur trade came more firmly under the control of the bourgeoisie. It was therefore in the towns primarily that the profit-centred commercial tradition of the original founders of French Canada was maintained.

Thus, both the urban / commercial and the agrarian / feudal elements of seventeenth-century France contributed to the founding of Canada and each left its mark on the colony. In the past, historians have often treated these two components of European society as antagonistic; traders were portrayed as struggling for progress and for freedom from lordly fetters on productivity. Lately, however, some scholars have argued that merchants and aristocrats were not essentially at odds.[3] Towns and the exchange economy, they assert, arose comfortably in the midst of medieval feudalism, their merchants indifferent to the way in which goods were produced as long as they could buy cheap and sell dear. Even in the early modern period, when French Canada was founded, a close but unequal relationship continued to exist in Europe between town and country, 'bourgeois' (literally, town dweller) and peasant; profits on exchanges, capitalist rents on land, interest on loans, and revenue from domestic crafts all tended to be drained from rural areas into the coffers of the merchant, giving the latter a substantial stake in the status quo.[4]

In early Canada, on the other hand, rural-urban relations of this sort seem to have been less important. The cities were so small and European trading partners so well supplied with grain that there was little market demand for agricultural produce until well into the eighteenth century. Moreover, merchants had a more profitable field of enterprise at hand in the fur trade and the haphazard staffing system of this commerce had only a limited effect on rural Canada until the late eighteenth century. No wonder then that Louise Dechêne concludes her study of seventeenth-century Montreal by emphasizing the duality of the region's economy and society; 'habitant' and 'marchand' lived at close quarters for many years without establishing intimate relations.[5] Not until the second half of the eighteenth century did Canada's merchant community begin to take an interest in the agrarian hinterland. Traders then went out into the countryside to sell imported goods, to buy grain, and to hire men for the fur canoes, and one of their favourite haunts was the area near the mouth of the Richelieu River, settled in Colbert's day by discharged soldiers.

MILITARY SETTLEMENTS ON THE ST LAWRENCE

As part of his program to establish a secure settlement colony on the foundation laid down by the fur trade, Louis xiv sent the Carignan Salières regiment in 1665 to protect Canada against its deadly enemy, the Iroquois confederacy. Fortified posts were established along the Richelieu River, traditional entrance to the St Lawrence valley for invaders from the south, and an expedition to the Iroquois country in 1666 brought the first solid victory for French Canada. From that time on the colony was no longer threatened with annihilation, although it remained vulnerable to locally devastating raids for another fifty years. Once the Iroquois had been defeated, it soon became official policy to use the Carignan Salières men to strengthen Canada in a different way, this time by building up the colony's rural population. Soldiers willing to marry and become permanent settlers were discharged and given land and other assistance, while officers, most of them nobles, generally received seigneuries, large estates under feudal tenure considered appropriate for military gentlemen. Soldier-colonists on the Roman model, these officers and men were established on the Iroquois frontier in the tongue of land where the Richelieu angles in to the St Lawrence. Varennes, Verchères, Contrecoeur, St Ours, Sorel, and Chambly were all Carignan settlements named after their officer-seigneurs.[6] Paternal links forged in the army were not abandoned in civilian life as the men of each company tended to cluster around their former captain, who usually provided each man with a farm-size lot in his seigneurie.

About seventy-five kilometres northeast of Montreal at the mouth of the Richelieu, the rural community of Sorel (or 'Saurel') grew up around the fortified post set up by Pierre de Saurel's company of the Carignan regiment in 1665. Even before it was settled, however, the site was one of considerable commercial and strategic importance. On the nearby island of St Ignace, Europeans and Indians used to meet at annual fur-trading fairs in the early seventeenth century, before the founding of Montreal. Iroquois war parties frequented the area and it was here that Samuel de Champlain and his allies first clashed with one in 1609. Several skirmishes followed; a French fort was built in 1642 and later abandoned, but French-Canadian control of the area really began only with the arrival of Pierre de Saurel and his men. Soon the transition from military outpost to rural settlement began; men married Canadian girls, built cabins, and attacked the tall pine forests that still stood in the way of the plough. 'Le sieur de Sorel,' the king was informed, 'a mis beaucoup de son bien et celui de ses amis à défricher les terres auprès du fort ... sur une concession qu'il demande pour se faire canadien perpetuel ...'[7] Twelve kilometres up the St Lawrence, Saurel's fellow officer, Pierre de St Ours, was at the head of another company of soldier-pioneers. Soon settlers from older Canadian communities were joining the Carignan men and their families at Sorel and St Ours.

A soil expert might well have deplored the choice of Sorel and St Ours as sites for agrarian settlements; there were certainly far richer lands awaiting colonization in New France. The south bank of the St Lawrence in this area is made up of a light, sandy soil unsuited for growing grain as it cannot hold moisture through the hot summer. But this was not a major problem in the early years. Virgin soils are always extremely fertile when first brought under cultivation and the sandy structure of those along the St Lawrence probably had the advantage of being easy to drain and easy to plough. To Gédéon de Catalogne, touring the colony in 1709, the lands around Sorel seemed 'très belle,' though later observers, visiting after the initial fertility had been exhausted, considered them among the poorest in the St Lawrence valley.[8] Sorel had an additional advantage in the archipelago of islands and shifting sand bars formed where the St Lawrence slows down as it enters Lake St Pierre. These islands, about half of them included in the seigneurie of Sorel, were a rich source of fish and wildfowl. 'Coastal' St Ours was not so well endowed but the seigneurie granted to Pierre de St Ours extended almost forty kilometres back from the St Lawrence, across the Richelieu, and as far as the Yamaska River. When the Richelieu valley was finally colonized in the eighteenth century, settlers encountered the rich soils formed of clay deposits left in prehistoric times by the receding Champlain Sea.[9] Unlike Sorel, St Ours eventually would have a thriving agricultural base but, in the seventeenth century, settlement was restricted to the seigneurie's worst lands.

Sorel and St Ours were in fact at the junction of two distinct natural regions, the St Lawrence-Lake St Pierre region and the Richelieu valley. Human geography eventually conformed to the environment: links tended to form through migration, intermarriage, and trade between Sorel and other communities on the St Lawrence such as Berthier and Yamaska. As population in the seigneurie of St Ours moved from the St Lawrence to the Richelieu, its fate was increasingly tied to that of villages (such as St Denis and St Antoine) further upstream. Contrasts developed between the rural societies of the St Lawrence and the Richelieu areas that provide some interesting opportunities for historical analysis.

Although a sensitivity to regional variations is vital, we should also recall some of the common characteristics of the climate and topography of the entire St Lawrence Lowlands (that is, all the settled area of New France). The surface of the land here is generally flat, favouring the unbroken extension of agrarian settlement. Rainfall is plentiful enough that irrigation is seldom required, whereas drainage is often a problem. Winters are long and cold, while the short summers are very hot. The Lower Richelieu has one of the mildest climates in Quebec, but the growing season is still only 190 days with a frost-free season beginning in the middle of May.[10] This climate dictates haste in sowing, ploughing, and harvesting between the departure and the return of winter; it also requires large quantities of fodder for stall-feeding livestock over an extended period. The settlers of the Lower Richelieu found various ways of adapting to this natural environment as they changed from soldier-pioneers to genuine peasants.

This adaptation and colonization took place within the legal and social framework of the seigneurie. Seigneurial institutions were of course neither ordained by God nor by nature; rather they were imposed on the Canadian countryside by deliberate government policy. Had it wished to do so, the government of Louis xiv could have used salaried officials to supervise the distribution of lands directly to settlers under allodial ('free') tenure. Indeed, more than one anti-feudal intendant proposed the abolition of seigneurial tenure as an obstacle to the development of New France.[11] The seigneurie never functioned as a unit of government administration and seigneurs were never, as some have argued, 'colonization agents' or local representatives of state power.[12] Instead, the colonial government, like the government of early modern France, relied on its own officials, as well as priests and militia officers, when dealing with rural communities.

Why then was seigneurial tenure established in Canada? To serve the same purpose it did in Old France, that of supporting an aristocracy by appropriating to it the surplus of peasant-producers. It seems only natural that representatives of the aristocrat-dominated French state would conceive of a settlement colony in accordance with a thousand-year-old view, still common in the seventeenth century, that saw society as properly composed of those who work, those who fight, and those who pray, the first group giving obedience and material support to the others.[13] If New France were to consist of more than fur traders and independent peasants, that is, if there were to be an ecclesiastic and lay aristocracy, feudal institutions would be an absolute necessity. The preamble to the title deed of Pierre de St Ours' fief makes it quite clear that this and other seigneurial concessions were designed to attract aristocrats to the colony and enable them to live 'nobly.' 'Sa majesté ... a fait passer en ce païs bon nombre de ses fidèles sujets officiers de ses trouppes dans le regiment de carignan et autres dont la pluspart se conformans aux grands et pieux desseins de sa Maté. voulans bien se lier au païs en y formant des terres et seigneuries d'une estendue proportionné à leur force ...'[14] In the early years there would, of course, be little surplus to extract from the settlers, and later, throughout most of the French régime, revenues from the land remained meagre due to the limited development of agricultural markets. This forced aristocrats to find other sources of income outside their estates. Nevertheless, seigneurial institutions did have the effect of transferring wealth – however small the aggregate amount – from direct producers to landlords.

Pierre de Saurel was one of the first to receive a seigneurie from the king. Though not, strictly speaking, a noble, this gentleman-warrior from Dauphiné had the ambiguous official status of one 'living nobly.' By acquiring a seigneurie and marrying Catherine LeGardeur, a daughter of a family by then already well established as a pillar of the Canadian noblesse, Saurel carved out a secure niche for himself in the colonial aristocracy. In 1668, three years after his arrival at the mouth of the Richelieu, Saurel had a manor house built there. A small log structure, it would have seemed rather modest standing next to a Loire chateau, but it was still three or four times the size of the settlers' cabins that surrounded it. Soon stables, a stone windmill, and a chapel were added to the collection of buildings in the 'fort de Saurel,' while colonists laboured to clear fields outside the walls. Mother Marie de l'Incarnation, writing in 1670, was clearly impressed:

Au fort de Chambly et à celui de M. de Saurel, qui sont de fort honnêtes gens [ie, well-born], on vit de ménage; on y trouve des boeufs, des vaches, de la volaille ... Ils ont de beaux lacs poissonneux et la chasse abonde en tout temps. L'on fait des chemins pour communiquer d'un fort à l'autre, les officiers y ont de fortes belles habitations et avancent leurs affaires par leurs alliances avec les familles du pays.[15]

It was only in 1672, however, that Pierre de Saurel was actually granted the lands at the mouth of the Richelieu as a fief. By this time he had been calling himself 'seigneur' and acting as such for several years. His ascendancy apparently was based largely on pre-existing (military) habits of subordination.

Saurel's neighbour, Pierre de St Ours, had an undisputed title to nobility. The oldest son of a Dauphiné family that could trace its noble status back to 1339, St Ours followed his ancestors into the profession of arms. Ordered with his regiment to the New World, he ended up settling in Canada even though he inherited an estate in France.[16] Unlike Pierre de Saurel, he fathered a large family, thus founding a dynasty of rich and powerful landlords and military officers that would play an influential role in Canadian affairs until the middle of the nineteenth century. For the patriarch himself, life as a seventeenth-century seigneur was anything but luxurious. Even though he was granted two fiefs, L'Assomption and Deschaillons, in addition to St Ours, Pierre de St Ours found it impossible to maintain an aristocratic level of existence on the paltry revenues they provided. In 1686 a sympathetic intendant wrote to the colonial minister:

Je dois rendre compte de l'extrême pauvreté de plusieurs nombreuses familles qui sont à la mendicité et toutes nobles ou vivant comme telles. La famille de M. de Saint-Ours est à la tête. Il est bon gentilhomme du Dauphiné ... chargé d'une femme et de dix enfants. Le père et la Mère me paraissent dans un véritable désespoir de leur pauvreté. Cependant ses enfants ne s'épargnent pas, car j'ai vu deux grandes filles couper les blés et tenir la charrue.[17]

This document is often cited by historians anxious to suggest that, far from exploiting the peasantry, the seigneurs of New France were beggars who worked the fields shoulder to shoulder with habitants, virtually their equals.[18] What is often forgotten is the class-specific nature of the definition of 'extrême pauvreté.' A noble would be viewed as indigent in circumstances that would be considered luxury for a peasant. Moreover, the incident of the daughters working in the fields was reported as though it were unusual and shocking rather than typical. The minister was being asked to do something about an intolerable situation and his response was generous; Pierre de St Ours received a gift of 100 écus from the royal treasury; later he and his sons were given lucrative positions as officers in the colonial troops as well as various fur-trading monopolies. Only by the second half of the eighteenth century could the seigneurs of St Ours lead a genteel existence on the revenues of their fiefs alone. In the seventeenth century, populations were so small, and the agrarian economy so undeveloped, that seigneurial incomes were necessarily low.

Since rental revenues were inadequate, demesne farms assumed a special importance for supplying the needs of seigneurial families. In

1681, Pierre de Sorel had 150 arpents of his own land under cultivation or in meadow. This was about twenty times the average arable of his habitant-tenants; it amounted to more than one-third of all the cleared land in the seigneurie. Besides providing grain, the demesne farm supported forty-three head of cattle, sixty-two sheep, and eighteen goats.[19] Considerable labour was required to work on an establishment of this size and the seigneurs of seventeenth-century Canada had at their disposal hired hands – often indentured servants – as well as corvée labour, in some cases where they were able to impose that feudal labour service on their peasants, and, occasionally, the efforts of members of the seigneurial family. Pierre de Sorel had six servants and his neighbour St Ours had three in 1681.[20] Demesne agriculture was not a truly seigneurial enterprise, but rather a direct exploitation of private property, a supplement to deficient seigneurial revenue. As rent-paying peasants became more numerous in the eighteenth century, and as indentured labour ceased to be available, demesne farms quickly declined in importance.

Although the prevalence of demesne agriculture suggests that the frontier seigneurie was economically weak, it was by no means a negligible social institution in the seventeenth century. Living in the midst of settlers, many of them former military subordinates, the first seigneurs of Sorel and St Ours did their best to organize community life around the manor house. The house itself seems in fact to have been far more than a private residence; a certain number of inhabitants lived as dependants under the lord's roof and the earliest religious services were celebrated there. Several elements of the economic infrastructure were provided under seigneurial auspices and served to reinforce the preeminence of the manor. The banal gristmill was the most important of these; Monsieur de Saurel had a windmill built next to his house as early as 1668 and his counterpart at St Ours followed suit in 1709. Pierre de St Ours even attempted to form a village settlement that would gather all his habitants around the manor. The settlers' passive resistance and the practical advantages of dispersed residence nullified that scheme, but the seigneur was more successful in his project of establishing a common pasture. In the early eighteenth century, he had a strip of land along the St Lawrence fenced off as a commons and began to charge adjoining tenants one day's corvée for the right to use it. This action too brought conflict with the habitants and a mass exodus to a different part of the seigneurie. Those who stayed apparently succeeded in having the degrading labour service removed, for, as of 1736, the records show a money payment of three livres being levied for the commons.[21] In Sorel too a common pasture under seigneurial auspices was a prominent feature of local agriculture in the seventeenth century, but it fell into disuse in the eighteenth. Justice was another seigneurial function exercised only in the early years of the settlement of the Lower Richelieu. Sorel and St Ours both appointed judges to settle disputes between habitants but, after 1711, there is no further mention of them.[22]

As a unit of society, the seventeenth-century seigneurie was important largely because of the weakness of other structures of authority; the state and, above all, the Church, were not strongly represented in the newly settled Lower Richelieu. Population being so scattered and the resources of the region so limited, there could be no question of establishing a resident curé in each village. Instead, missionaries, either secular priests or members of religious orders, did their best to minister to people in several seigneuries scattered over a wide area. Along with the fact that few missionaries remained long in the area, this arrangement naturally tended to minimize clerical influence in the countryside. According to a document dated 1683, both Sorel and St Ours happened to be bases for itinerant clerics.[23] One young missionary, appropriately named Monsieur Volant, was responsible for Rivière du Loup, Berthier, Autray, and St François, as well as Sorel where, in theory, he resided. In such circumstances, the most energetic pastor could have exercised little influence in the affairs of all these communities; even collecting his tithes would have been enormously difficult. Stationed nearby at St Ours was a Monsieur Duplein, who covered that seigneurie as well as Contrecoeur, Verchères, Lavaltrie, and Chambly. This priest boarded at the house of the seigneur, clearly a more important local figure. By this time (1683), there was a small wooden chapel, about the size of an eighteenth-century habitant's house, although originally mass was apparently celebrated in the manor house. The little churches at both St Ours and Sorel long remained in the shadow of the manor and Pierre de St Ours liked to refer to one of them as '*my* church.'[24]

For all his pre-eminence, the seventeenth-century seigneur was no local despot. Besides being controlled to some extent by the state, seigneurs were restrained by an aristocratic view of the world that stressed the obligations of the wealthy and powerful towards the 'humble folk.' In his will, written in 1721, shortly before his death, Pierre de St Ours set out instructions for his heirs that reflect conventionally paternalistic attitudes. 'Quant à ce qui regarde nos habitans je vous commande de les regarder comme vos propres enfants et de ne les molester pas et de les porter toujours à l'amour et à la paix.'[25] The cantankerous old seigneur doubtless meant this sincerely, but there was only one sense in which he lived up to his own precepts: he had treated his peasants as he treated his children, being sporadically at war with both groups during the last twenty years of his life. With his sons and daughters, Pierre de St Ours had disputes (over inheritance matters and over his decision, at the age of sixty-eight, to marry a seventeen-year-old girl) that could only be settled by the highest courts in the colony. Judicial records also have traces of conflicts with his 'censitaires' (as those who paid seigneurial dues were often called) over common pastures and over hunting and fishing rights. Early St Ours certainly was not a harmonious utopia in the wilderness, and to some extent this probably was due to the obstreperous character of its first seigneur.[26]

Although Pierre de St Ours did much to inflame relations with his habitants, he did not create the fundamental tensions. Since their relationship was, at bottom, one of subjection and exploitation, the interests of seigneurs and peasants could only be antagonistic, even if their relations were softened and regulated by routine deference and paternalism. Furthermore, the two groups often had different views on how the life of the community should be organized. The early seigneurs might consider themselves authorized to arrange things their own way but, like the curés of a later period, they often found their plans frustrated by the resistance of the habitants. In matters such as the attempt to form a nucleated village, peasant opposition emerged triumphant. Lest anyone attribute this to the 'Free Spirit of the Frontier,' I should add that such peasant opposition was just as strong – in many cases, much stronger – in hidebound old Europe.[27] Habitant resistance, then, was an additional factor, along with state regulation and ideological inhibitions, that limited the power of early seigneurs. Although the seigneur was no absolute ruler, the seventeenth-century seigneurie was, all the same, an institution of prime importance, the basic framework within which seigneurs and habitants, sometimes collaborating and sometimes contending, shaped the emerging communities of Sorel and St Ours.

For all its social and political importance, the early seigneurie could not extract any substantial revenues from a handful of unstable settlers. The emergence of a real landed aristocracy had to await the formation in the eighteenth century of a true peasantry with sedentary ways and an agrarian vocation. The original settlers were mostly soldiers and a disproportionate number of these had urban or, at least, non-agricultural backgrounds. There were, according to the 1681 census, three shoemakers, two surgeons, two weavers, two carpenters, a mason, a tanner, a ropemaker, a powdermaker, a toolmaker, a cooper, and a baker among only forty-nine heads of households in Sorel and St Ours.[28] Like all the other settlers, these men cleared and worked some land but they devoted much of their time to other pursuits. For example, Jean Réjasse dit Laprade of St Ours must have been more than a casual hunter for he hired his carpenter-neighbour Jean Duval to build a house and agreed to pay in game – six geese, eighteen ducks, and two dozen teal. The fur trade with the western Indians and the contraband commerce with Albany, New York, occupied other habitants, not to mention the seigneurs of Sorel and St Ours themselves.[29] This activity simply added to the population mobility normal in a frontier settlement. The records of a local notary show traces of this coming and going: a man sells all his property before moving to Acadia, another leaves his land to the local church in preparation for a journey 'ordered by the king', with the stipulation that he may reclaim it should he return alive. Frequent land sales also reflect the high degree of mobility.[30]

The conquest of the Lower Richelieu wilderness did not proceed rapidly in the seventeenth century. By the time of the 1681 census, when rural settlement was well established and population was growing rapidly on the lands around Montreal and Quebec, Sorel and St Ours had only twenty households each. Each settler had only three or four head of cattle and two to twelve arpents of cleared land. The mean extent of arable and meadow was only six and one half arpents in St Ours. Population growth was, for many years, not just slow, but indeed negative. Census figures, many of them imperfect for this period but good rough indicators all the same, show a downward trend in the last two decades of the century (see Appendix 1). To some extent this might be explained by the shortage of women in early New France. The census of 1681 indicates a combined sex ratio of 108 for Sorel and St Ours, admittedly only a moderate imbalance, but this figure includes a large number of small children; among adults the surplus of males was considerable and fourteen of the region's forty-eight households (29 per cent) were composed of single men living alone. A much more fundamental cause of stagnation was the continuing Iroquois menace, which led many habitants to abandon the area and move to more secure parts of New France.

Until the beginning of the eighteenth century, the Lower Richelieu was still an exposed frontier. In 1691, for example, Iroquois raiders burned several houses in St Ours and Contrecoeur and carried away nine captives. Travelling up the St Lawrence ten years later, an officer from France was evidently quite nervous as he passed Sorel's islands at the entrance to Lake St Pierre.

Lors que l'on a quitté cet Archipel qui sert de retraites aux Iroquois, on trouve du côté sud la Seigneurie de Sorel. Tous les habitans de ce gouvernement sont renfermez dans des Forts, palissadez de pieux, de douze à quinze pieds, pour être à l'abris des Iroquois; de sorte qu'il y a très-peu de maisons à la campagne. Le Fort de Sorel est à l'embouchure de la rivière de Richelieu ... que l'on apelle encore la rivière des Iroquois ...[31]

Because of its strategic importance, Sorel had a fortified post and a small garrison through all of the French régime and much of the British as well.

FRENCHMEN INTO PEASANTS

In the early eighteenth century, when Indian incursions ceased, habitants began moving out of the fort and setting up houses by the water's side on their long narrow farms. The habitants of St Ours acted similarly, much to the annoyance of their seigneur, whose plans called for a compact village. Partly in reaction to the imposition of the commons charge on lots along the St Lawrence, many began moving further from the proposed village, across the narrow neck of land to the shores of the Richelieu. Another motive for relocation was probably the superior quality of Richelieu soils in the area now freed of Iroquois terror. As of 1721 there was only one St Ours family living on the Richelieu but twelve others were clearing farms there while continuing to reside on the St Lawrence.[32] Within ten years the balance of population had shifted in favour of the new settlement, now called 'Petit St Ours.' A church was established on the Richelieu in 1740; later it was surrounded by a village as colonization in the seigneurie pushed further to the southeast. By the time of the English conquest, little was left of the original settlement, misleadingly christened 'Grand St Ours.' 'Most of the habitations are abandon'd,' observed a passerby, 'except eight or ten which are so very miserable that they scarsly deserve to be number'd.'[33]

This mini-migration within the seigneurie of St Ours was part of a larger stream of population into the Richelieu valley. Beginning about 1720, colonists started occupying the area from Sorel up to the once isolated seventeenth-century settlement of Chambly; they lost no time in establishing farms and pushing the forest back from both banks of the river. By 1749, Peter Kalm remarked that the Richelieu was as densely populated as the St Lawrence.[34] The movement of population was never massive; people came, it seems, as families, not in large groups. This was a time when immigration from France had largely ceased and, accordingly, most of the newcomers were Canadian-born. Most, in fact, came from nearby parts of the colony. To the south of St Ours, Contrecoeur habitants settled the back of their seigneurie where it ended at the Richelieu (this part of the seigneurie would later form the parish of St Antoine). Across the river from Contrecoeur (St Antoine) and adjacent to St Ours, the seigneurie of St Denis received its first pioneers in 1720, most of them coming from the Carignan settlements on the St Lawrence between Varennes and St Ours. In 1740, there were twenty-one families at St Denis and all the lands along the river had been occupied.

Thus, St Denis was an eighteenth-century seigneurie even though it had been granted by the Crown in 1695 when it was still wilderness.[35] Its development differed significantly from that of Sorel and St Ours, colonized eighty years earlier. Smaller and blessed with more fertile soils than the other communities, St Denis began life only after the region had been secured against Iroquois raids. Its settlement therefore was quite rapid and, presumably, it was a paying proposition for the seigneur from an early date. On the other hand, the seigneur and the seigneurie seem to have played a less significant role in shaping the rural community here than they did in Sorel and St Ours. This is partly because St Denis did not have a resident seigneur until the nineteenth century. As soon as the fief had enough settlers to make it worth selling, it was sold, in 1736, to Claude-Pierre Pécaudy, seigneur of Contrecoeur and grandson of a Carignan Salières captain. For as long as seigneurial tenure survived in Quebec, St Denis remained in the same family line and, for many years, it essentially formed a rear annex to the seigneurie of Contrecoeur. A second factor explaining the weakness of the seigneurie as a community institution is the rapidity with which a strong parish organization was established, only twenty years after the first settlement. Although they were never important local leaders, the eighteenth-century seigneurs of St Denis nevertheless benefited materially from the region's rapid development.

In the first half of the century, the development of the Lower Richelieu meant, for one thing, the expansion of a rural population, an expansion that not only colonized new areas like St Denis, but also increased the density and solidity of the old settlements like Sorel. As life became more secure, a trickle of immigrants came to the area and fewer residents departed. Natural increase was a more important source of demographic growth, however. Population grew and so necessarily did the region's agricultural production. Hunting and fishing could not support a dense

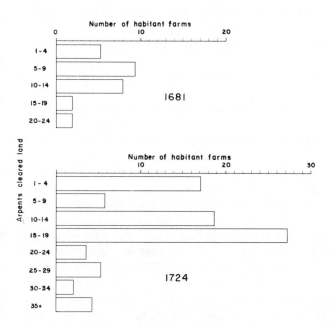

FIGURE I

CLEARED LAND ON HABITANT FARMS, SOREL, 1681, 1724.

population, even assuming that the seigneur would permit it. The fur trade provided limited opportunities for employment and these were increasingly monopolized by men from the Montreal and Trois-Rivières areas. Accordingly, farming became the main – almost the only – economic activity of the habitants of the Lower Richelieu. For the most part, they raised crops and animals to supply their own household consumption needs and meet the seigneur's demands, while perhaps selling any surplus when this was possible. As of 1720, land concession deeds in the seigneurie of St Ours began to specify annual rents mainly in measures of wheat. Clearly this was a favour to cultivators who had difficulty making payments in any other form; other deeds mention a penalty for paying money dues in grain.[36] Habitant society was, by this time, thoroughly agrarian.

This development is reflected in the records on land use as well. Between 1681 and 1724, the number of habitant farms in Sorel increased significantly and so did the size of cleared arable per holding (see Figure 1).[37] There was a good number of settlers in the initial stages of establishing a farm at the later date but, in the older parts of the seigneurie, the tendency was for cleared areas to cluster in the fifteen to nineteen arpent range, about the size of arable needed at this stage to support a family comfortably. Leaving aside the large seigneurial demesne, the mean extent of land under cultivation and in meadow was 16.1 arpents for Sorel's eighty-two households in 1724, up from 9.2 arpents four decades earlier. Somewhere between 1681 and 1724, it seems, Sorel's settlers crossed the threshold leading to agricultural self-sufficiency.

Just when the seigneuries of the Lower Richelieu became more densely populated and more thoroughly agricultural in the first half of the eighteenth century, beginning to provide important revenues to their seigneurs, the seigneurie gave way to the parish as the main unit of community life. It was only in 1722 that Sorel and St Ours, like most areas of rural Canada, were organized into parishes. Parochial boundaries followed the long-established seigneurial geography quite closely. A small point of land in the seigneurie of Yamaska but accessible only from Sorel was added to the parish of Sorel, but otherwise parish and seigneurie coincided for many years. Pieces were eventually detached from the sprawling seigneurie of St Ours in 1749 and 1822; Sorel too was subdivided in the 1840s, while St Denis' boundaries remained those of the seigneurie for more than a century after the establishment of the parish in 1740. Although the parochial organization was originally superimposed on the pre-existent seigneurial framework, the parish became a more important unit of community life over the course of the eighteenth century. For many years after 1722 it was still common for curés to be assigned two adjoining parishes, but gradually, as trained clergy became more numerous and as population and agricultural productivity increased, priests could be attached to individual parishes and subsist on the tithes they provided. With a permanently established full-time officer, the ecclesiastical unit took on added weight. There was also a very important lay component to eighteenth-century parish life. Official vestries were established in the Lower Richelieu in this period; larger and more solid churches and rectories were built with all the elaborate financing and assessment procedures that implied. At the end of the century, the church and even the rectory were the most prominent local landmarks, dwarfing the seigneurial manor house in those villages that still had resident seigneurs.

In 1740, when St Denis and 'Petit' St Ours on the Richelieu were set up as parishes, the transformation of the Lower Richelieu from a collection of insecure encampments to a firmly rooted facsimile of western

European rural society was more or less complete. The initial assault on the wilderness was over, and, after seventy years of colonizing efforts, almost all the river-front lands had been occupied in the three seigneuries of Sorel, St Ours, and St Denis. In a few years new farms would begin to emerge along a second row, back from the Richelieu in St Denis. Down the river in Sorel, on the other hand, there was still a virgin stand of red pine extending over a league that was reserved to supply masts for the king's navy. Generally, however, someone travelling past in a boat would have seen a regular succession of small log houses and fairly continuous fields that went back 200 to 300 metres, occasionally as far as a kilometre.[38] An entire generation had grown up free from the menace of Iroquois attack. With security came greater stability and a rising population, its expansion fed primarily by a vigorous natural growth, but also by some immigration from older Canadian settlements. Agriculture was now the chief pursuit of almost all the inhabitants of the area; the original craftsmen and army veterans-turned-settlers had been replaced by a new generation of Canadian-born peasants for whom hunting, fur-trading, and smuggling were at most marginal activities. A European rural society had emerged in this corner of the New World and it was one whose life centred on the self-sufficient peasant household.

2

The peasant family household

Almost all the land in the eighteenth-century Lower Richelieu was in the possession of the peasantry. At the time of the 1765 census, there were two parish priests in the region and neither had any land. The seigneurs of Sorel and St Ours owned demesnes that were not much larger than a habitant farm and one shopkeeper possessed a lot of about the same size. Otherwise, cleared land belonged to the peasants themselves, subject of course to the lordship of a local seigneur. Moreover, not only did the land belong to the peasants, the great majority of peasant families possessed land. Leaving aside the priests and seigneurs, the census lists 312 households in Sorel, St Ours, and St Denis and only twenty of these (6.4 per cent) lacked real property.[1] Since many of the landless were likely artisans, it seems clear that agricultural families in the region were, with very few exceptions, land-owning families.

Not only did the land belong to the peasants, it was distributed among them fairly evenly. Once more the 1765 census is our source. It indicates that, at a particular point in time, the size of farms in each of the three seigneuries tended to cluster within a certain range, sixty to seventy-nine arpents in Sorel, and 100 to 149 arpents in St Ours and St Denis (see Table 1). This was certainly not complete uniformity. Some families held properties far larger than the local average but, as we shall see, extensive holdings did not normally represent large-scale farming so much as temporary concentrations intended to be divided among several sons. Even though there was a certain degree of variation, it is notable that very few habitants had less than sixty arpents or more than 250. In the context of eighteenth-century Canada, these two values could be

TABLE 1
Habitant land holdings: Sorel, St Ours, and St Denis 1765

Arpents	Sorel (%)	St Ours (%)	St Denis (%)
0–19	3	2	2
20–39	5	1	0
40–59	9	4	2
60–79	38	10	8
80–99	20	30	16
100–49	17	36	34
150–249	8	15	32
250 +	0	2	6
	100	100	100
Habitant households	130	93	50

considered the lower and upper limits of a family farm; less than sixty arpents would not normally support a household while more than 250 would require more labour than a family could handle. Unlike rural France in the eighteenth century then, with its fragmented peasantry composed of rich 'laboureurs,' landless proletarians, and an array of 'haricotiers,' 'bordiers,' and other intermediate groups scrambling to get by on a combination of revenues from handicrafts and the produce of their own small plots, the Lower Richelieu was inhabited by a largely homogeneous class of cultivators living in self-sufficient households, each possessing enough land to live on but not enough to dominate others.

Who lived in an eighteenth-century habitant household? To date, no analysis of rural household structures has been undertaken, mainly because there are no nominal census rolls for the period between 1681 and 1851. Local listings may exist for the intervening years, but none was located for the parishes of the Lower Richelieu. Instead we are left once more with the laconic census of 1765. Although they provide no information on ages or kin relationship, the 1765 census rolls do give some indications of household composition. For each household, members are classified under the following headings: men, women, male children, male servants over fifteen, male servants under fifteen, female servants, and strangers. The last category, 'étrangers,' clearly does not mean 'foreigners' since they are scattered fairly evenly, one here one there, through the rural parishes of Canada in houses where the family head has a French name; instead, the term seems to denote visitors or lodgers, people who are neither blood relatives nor hired employees. There are

TABLE 2
(Married) men and women per habitant household, Sorel 1765

	N	Per cent
0 men, 1 woman	3	2.3
1 man, 0 women	9	6.9
1 man, 1 woman	97	74.6
1 man, 2 women	2	1.5
2 men, 0 women	1	0.7
2 men, 1 woman	9	6.9
2 men, 2 women	7	5.4
3 men, 1 woman	1	0.7
3 men, 2 women	1	0.7
	130	99.7

not very many of these strangers (four in all the Lower Richelieu), but the fact that the census had a column for them suggests that the remaining categories concern kin and servants only. The 'men' and 'women' enumerated in the returns therefore would be related to the household head and, furthermore, they were probably all married or widowed since unmarried sons or daughters would appear in the columns for 'children.' 'Strangers' were very rare and servants, as we shall see, were not very common in the peasant households of the Lower Richelieu. It therefore seems reasonable to conclude that the habitant household was primarily a kin grouping; in other words, 'family' and 'household' denote virtually the same thing.

Household size and structure is another subject for which the 1765 census provides information that is suggestive but not susceptible to precise quantitative analysis. It shows us, for example in the parish of Sorel, that 75 per cent of the peasant households had one 'man,' one 'woman' (presumably a married couple) plus their children and any servants (see Table 2). There were a few families headed by a single man or woman (mostly widows) as well as a substantial minority (15 per cent) of households with two men and / or two women. The latter configuration likely signals family households with two generations of married people: an elderly father, mother, or both, if they survived, living with a son or daughter and their spouse and children. Since less than 2 per cent of the households had three men (none had three women), it does not seem to have been common for more than one grown offspring to stay with retired parents. Instead, the nineteen three-generation households suggest a 'stem-family' pattern where a single child would inherit the family farm and stay with his parents while his brothers and sisters would leave home on marrying. Since it was less common than the single-couple household, it might appear that the stem family was unusual or abnormal, but research on other peasantries suggests that, even where the stem pattern predominates, a static listing like a census neglects the mutations that alter a family's structure as it develops through certain stages. Thus the 'snapshot' of Sorel in 1765 may mask the fact that many (or most) of the single-couple households either had previously included parents who had died or would later be joined by elderly parents.

The next chapter will deal with the ways in which the habitant household was reproduced from one generation to the next, but it is important to note here that, even in the shorter term and within a particular family, the evolving 'developmental cycle' altered the shape of a household and was an important factor conditioning the peasant economy. As a couple marries and begins to have babies, the number of mouths to feed or, more generally, the family's consumption needs, grow. Eventually the children become big enough to help out with farm work. Later the children will tend to marry and most of them will leave home. Thus the household's consumption requirements expand and contract over the years and so does its labour supply, but not simultaneously. The Russian economist A.V. Chayanov saw the changing ratio of consumers and workers as the central problem of the peasant economy and he argued that adjustments in the extent of land holdings helped to maintain an equilibrium.[2] Chayanov has been criticized for neglecting the ambient society, with its landlords and day-labourers, that influences the peasant household; still, there is no denying the significance of his insights into the ways in which the demographic dynamics of the peasant family make it much easier for a family to feed its members and produce a surplus at some stages of its development than at others. Thus, when we encounter evidence of inequalities of wealth, of land holdings, or of agricultural production among the habitant families of the Lower Richelieu, we must remember that the discrepancies to some extent reflect different points in the progress from newlyweds to dotards.

What about 'servants,' hired labourers living and working with a peasant family? The main thing about servants in the eighteenth-century Lower Richelieu is their scarcity. They accounted for 4.1 per cent of the region's population in 1765 and 3.6 per cent in 1784.[3] Viewed from a different angle, 13.5 per cent of the 273 habitant households of Sorel, St Denis, and Petit St Ours had one or more servants in 1765. Why did some families have employees while most did not? One hypothesis would be that servants were hired to make up for deficiencies in the family labour force resulting from sterility, premature death, or the vagaries of the developmental cycle. If this were the case, families with servants should tend to be smaller than those lacking them. The evidence does not bear this out however:

	N	Mean size	Standard deviation
Families with servants	37	4.89	2.52
Families without servants	236	4.81	2.42

Thus it is not clear what led some habitants to hire unrelated workers to share their homes and their chores, but it is clear that they were not numerous.

This does not mean that all the work around habitant farms was always done by family members alone. Census figures on resident workers only tell part of the story here. Day labourers were commonly hired for short periods, particularly at harvest time. It was not always the poor working for the rich either; sometimes habitants lacking oxen had to pay a more fortunate neighbour to come and plough their fields.[4]

The wage relationship between employer and worker would often be bound up with personal connections of a different sort. There was, for example, a lawsuit about the time of the British conquest of Canada that arose from a misunderstanding about the arrangement between a habitant and his helper. We hear about it from the point of view of the defendant, a habitant who was being sued for wages by a young man named Jean-Marie, 'un garçon ambulant et traficant.'[5] The peddlar had stayed with the peasant family for three months, using their home as a base as he went out selling his wares. In return for being fed and housed and having his washing done, Jean-Marie was glad to help out around the farm. (So says his 'host,' our informant, at any rate.) He even 'lent a hand' during the harvest but then, to the peasant's surprise, he expected payment beyond the hospitality he had already received. What the judges decided in this case is not known, but that does not alter its value in illustrating the uncertain nature of wage labour in this pre-capitalist rural society. Was Jean-Marie a guest or a servant? As long as the categories remained ill defined, there could be no simple answer to such a question. The wage connection was known here but it did not dominate society;

instead society dominated it. Work was normally a duty towards a human group, in this case the peasant household to which Jean-Marie temporarily attached himself, not a commodity to be bought and sold.

Work, then, was primarily, though not exclusively, a family affair. Not only was wage labour fairly unimportant, but French-Canadian agriculture had hardly a trace of the communal practices that were so common in Western Europe and even in early New England. Farmsteads in the Lower Richelieu were entirely self-contained and surrounded with post and rail fences. Although officials and agricultural reformers complained throughout the eighteenth century of the custom of *vaine pâture* by which animals were allowed free access to all fields between October and May, this practice was limited to the vicinity of Montreal except in the early years of New France.[6] In the Lower Richelieu, enclosure was always the rule and the only departures from 'agrarian individualism' were the common pastures and meadows established by the seigneurs of Sorel and St Ours in the seventeenth century. In Grand St Ours, peasants could graze their cattle on a strip of land along the St Lawrence and could cut hay on an island in the river, but only those living near these facilities – a small proportion of the seigneurie's population – ever made use of them. The island pasture of Sorel was no longer used at all by the end of the eighteenth century.[7] No doubt there was some co-operation among neighbouring and related families, but I found no mention in the records of the Lower Richelieu of the 'bees' that were so often remarked upon by observers of pioneer life in Upper Canada and the American Mid-West. Here, much more than in most rural societies, the family household was the fundamental unit of agricultural production. Consequently, the habitant family and the farm that was its material base deserve close scrutiny; one means of dealing with them is by describing a specific example.

Théophile Allaire was the legal head of a typical rustic household in mid-eighteenth-century St Ours. His family may have been somewhat poorer than average, but its farm was laid out and operated in essentially the same way as those of other habitants of the period. Born in 1722 at St François on the Ile d'Orléans near Quebec, Théophile was the twelfth of fifteen children. The Ile d'Orléans was one of the oldest rural settlements in Canada and it was already showing signs of overcrowding in the early eighteenth century; the family moved west when Théophile was three years old and settled in the seigneurie of St Ours on the left bank of the Richelieu, where settlement had only begun about five years earlier.[8] The youngest of five boys surviving to adulthood, Théophile did not enjoy all the advantages conferred on his older brothers; he was fairly old when he finally received a modest portion detached from his father's large concession. Accordingly, Allaire only married in 1753, when he was thirty-one years old. His first wife, Amable Ménard, died six years after the marriage but Théophile remarried, to Félicité Audet, in 1761. Another six years passed and another death occurred, this time Théophile's (1767). Two deaths in one decade meant two inventories of the possessions owned jointly by Théophile Allaire and each of his wives.[9] The inventories, notarized documents required by the laws governing inheritance, along with the intervening census report of 1765, give us an opportunity to examine the material basis of one habitant household and its changes over time.

The inventory of 1762 shows that Théophile Allaire's farm was only sixty arpents, small by St Ours standards, but quite adequate to support a family in this very fertile section of the parish. A long and narrow rectangle like all Canadian farms, the lot occupied only two linear arpents along the Richelieu, but stretched westward back from the river fifteen times that distance; Théophile could have stridden across his domain without taking much more than a hundred paces but he would have had a mile hike going from front to back. The elongated shape of their farm had a number of advantages for the Allaire family. Of course, it gave them access to the river, the most important transportation corridor and a source of drinking water, but it also had other features that made it useful to the habitants who were then settling new rows of long lots away from the river. Surveying a whole row of lots was a simple matter of laying out one frontage line and placing markers along it. The burden of road-building and maintenance, a legal obligation of proprietors whose land was crossed by the right-of-way, was minimized. Even agricultural work was lightened as long furrows could be ploughed with a minimum of troublesome turns.[10] Moreover, fields received plenty of sunlight, even in the early stages of colonization for, unlike nineteenth-century Upper Canada where settlers often began with gloomy clearings in the middle of a squarish lot, clearance was normally continuous on adjoining farms, leaving a broad swath of arable that was gradually expanded back into the retreating forest. Socially, the French-Canadian cadastral pattern had the effect of facilitating contacts between neighbours. Since houses were always built at the front of farms, near the road – which in Allaire's case passed along the edge of the Richelieu – it would seldom be more than one or two hundred metres from one door to the next. On their doorstep, Théophile and Félicité then would have been within sight of a large number of farmhouses and they would have been able to carry on a shouted conversation with their nearest neighbours. Relations with their next-door neighbour, Nicolas Thibault, seem to have been particularly close; he witnessed their marriage contract and married Théophile's sister. The arrangement of land in rows of long thin lots produced rural communities that combined some of the sociability of village life with the practical convenience of residence at the place of work.

Since they lived far from the seigneurial commons, the Allaires would have had to graze their animals on their own land, on the arable after the grain harvest, and in the woods and brush at the back of the lot in other seasons. About half the farm (thirty-three arpents) was still un-cleared forest at the time of the inventory of 1762. Nevertheless, it con-stituted a vital resource and was used, not only as wasteland pasture, but also as a source of firewood, fencing, and building materials and perhaps, if the Allaires were lucky enough to have some maples, of sugar. Woodlots at the back of a farm or on a separate property were the only source of wood in the Lower Richelieu since hedgerows and shade trees were never permitted near the house and arable. French-Canadian settlers seemed determined to eradicate all traces of their old enemy, the forest, and the treeless vistas of much of rural Quebec today show how successful they were. One estimate has suggested that a seventeenth-century family would need a thirty-arpent woodlot to main-tain a continuous and self-renewing supply of wood and so the Allaires' uncleared land would have been just about the right size.[11] Shortly before he died five years later, Théophile cut down all the trees in his woodlot and expanded the arable to thirty-five arpents, leaving the rest in brush. He only did this after assuring a new fuel supply by obtaining an eighty-arpent lot across the river in a newly opened section of the seigneurie. Two boys had been born since 1762, Félicité's and Théophile's first male children, and they may have had their sons' futures in mind when they acquired a second piece of land.

The cleared land (twenty-seven arpents in 1762) was divided into several sections, ploughland, fallow, meadow, and garden, with rather impermanent fences marking the limits of each. Fences seem to have been moved or replaced quite frequently to allow cattle into the grain fields after the harvest and to adjust the size and location of the different parts of the arable. A crucial element in the family's provisioning system, the garden occupied a small patch of ground – perhaps half an arpent – near the house. Another five or six arpents of the Allaire farm would be a meadow, producing the enormous quantities of hay required for winter stall-feeding. At least part of this probably would be natural meadow by the side of the river but, if the Allaires were like most habitants on the banks of the Richelieu, they had to create an area of artificial meadow as well to produce an adequate supply of grass.[12] About twenty arpents were left then in 1762 for the growing of grain, particularly wheat. At the most, however, half this area was under crop in any particular year. This raises the subject of crop rotation and takes us beyond a description of farm layout, into the subject of how the land was used to raise crops and livestock. In examining the seasonal round of agricultural tasks, our main source will be a collection of estate inventories listing the property of seventy-nine Lower Richelieu habitants from the middle and the end of the eighteenth century.[13]

THE AGRICULTURAL CALENDAR

Spring comes late in the Lower Richelieu and normally it was only in April or early May that the snow had disappeared and the soil was dry enough to plough. One of the major chores of the agricultural calendar, ploughing required equipment and a team of animals that were beyond the reach of many French peasants – perhaps a majority – in the eighteenth century. In Canada, by contrast, few habitants were without a plough, though often, the estate inventories suggest, it was in rather poor condition. The design was essentially uniform until the nineteenth century when swing ploughs became common. Until then, the heavy wheeled plough, typical of northern Europe, was used. Habitants made the beam, axle, and handles from wood and fitted them with two wheels, a chain, an iron coulter, and a small iron ploughshare. In May, after ploughing was finished, grain would be sown and the seeds covered by the passing of a harrow, a crude device made with wooden pegs mounted in a simple frame.

Ploughs in this period might be pulled by oxen or by horses, or by mixed teams of oxen and horses. The animals were of the 'canadien' breed, rather small but quite hardy. The fast-stepping horse was preferred in Sorel, where the light soil did not require the slower but more powerful ox. Elsewhere, oxen were more common in the mid-eighteenth century but, in St Ours and St Denis, they tended to be replaced by additional horses towards the end of the century. Whether composed of horses, oxen, or both, the plough teams of the Lower Richelieu were not large; indeed, they may not have supplied enough traction to cut very deeply into the ground, particularly in heavy soils. A British visitor of the early nineteenth century considered the Canadian habitants 'miserable farmers' who 'plough so very slight and careless, that they continue, year after year, to turn over the same clods which lie at the surface, without penetrating an inch deeper into the soil.'[14]

Oxen had the advantage of providing their owners with valuable beef and hides, whereas a dead horse was simply a carcass. On the other hand, aside from ploughing and hauling wood, the bovines did little through most of the year except consume fodder. It is the greater versatility of horses that probably explains why most habitants came to prefer them. No doubt the development of a local road network hastened the changeover from ox to horse in St Ours and St Denis. Besides the ploughs, carts, and sledges that would be pulled for strictly agricultural work, most eighteenth-century inventories also list both a buggy ('caleche') and a sleigh ('cariole') for human transportation. These vehicles were generally home-made, except for the wheels; an original French-Canadian design emerged in the late seventeenth century or early eighteenth century for sleighs and carriages that carried two or three adults and could be pulled by a single horse.[15] Residents of the islands of Sorel of course had little use for road transportation. Inventories from this section therefore often mention a sleigh and a canoe, but no carriage. No saddles were found in any of the Lower Richelieu inventories; apparently the habitants did not ride their horses.

Another springtime job besides ploughing was tilling and planting the kitchen garden. Gardens supplied the herbs and vegetables that formed an important part of the habitant diet. Men normally ploughed the soil every year and spread manure from time to time but, otherwise, the garden was a female responsibility. Helped by her small children, a woman like Félicité Allaire would plant the seeds, water the ground, remove weeds, harvest the produce, and prepare it for the table or for storage. Squash, onions, cabbage, and tobacco were among the most important garden crops but the sources tell us next to nothing about the quantities grown. Gardening was only one seasonal task that came in addition to the routine duties that kept women busy the year round. Besides cooking, baking bread, washing clothes, and cleaning the house, women made butter and took care of the poultry and dairy.

With the advent of summer, Théophile Allaire and the other men of the Lower Richelieu would be busy setting up fences around the newly planted grain fields.[16] The rest of the summer would be devoted to various outdoor jobs such as whitewashing and repairing the house, and outbuildings. One of the most demanding chores was digging and main-taining drainage ditches. One particularly detailed inventory from St Ours (dated 1791) mentions ditches with a total length of 2.6 kilometres drain-ing a moderate-sized forty-four arpents of cleared land.[17] There were ditches running lengthwise down each side of the lot and one in the middle, as well as four others traversing the lot. Digging these by hand must have been an enormous task but it was not one that exempted a habitant from further efforts. A farm lease from St Antoine spells out the tenant's duty to 'recaller tous les deux ans les fossets de travers et du milieu de la terre et à l'égard des fossets de ligne il les entretiendra et recallera à la demande de ses voisins.'[18]

In mid-summer, scythes were sharpened for the haying season. The tons of cut hay were then pitched into carts and transported to the barn. Most eighteenth-century habitants had a cart and several had two or three. These were simple home-made devices, except for the spoked wheels, which may have been bought from a specialized craftsman. Wheels were often removed and attached to various chassis for the different functions of carrying hay, peas, or sheaves.[19] Most farms were also equipped with a smaller tip-cart ('tombereau') for emptying stables and for other minor jobs. The grain harvest was in September and, in the Lower Richelieu as in other agrarian societies, it was a time of intense activity requiring an unusually large labour force. Women aided hus-bands and grown sons; where possible, labourers were hired. Many eighteenth-century inventories list five, six, and as many as nine sickles, often more than enough for every member of the family. The use of scythes might have made the cutting faster but French-Canadian peas-ants, like their European counterparts, preferred the sickle because it left longer straw for stubble grazing and because it was a more delicate instrument causing less grain to be lost on the ground. Bound into sheaves, wheat and oats were carted to the barn where they were stored – unless some grain was needed for immediate consumption – for several months before being threshed.

After the harvest, internal fences were removed so that animals could graze over the entire farm. Later, fall ploughing began. Available sources for the eighteenth century give no indication as to whether all the fields were ploughed at this time or only the areas to be planted in grain the following year, but we do know that the Canadian climate did not leave much time for this activity. We lack precise information also on crop rotation schemes but all indications are that they were quite primitive. Visitors to Canada reported that the habitants normally grew grain on half their land while leaving the other half to 'rest' as fallow and alternating the fields every few years. This simple rotation was taken seriously enough that farm leases invariably added the phrase 'sans le désaisonner' after insisting that the tenant care for the land 'en bon pere de famille.'

There were certainly 'better' ways of farming known in the eighteenth century and used in some parts of England and the Low Countries; by reducing or eliminating the fallow, these rotation schemes had made it possible to extract much more produce from a given area. Commentators who sneer at the habitants as unenlightened cultivators, however, fail to appreciate the importance of labour, the other ingredient, along with land, of agricultural production and the factor which best explains why, in many societies around the world, 'primitive' rotations have been preferred even when more intensive methods were well known. A leading theorist of agricultural economics has explained that, in relation to labour input, production actually declines as cultivation becomes more land-intensive. Shorter fallows and more elaborate rotation schemes give greater output per unit of land, writes Ester Boserup, but less output per unit of labour. Peasants will only adopt more 'advanced' methods, she continues, when forced to do so by population pressure or, more often, one might add, when coerced by landlords, governments, or creditors.[20] Compared to Europe, French Canada of course had an abundance of land and a shortage of labour, particularly in the eighteenth century. Moreover, it had a severe winter climate which made the growing of autumn-sown grain quite risky. This meant that the three-course rotation used by peasants in northwestern Europe since the Middle Ages to coax more grain out of a given territory could not be adopted. The habitant's practice of planting grain in only half the arable while leaving the rest under a natural cover of grass and weeds was certainly an inefficient use of natural resources but, from the point of view of a family concerned above all to feed its members with the fruits of their own labour, it was far from 'irrational.'[21]

With the onset of winter, habitants selected some animals – perhaps two pigs, a few sheep and calves or, occasionally, a cow or an ox instead – for slaughtering. Killing at this time of year saved on winter fodder and permitted some meat to be preserved frozen. Care was taken to fatten the hogs, often on peas, before slaughtering and the result was a high-quality pork. Sheep, on the other hand, were generally valued more for their fleece than for their flesh. Fresh meat appeared on habitant tables just in time to make up for the loss of another source of protein, eggs. Estate inventories tell us that most farms had their little flock of 'fowl,' consisting usually of one or two dozen hens who laid 'from spring to autumn,' a rooster and (rarely) a turkey. Milk was another protein source that tended to disappear in the winter. Peasant women made butter but, in the period before 1840, there is no mention of local cheese production.

On the whole, habitant animal husbandry struck non-peasant observers as negligent. No care was taken in breeding, it was claimed, and races degenerated as a result. Another accusation was that the quality of meat suffered by the habitant's failure to castrate sheep and cattle at an early enough age. One seigneur, writing in the 1780s, also lamented the common practice of letting rams and ewes run together throughout the year, so that many lambs were born in the winter when their chances of survival were low.[22] On the other hand, the canadien breeds of horses, sheep, and cattle found everywhere in Quebec had many admirable characteristics when properly cared for. Though smaller than many foreign races, they were generally quite hardy. The cows were good milk producers and the horses 'robustes et pleins de feu.'[23]

After the slaughtering season, there was plenty of time left for threshing, the main winter occupation of habitant men. In Europe, grain was normally threshed in the fall; Baron de Lahontan explained the tardier Canadian schedule, declaring that grains were most easily disengaged when the weather was coldest.[24] This may be true but more likely threshing was delayed because the Canadian climate left little time for anything but ploughing after the harvest and because the comparatively abundant Canadian food supply made threshing less urgent than it may have been in France. In January and February then, men could be found in the barns of the Lower Richelieu wielding their flails on the threshing floor, near the door. Soon after this, and before the spring thaw made roads impassable, habitants usually loaded their surplus grain into a sleigh and delivered what they owed to the curé, the seigneur, and the merchant. Besides threshing, men spent much of their time in the winter cutting firewood and fencing materials. Wood was brought in from the woodlot on horse-drawn sledges ('traines').

Women were certainly not idle during the winter months. This was a time to catch up on spinning, weaving, sewing, and knitting. Homespun shirts, woollen stockings, rugs, quilts, and sheets were some of the products of habitant handicrafts. Essential as they were, the winter activities of both sexes were conducted at a more leisurely pace, less rushed than were the harvest, ploughing, and planting by Nature's relentless schedule. Accordingly, winter was also a season of festivities. This was the favourite time of year for weddings and they, along with New Year's Eve and several religious holidays, were occasions for visits, parties, drinking, and dancing. There was a festive atmosphere in early spring as well when many habitants collected maple sap and boiled it down to make sugar. With the return of warm weather, it was again time for the heavy work of ploughing and sowing and the cycle began once more.

The first and most obvious conclusion to be drawn from this sketch of the agricultural calendar of the eighteenth-century Lower Richelieu is that agrarian life followed a pronounced seasonal pattern. The same could of course be said of contemporary rural societies of the United States or Europe, but the contrast between the seasons is more pronounced in Canada. This tendency towards climatic extremes, joined with the relatively long winters, imposed some special constraints on agriculture in the St Lawrence colony. There was little time for ploughing, certain crops such as corn and winter wheat did not flourish, and livestock needed a great deal of fodder. Another, more significant determinant of agricultural practices than the climate, however, was the household economic organization that Lower Richelieu habitants had in common with peasants everywhere. Relying essentially on a family labour force, cultivators had to devise procedures for extracting a living from the soil with a minimum of effort. This precluded the intensive cultivation and elaborate division of labour possible with larger enterprises. Moreover, family members could not be 'laid off' and therefore seasonal underemployment inevitably alternated with seasonal shortages of workers. Not only was the labour supply limited and inflexible, capital was quite scarce. There were no banks and wealth was unlikely to accumulate in the hands of a peasantry. Feudal exactions and restrictions on habitant land ownership certainly worked against any such capital formation, as did the demands of social reproduction. Accordingly, there was little possibility of taking up 'advanced' techniques requiring investments in fertilizer, livestock, or land. Finally, the need to produce a wide range of products for direct domestic consumption precluded the efficiency that goes with specialization. Nevertheless, in spite of its 'faults' and of the handicaps it had to contend with, Lower Richelieu agriculture did not do badly. It supported the local peasantry as well as the lay and clerical feudal classes and even produced an additional surplus to feed a considerable grain export trade.

It may be somewhat misleading to speak of the household economy as a 'constraint' limiting agricultural productivity, since this presupposes an abstract and 'external' point of view. It implies that, without 'artificial' barriers, the fruits of the soil should have increased. The problem with this approach is that it scorns the peasant's perspective in favour of that of the merchant and the official. In rural French Canada, the household framework defined the purposes of cultivation and stock-raising. Habitants had to sell produce for various reasons, but their efforts were directed, in the first instance, to preserving and reproducing the family unit; in other words, 'subsistence' in the broadest sense of the term was the end of agriculture. As we shall see in the pages that follow, production was closely connected to consumption in the eighteenth-century Lower Richelieu.

CONSUMPTION

Patterns of consumption do not, of course, appear in documents, such as inventories, designed to give a static view of possessions and we must turn to a different source, notarized deeds of gift ('donations-entre-vifs'). The *donation* was a common arrangement in the eighteenth century for transferring the ownership of a habitant farm from parents to children while the former were still alive but too old to work. In the next chapter I shall examine this system in the context of inheritance practices but, for the moment, it is sufficient to note that the transfer of property to a son or daughter was generally accompanied by a requirement to feed, house, and maintain the retiring parent or parents. Usually this obligation was spelled out in a precisely enumerated 'pension alimentaire' and it is this clause that gives an indication of habitant consumption needs.[25] For example, there was a deed of gift in 1760 in the Thibault family, neighbours of the Allaires in St Ours.[26] The widowed mother gave her portion of the family farm to her son Toussaint and he agreed by the contract to allow her to live in the house for the rest of her life and to provide heat, light, and clothing plus sixteen minots of flour, a quarter minot of salt, and 120 pounds of salt pork every year.

The Thibault *pension alimentaire* is fairly typical for the period around the Conquest but, towards the end of the eighteenth century, deeds of gift became more common and the *pensions* in them more detailed. Obligations to provide heat and light, for example, are spelled out as so many cords of wood and so many pounds of candles. 'Store-bought' items are also more common in the later deeds of gift. This probably reflects a real change in consumption habits, and not just greater contractual precision, as we know that retail commerce increased greatly in the second half of the eighteenth century. *Donations* from the 1790s are nevertheless of great interest because they seem to give a relatively complete picture of peasant consumption needs. We must bear in mind, however, that they portray habitants who were somewhat more dependent on imported merchandise than were their ancestors of Théophile Allaire's generation. Since each deed of gift has its peculiarities, quantitative analysis seems less helpful than an examination of a typical *pension* and variations.

Joseph Blanchard and his wife Marie Daigle of St Ours ceded their farm to their son Joseph fils in 1791.[27] Besides providing a furnished room, washing and mending, and other services, young Joseph and his wife agreed to maintain a milk cow and six hens with a rooster and supply the following *pension alimentaire*:

30 minots wheat ground into flour
200 pounds pork or 150 pounds pork plus one quarter beef
1 fatted sheep
2 minots peas
1 minot salt
1 pound pepper
100 heads of cabbage
3 *pots* rum
3 *pots* wine
25 pounds maple sugar
1 pound tea
200 onions
10 pounds candles or 3 *pots* lamp oil
30 pounds tobacco
10 pounds butter
25 cords firewood
3 pounds wool
4 shirts of homespun and a complete suit of work clothes
sheets and shoes ('souliers de boeuf') as needed
a set of Sunday clothes purchased from the merchant every three years.

Wheat is certainly the principal element of the diet suggested by this and other eighteenth-century *pensions*. If the Blanchards were to receive almost twice as much as the widow Thibault thirty years earlier, this was of course because there were two of them. (Most *donations* specified that the ration would be reduced by one-half on the death of one parent.)

In both cases, the amount was normal: in thirteen eighteenth-century deeds of gift selected arbitrarily from the notarial archives, wheat supplies ranged from twelve to fifteen minots per person. This was certainly a generous ration, slightly larger than the widow's allowances specified at about the same time in farmers' wills in a grain-rich area of Pennsylvania (mean 13.2 bushels = 12.0 minots), and well above the six to ten bushels that one historian has estimated to be the basic requirement for people subsisting primarily on bread (a bushel is slightly smaller than a minot).[28] Bread was indeed the main element in the habitant's diet, as many visitors to the country noted; it seems to have been eaten in copious quantities and, being exclusively wheaten, it would have been nutritionally superior to the breads eaten by most European peasantries.[29]

Pork was the main meat in the Lower Richelieu; most deeds of gift called for one fattened hog per year. This meant fresh meat in slaughtering season and perhaps some sausages, but most of the flesh was salted in barrels to be used through the year to add fat and flavour to soups and other dishes. Beef was less common in the habitant diet, particularly after the late eighteenth century when oxen ceased to be the favoured draft animal. One or two minots of peas, the basic ingredient for soup that was eaten on a daily basis, were an element of every *pension alimentaire*. Salt was also generally required and one minot was the usual quantity; obviously this was used to preserve meats as well as to flavour dishes. Less prosperous peasants than the Blanchards did not ask for pepper, wine, and tea, though many *donations* insist that wine and chicken be provided to the parents in case of illness. Rum, on the other hand, seems to have been a common beverage in the post-Conquest period. Wheat bread, pork, peas, and garden vegetables were the staples of the habitant diet in the eighteenth century, but meals were not as monotonous as the strictly agricultural deeds of gift suggest. In Sorel particularly, with its myriad of islands and marshes, fish and game birds were also eaten; hence the fishing nets and hooks, guns and traps in the inventories of river-front habitants. 'This must be a good land in time of peace,' wrote Baroness von Riedesel, who lived in Sorel at the time of the American Revolution. 'All sorts of food are to be had, and for the most part there are lots of good fish and many doves.'[30]

Returning to the Blanchard *pension alimentaire*, we note several non-food requirements. Sheets and clothing for everyday use were to be of homespun made from the flax that was grown on all habitant farms. Shoes – 'souliers sauvages' or 'souliers de boeuf' – also seem to have been home-made. Only special outfits for public occasions were purchased. Like most habitants of both sexes and all ages, the Blanchards appear to have been great smokers; their annual supply of tobacco would have come from the farm's garden.

One striking feature of the Blanchard deed of gift is the extent to which it indicates a pattern of family consumption that could be satisfied by family production. Salt, rum, wine, pepper, tea, lamp oil, and Sunday clothes would have to be purchased but poorer families like the Allaires would have done without most of these items. Everything else was provided by the farm, including all the food and most of the clothing. Exotic beverages and imported fabrics had a place in the homes of many peasants but, in its essentials, household consumption was bound closely to household production.

PRODUCTION

There is little precise information about the production of many of the goods needed to sustain an eighteenth-century habitant family but the census of 1765, some scattered tithe records, and notarial documents do provide quantitative data on the grain crops and livestock herds that were the principal sources of food. The census actually lists only the amount of grain *sown* by each household without specifying which particular grains were planted and in what proportions and without giving any hint as to the amounts harvested. It tells us, for example, that Théophile Allaire planted fifteen minots in 1765 but it leaves us in the dark as to how much wheat, peas, and oats this produced to feed the Allaire family and its livestock. Fortunately, other sources help to fill the gap by giving some indications of crop yields and of the proportions of specific grains in the total harvest. On the question of the composition of Lower Richelieu harvests, parish tithe figures show that fairly consistent proportions of the three principal grain crops were grown (see Table 3).[31] Of course, even with a certain consistency in the total harvest of an entire parish, there could be tremendous variations at the level of individual farms. And yet it does appear that every household grew the same crops and in roughly the same proportions. At this level, our only source of information is estate inventories which occasionally provide figures on the quantities of various grains sown or harvested (see Table 4).[32] Variations in the total volumes planted and reaped may be related to family size, although this is an untested hypothesis. Differences in the proportion of oats, on the other hand, are clearly connected with

TABLE 3
Composition of Lower Richelieu harvests: parish aggregates

Date	Locality	Total (minots)	Wheat (%)	Peas (%)	Oats (%)
1739	Sorel	3880	67	5	26
Early 1780s	St Ours	27,040	72	8	19
Early 1780s	St Denis	20,800	75	6	19
1789	St Ours	26,312	67	5	28

TABLE 4
Composition of Lower Richelieu harvests: individual households

Date	Locality	Total sown	Total reaped	Wheat	Peas	Oats
1746	Sorel	29		65%	7%	28%
1748	St Denis		152	72%	20%	8%
1764	St Ours		60	67%	0%	33%
1793	St Ours	24		62%	0	37%
1795	St Ours	50		60%	4%	36%

the adoption of horses as draft animals. What remains striking is the high degree of uniformity in the composition of harvests from year to year in the eighteenth century and from one farm to the next. Thus it seems safe to assume that, of the fifteen minots Théophile Allaire sowed in 1765, about ten would have been wheat, one peas, and the remaining four oats.

After sowing this much wheat, peas, and oats, what would the Allaires have reaped? This is a very difficult question since not only does the 1765 census give no harvest data, but there are no crop yield figures for the eighteenth century that would permit any precise estimate. Nevertheless, we can get a rough idea, of the wheat output at least, by using Cole Harris' estimated seed-to-yield ratio of 1: 5.8 for all of Canada in 1739.[33] On this assumption, Allaire would have reaped fifty-eight minots of wheat in a 'normal' year. Of this, ten would be set aside for seed and another 3.4 minots would have to be turned over to the seigneur's miller to have the rest ground into flour. This would leave the flour produced by 44.6 minots of wheat to feed the family and pay its feudal dues for one year. At this time (1765), the Allaires had four small children and, assuming they ate about half as much as grown-ups, the equivalent of four adult rations would be needed. The net proceeds of the wheat harvest divided by four gives 11.2 minots of wheat, slightly less than the annual supply specified in most eighteenth-century deeds of gift. The seed-yield of peas was probably about the same as or slightly less than that of wheat, suggesting a net harvest of roughly five minots, again not far from the one minot per person specified in the Blanchard deed of gift. The Allaires, then, seem to have grown about enough to supply their own domestic needs in 1765, but not much more. Nevertheless, they still had to pay the tithe, seigneurial rent, and other feudal dues, as well as pay for any purchases. I will discuss the impact of these exactions on the peasant household economy in a later chapter. For the moment, it is enough to note how close to the edge the Allaires found themselves. With an exceptional harvest or with some skimping on bread consumption, they might have had a little grain to sell in some years; otherwise they must have struggled to meet obligations by selling a calf, a few eggs, or some butter and by working for richer neighbours from time to time.

The Allaire family was comparatively poor but not too far short of the St Ours average for per capita wheat production in 1765. Similar calculations for all the ninety-nine habitant families for which the 1765 census provides data suggest a wheat supply of fifteen minots per 'adult equivalent.' This amount – the annual ration set out in the most generous *pensions alimentaires* – was available to the local peasantry before priest, seigneur and merchant had been paid. In a 'normal year' then, where the seed-yield ratio was 1: 5.8, there was not a very wide margin between wheat production and wheat consumption. The picture is much more complicated when we take account of inequalities within the local peasantry and of the vagaries of the harvest.

It is well known that agricultural outputs vary greatly from year to year. This is particularly the case in pre-modern agrarian régimes, vulnerable as they are to natural accidents. A late frost, a flood, or an infestation of insects could have a devastating effect on harvests. In the second half of the eighteenth century, for example, there were serious grain shortages on at least four different occasions (that is, not including the crisis connected with the Seven Years' War: 1769, 1783, 1789, and 1796). A St Denis merchant wrote in the spring of 1784 of the previous harvest, 'The crop has failed here abouts in particular. What little wheat the Inhabitants sell now is from 7 to 8 Livres pr. minot,' and, in another letter: 'I never saw a year so distressing amongst the inhabitants as this is. Above one third of them have not seed to sow. The Priest who used to have 1200 minots of wheat for his Deem [ie, tithe] has this year about

TABLE 5
Farm animals belonging to Théophile Allaire and Félicité Audet, St Ours 1762-5

Animal	1762 (inventory)	1765 (census)	1767 (inventory)
Horses	2	2	1
Oxen	0	0	0
Cows	2	2	3
Heifers	1	0	0
Sheep	1	2	4
Pigs	1	2	3

350 minots.'[34] The shortage of 1768–9 was probably even a greater disaster for the population of St Denis.[35]

Fortunately, Canadian peasants did not live by bread alone. As noted earlier, farm animals played a vital role in the household economy, both as sources of food and as traction power. The Allaire family was one of those that did without oxen. Théophile and Félicité in fact managed to make do with a rather modest complement of farm animals. Two inventories and a census allow us to follow in some detail the changing size of their little herd over the space of five years (see Table 5). At best, these beasts would barely provide the meat, butter, and traction required by the family, although there might be some butter or pork to sell if the Allaires stinted themselves. Changes over time suggest a strictly subsistence function. Between 1762 and 1767, the household's consumption must have expanded greatly as four children were born and they, as well as their two older half-sisters, grew bigger every day; accordingly, the need for milk, wool, and meat must have increased, forcing the Allaires to keep more cows, sheep, and pigs than earlier. On the other hand, one of the two horses died after 1765 and it was not replaced before 1767. This suggests that the growth in the overall number of animals reflects only greater subsistence needs and not increased prosperity. But how typical were the Allaires in this regard?

Two different sources can be used in studying habitant livestock holdings on a wider scale and, unfortunately, neither of them is perfect. Several censuses have data on animals but, in some cases (the censuses of 1784 and 1790) only parish aggregates are available, with no indication of the holdings of individual households. A further problem stems from an inconsistent use of categories. When a census-taker notes that a farm had six head of cattle, for example, it is not always clear whether he counted only full-grown animals or whether he included calves as well. All indications are that the two most complete censuses in our period

– those of 1765 and 1831 – used quite different criteria on this point, the earlier census enumerating only adult animals while the later one, less helpful, lumped together beasts of all ages.[36] The sample of estate inventories does not suffer from this weakness for each listing provides details on every single animal owned by a family. This permits reliable comparisons between localities and periods, as the researcher may arrange the data in uniform classifications, leaving aside piglets and colts and counting only useful adult animals. On the other hand, the number of households covered by the inventory sample is rather small. However, when figures from the 1765 census and inventories from about the same time are confronted, as in Table 6, the results are reassuring. For each animal and within each parish, the distribution of livestock is quite consistent, whether one looks at all habitant households by means of the census or only at the thirty-nine families whose property was described in estate inventories. This similarity tends to support the claim that inventories represent a good cross-section of the entire community.

Substantively these data suggest a remarkable uniformity in the size and composition of habitant herds. In the middle of the eighteenth century, a sizeable majority of the peasant households of the Lower Richelieu had either one or two horses, two to four cows, two oxen or less, and so on. Only where sheep are concerned was there anything approaching specialization. A good number of families had no sheep at all and probably obtained wool from neighbours; on the other hand, one or two peasants had relatively large herds (the biggest was twenty-two head, still quite modest by most standards). Otherwise, farmyard populations were strictly limited. No one covered by either the census or the inventory sample had more than five horses, nine cows, eight oxen, twenty-two sheep, or twenty-two pigs. Obviously, there were environmental factors – particularly the long, cold winters which kept animals in the stable and in need of large amounts of fodder – that tended to keep herds small. The point is that there is little indication of any specialized production for the market in these figures.[37] Some families had more animals than others because some families were larger or more comfortable than others, but all had essentially the same complement of livestock. Like grain production, animal husbandry was apparently conditioned primarily by domestic consumption needs.

THE HABITANT AT HOME

The peasant economy revolved around the household; the latter was of course more than simply a unit of production, consumption, and labour,

TABLE 6
Distribution of horses, cows, oxen, sheep, and pigs, Lower Richelieu 1740–69 (per cent)

	Sorel		St Ours–St Denis	
	Census	Inventories	Census	Inventories
Habitant households	130	16	143	23
Horses				
0	15	12	3	9
1	18	31	22	52
2	56	37	50	26
3	10	12	19	13
4	2	6	5	0
5	0	0	1	0
Cows				
0	12	6	5	4
1	17	12	18	17
2	20	50	24	30
3–4	39	12	41	39
5–6	10	19	8	9
7–9	2	0	4	0
Oxen				
0	81	81	38	44
1–2	17	13	43	39
3–4	2	6	14	17
5–6	0	0	3	0
7–8	0	0	1	0
Sheep				
0	43	44	34	35
1–2	14	12	16	30
3–5	24	6	36	17
6–10	18	19	13	17
11–20	2	13	1	0
21–5	0	6	0	0
Pigs				
0	14	19	2	22
1–2	18	25	23	57
3–5	47	31	64	17
6–10	21	19	10	4
11 +	0	6	1	0

it was also the framework of domestic existence. In the absence of letters, diaries, and the like written by habitants, there is a limit to how much we can know about the 'home life' of the rural masses of the eighteenth-century Lower Richelieu. However, estate inventories which describe the physical circumstances of domestic life are a valuable source of clues in this regard. Together with other documents, they tell much about such aspects of material culture as domestic architecture, furniture, and cooking utensils, as well as revealing a good deal about habitant daily life.

The physical centre of family life on an habitant farm was the house and, by the second half of the seventeenth century, a standard domestic architecture had emerged in rural New France. A French officer stationed in the colony shortly before the Conquest described the basic pattern and its variants.

Les maisons sont pour la plus grande partie en bois aussy et couverte de chaume ou de planches et les cheminées de terre ou de pierres. Les plus belles maisons sont en pierres, mais ce ne sont pas les plus nombreuses; chaque habitant a un petit four en terre; leurs maisons en général sont peu de chose, plusieurs n'ont qu'une chambre, et les mieux en ont deux avec quelque petit cabinet de décharge dans le fond; ils couchent tout l'hiver dans l'endroit ou est le poêle.[38]

If there were one or two stone houses in the Lower Richelieu at this time, they belonged to priests and merchants. For habitant homes, the style called 'pièce-sur-pièce' was nearly universal until the middle of the nineteenth century. This characteristically French-Canadian construction technique used roughly squared logs stacked horizontally and secured by dovetail joints or vertical posts at the corners.[39] The Allaire house was likely a log cabin of this sort with a steeply pitched roof covered with overlapping boards. On the other hand, it may have been one of the few 'poteaux-debout' still standing in mid-eighteenth-century St Ours as relics of an earlier age of primitive pioneer shelters.

Pièce-sur-pièce houses were certainly unostentatious and they may have seemed 'peu de chose' to a Frenchman, but they represented an excellent adaptation to a country with a cold climate and relatively abundant supplies of timber. Simple to construct, these dwellings were also easily altered. Once the cracks between logs were stuffed, pièce-sur-pièce buildings were also quite warm, particularly in comparison with stone houses. Strictly practical considerations guided habitant architecture to the exclusion of any concern for expressing individual pretensions or ambitions. Accordingly, houses were roughly uniform, within a given period, in size as well as in design. Inventories dating from 1740 to 1769 give the floor dimensions of twenty Lower Richelieu houses; they ranged from 4.8 by 3.2 metres up to 9.7 by 8.1 metres. Though smaller, on the whole, than nineteenth-century houses, these buildings were larger than most of the cabins of seventeenth-century Sorel and St Ours. In fact, over the centuries there seems to have been enough steady progress in rustic accommodation to gratify the most Whiggish historian.[40] Measuring only 5.2 metres square on the floor, the Allaires' house was quite small, even by mid-eighteenth-century standards. It probably only had one room on the main floor, though larger houses had two or three rooms, divided by thin board partitions. Upstairs, under the sloping roof, would be room for storage of foodstuffs and an area where the children slept.

Behind every house was a barn and usually several smaller outbuildings as well. Around the middle of the century, Lower Richelieu barns were all of the primitive poteaux debout style, made with cedar, spruce, or pine posts simply planted in the earth and standing side by side as close together as possible; pieces of split wood filled the cracks and helped to hold the structure together. By the 1790s this style had disappeared and the more solid pièce-sur-pièce was in use for barns as well as houses. Throughout the century, all barns seem to have been roofed with straw thatching. Several inventories mention a wooden threshing floor ('batterie'), suggesting that the ends of the building where sheaves were stored had only a dirt floor.

Under the same roof as the barn was often a cow-shed. For the most part, however, Lower Richelieu farmyards seem to have had a collection of various detatched outbuildings. Dairies, horse stables, pig-sties, sheepfolds and wood-sheds can be found in many inventories, although they are seldom described in detail. Few farms had all these structures. The geographer Pierre Deffontaines has pointed out that an arrangement under which buildings were grouped together around a central courtyard would have made access easier and given better protection against the wind.[41] The dispersal of outbuildings, he argues, is mainly due to the attachment of Canadian colonists to the traditions of western France. Probably more important than any 'vieil atavisme,' however, was the concern, quite reasonable in a land of wood and thatching, to prevent accidental fires from spreading. Farm buildings were also dispersed in Early Modern Sweden, another country where wooden structures predominated.[42]

Inside the Allaire home, the furnishings were Spartan – three old chairs, a pine chest, and a wooden sideboard – except for what sounds like quite a sumptuous bed: 'un lit de plume pesant environ avec le traversin et les deux oreillers vingt quatre livres avec un drap, une courtepointe, une paillasse et sa couchette.' Baroness Von Riedesel remarked that 'the dwellings are very comfortable and one finds the beds remarkably good and clean.'[43] All the furniture was of course of domestic construction, including the bed linen and quilt. Most kitchen utensils, on the other hand, were not home-made. There were four pots and three frying pans of various sizes, as well as a pair of pressing irons, all made of cast iron. An earthenware platter, two jugs, five milk bowls, and a few pots and bottles were probably obtained from one of the potters of St Denis, and the lamp, tin candlestick, tin coffeepot, and two copper cups were likely made by local craftsmen as well. There were also three wooden buckets for carrying water, a saltbox, a basin, and a wooden washtub up in the attic that may well have been made by Théophile himself. Like most habitants, he was obviously handy with woodworking, as the hammer and chisels mentioned in the inventory suggest. There is evidence, in the nineteen pounds of yarn and the two pounds of 'fil d'étoupe' found in the attic, that Félicité too engaged in craft work; she may have been busy with a quilt or a 'catalogne,' a bed covering common in French Canada since the seventeenth century and made from discarded bits of cloth twisted and woven together with thread.[44]

If there was a table in the Allaire house, the 1762 inventory does not mention it. More well-to-do eighteenth-century habitants would have at least had a place to sit down for meals and they would have had a more elaborate collection of eating utensils. Théophile and Félicité had only two tin goblets, two cups, and five steel forks. Some habitant inventories from this period list silver goblets and large quantities of dishes and cutlery, but this family does not seem to have possessed plates; presumably everyone here ate straight from the pot.[45] Little else was to be found in the Allaires' home other than a few agricultural implements and a trunk full of women's clothes – a dress, two petticoats, a pair of embroidered moccasins, a shawl, a cape, and a nightcap. Théophile must have had some extra shirts and other clothes but, as the personal apparel of the surviving spouse, they were not included in this inventory of the couple's common property.

Modest as the interior of the Allaire house may have been in most respects, it did hold one prized possession that would have seemed an amazing luxury among peasantries in other parts of the world. The Allaires had a stove, a box-type cast-iron stove with its sides stylishly embossed 'à la samaritaine,' and it must have kept their small log cabin perfectly warm during the coldest winters. Even though the top had been broken and repaired, it was valued at 140 livres, about one-third the value of all the household possessions (445 livres) and considerably more than the estimated worth of the house itself (80 livres). It was probably made at the St Maurice Forges near Trois-Rivières, where the founders had been casting stove parts for about twenty years. This was the one sign of comparative comfort in a rather poor household; cast-iron stoves were common in the mid-eighteenth-century Lower Richelieu but by no means universal; one-third of the thirty-nine inventories for the period 1740–69 mention them. Many habitants made do with cheaper substitutes; four had sheet-metal stoves and nine had 'plaques de poele,' cast-iron plates that stood on brick or stone sides to form a rudimentary stove; only six households did without any sort of enclosed heating device. Over the years, plates and sheet-metal stoves tended to disappear while cast iron stoves became increasingly common. By the end of the eighteenth century most families had at least one and many had two; those who could not afford the considerable investment needed to buy an iron stove borrowed or rented one.

Stoves were certainly known in Europe long before 1740 but they were not widely used; in England, France, and English America, most people, even the rich, warmed themselves around open fireplaces until the nineteenth century.[46] As a source of heat the fireplace is definitely inferior to the stove, warming only one small corner of a room while generating chilling drafts everywhere else. An iron stove, by contrast, is safer, more portable (that is, it could be removed in summer), and a far more efficient heater.[47] It can easily warm an entire room and, with a good length of stovepipe, it could raise the temperature of a whole habitant house, even one bigger than the Allaires'.

Despite the cost of iron stoves, habitants quickly recognized their advantages and adopted them quite rapidly after the middle of the eighteenth century in the Lower Richelieu and, according to the comments of foreign visitors, throughout French Canada. The result was a relatively even temperature throughout the house and a radical differentiation of indoor and outdoor climates in the winter. This precociously modern situation astonished Englishmen accustomed to fires that warmed one's body occasionally but not one's house permanently. About habitant houses they were told that, 'in winter, by the aid of a stove, they are rendered completely uninhabitable by an European. The excessive heat in which the Canadian lives, within doors, is sufficient to kill anyone, not from his infancy accustomed to that temperature.'[48] English visitors to Canada complained of the hot (one actually measured 73 degrees F!), stuffy houses. They were certain that the lack of fresh air and the sudden temperature change on entering or leaving could only be fatal to the health. People went about indoors without coats on and the very walls were so warm that no condensed moisture could be seen trickling down them![49]

Until the second half of the nineteenth century, stoves were used exclusively for domestic heating; cooking was still done over an open fire. The majority of fireplaces described in mid-eighteenth-century inventories were of field-stone construction, but there was also a certain number of 'cheminées de terre' made of wood covered with clay. Being comparatively poor, the Allaires probably had a clay fireplace and here Félicité must have boiled soups and other dishes in a big iron pot and, on the special occasions when fresh meat was on the menu, she would roast it over the wood fire. Bread, on the other hand, the most important element in the family diet, would be baked in an outdoor oven.

Not only domestic utensils, but agricultural equipment too was found in the Allaire house: axes, pickaxes, sickles, a scythe, and an old garden cultivator. Clearly the radical distinction between 'living' and 'working' environments was foreign to this pre-capitalist household. Other habitant inventories give a similar impression. Within the house, space was scarcely specialized as to function and so it is common to find pots, sickles, spinning wheels, and beds all in the same room.

Habitant houses then, that of Félicité and Théophile Allaire included, were small and modest, the furnishings were rather rough, but they were warm and well equipped for activities such as cooking, eating, sleeping, socializing, and craft work. They were built for the basic security and comfort of family members, not for projecting an impression of status. Above all, the buildings themselves, as well as their contents, were for the most part made by habitants for habitants. Peasant houses were certainly not immutable structures. Inventory descriptions imply that, over the years, many were expanded by the addition of wings or lean-tos, no doubt to accommodate growing families. For the habitant family was never a static entity; indeed, it was constantly in flux, expanding and contracting as one generation succeeded another.

3

Generations of peasants

There is a dynamic to peasant life that is demographic, ecological, and economic. For the peasantry to survive, old and dying individuals must of course be replaced through procreation, but there can only be continuity of the basic social and economic organization if this biological process is contained within the framework of the family household. Hence, in order to understand the habitants of the Lower Richelieu, we must intrude into the most intmate aspects of their lives and observe them being born, dying, marrying, and copulating. 'Reproduction,' in its widest sense, involves much more than these matters alone, however. The family units that were forming and reforming over the years had to support themselves and this required, above all, land. One way for young habitants to obtain the land needed to establish a new family was to receive it from their aged or deceased parents. In a burgeoning population like that of the Lower Richelieu, inheritance alone could never provide farms for every member of the rising generation. Many were instead accommodated through the laborious business of colonization as forests were cleared and farms established in what had previously been wilderness.

MARRIAGE

Marriage, the ceremony establishing a new, culturally sanctioned family, is as good a place as any to begin. Weddings were great and joyful occasions in rural Quebec of the eighteenth and nineteenth centuries and, given the importance of the family unit in this society, this seems quite appropriate. Visitors to the country wrote of the large assemblage of guests at the church, the processions of carriages or sleighs through

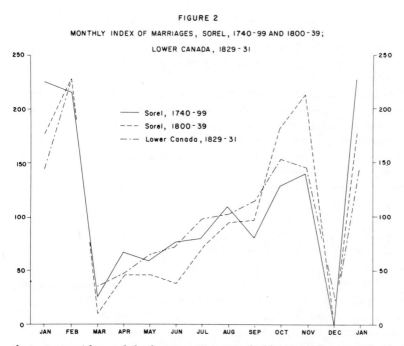

FIGURE 2
MONTHLY INDEX OF MARRIAGES, SOREL, 1740-99 AND 1800-39;
LOWER CANADA, 1829-31

the countryside, and the long parties attended by neighbours and relations. Wedding day festivities were preceded by other public and semi-public events such as the signing of a marriage contract and the publishing of the banns at the parish church. As in contemporary France, most weddings were held in the winter or, to a lesser extent, in the late fall months when agricultural tasks were not pressing and when fresh meat and other supplies were most plentiful (see Figure 2).[1]

We know little enough about habitant courting, the circumstances under which boys and girls met, or the semi-conscious 'rules' governing the choice of a mate. Painstaking analysis of parish registers or marriage contracts would reveal a good deal about, for example, degrees of familial and local endogamy. We do know, of course, that the Church, with its elaborate incest prohibitions, played a role in restricting the choice of spouses. People with blood ties, even some quite distant ones, or with pseudo-kin relationships through marriage or god-parentage, could not legitimately marry unless they received a special dispensation from the bishop.[2] In France, this posed a serious problem in many rural communities where the ramifying networks of kinship made a certain incidence of consanguinous matches inevitable.[3] By the early nineteenth century, the parishes of the Lower Richelieu began to face a similar situation. They were riddled with such relationships, the legacy of two and a half centuries of collective life, and the clergy were often faced with a thorny dilemma. Although his first impulse was simply to refuse to marry cousins, many a curé was inclined to be liberal and petition the bishop for a dispensation, fearing that the lovers, if thwarted, might approach a Protestant minister or else commit some other serious transgression. Playing upon these fears, couples seeking a dispensation often would simply set up housekeeping as man and wife, knowing that their parish priest would move quickly to quell the scandal by legitimizing their union.[4]

It was this same concern to avoid unsanctioned unions and the challenge they implied to the sacramental character of marriage that led the church to champion a generally 'liberal' policy on marriage; in the seventeenth century, for example, bishops fought the military authorities to allow soldiers to marry if they wished. While avoiding as far as possible any direct challenge to parental authority, the clerics also tended to favour the rights of young people to choose a spouse without being coerced by their families. A curé of St Ours noted in 1815 that he always insisted that prospective brides and grooms, even those aged over twenty-five and therefore legally independent, secure their parents' permission. 'Je n'ai point encore rencontré,' he added, 'un seul majeur ou une seule majeure qui ne soit convenu, qu'il étoit de son devoir de consulter ses parens et de solliciter leur consentement.' In the rare case of a refusal of permission, the priest advised postponement and conciliation through a third party, but, if the parents stubbornly refused without reasonable grounds, he would proceed with the marriage regardless.[5] However, the general impression given by the curé of St Ours is one of harmony between parents and children and this is not altogether surprising in a community composed mainly of peasants who lacked the motives – pride of class, dynastic diplomacy, the consolidation of large estates – that led the upper classes of pre-industrial societies to arrange their children's marriages. In the eighteenth-century Lower Richelieu, the only serious case of parental interference in the choice of a marriage partner involves the merchant Samuel Jacobs, who completely disowned one of his daughters for marrying against his wishes.[6]

Within the habitant class, differences of fortune were not great enough to give parents grounds for snobbishness. Moreover, the social, cultural, and economic importance of the family in early French Canada was such that parents and children would naturally tend to favour marriage for

TABLE 7
Mean age of first marriage in Sorel, by birth cohort

Period of birth	Births in sample	Linked to Sorel marriage		Mean age at first marriage
		Number	Percentage	
		Males		
1740–79	685	148	21.6	26.6
1780–1809	552	158	28.6	25.7
1810–39	610	152	24.9	24.1
		Females		
1740–79	639	144	22.5	22.4
1780–1809	500	167	33.4	22.1
1810–39	535	191	35.7	21.4

all with a minimum of impediments and delay. Demographic studies have indeed underlined the preference of the settlers of New France for married life, but they have not always explained this adequately. Although marriage patterns were fundamentally similar to European models, Canadians of the seventeenth and eighteenth centuries tended to be more likely to marry in the first place, more likely to marry at a relatively early age, and more likely to remarry soon after the death of a spouse.

Nubile brides of fourteen or fifteen were common in French Canada only in the period of extreme sex imbalance that ended around 1660. By the second half of the eighteenth century the mean age at first marriage in Sorel was 26.6 for men and 22.4 for women (see Table 7), fairly young by contemporary western European standards, but not exceptionally so. These figures seem quite typical in the context of early North America; in Hingham, Massachusetts, for example, the mean age at first marriage (1761–80) was 24.6 for males and 23.5 for females.[7] The New World may not have been a Garden of Eden, but it was a place where, in the seventeenth and eighteenth centuries, the economic and ecological restraints on early marriage operated with less force than they did in Europe. Land was of course the main factor determining age at marriage in these rural societies of both sides of the Atlantic and its comparative abundance in America allowed more people to establish new family households without the long delays needed to accumulate 'capital' or await the devolution of their parents' property. Nevertheless, North American practice – both French and English – only represents a variant on what has been called the '(Western) European marriage pattern';

nowhere on this continent do we find a predominance of very young brides and grooms such as occurred in many Asian, East European, and South American populations.[8]

Besides comparatively late marriage, the other main characteristic of the pre-industrial Western European pattern is the high incidence of permanent celibacy. The same factors that forced many to delay marriage until they were fairly old prevented many others from ever marrying at all. In the absence of 'family reconstitution' data or proper nominal censuses for the period between 1681 and 1851, no precise figures can be offered on the prevalence of 'definitive celibacy' in the Lower Richelieu. However, studies of the French-Canadian population in the seventeenth and early eighteenth centuries make it clear that this state was quite rare, much more so than in Europe.[9] (Of course, some early Canadians never married because they joined one of the male or female religious orders. Demographically, however, the numbers involved were not very significant in spite of the cultural importance of these institutions.) It seems safe to assume that this low incidence of celibacy remained in effect in the Lower Richelieu, at least through the eighteenth century; this certainly is the impression one gets in going through notarial records and other documents where references to old people who never married are conspicuously absent. Given the relatively easy access to the land normally required to establish a new household and given also the particular importance of the family in early Canada, it would hardly be surprising to find that few people remained spinsters or bachelors for their entire lives.

One final reflection of the importance of the family is the tendency of seventeenth- and eighteenth-century habitants to remarry if their husband or wife died and to do so with a minimum delay. Here again, only earlier studies based on family reconstitution can provide precise data. In early eighteenth-century Canada, widows waited on the average only 38.4 months before remarrying and widowers only 25.5 months. At that time, 27 per cent of all marriages involved at least one previously married partner, down from 39 per cent in the seventeenth century.[10] There seems to have been a general downward trend in this proportion as only 18 per cent of the weddings celebrated in Sorel between 1740 and 1840 involved a widow or a widower.[11] Although this percentage changed little over the course of a century, the proportion of men and women did evolve considerably. In Canada generally, the predominantly male immigration of the seventeenth century created a sex imbalance that gave women a decided advantage in the 'marriage market.'

TABLE 8
Marital status at marriage, Sorel (in percentages)

	Spinsters	Widows	Undetermined	All brides
1740–79 (224 marriages)				
Bachelors	82.1	8.9	1.3	92.4
Widowers	5.4	1.8	0.0	7.1
Undetermined	0.0	0.0	0.4	0.4
All grooms	87.5	10.7	1.8	100
1780–1809 (179 marriages)				
Bachelors	83.2	3.9	1.1	88.3
Widowers	8.4	2.8	0.0	11.2
Undetermined	0.6	0.0	0.0	0.6
All grooms	92.2	6.7	1.1	100
1810–39 (215 marriages)				
Bachelors	80.9	3.3	1.4	85.6
Widowers	11.6	1.4	0.0	13.0
Undetermined	1.4	0.0	0.0	1.4
All grooms	93.9	4.7	1.4	100

Weddings joining widows and bachelors were therefore more common than those uniting widowers and spinsters.[12] In Sorel, widows were still not shunned by bachelors in the middle of the eighteenth century; in fact they were more likely to find a second mate who had never previously married than were the parish's widowers (see Table 8). By the end of the century this was no longer the case, and, by the 1810–39 period, widowed men were in the privileged position they had long enjoyed in France.[13]

While the social and demographic aspects of marriage are important, marriage always has an economic side as well. In early French Canada, the 'marriage community' ('communauté de biens') was the socio-legal entity governing the material relations of husbands and wives. 'Hommes et femmes conjoints ensemble par mariages, sont communs en biens meubles et conquêts immeubles ... ,' states the Custom of Paris, one of France's regional legal codes and the basis of Canadian civil law from the middle of the seventeenth century.[14] Except for immovable property (basically land) owned by the husband or wife before their marriage or inherited later ('propres'), all possessions were owned jointly by a married couple, legally forming a communauté de biens. Through the use of a marriage contract, fiancés could renounce the communauté system (though I know of no Canadian habitants who took this option) or they could reserve certain items or sums of money for one partner or for the eventual survivor after the death of one spouse. Although the man was legally 'master of the communauté,' the wife being unable to undertake transactions on her own, he was nevertheless constrained by the obligation to secure the written consent of his partner before selling, mortgaging, or alienating any of their joint property. The notarial records of the Lower Richelieu suggest that this formality was observed quite scrupulously but there is no evidence that wives ever exercised their theoretical right of veto, at least not in any formal way.

In practical terms, the communauté de biens played an important role only at the point of its dissolution following a separation or, more commonly, the death of one of the spouses. Theoretically, the widow or widower would receive half the real property and half the value of the moveables as established by an inventory, along with the burden of half of any debts; the other half would go to the heirs (children) of the deceased. A widow had the right, however, to refuse her portion should she find the debts outweighing the assets; a man had no such option. With the consent of the children, it was also possible for a man or woman to continue the communauté after the death of his or her spouse, postponing the inventory and dissolution until the death or remarriage of the survivor. Thus, land records often have entries for farms owned by, for example, 'widow and heirs of the late Jean Cournoyer,' indicating that the property belonged jointly to all the sons and daughters and the mother in a continuing communauté de biens.

Although these rules are fairly straight forward, the issue was complicated considerably by special arrangements specified in marriage contracts or by habitant customs that modified procedures set down in the Custom of Paris. It seems to have been normal in all classes of French-Canadian society to sign a contract before marrying.[15] The primary function of the marriage contract in rural Quebec was to provide some protection for women in the event their husbands died first. This was achieved mainly by means of the 'douaire préfix,' a specified sum that the groom 'gave' to the bride. The marriage contract of Théophile Allaire and Félicité Audet, for example, mentions a douaire préfix of 150 livres, a common figure for habitant contracts of the mid-eighteenth century. This meant that, on the death of her husband, Félicité would have a claim to that amount out of his half of the communauté. Essentially the 150 livres came out of the inheritance of their children, but only for the duration of the widow's life; on her death, it would of course return to the heirs. The douaire could be particularly important to the widow of a man who died deeply in debt. She could then refuse the communauté while salvaging her douaire since the marriage contract gave her priority over other creditors of the estate for this amount. The 'préciput' was an additional safeguard mentioned in most marriage contracts and giving the surviving spouse, whether male or female, a claim for a certain amount against the communauté prior to the division. In most cases, the préciput represented half the value of the douaire – seventy-five livres in the case of the Allaires. It seems, in general practice, to have allowed widows and widowers to retrieve their bed, clothes, and personal effects from the communauté before the inventory, division of inheritance, and payment of debts.[16]

The marital history of the Allaires of eighteenth-century St Ours helps to illustrate some of these points. Théophile first married in 1753 to Amable Ménard when he was thirty-one years old and she was twenty-one. The couple had five children in the next six years but only one survived beyond infancy. Amable herself died in 1760. Now a widower with a little girl five years old, Théophile soon hired Félicité Audet, a widow from the Quebec region, to keep house for him. Félicité also had a young daughter, the legacy of an earlier marriage. Within three months, she and her employer were man and wife. By their marriage contract, each promised to care for the other's child should one of them die, feeding and raising the orphan and instructing her in the Catholic religion.[17] Théophile and Félicité lived together for six years and had three children together before the family was again broken up, this time by the death of the husband at the age of forty-five. Félicité then found herself a widow once more, but now she was responsible for five children, from three months to fourteen years old. Within a year of her second husband's death (1767) she was once again married, to Etienne Ledoux, a St Denis habitant. At least three sons were born to the couple but, after twelve years, this family too broke apart, not because of a death, but through what is now called 'marriage breakdown.'

Separations are not common in the rural society of eighteenth-century Quebec,[18] but the story of Félicité's break-up with Ledoux is interesting all the same for the light it sheds on marital relations and the position of women. Instead of going through the expensive process of obtaining a legal separation, Etienne and Félicité simply called on the local notary to draw up a contract specifying the conditions of their separation, 'en attendant que Dieu leur fasse la grace de rétablir la concorde et la paix dans leurs coeurs, ainsi qu'ils ont fait la première année qui [sic] lui a plu de les unir ensemble ...'[19] Félicité was to leave their home in St Denis, taking with her one of their sons while their father kept the other two, promising to 'les faire représenter à leur mère toutte fois et quantes qu'elle souhaitera.' No mention was made of the children from Félicité's earlier marriages; presumably they went with their mother, although some of them must have been fully grown by this time and at least one had already married a year earlier. By the terms of the separation agreement, she took with her one cow, one pig, a bed, and several smaller items; she was also entitled to half the grain harvest, half the garden produce, and one-quarter of the hay from the family farm. In addition she and her son were each to be supplied with one minot of wheat per month for four months. To dissolve the couple's communauté de biens, Félicité would also receive about sixty arpents of land, part of the family farm. Within two weeks she had sold this land to a neighbour and used the proceeds to purchase a farm in nearby St Hyacinthe as well as a loom, 'pour pouvoir travailler et gagner sa vie.'[20] At this point Félicité Audet disappears from the records, leaving the impression somehow that she managed quite well on her own.

Félicité may have been an unusual woman, but the incidence of death and remarriage was such that her experience as wife to three successive husbands and mother to three different sets of children cannot have been extraordinary. Her separation agreement certainly suggests a need to qualify traditional views about the 'equality of women' under the Custom of Paris.[21] The document does indeed imply some recognition of the wife's contribution to the agrarian economy in the clause turning over half the harvest. Moreover, Félicité also got a good-sized piece of the family farm, although it was no more than she brought to the marriage and was probably less than half the couple's total holdings. It should be noted, however, that the language of this document presumes the legal mastery of the husband and father: Etienne Ledoux *permits* his wife to go and live wherever she wishes; he *gives* her a certain quantity of land. The relationship between the spouses was clearly unequal, but the communauté de biens, the fundamental principle governing marital property arrangements, gave women legal protection and a stake in family possessions that could not be ignored by any male 'head of household.'

'Outside the family, there is no salvation,' could almost be the motto of the Lower Richelieu habitant. Everything in the social and economic environment conspired to push men and women into the married state. There were individuals like Félicité Audet who resisted the pressure, at least for a time, but they went against the grain of rural life. With hired help comparatively rare, the peasant household and the biological family tended to coincide quite closely in this part of the world and it was the family household that formed the basic unit of material production and consumption. A solitary life in the country was virtually impossible for anyone without independent means. Furthermore, it was easier here than in Europe for young people to obtain the land needed to support a new family and, accordingly, marriage tended to occur at an earlier age and to be more nearly universal. Of course marriage is something more than an economic arrangement, but it is striking to notice how the cultural side of matrimony blended harmoniously with the material life of the peasantry. Permissive parental attitudes about the choice of a mate, clerical co-operation, and egalitarian inheritance customs all tended to facilitate the union of men and women, while popular attitudes towards sexual morality tended to direct physical passions along channels that reinforced rather than threatened the family.

SEXUAL MORALITY

The purpose of marriage, according to Christian doctrine, was procreation and only in marriage was sexual intercourse permissible. In the Catholic society of the Lower Richelieu, the ideal of confining sex to marriage seems to have been accepted by the community as a whole. Although most people acted accordingly, there were always enough exceptions to convince the local clergy of the need for constant vigilance. The curés' correspondence contains just enough sex scandals – surreptitious liaisons and defiant cohabitations – to prove that eighteenth- and early nineteenth-century French Canada was not a society of saints, even in the countryside.[22] It was primarily the 'concubinaires publics' that captured the priests' attention since the flagrancy of their sin seemed most threatening to public order and morality, but such cases were rare enough to be shocking.

For the men of Sorel, when that parish was a major supplier of fur-trade labour, the most common form of sexual deviance occurred in the distant northwest, where they formed unions with native women. Although they were not sanctioned by the Church, these relationships were not promiscuous. The parish registers of Sorel record the baptisms of ten Métis children between 1795 and 1827; all were born of Sorel fathers and Cree, Sioux, Saulteux, or other 'sauvagesses.' The children's ages, recorded in half the cases, ranged from six to twelve years, suggesting that their parents had established fairly stable families.[23]

One index commonly used to obtain some measure of sexual mores in a community is the ratio of illegitimate to legitimate births. While useful, such figures should not be treated as precise and absolute indicators since they reflect several extraneous factors, such as the demographic composition of the population, in addition to moral behaviour.[24] Using a transcript of the parish registers of Sorel, I counted legitimate and illegitimate infant baptisms, considering a baby 'illegitimate' if it was listed as a foundling or if its mother was identified and its father listed as 'unknown.' The resulting illegitimacy ratios are as follows:

	Infant baptisms	Illegitimate births	Ratio
1740–99	2556	47	1.84%
1800–39	6747	148	2.20%

The slight rise between the eighteenth and early nineteenth centuries may be connected to Sorel's importance in the second period as a river port and a stopping place for immigrants. In any case, the ratios in both periods are fairly low compared to most contemporary European populations.[25]

What was the fate of Sorel's bastards? In a minority of cases (one out of four in the eighteenth century), unmarried mothers openly kept their babies in spite of strong public censure. At a time when women supervised most aspects of child delivery, however, it was not always the girl and her family who were stuck with the obligation of raising an illegitimate child. Marguerite Paul Hus, a Sorel midwife, once managed to persuade a young and unmarried girl, 'durant les douleurs d'enfantement,' to identify the father of her baby. The fear and pain that accompanied this avowal, like a confession under torture, apparently served to guarantee its authenticity. Her job complete, Marguerite promptly departed for St Joachim where the young man lived and deposited the infant with his family.[26] More commonly, illegitimate children were secretly left at the door of the church. The fate of these foundlings was simple enough; deprived of proper care, the great majority died within a few days. At least these infants received the sacrament of baptism. This would not have been the case for any babies born out of wedlock and, not simply abandoned, but deliberately killed by unwed mothers wishing to escape shame and rejection. At least one historian argues that infanticide was a substitute for abortion practised to a significant extent by married couples as well as single girls in pre-industrial Europe.[27]

While there is no evidence that infanticide was ever common in French Canada, here as in Europe, there was a horrified fascination with the image of the unwed mother compounding her sins by depriving her unbaptized baby of both life and salvation.[28]

Of course not every unmarried woman who became pregnant ended up giving birth to an illegitimate child; many married during the period of gestation. To gain a rough idea of the extent of pre-marital conception in Sorel, I took the couples in the marriage sample described earlier and searched the parish registers for births recorded within eight months of the wedding.

	Marriages	Pre-marital conceptions	Rate
1740–79	224	15	6.7%
1780–1809	179	8	4.5%
1810–39	215	18	8.4%

Ordinarily rates of pre-marital conception give the number of early first births as a proportion of all first births but this requires data that can only be found through family reconstitution. By using marriages instead of first births we certainly underestimate the rate of pre-nuptial conception, perhaps by as much as one-half, because we do not account for the couples that may have married in Sorel but who were either childless or who baptized their first baby in another parish. Even if the figures are doubled – and this is probably going too far – they are still fairly low by contemporary French standards and far below the rates of pre-marital conception found in England and the United States. On the other hand, pre-marital conceptions were much more frequent in Sorel after 1740 than they were in seventeenth- and early eighteenth-century Canada, but their incidence in Sorel did not increase sigificantly between 1740 and 1839.[29]

Whether we view sexual behaviour through the medium of priests' correspondence or through illegitimacy and pre-nuptial conception rates, the conclusion is essentially the same: without being totally 'pure,' the people of the Lower Richelieu tended to keep sex confined to marriage. The French-Canadian pattern of marriage mentioned earlier must have reinforced this. Compared to contemporary Europeans, eighteenth-century Canadians spent a smaller portion of their life with no legitimate outlet for their sexual urges. Pierre de Sales Laterrière declared (with considerable exaggeration) that there was no 'immorality' in rural Lower

Canada but, he explained, this was because people 'are unexposed to temptation.' 'They marry young; are subject to no restraint; and can therefore exercise no virtue.'[30] Laterrière to the contrary, habitants clearly did have to 'exercise virtue' during the ten years or so that usually intervened between puberty and marriage, as well as during any period of widowhood. They generally accepted the notion that sex was permitted only between husband and wife and there are even hints that they considered it mandatory within marriage. One man tried to have his wife barred from the church for refusing to share his bed. Writing to the bishop, he complained of the scandal caused by her behaviour and of the open mocking he encountered in the parish.[31] Besides illustrating the lack of privacy characteristic of pre-modern village life, this anecdote suggests, through ridicule of a deviant case, how the community felt the roles of husband and wife should properly be carried out. The family then was not only the basic unit of habitant production and consumption, it was also the primary locus of erotic life and of procreation.

DEMOGRAPHY

Habitant families were indeed fruitful. Year after year, births were more numerous than deaths and the result was a rapid and sustained natural growth that soon filled the region with as many households as it would support. The early French-Canadian population has of course long been viewed as exceptionally expansive,[32] and factors such as the influence of the Church and the national spirit have been proposed to explain this characteristic. Recent research, however, suggests that French Canada's demography was never unique, except perhaps during the period of intense immigration before 1660.[33] On the whole, demographic patterns were essentially similar to those of pre-industrial Europe. In New France, as in colonial New England, New World circumstances tended to produce an 'American' variant with levels of fertility and mortality encouraging growth. Still, departures from the western European model were more a matter of nuance than of basic structure and, before 1840 at least, they resulted more from the relative abundance of land than from any 'spiritual' causes.

Fertility, that is the incidence of births, and mortality, the incidence of death, are the two basic characteristics governing the rate of growth of a population and to isolate each and measure it precisely would require family reconstitution data. The blunter instruments employed on the

TABLE 9
Marital fertility, Sorel, St Ours, and St Denis 1740–1829

	Sorel	St Ours	St Denis
1740–9*	9.47		12.18
1750–9		11.09	10.98
1760–9		7.63	8.80
1770–9		6.48	8.63
1780–9	7.30	6.24	7.72
1790–9	6.36	6.17	7.53
1800–9	5.86	7.04	6.92
1810–19	7.63		6.44
1820–9	7.17		7.51

* Marriages 1740–9 divided by baptisms 1745–54, etc.

censuses and parish registers of the Lower Richelieu still give useful, though somewhat rough, indicators of fertility and mortality. Essentially they suggest that the typically 'American' population of the region had levels of fertility that were somewhat higher and levels of mortality rather lower than most contemporary European populations.

The crude birth rate around 1831, when reliable census figures are available, was 47.7 per thousand in Sorel (Catholics only), 48.9 in St Ours, and 51.8 in St Denis. Figures this high could be found in many localities in pre-industrial Europe, but thirty-five per thousand was probably closer to the average there.[34] On the other hand, birth rates in the United States were about the same as those of the Lower Richelieu (forty-five to fifty per thousand around 1830) and, in the Brazilian province of Parana, they were considerably higher (fifty-six per thousand, 1800–22, whites only).[35] Another rough indicator of fertility can be calculated by dividing the number of births in a decade by the number of marriages in an overlapping decade, five years earlier (see Table 9). In this case, the results are seriously distorted for the period before 1760 when immigrants married outside the region made up a sizeable proportion of those bringing their babies to be baptized at Sorel, St Ours, and St Denis. By this measure also, fertility in the Lower Richelieu was higher than in contemporary Europe, and about the same as in early New England.[36] The histories of fertility are not exactly parallel in English and French North America, however. Indices of fertility began to decline quite sharply in New England as soon as the land in a locality was fully settled,[37] whereas the number of births per marriage remained virtually unchanged in the Lower Richelieu, even into the nineteenth century when 'frontier conditions' had disappeared.

Why was fertility high in French Canada compared to eighteenth-century Western Europe? Birth control was not an important factor since it was not practised to any significant degree, except in a few areas of France late in the century; moreover, even where contraception was clearly not used, French fertility was generally lower than Canadian. On the other hand, marriage patterns, the Lower Richelieu tendency to marry at an early age and to remarry promptly after the death of a spouse, must have helped to keep fertility high. If married couples had babies every two years or so in a pre-industrial population, then the prevalence and duration of marriage would naturally affect fertility. Thus, adult mortality – comparatively low in the eighteenth-century Lower Richelieu – would have reinforced the effects of French-Canadian marital behaviour in maximizing the population's reproductive capacities.

Population growth is conditioned as much by mortality as it is by fertility and, in this case too, all we have for the moment are rough-and-ready indicators. In a pre-industrial population, the number of deaths may fluctuate dramatically from one year to the next, with unusually large numbers occurring in occasional 'demographic crises.' This 'crisis mortality' is therefore studied separately from 'structural mortality,' that is, the normal incidence of death.

Sorel, St Ours, and St Denis certainly had their mortality crises, in 1784 for example, and again in 1832, when there were twice as many deaths as in preceding years. Moreover, several of the peaks in the death curves (Figures 3–5) correspond to temporary dips in the number of births and marriages which reinforced the negative effect on population growth. In this respect, the agitations on the Lower Richelieu graphs mirror the classic pattern of the 'mortalités' of Old Régime France.[38] However, these are in fact quite minor affairs compared to the much more devastating catastrophes to which European populations were regularly subjected. In French Canada, as in colonial New England, the number of deaths even in the worst years never went soaring beyond the birth curves as they did across the Atlantic.[39] Less severe than the Malthusian catastrophes of Europe, the mortality crises of the Lower Richelieu seem nevertheless to have been essentially similar events with similar causes.

The mortality crises of Old Régime France have received intensive scrutiny from historians and, though some insist that epidemics and not starvation were the killer, most experts now agree that food shortages were at the root of many crises. There was a precarious balance between agricultural production and subsistence needs; grain harvests being quite

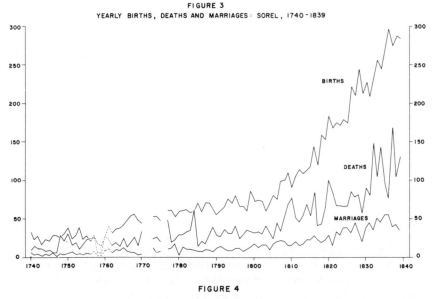

FIGURE 3
YEARLY BIRTHS, DEATHS AND MARRIAGES: SOREL, 1740-1839

FIGURE 4

YEARLY BAPTISMS, MARRIAGES, AND BURIALS: ST.OURS, 1751-1840

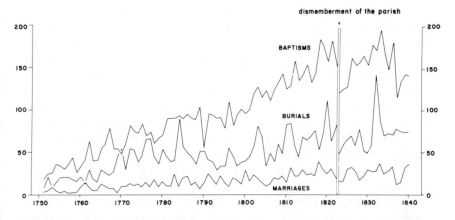

vulnerable to climatic accidents, it only took a late spring frost or heavy fall rains to curtail supplies severely and increase grain prices far beyond the means of the urban and rural poor. Clear evidence of outright starvation is rare for seventeenth- and eighteenth-century France, however. It was actually disease that finally claimed so many lives during these recurrent 'disettes.' Undernourishment and the consumption, in des-

FIGURE 5

YEARLY BAPTISMS, MARRIAGES AND BURIALS : ST. DENIS, 1740-1840

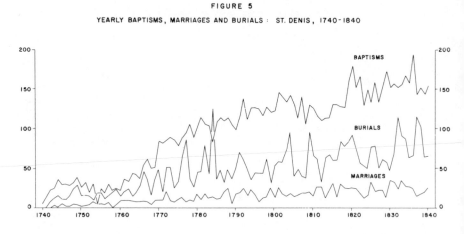

peration, of unripe and unwholesome foods weakened people's resistance to infection, and illness soon finished off what hunger had begun.[40] The European subsistence crisis was therefore a complex event in which disease was the epiphenomenon of food shortage.

Were there ever genuine subsistence crises in French Canada? Although the term 'famine' has been applied to some of the bad years in eighteenth-century Quebec,[41] there is no trace of anything so dramatic in the history of our region. Certainly agricultural production was no less subject to shortfalls than European agriculture and grain was in dangerously short supply on more than one occasion. Moreover, correspondence and other 'qualitative' sources suggest that hunger was sometimes severe in poor and isolated communities in the eighteenth and early nineteenth centuries. Poor harvests did not go unnoticed in the annals of the Lower Richelieu either, but local priests speak of economic rather than of biological hardships. Parish vestries sometimes gave emergency relief at such times, but it was a matter of loaning seed grain, not of relieving starvation.

What about the quantitative record? Most of the sharp peaks on the death curves of Sorel, St Ours, and St Denis coincide with epidemic years. There were outbreaks of smallpox in 1770 and 1784. The latter epidemic was one of the cruelest in the region's history. As smallpox often does, it carried off a disproportionate number of children. In 1809–10 the Lower Richelieu and most of Quebec was struck by 'fièvres,' apparently typhoid.[42] St Denis was affected quite badly and earlier than most other parishes. In November 1809, the curé wrote: 'La mort depuis

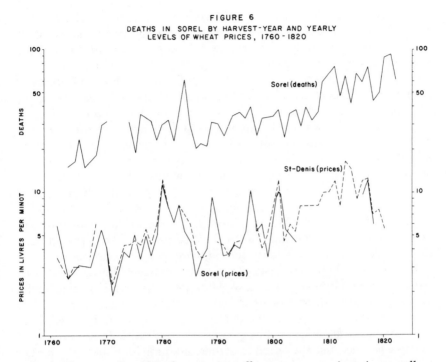

FIGURE 6
DEATHS IN SOREL BY HARVEST-YEAR AND YEARLY
LEVELS OF WHEAT PRICES, 1760-1820

près de deux mois, y fait des ravages allarmans: en quinze jours, elle a enlevé quinze adultes; depuis samedi dernier, treize ont été administrés et presque tous annoncent une fin prochaine.'[43] The famous cholera epidemic of 1832 – which allegedly hit Lower Canada more severely than any European nation[44] – took a heavy toll in all three parishes, but only Sorel seems to have had an unusual number of deaths during the second cholera year, 1834. Eighteen thirty-seven was a year of influenza, as well as rebellion, in the Lower Richelieu.

There also seems to be a connection between mortality and grain prices, particularly when deaths are grouped in harvest years to correspond more closely to the agricultural calendar (see Figure 6). One notices bumps in Sorel's death curve that coincide with relatively high wheat prices in 1769, 1784, 1789, 1796, 1801, 1811, 1813, and 1817. Viewed in this light, the smallpox outbreaks of 1770 and 1784 look more like examples of the classic pre-industrial syndrome of food shortage combined with disease epidemic. The year before the smallpox of 1770 had been 'une année de la plus grande disette ... depuis vingt huit ans,' and the curé of St Denis noted that the habitants were forced to reap their grain while it was still green.[45] And yet, one hesitates to characterize some of the tiny irregularities in the mortality graphs as subsistence crises, much less 'famines.' Certainly the most important crisis of the 1740–1840 period was the cholera of 1832, a 'pure' epidemic. With these qualifications in mind, we may still conclude that, in French Canada as in France, mortality was influenced by food supplies, although the Lower Richelieu was spared the more severe forms of Malthusian crisis.

Crisis mortality was likely attenuated by two factors in rural Quebec before the nineteenth century. One was a relatively low population density that put less pressure on the food producing capacity of the environment. When wheat crops failed, habitants of the Lower Richelieu were close to forests and marshes where they could find berries, fish, and wildfowl. Second, French Canada long remained a river-front civilization and, in the days before railroads, this meant that transportation was comparatively easy and that local shortages could be supplied from the outside with less difficulty than in many parts of Europe.

In the years between crises, the Lower Richelieu had a pattern of structural mortality that also followed European patterns in its essentials. This aspect of mortality is very difficult to measure, particularly where adult deaths are concerned. Aside from any technical difficulties, there is the major problem caused by people whose deaths do not appear in the registers because they died elsewhere after moving out of the parish or during a temporary absence. Children, however, are not generally as mobile as adults and their mortality therefore can be estimated with a greater degree of confidence through the use of family reconstitution or by means of a 'short-cut' technique devised by Pierre Goubert.[46] An adaptation of Goubert's method was applied to the Sorel parish registers. It involves following the progress of a birth cohort over twenty years to discover how many of its members die and at what ages (see Table 10). Because a certain number of juveniles, particularly adolescents, likely die outside the parish, this procedure underestimates mortality slightly but Goubert found it gave results quite close to those obtained from family reconstitution data.

Mortality in the first year of life was substantial in Sorel, at least in the middle of the eighteenth century. Once a child had passed its first birthday however, it seems to have had a much better chance of surviving in the Canadian than in the French parish. The comparison with Auneuil in the 'tragic' seventeenth century is perhaps unfair but other figures for French populations in the second half of the eighteenth century indicate substantially higher juvenile mortality than was found in

TABLE 10
Child and infant deaths by birth cohort

	Sorel 1730–55	Sorel 1785–90	Sorel 1816–19	Auneuil 1656–1735
Births	153	395	596	2155
Deaths under 1 month	17.6%	7.6%	6.7%	
" under 1 year	24.8%	18.7%	17.6%	28.8%
" 1–4 years	2.6%	3.5%	9.1%	14.5%
" 5–9 years	2.6%	2.0%	2.7%	3.8%
" 10–19 years	2.0%	1.0%	2.7%	4.0%
" under 19 years	32.0%	25.3%	32.0%	51.1%

TABLE 11
Infant mortality (per thousand live births)

Canada 1630–1739	211
Canada 1700–50	246
Sorel 1740–79	276
Sorel 1780–1809	222
Sorel 1810–39	171
France (females) 1740–79	254–75
France (females) 1780–99	234–65
Crulai (France) 1720–89	172
Rural Finland 1749–73	197
Sweden 1751–60	206
Sweden 1791–1800	193
Colyton (England) 1750–1837	122–53

Sorel.[47] It seems reasonable to suppose that adult structural mortality was also lower in the New World.

One element of Sorel's structural mortality that would have given Europeans no grounds for envy was infant mortality. For the eighteenth-century cohorts listed in Table 10, an unusually large proportion of the deaths under twenty years occurred in the first year of life. More complete figures for the entire 1740–1840 period confirm the impression that infant mortality was quite high (see Table 11).[48] Well over one-quarter of the babies born in the years before the American Revolution did not survive to their first birthday. To some extent, this was probably a reflection of French Canada's rather high fertility, since infant mortality increases with family size.[49] Other factors commonly associated with high infant mortality – genetic defects, accidents during delivery, and poor conditions of hygiene and sanitation – must have been more important. Understanding the 'whys' of infant mortality and other aspects of the Lower Richelieu demographic régime requires us to leave the parish registers and censuses and turn to sources that tell more about conditions of life, sanitation, and medical care in the eighteenth and early nineteenth centuries.

Child delivery at the time was handled by midwives. Respected local women, midwives had religious as well as medical responsibilities and they were authorized by the priest to perform emergency baptisms on babies in danger of dying. In Canada, as in other countries, they came under attack in the late eighteenth century from physicians (male, of course) seeking to assert control over this function. A Dr John Connor of Quebec argued in favour of state regulation of all aspects of medicine:

I'll not except midwifery in which we daily see the greatest cruelty committed on the deplorable [sic] mothers and innocent children. These practitioners take up the first utensil they find to serve in the room of a blunt hook or crochet to extract fetuses limb by limb ... and by their untimely and imprudent assistance cause children to present in a wrong which if left to nature would come in a natural position.[50]

Although he was not a detached observer, the infant mortality figures suggest that Dr Connor's criticisms of midwifery were justified. On the other hand, this does not necessarily mean that he and his colleagues would have been any more effective in saving infant lives. The international assault by 'qualified professionals' against midwives and 'ignorant empirics' was more a matter of propaganda than of proven perform-ance.[51] It was directed against practitioners who were closer to the people they served and perhaps just as efficacious as those who considered themselves their superiors.

Members of the habitant community itself dealt with many routine medical problems as well as with childbirth. The documents provide few details about popular medicine, but they make it clear that a strong folk tradition existed in the Lower Richelieu. There apparently were paid local specialists such as the widow Lafresnai who claimed three livres from one estate, 'pour médicament.'[52] Habitants derived a number of remedies from various evergreen trees, perhaps in imitation of the Indians; pine resin, for example, was used as an ointment for cuts.[53] Wine and rum were favourite medicines for people sick in bed. When lives were in danger however, doctors were normally called for.

There were always surgeons or doctors in the Lower Richelieu and the habitants seem to have made use of their services. From the late eighteenth century on, most aging peasants who turned over their farms by deed of *donation* required the beneficiary to fetch the doctor in case of illness. Probably this was meant to apply only to the most serious cases, since the priest usually had to be summoned as well as the doctor. Estate inventories frequently list debts owed to doctors, 'pour soin pendant sa maladie.' Forty per cent of the inventories in our sample of 110 mention such debts, but the proportion varies greatly over time: 1740–69 – 30 per cent; 1790–9 – 20 per cent; 1830–9 – 75 per cent. Apparently recourse to 'qualified' medical aid increased greatly in the early nineteenth century. Moreover, that aid was of a different sort than what was available in earlier years. Most local practitioners in the eighteenth century were surgeons, whereas university-trained physicians predominated in the later period.

How much did professional medical care affect mortality conditions in the Lower Richelieu? Hardly at all, if the figures from Table 10 are any guide. Death rates for the 1816–19 cohort, that is for the period when physicians' visits were most common, were worse than those of the eighteenth century for every age except infants. Even the improvement in infant mortality was probably not due to improved medical care, since doctors seem to have been called mainly to help adults and were not normally present at deliveries. Moreover, the infant mortality rate was substantially the same in 1816–19 as it was in 1785–90, when doctors were mentioned in very few habitant inventories. Medical care by professionals and by popular healers may have relieved suffering and may have saved some lives, but it does not seem to have altered the mortality structures of the Lower Richelieu substantially. This is no particular slur on early Canadian medicine; some experts have argued that, everywhere in the past, doctors, surgeons, and hospitals did as much harm as good and that they only began making significant contributions to the death rate with the advent of sulpha drugs in the 1930s.[54] Up until then, environmental factors – diet, sanitation, hygiene – were far more important.

By modern standards, sanitary conditions were appalling in rural Quebec in the eighteenth and early nineteenth centuries. Habitants drank more than one from the same cup, they passed pipes from mouth to mouth, they spat on the floor, and they chewed food before transferring it to their babies' mouths. Dead animals were left to rot where they dropped in the fields. Latrines were virtually unknown as late as the 1830s.[55] Moreover, wells were regularly polluted when the spring run-off flushed barnyard mess into the drinking water. Those who could afford it brewed beer for their families when the snows melted, but this was not always possible and one observer blamed the outbreak of deadly fever at St Denis in 1809 on 'les mauvaises eaux que les habitants des concessions ont été obligés de boire.'[56] Residents living near the rivers would not have been affected since they presumably drew their drinking water from the stream.

This may in fact be the key explaining the apparent deterioration of French-Canadian mortality over the course of the eighteenth century. As rural settlement filled the banks of the St Lawrence and its tributaries and began expanding inland, an increasing percentage of the population must have depended on wells and thus found its water supply subject to contamination. This hypothesis seems to be confirmed by a shift in the seasonal incidence of mortality between the seventeenth century, when few settlers would have needed wells and when the largest number of deaths occurred in the winter months, and the second half of the eighteenth century, when more deaths occurred in the summer. Since winter deaths are commonly caused by respiratory illnesses and summer deaths more likely to result from the gastro-intestinal complaints often associated with contaminated water supplies, polluted wells are a likely culprit.[57]

Was rural Quebec, with its polluted wells and spittle-covered floors, an exceptionally unhygenic pre-industrial society? By no means! In other parts of the eighteenth-century world, conditions were just as bad, if not far worse.[58] In this respect too, the conditions of life of the peasantry of the Lower Richelieu were similar to those of Western Europe. Consequently patterns of mortality were also essentially the same. If mortality was somewhat less severe in North America, it was probably because the food supply there was a bit more nourishing, plentiful and secure, not because of any superiority in hygiene or medical care. The eighteenth-century diet of wheaten bread, pea soup, and salt pork described in the last chapter was good hearty fare.

The eighteenth-century Lower Richelieu then was subject to a pre-industrial demographic régime essentially similar to that of Western Europe. A slight edge in fertility and mortality, due to the relative abundance of land in North America, tended to favour high rates of natural increase. As a result, each generation was of course larger than the last and, for the economy to remain one of household consumption and production, there had to be land for young adults to establish and support their new families. The economic counterpart of biological reproduction was, in the first instance, inheritance, the transfer of property from parents to children.

INHERITANCE

In a peasant society like that of the Lower Richelieu the devolution of land is the central element in the process of economic reproduction, although livestock, buildings, and equipment are also important. The term 'inheritance' is used for want of a better name, but it has the unfortunate tendency of implying a simple post-mortem transfer from parents to offspring. In fact, inheritance is a complex process involving the transmission of property on various occasions, the death of one parent, the remarriage of a widowed parent, the death of the last parent, the marriage of an heir, or the retirement of the parents from productive activity. In rural French Canada, part of the patrimony could devolve on any or all of these occasions. In theory, inheritance here was governed by the Custom of Paris and an understanding of that legal code is a necessary first step in studying actual inheritance customs which modified the law in line with changing attitudes and circumstances.

Under this code, arrangements were quite different for 'noble' lands, that is, seigneuries, regardless of the status of their owners, and 'commoners'' lands. While equal division was the basic rule for the latter, a partial form of primogeniture applied to fiefs. On the death of a seigneur, half his or her estate, along with the manor house, went to the eldest son, while the remainder was divided equally among the younger children. Without going to the extremes of English law, this was meant to protect the landed aristocracy against excessive splintering of estates. The subdivision of fiefs would have been fatal to the nobility had it been widespread, but this did not occur to any great extent in Canada, thanks partly to the law but also to the aristocratic spirit of the country's seigneurs, who made great efforts to avoid such an eventuality. For example, Sorel was kept intact after the death of the second seigneur, Claude de Ramezay, because his four children agreed to avoid a division. Roch de Ramezay, the son and principal heir, managed the estate and distributed shares of the revenue to his three sisters.[59]

Relations were not so harmonious in the family of Pierre de St Ours. For some years after his death, the seigneurie remained, like Sorel, 'indivise,' but in 1734 the heirs finally decided on a partition.[60] The division was frightfully complicated as the estate was made up of three seigneuries, St Ours, L'Assomption on the north shore of the St Lawrence, and St Jean Deschaillons near Quebec; moreover, Pierre had left six heirs at his death ten years earlier and two of the daughters had died since then, leaving sons or widowers to claim their portions. Where St Ours itself is concerned, every effort was made to distribute the good and the bad lands fairly by dividing each section into small parcels and having the heirs draw lots to determine which they would receive. The proportions specified by the Custom of Paris were rigidly adhered to, however: Jean-Baptiste St Ours de l'Echaillon, as first son, was awarded the manor and half the territory, while the other heirs got one-tenth each from a checkerboard of bits and pieces. The subsequent history of St Ours saw the gradual reintegration of the seigneurie under the ownership of Jean-Baptiste's heirs, the 'principal seigneurs.' One of them bought banal rights for the entire fief in 1770. Acquiring the five minor sections of the estate itself was a long and arduous process covering 113 years and requiring several purchases and, on one occasion, the 'retrait féodal' to nullify a sale to a third party.[61] Along with the retrait féodal, the rule of partial primogeniture gave the senior line of a seigneurial family a considerable advantage in its efforts to preserve the integrity of an estate without disinheriting cadets.

Where 'commoners' lands' were concerned, the intent behind the Custom of Paris was not to maintain large, revenue-producing estates, but to provide for the maintenance of as many offspring as possible. Although the basic idea is one of equal division of land and moveables among all the children of a deceased parent, there were several qualifications favouring preferential treatment. Commenting on the work of a French legal historian, Emmanuel LeRoy Ladurie suggests that the Custom of Paris and other codes of the Ile de France represent a compromise between the radical egalitarianism of the western parts of the kingdom and the partriarchal authority and single heir practices of the south.[62] LeRoy Ladurie is interested mainly in the fate of children endowed with a marriage portion or otherwise favoured, and he finds evidence of an egalitarian spirit in the rule that allowed previously advantaged heirs the option of returning any property they received to the estate in order to share equally in the entire property. Heirs in this position had the choice of returning their endowment or keeping what they had received before the parents' death; their interest would obviously be to participate in the division only if they had been given less than their share of the property. What LeRoy Ladurie fails to note is the potential under this rule, unlike the western customs which made restoration mandatory, of considerable inequality among heirs if one child were given much *more* than his share while the parents were still alive. The problem is that this author seems to assume that there is a necessary connection between endowment and departure from the parental home. In French Canada, under the Custom of Paris, habitants often endowed a stay-at-home, turning over before they died the greatest part of their property to one son or daughter.

The 'légitime' was a right that, in theory, limited any such preferential treatment. The légitime was one-half of what each child would have received in an equal division of the family property had it been undiminished by any endowments or bequests; every heir had a right to demand this much as a minimum inheritance and brothers and sisters who had been given endowments to the prejudice of siblings' légitimes would have to compensate them.[63] A parent had the right to make bequests in a written will but only if these did not infringe on the légitime of legitimate heirs and only for the value of movable property and one-fifth of inherited land. In other words, the power to dispose of wealth in this way was so restricted that very few eighteenth-century habitants bothered to draw up a will. The basic rule then is equal division among all children of property left at the parents' death, some protection through the légitime against bequests and pre-mortem endowments that might deplete the estate excessively, and the option for endowed offspring of returning endowments and participating in the sharing of the estate.

The actual settling of the estate of a deceased parent was complicated by the existence of a communauté de biens that may or may not have been dissolved at the same time and by the presence, in many cases, of underage children who could not handle property on their own. With the consent of all parties, the communauté de biens might be left intact after the death of one parent, so that a dissolution and a real division of property could occur much later, commonly after the death or the remarriage of the second parent. In the various transactions of the settlement, the rights of minor orphans would be looked after by a legal guardian, usually a relative of the child. Depending on whether the division was held after one or both parents died, the heirs would share half the property (less the value of any douaire or préciput) or all of it. This meant auctioning off movable wealth and dividing the proceeds, as well as dividing the land, or rather (since few families had enough land to go around without reducing each share to an uneconomic fragment), transferring land and credits so that one or two heirs got the farm and the others were compensated with cash or other benefits.

In her account of inheritance practices based on a thorough study of

the notarial records of seventeenth-century Montreal, Louise Dechêne
emphasizes the pragmatic and egalitarian spirit that led the early settlers
of New France to go beyond the letter of the Custom of Paris in arranging
equitable settlements,[64] while sensibly avoiding any excessive fragmentation of holdings. Genuine solidarity within the family, together with
a democratic habit of involving all members, male and female, young
and old, in estate arrangements, ensured that the allocation of land and
other property would be done in the interests of all concerned. A similar
equality and harmony seems to have prevailed in the Lower Richelieu
early in the eighteenth century when abundant land was still close at
hand and when agricultural markets were quite limited, but in later
periods land came to be difficult to obtain and grain sales were more
common; inheritance arrangements then became less democratic in their
procedures and less equalitarian in their effects.

At all times it was normal to provide all sons and daughters with a
small endowment of household goods when they married and left home.
To take one typical example, three children, a boy and two girls, were
already endowed and 'established' in 1791 when an inventory was made
of the estate of Jean-Baptiste Cardin and Jeanne Carie of Sorel and the
records show that each had taken a bed, a cow, a sheep, and a pig.[65]
The son also received a horse and the daughters took a sideboard and
a spinning wheel. In this and in other cases, the value of moveable
goods was about equal for departing children of both sexes but endowments of land were frankly discriminatory. Habitants sometimes gave
a piece of land to a son about the time he married but daughters almost
never benefited from such liberalities (except of course indirectly through
their husbands). The law gave women a share in land and other property
when their parents died so that, in the mid-eighteenth century, they
really did receive part of the family estate. In pre-mortem distributions,
however, parents thought first of 'establishing' their boys and assumed
that sons-in-law and and their families would look after their daughters.
Since the tendency was for habitants increasingly to dispose of their
property before they died, transmission through the female line all but
disappeared by the turn of the nineteenth century.

As far as land is concerned, genuinely partible settlements, with
daughters benefiting as much as sons, were possible in the early period
because habitants were often able to secure huge holdings that were
clearly intended for no other purpose than to provide future farms for
a large family. The prime example of this is the patriarch Paul Hue (or
Hus), who secured from the seigneur of Yamaska in the 1670s the conces-

sion of an entire peninsula separated from the rest of the seigneurie by the swampy Baie de la Vallière, as well as the Ile du Moine, separated from the peninsula by a narrow channel. Hue rounded out his domain with a few adjacent rotures in the seigneurie of Sorel and, before he died, he divided up his kingdom into thirteen large farm lots, with common grazing privileges on the Ile du Moine attached; he gave them, one to each of five sons, three sons-in-law, one unmarried daughter, and four grandsons.[66] His descendants were legion and spread throughout Sorel and beyond in the following century.

Etienne Allaire, Théophile's father, is another example, less dramatic though more typical than Paul Hue. In 1745, he had a lot of 255 arpents in St Ours, though only forty arpents were cleared. This was far more than one household could make use of but Etienne had six daughters and five sons, only one or two of them established on their own farms. The need to provide for these offspring, the young men particularly, made the father willing to pay seigneurial dues for such a large and, for the moment, useless piece of property. When Etienne died in 1753, each of the eleven children – most of them were grown and married, the daughters therefore being officially represented by their husbands – were duly awarded a portion of some twenty-three arpents. This was not enough land for a Canadian farm and certainly no one dreamed that such a division would be more than a temporary legal fiction; accordingly, the Allaires used their shares to negotiate a complicated series of transactions. Without going into all the details, we might note that Théophile Allaire bought out the shares of one of his brothers and one sister who were both married and established on farms nearby; he raised the 370 livres to make this purchase by selling to his father-in-law his wife's share in her mother's estate. No sooner was this transaction complete than he turned around and gave land purchased from his brother to a sister and brother-in-law in exchange for a plot that rounded off a consolidated sixty-arpent farm for him. Looking through the notarial records, one might almost get the impression from hundreds of sales and exchanges of this sort that the Lower Richelieu was the scene of intense real estate speculation, more like the downtown core of a booming metropolis than a quiet countryside. But this is a misleading impression. A closer look at these transactions, for example, shows that Théophile and Amable Allaire had already lived and worked for years on the land they 'bought' in 1755; adequate compensation had to be worked out for siblings with an interest in the estate but clearly there was no question of banishing the couple from their home.[67] In the end, all of Etienne

Allaire's descendants shared his small fortune after the old man's death; his extensive land holdings were broken up into smaller units, as he doubtless intended they should be; but elaborate arrangements were made to avoid the excessive fragmentation that would have accompanied an equal division of the land.

While settlements of this sort remained the rule well into the nineteenth century for those who died still in possession of their property, the overall process of property devolution changed considerably over the years. Habitants turned increasingly in the eighteenth century to a pattern centring on the deed of gift ('donation-entre-vifs') to pass on their land and goods to the succeeding generation *before* they died, and so avoid a post-mortem division. Consequently, when they died there would be little or nothing left for any heirs to divide. This is why one encounters few deeds dividing up estates ('partages') and a great many deeds of gift in the notarial files of the late eighteenth and early nineteenth centuries. The Sorel estate role of 1795 lists eighty-five lots acquired by the current owner from a relative and forty-five of these (53 per cent) were transferred by gift; another nine lots were acquired by gift from unrelated individuals. As mentioned earlier, these were not really gifts in the normal sense of the word. The son or daughter receiving land and other property from elderly parents invariably had to accept a certain number of obligations, primarily that of supporting the donors. A French commentator writing in 1786 remarked on the trend to deeds of gift in tones of the strongest disapproval.

Une manie depuis longtems Introduite parmi les habitans Canadiens ... porte a l'agriculture de la province, un prejudice des plus notables.

A peine un chef de Famille Rustique est Parvenû à Sa 45e année, que pour s'abreger toute culture, et vivre dans l'oisivité, *ce quils qualifient de repos*, delaisse tout, ou Majeure partie de son bien à quelqu'un de Ses enfants; Quelquefois même a des jeunes gens qui lui sont Etrangers, Moyanant une pension viagere, Plus souvent superieure au revenu liquide du bien qu'il delaisse, transaction quils qualifient de donation *entre vifs*, dont l'espece même est presque inconue a la Coutume de Paris ...[68]

Arrangements of this sort were certainly not unique to early French Canada. In every society of cultivators, there must be a certain number of cases where control passes, de facto if not always de jure, from the older generation to someone in the younger before the death of the former. Fathers in colonial Andover, Massachusetts, used deeds of gift in this way, although they tended to delay the transfer of farms that had been worked by sons for many years, relinquishing legal control only after their children had reached middle age.[69] A precise study of French-Canadian transfers has yet to be undertaken but evidence in the deeds of gift themselves suggests that retiring habitants tended to cede their land to sons or daughters who were fairly young and who had married recently. Parental control (under the régime of the communauté de biens, the term 'patriarchal' would not apply here as it does in early Massachusetts) was guaranteed by conditions inserted into the deed. Determined to avoid the fate of King Lear, Lower Richelieu habitants loaded down their *donations* with a multitude of conditions and obligations designed mainly to ensure their own maintenance once they had ceded legal ownership of their farms. They often stipulated benefits for brothers and sisters of the beneficiary but this was by no means universal. The basic effect of the deed of gift was to favour one heir at the expense of the others.

In the present state of research we do not know what determined the selection of a beneficiary for a deed of gift. Some were certainly given to married daughters and their husbands and in one case a widow passed over sons and sons-in-law to leave her farm to an unmarried daughter.[70] The great majority of *donations*, however, were directed towards sons. If there were many sons, which one was chosen? Since many deeds speak of both older, married brothers and of younger brothers still at home, it seems clear that no rigid rule of primogeniture or ultimogeniture was applied; more likely parents left their farm to whichever son reached maturity and married when they were ready to forsake active farming. On the other hand, less readily apparent factors such as affection, reliability, or loyal services in the past doubtless played a role. One old woman began her deed of gift with these words: 'Laquelle attendu son grand âge et infirmité, la tranquilité et le repos dont elle a besoin et reconnoisant la bienveillance et amitié que luy témoigne visiblement et sensiblement depuis quelques années Antoine Lacoste dit Languedoc son fils ...'[71] Eighteenth-century *donations* tend to keep the inherent favouritism of this arrangement limited, showing considerable concern for the rights of co-heirs. In many cases, they are the work of a widow and therefore involve only the half the family property that came into her possession when the marriage community dissolved on the husband's death. In others, there is an insistence that the ceded property be effectively restored to the estate on the death of the parents, an equal division worked out (at least, on paper) and compensation given to the unendowed siblings. This was the provision in the 1759 deed by which Louis Poulin left his St Denis farm to his son Louis-Marie-Joseph: 'à la charge par ledt. donataire de tenir compte à la succession des dits donateurs un compte de ce que pourra luy revenire lors que partage se fera, ladite terre ayant été estimé à la somme de cinq mille livres ...'[72] Few deeds of gift from this period are quite so scrupulously egalitarian, but most provide for some compensation to co-heirs. Pierre Plante and his wife, when turning over all their property to their son Antoine, at least thought it necessary to note that, 'au regard des autres enfants desdts. donateurs attendu que les uns sont pourvus et les autres en état de gagner leur vie ...'; even so, Antoine had to provide a cow for each of his brothers and sisters as they left home and pay each fifty livres on the death of his parents, 'pour leur tenir lieu de légitime.'[73] Once again, the law is honoured in the breach since fifty livres and a cow was likely far less than a proper légitime, but at least the Plantes were aware of the concept. One common provision made the beneficiary responsible for maintaining younger brothers and sisters still at home and for giving them the customary endowment when they married.

If the Plantes and other habitants sinned against the Custom of Paris and left all or most of their belongings to one child, it was not generally out of any capricious favouritism, or out of a desire to found a family fortune, but simply to preclude excessive fragmentation and preserve intact a holding capable of supporting a family (including one or two retired parents, of course!). It is because of this practical consideration, no doubt, that the excluded heirs generally gave their consent to deeds of gift in the eighteenth century. In many cases from that period, brothers and sisters of the beneficiary ratified the deed of gift, waiving their future rights to the estate, and in others the consent of the co-heirs was at least noted, even if no signatures were secured. By the 1830s, however, as we shall see, co-heirs were rarely consulted and parents felt free to convey all their wealth to a single child, leaving the rest to fend for themselves.

The obligation to maintain the donors that accompanied almost every gift of a farm was spelled out in varying degrees of detail. Some of the early deeds simply call on the beneficiary to 'lodge, feed and maintain the donors in sickness and in health for the rest of their lives,' and specified an annual indemnity in money and produce to be paid if, 'by incompatibility of temperment,' the old folks found it necessary to live elsewhere. Most were more elaborate than this, however, and from the age of the Conquest to that of the Rebellions, the tendency is for parents to spell out their exactions in ever greater detail. Food requirements have already been discussed in the previous chapter but, in addition to these, a great many other payments and services found their way into Lower Richelieu *donations*. In 1769 a deed might insist simply on heat and light for the retirees but, by the end of the century, it was common to specify an annual supply of, for example, ten pounds of candles or three *pots* of lamp oil, plus twenty-five cords of wood, spruce and hardwood mixed, cut into stove lengths and delivered to the parents' room. Similarly, early deeds might require the beneficiary to pay for the donors' funerals, whereas the later gifts set down exactly how many masses were to be said for the repose of their souls. Parents were leaving nothing to chance for the rest of their lives, and beyond. Besides food, fuel, and clothing, many late eighteenth-century *donations* required washing, mending, the use of a horse and carriage, and special care in time of illness. Deeds of gift from the 1830s are even more detailed than the already quite demanding ones of the 1790s.

When we recall that these are contracts between parents and their children, the question soon arises, were all these stipulations meant to be enforced or were they simply formalities inserted by notaries anxious to protect their clients? Surely relations between a mother and son living under the same roof would not have permitted such nice calculations or even the expectation that the annual supply of flour would ever be measured exactly. There are, however, clear indications that the lists of conditions were not drawn up arbitrarily; instead they seem to have been carefully thought out by the habitant, not by the notary. I came across one *donation* in which the notary left a piece of paper with a badly misspelt set of instructions, obviously written by one of the retiring parents, setting out all the elements of an elaborate *pension alimentaire*.[74] Every deed of gift is unique, despite a rough similarity among the *pensions* of a particular period, and they seem to be related to the productive capacities of the farms transferred. Also, many *donations* were annulled after a year or two because the young people found the annual obligations too burdensome. Finally, many *donations*, particularly the more elaborate ones from the late eighteenth and early nineteenth centuries, stipulate dates connected with the seasonal routine of farm life for the delivery of each element in the *pension*.[75] Obviously, there must have been families in which the supplies and services were less strictly exacted than in others, but the fact remains that the various conditions found in deeds of gift were set down with serious intent. The tendency for deeds to be loaded down with more and more conditions over the century 1740 to 1840 seems then to betoken real changes in customs of land transmission and in parent-child relations.

A number of trends in fact emerge from this summary of a collection of Lower Richelieu deeds of gift. First, in the eighteenth and early nineteenth centuries, deeds of gift gradually became the predominant mechanism of property transmission. Second, they tended to channel an increasing proportion of habitant family fortunes to one individual or couple, as co-heirs were more and more frequently left unprovided for. Third, there was a parallel trend for parents to act unilaterally, neglecting to secure the approval of disinherited sons and daughters. Finally, the conditions imposed on beneficiaries became more numerous and more strictly defined over the years.

These trends, evident in the *donations* themselves, suggest some more general tendencies in habitant family relations and inheritance customs. There seems, for example, to have been a deliberate effort to replace a partible pattern with an impartible scheme, for moveable wealth as well as for land in many cases. This claim needs to be qualified because many early inheritance settlements were imperfectly partible in the end and because some rich peasants in the later period provided for more than one child by using several deeds of gift to distribute extensive land holdings; even so, it does seem that the légitime guaranteeing the rights of all heirs faded into the background. This presumably tended to reinforce a form of stem-family structure, in which one married offspring with his spouse and children co-habited with his aged parents and unmarried siblings while the other brothers and sisters left the parental home when they married. Not only did property tend increasingly to devolve on one heir, but that individual was usually a son. The trend to neglect the rights of co-heirs was therefore particularly injurious to daughters. Of course, through the régime of the communauté de biens, married women still had a right to half the property their husbands acquired,[76] but the use of gifts to favour sons nevertheless effectively channelled family wealth through the male line. Deciding whether the beneficiary was to be a boy or a girl, an older son, a younger son or a nephew, seems to have fallen increasingly to the parents alone. An additional development suggested by the deeds of gift would therefore be the increase in parental authority over the devolution of family property. Moreover, parents seem to have used this power to exact increasingly onerous duties from the 'lucky' beneficiary.

Why did inheritance customs evolve in this way? The best explanation would probably include a combination of three complementary factors, one environmental, one institutional, and one economic. The most obvious explanation is the changing ratio of population to land; after the middle of the eighteenth century, very few habitants had the wide expanses that allowed Paul Hue and Etienne Allaire to provide equal portions for all their offspring. Maintaining farms as viable productive units in these circumstances imposed impartible settlements, or something close to it, on the vast majority of the agrarian population. Moreover, control over an increasingly rare resource must have enhanced parental authority in the inheritance process. A second factor, the transfer of Canada to British jurisdiction in 1763, may also have played a role. While officially the seigneurial Lower Richelieu remained subject to the Custom of Paris (at least after the Quebec Act of 1774), there may have been a tendency for judges – most of the early ones were English – to view inheritance cases from an English point of view, favouring the rights of fathers to dispose freely of property by a will or otherwise.[77] If so, this could have encouraged parents to play fast and loose with the Custom of Paris and with the rights of co-heirs; also, notaries might have been more inclined to permit arrangements of this sort in the contracts they drew up. If indeed English juridical influences played a role, they must have done so gradually, for it was only in the nineteenth century that wills became common among the Lower Richelieu peasantry. Finally, there is a third factor that may have been the most important one in some parts of the region militating against equal division of estates and tending to make relations between parents and children more businesslike than they were in the past. This was the development of the grain trade in St Ours and St Denis during the second half of the eighteenth century. With the establishment of local merchants and the expansion of commerce, it became important to maintain farms large enough to produce some surplus beyond subsistence and rent requirements. A fuller discussion of this limited commercialization and its impact on inheritance practices follows in a later chapter.

Even in the eighteenth century, many habitants did not receive land from their parents and, even among those who did inherit plots, many found themselves with undeveloped forest. Consequently, the reproduction and multiplication of peasant household units implied a long-term campaign of land clearance.

COLONIZATION

From the seventeenth century to the early nineteenth, the Lower Richelieu was the scene of almost continuous colonization. As population grew, trees were felled, scrub was burned, and rocks dislodged to bring new lands under cultivation and to accommodate more and more habitant family farms. Spreading along the islands and the shores of the St Lawrence and the Richelieu through most of the French régime, settlement began to penetrate into the interior about the time of the Seven Years' War when new farms were established behind the waterfront row of lots. Five rows ('concessions' or, as they were called in the nineteenth century, 'rangs') were eventually laid out in St Denis and by the 1780s they were all occupied by settlers. St Ours and Sorel were much larger seigneuries that took longer to fill. They still had unconceded lots in the 1820s and 1830s respectively, although the best lands were settled long before that. It took centuries for the seigneurs to divide up these vast territories and distribute them to habitants but the process of clearing the land and bringing it into agricultural production was even slower, and nowhere more so than in Sorel.

In 1770, the new English seigneurs of Sorel ordered a complete survey of their estate and a map was carefully drawn up by the surveyor (see Appendix 8).[78] This document is unique in showing, not only property lines, but also buildings, fields, and woods. One feature emerging from the map is the way in which both concession lines and cultivated surfaces follow the local hydrographic pattern with no regard for 'geometric order.'[79] The doctrinaire imposition of a geometric pattern regardless of topography was characteristic of nineteenth-century English Canada much more than of early French Canada. Even more striking, however – particularly when one realizes that this map portrays a community occupied for more than a hundred years by a rapidly expanding agrarian population – is the narrowness of the bands of cleared land. The impression is of an immense forest pushed back only slightly at the edges. In the decades following 1770, new sections of Sorel were opened to settlement and clearing proceeded apace. Still, it is instructive to note how slow and painful the human assault on the wilderness could be.

Colonization was a movement with two distinct aspects, legal and physical. Settlers had to gain recognized possession of land and they had to transform it from wilderness into arable. Since the entire territory was organized into seigneuries, the legal aspect of land acquisition revolved around the seigneurs of the Lower Richelieu who granted farm-lots ('rotures') to habitants while retaining seigneurial domain. By the royal edicts of 1711 and 1732, seigneurs in New France were obliged to grant land under prevailing conditions to any legitimate settler who asked for it. As Cole Harris has observed, however, these laws did not transform seigneurs into land agents of the government; rather they sanctified long-standing Canadian practice.[80] After all, the granting of vacant lands to all comers in return for perpetual rents was the best, if not the only, way for a seigneur to derive any benefit from his estates in a new colony like Canada. Despite the legal restrictions and economic incentives, seigneurs had real power over the colonization process; it was under their auspices that wild lands were surveyed and allotted to settlers and it was they who awarded the legal title that transformed a piece of the natural environment into private property.

Once the river-front lands had been occupied, settlement could only proceed as fast as the seigneur had new concessions surveyed (legitimate settlement that is; pre-emptive squatting was not unheard of). This meant that people often had to wait several years until the seigneur felt that there was enough demand to justify arranging a survey. A surveyor would be brought in and he would trace a line through the forest, setting up stakes every three arpents or so to indicate the limits of the long rotures. At this point, young men in the fief who had been promised land would be given lots (often fathers made the arrangements in favour of their sons) and, if there were any lands left over, people from outside the seigneurie might be invited to apply for concessions. In spite of the demographic pressure, the response to these offers was not always massive.[81] Habitants hesitated to accept unnecessary grants because these were not really free lands. Besides the annual rents required from the date of possession, there was the surveyor's fee, payable immediately, and the notary's charge for drawing up a deed of concession to formalize the title; both charges were paid by the habitant, even though a copy of each document had to be supplied for the seigneur's files.[82]

Seigneurial concession was not the only way of obtaining a farm lot on the edge of settlement; many habitants purchased rotures that were still forested or only slightly developed, usually for a low price. A high mobility of property and population is of course characteristic of 'frontier society' in French and English North America. Before human roots have been sunk in the soil and before improvements have been made to the land, there is little to hold settlers to their new homes, particularly when they find soil quality disappointing or rents difficult to pay. Add to this normal instability, the operations of land speculators, including the seigneurs themselves, and it is little wonder that almost as many peasants acquired lots in the new rows by purchase as by seigneurial grant. The Sorel estate role of 1795 lists, in most instances, the means by which the current owner acquired each lot in the seigneurie. Of 146 lots originally conceded since 1770, fifty-two (36 per cent) were purchased and sixty-six (45 per cent) were still in the hands of the original grantee.[83] Whether they bought new land or were granted it, habitants never encountered free land in the eighteenth-century Lower Richelieu. Furthermore, this process of gaining legal title was only one step in creating a self-sustaining family farm. The land had to be cleared and brought under the plough, a house and barn had to be built, and livestock and equipment had to be obtained before a new household could be secure and independent.

Louise Dechêne has already provided an excellent description of the operations of land clearance in the seventeenth century and there is no reason to doubt that colonists in the eighteenth-century Lower Richelieu would have followed the same basic procedures.[84] If the seigneur had not previously stripped the area of timber, trees were felled in an arpent or so at the front of the lot, leaving only the largest ones to be girdled and left to die over the course of four or five years. Branches and scrub were then burned and a small clearing would be ready for rough cultivation between the stumps by a pick-axe. At a rate of perhaps two arpents per year, the forest would slowly be pushed back. Eventually stumps would have rotted enough that the final and most difficult stage could be undertaken, that of removing roots and rocks to permit ploughing. Creating a farm was a lifetime's work and we can see evidence of land clearance in progress in many habitant inventories where there is mention of the ragged zone of partial clearance between forest and fields. Of Pierre Ledoux's ninety arpents in St Denis for example, there were in 1764, seventeen arpents of ploughland ('en valeur'), $2\frac{1}{2}$ arpents of felled timber ('d'abattis et souche'), two of meadow, and $13\frac{1}{2}$ of brush, some of it burned ('en brulé et ferdoche').[85]

Under any circumstances, the creation of a new farm called for tremendous physical exertions but, for colonists far from sources of assistance, it also required a good bit of money or credit for subsistence during the initial seasons before any crops were harvested. For French immigrants to seventeenth-century Canada and for Anglo-American pioneers bound for distant western territories this often dictated, in the absense of cash assistance from their families, prolonged periods of wage labour to accumulate a nest-egg before seeking land. There was a system of family colonization common in the eighteenth-century Lower Richelieu, however, that eased the transition from dependence to independence and obviated the need to accumulate a small capital. If a young man could acquire a wilderness lot, on his own or through his father, in the vicinity of the paternal home, he and his relatives could work at clearing the land and putting up the necessary buildings, using his parents' house as a base. We can see this process at work in the estate inventory of Etienne Ledoux of St Denis (Félicité Audet's third husband). When his first wife died in 1767, Ledoux had eight children, three of them teenaged boys aged seventen to twenty. In addition to his farm on the banks of the Richelieu, this habitant owned a forested lot in the second concession and it was doubtless intended for one of the boys. A barn had already been built there and a house was under construction.[86] Residents of Grand St Ours who moved from the St Lawrence to the Richelieu proceeded in a similar way; in 1721 thirteen families were busy clearing lands in the new area, but only one actually lived there; the rest presumably 'commuted' the five kilometres between their old and new homes.[87]

If this form of gradual, family-assisted colonization was widespread it might help to explain what seems to have been the limited range of agrarian migrations in French Canada. Alexis de Tocqueville was interested in colonization when he visited Canada in 1831. Asking Mr Quiblier, the superior of the Montreal seminary, whether the French-Canadian race was expanding, he received the reply,

Oui. Mais lentement et de proche en proche. Elle n'a point cet esprit aventureux et ce mépris des liens de naissance et de la famille qui caractérisent les Américains. Le Canadien ne s'éloigne qu'à la dernière extremité de son clocher et de ses parents et il va s'établir le plus près possible.[88]

At the time of Tocqueville's visit, as well as in earlier and later centuries, there was plenty of long-distance migration in Quebec on the part of habitants seeking new lands to settle; Théophile Allaire's parents, for example, had come all the way from the Quebec City area and many of his neighbours were Acadian refugees.[89] And yet, Mr Quiblier does seem to have had a point, one that was echoed by many nineteenth-century observers, when he implied that short gradual movements were the norm rather than long jumps of this sort. Land settlement tended to spread from one area to the immediately adjoining wilderness, from Contrecoeur to St Antoine, for example, and from there on to St Denis and St Hyacinthe.[90] By way of contrast, non-inheriting sons from colonial Andover, Massachusetts, scattered far and wide, settling in various parts of New Hampshire, Connecticut, and western Massachusetts, guided in their wanderings largely by land prices.[91]

Some indication of migration patterns within the Lower Richelieu can

be found by tracing the dispersal in 1831 of household heads belonging
to four of the region's more numerous families (see Figure 7). At the
time of the 1765 census, there were five Peloquins in Sorel, four Bousquets
in St Denis, and an Arpain and a Lamoureau in St Ours. Over the next
sixty-six years, the number of household units carrying these names
through the male line had grown tremendously and many of them occupied lands that had only been brought under cultivation during the
great colonization movement of that period. No doubt many moved far
from the Lower Richelieu but, of those who stayed in the region, few
strayed far from their families' point of origin. To some extent, the 1831
settlement pattern suggests that seigneurial control of land granting
tended to keep habitants in their home seigneurie. It also suggests that
the native parish, the 'clocher' mentioned by Mr Quiblier, exercised a
strong attraction on settlers. But, more important than either of these
institutional factors, was simple proximity to the family of origin. Members of the four families tended to cluster in particular areas that coincided partly, but by no means completely, with the seigneurial and
parochial geography of the region. The Lamoureux stayed in the south-
western portion of the parish and of the seigneurie of St Ours while the
Arpains were limited mainly to the northeast and to adjacent sections
of Sorel. The numerous Peloquins were located all over Sorel but they
were also represented in bordering regions of the seigneuries of Yamaska
and St Ours; there were no Peloquins in St Denis and none in the more
distant half of St Ours. Other evidence reinforces the suggestion that a
desire to keep migrations short was just as important as any loyalty to
parish or seigneurie. For example, the 1831 census lists for the Prescott
section of Sorel, the area furthest from the centre of the parish in the
south, where it borders on St Ours, show the presence of a large number
of recognizable St Ours names in addition to the two Arpains noted on
the map. Moreover, while people from St Ours were moving into this
part of Sorel in the early nineteenth century, the rear sections of their
own seigneurie – at the time, it was still part of their parish also – were
being settled by newcomers from St Hyacinthe, across the Yamaska
river.[92]

Why did these habitant-colonists prefer to set up their new households as close as possible to their parental homes? Mr Quiblier, as well
as many other observers, would suggest that it was because of a timid
outlook that stressed family and community ties and feared risky
undertakings under unfamiliar skies.[93] What they fail to note are the
material imperatives behind this behaviour. The young man wishing to

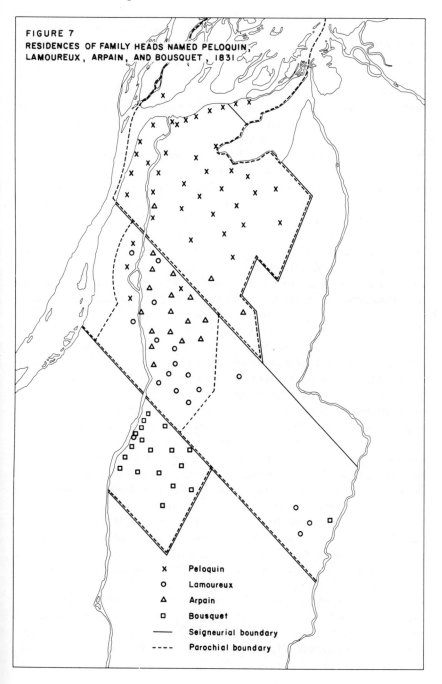

FIGURE 7
RESIDENCES OF FAMILY HEADS NAMED PELOQUIN,
LAMOUREUX, ARPAIN, AND BOUSQUET, 1831

x	Peloquin
o	Lamoureux
△	Arpain
□	Bousquet
——	Seigneurial boundary
- - -	Parochial boundary

marry and set up a farm, but lacking the capital needed to acquire and clear a lot in a distant region, had every reason to look for land that he could develop gradually without leaving home.

Upper-class contemporaries and later historians have been divided in their views about the early Canadian habitant. Some pronounce him 'the most independent man in the world,' while others stress his subjection to Church, state, and aristocracy.[94] The tendency is, of course, always to focus on the male individual, torn from his familial setting, but even if we ignore this distortion and pretend that it is the habitant family that is under discussion, we still find an interesting contradiction in the literature. Were habitant households independent or dependent? Their treatment in the preceding pages, where classes and institutions other than the habitant family itself are conspicuously absent, would seem to lend support to the 'independence thesis.' It is striking that most aspects of peasant society and economy can be understood with reference to the peasantry alone. This is because peasant families are truly 'independent' in an important sense. They normally run their own affairs, supporting, maintaining, and reproducing themselves mainly with the fruits of their own collective labour with land and equipment under their own immmediate control. In this sense, a peasant family is quite unlike a slave or a modern worker. While the latter cannot undertake productive labour without the facilities and direction provided by a 'master,' peasants are quite capable of functioning without the intervention of any superior class. Indeed, most would likely have been happy to dispense with the paternal care of their 'betters,' but of course few were fortunate enough to escape it. Even when peasants are weighed down by an oppressive dominant class, however, they maintain a basic autonomy, denied to slaves and proletarians, within the realm of production. Since they were able to run their own affairs – within wide limits – and to marshal the human and natural resources needed to produce goods then, the habitants can fairly be called 'independent.'

On the other hand, outside the circumscribed sphere of the household economy, the habitants did have to have dealings with more powerful aristocratic and mercantile classes. Economically and politically, this was an unequal relationship and, from this point of view, it is difficult to sustain any notion of an entirely 'independent' peasantry. Basically self-sufficient within the realm of production and consumption, the habitants could survive well on their own, but they still felt the burden of 'extra-economic' domination. Hence the paradox of their simultaneous dependence and independence.

4

Aristocratic ascendancy

Superimposed on the Lower Richelieu network of peasant households were power structures that demanded tribute and obedience, and ensured that some of the produce of habitant labour was diverted to priests, seigneurs, merchants, and officials. This is a fate that the habitants shared with peasantries the world over; throughout history, peasants have found themselves under the thumb of some sort of superior class. Their subjection can take many forms, some of them quite brutal and others more subtle; their overlords might be mandarins, priests, or feudal warriors; but the common experience of subsistence cultivators is domination and exploitation. For the habitants of the Lower Richelieu this meant that some of what they grew was siphoned off for the support of local seigneurs and clergymen in the form of rents, tithes, and other dues. There was nothing very mysterious about this appropriation: some of the wheat from a habitant family's granary, some of their money, or some of their labour was simply demanded by these aristocrats and, except where they found the means of evasion or defiance, the peasants had to turn it over. They had to because they were subject to the authority of their own exploiters. The relationship between peasant and priest or between peasant and seigneur was generally peaceful, with genuine paternalism on one side and real deference on the other softening the harsh economic realities; nevertheless, habitant deference and habits of compliance grew out of and were based upon the superior power of the dominant classes. Thus, the economic ascendancy of the 'aristocracy' was intimately bound up with its political ascendancy. Of course the same thing could be said of any 'ruling class,' but in the feudal society of the Lower Richelieu, unlike, for example, contemporary Canada, the power of superiors over inferiors had to be immediate, personal, and overt. There could be no admission that peasants, clerics, and seigneurs were equal.

Let us begin then by examining the 'political' side of the feudal relationship, insofar as it can be separated from more strictly economic topics, such as the structure of seigneurial revenues and their impact on peasant budgets, which will be taken up in the next chapter. What was the nature and extent of the clerical and seigneurial power that guaranteed those revenues and what sort of countervailing power, if any, did the habitants dispose of when the limits of their acquiescence were reached? The two most important local institutions of aristocratic domination were the seigneurie and the parish. The emphasis here will be on the former, not because it was the more important of the two, but because seigneurial tenure is such a difficult subject and one about which so much utter nonsense has been written.

Although historians of seigneurial Canada have generally abandoned the narrow legalism of earlier studies, there is still a tendency to see seigneurial tenure as a phenomenon with a reality all its own. It might have been set in motion and, to some extent, regulated by the state; it might manifest special characteristics in various circumstances and periods; it might be more severe, more lucrative, more efficient at some times or in some places than in others. Nevertheless, according to this view, there was a 'seigneurial *system*,' a mechanism with an autonomous and more or less coherent set of rules. It follows logically from this that the 'system' itself should be the primary object of study.

But seigneurial tenure was not a *thing*; it was rather a form of *property* and, as such, it had to do with relations between different classes of people. 'Property rights,' according to the anthropologist Irving Hallowell, 'are institutionalized means of defining *who* may control various classes of valuable objects for a variety of present and future purposes and the *conditions* under which this power may be exercised.'[1] The premise guiding this study of the seigneuries of Sorel, St Ours, and St Denis is that this type of property was in no degree self-sufficient; it can therefore only be understood as an aspect of a larger configuration of society. Since the seigneurie was not a system but a relationship, it follows that the focus of inquiry should shift from the institution to the relations between the agrarian classes of landlords and peasants.

It was the power of the absolutist state, in Canada as in France, that guaranteed the seigneurs' property and special privileges. Thus, if a peasant did not pay his rent, the landlord's ultimate recourse was to a lawsuit in a court provided by the king, upholding feudal law and able to back its decrees, if necessary, with military force. Seigneurial power was not exercised only at the level of the state, however, even if the state was its fundamental base. There was also a direct and local domination that seigneurs exercised over the land and people of their estates. Although habitants had basic personal freedom of a sort not found, for example, under régimes of serfdom and although they had overall control over the use of their lands, they were nevertheless subject to the authority of the seigneur in many important respects.

NULLE TERRE SANS SEIGNEUR

Even on the eve of the Revolution, there were places in France where free peasant lands (allods) had survived since the early Middle Ages, untouched by feudal lordship. In many regions, the legal assumption was that land was allodial in the absence of written proof to the contrary, but the rule in northern France was 'no land without a seigneur.' Even so, there were many patches of land that recognized no overlord. One recent work has gone so far as to assert that seigneurial control of all land 'was never achieved in any feudal social formation.'[2] Early French Canada was one society where the principle of 'nulle terre sans seigneur' was indeed scrupulously applied in practice and, until about 1791, seigneurial tenure was universal in the settled parts of the colony. In the Lower Richelieu it remained in force until the 1850s.

Before permanent settlements were established in the St Lawrence valley, the French monarchy granted large fiefs to individuals (most of them nobles) and to ecclesiastical bodies who thereby became seigneurs and, in a sense, 'owned' the lands. Though obliged to kneel and pledge homage on occasion to a representative of the king, the seigneur could sell his fief (seigneurie) or leave it to his heirs. In this sense he 'owned' it but still he could not dispose of it exactly as he pleased; instead, he had certain limited rights over different parts of his estate. According to the Edicts of Marly of 1711 and 1732, he had to concede plots of land to any settler who requested a grant under 'common' or non-seigneurial tenure ('en censive'). A section of the fief could be reserved as a demesne, however, for the exclusive use of the seigneur, as long as an effort was made to clear and develop it. The remaining unconceded lands were the seigneurial domain, the seigneur's property, but only, according to the theory expressed in the Edicts of Marly, until they could be sub-granted and occupied by habitants.

Until overcrowding made land speculation attractive, seigneurs were generally happy to concede land to all comers; they had no need of the Edicts of Marly to tell them that their interest lay in allowing habitants to convert their vast wilderness domains into rent-paying farms.[3] Meanwhile, the forest need not be entirely unproductive; some seigneurs contrived to extract a profit from it. Good timber from unconceded lands could be a lucrative resource for alert seigneurs. The de Ramezay family, seigneurs of Sorel in the first half of the eighteenth century, particularly the widow, Charlotte de Ramezay, were among the foremost producers of wood in New France; they furnished, for example, much of the timber used in the shipyards of Quebec City.[4] Besides Sorel, the de Ramezays owned other fiefs, some of them with no agricultural development, on the Yamaska and the upper Richelieu and they drew on the timber resources of all of them, transforming many of the logs into lumber in their Chambly sawmill. In the remote areas, the actual work seems to have been done by salaried workers, many of them soldiers, but it is quite possible that Sorel habitants owing corvée duties were enlisted to fell pine trees in that seigneurie.[5] Now there is no doubt that Charlotte de Ramezay was an enterprising lady who knew how to marshal people and resources to enhance her family's fortunes, but it would be misleading to suggest that the de Ramezays were therefore essentially bourgeois. Just because aristocrats adopt some bourgeois techniques for amassing wealth, they do not cease to be aristocrats who owe their preeminence to legal privilege and to their control over the land and rural populations. In this respect, the de Ramezays were no different from the noble seigneurs of the Toulousain and of Poland, who were also active in the timber trade.[6] This was anything but 'free enterprise': the seigneurs' political influence helped secure them vital government contracts and their vast seigneurial holdings gave them, not only access to supplies of raw materials, but also a legal monopoly over sawmilling. This then was an enterprise built on privilege and it was one that, in any case, only played a significant role in one Lower Richelieu seigneurie for two or three decades.

While the unconceded domain shrank over the years in the face of expanding peasant settlement, the demesne remained as an area of exclusive seigneurial control. Its size could fluctuate depending on whether the seigneur made any effort to acquire previously conceded and developed land from his habitants. In many parts of Early Modern France seigneurs consolidated ever larger holdings to the point where peasant property was eliminated and seigneuries became almost entirely demesne.[7] Sometimes this was done in the interests of establishing large-scale agricultural enterprises employing wage labour but, more often, particularly in the western part of the kingdom, the consolidation of large domains had no such 'progressive' thrust. Inefficient, small-scale productive units remained the rule; the dispossession of the peasantry served instead to permit seigneurs to impose more flexible, short-term leases that added ground rents to seigneurial dues, thus increasing the intensity of feudal exploitation. Canadian seigneurs, by contrast, showed little interest in establishing large demesnes.[8] As mentioned earlier, demesne agriculture in the Lower Richelieu was important only in the seventeenth century when indentured labour was available and when revenues from peasant lands were so meagre that seigneurs had to rely on demesnes simply to feed their families and entourages. Never a significant source of wealth (as opposed to subsistence), the demesne was allowed to stagnate or shrink in the eighteenth and nineteenth centuries when it became difficult to find labourers or tenant-farmers on advantageous terms and when strictly seigneurial revenues from sub-granted lands grew to be quite considerable.

There were still demesne farms in Sorel, St Ours, and St Denis in 1831, but they were small, about the size of a large habitant farm,[9] and they seem to have been anything but model farms. In the two older seigneuries, the practice had long been to lease the demesne to a tenant-farmer for either a fixed rent or for a share of the harvest. A share-cropping lease of Sorel's demesne farm dated 1759 shows the seigneur supplying all the equipment, livestock, and seed, as well as the land and buildings, and exacting from his 'métayer' half the grain harvested, as well as four pigs, twenty-four chickens, twenty-four dozen eggs, ten pounds of butter, and a share of various other animal products every year. With seed and tithe deducted, the half-share of grain production reported five years later would scarcely have kept the farmer's family alive and would have added little to the seigneur's overall income from Sorel.[10] This lease portrays a farm that was fairly large but not particularly well equipped; nor did the contract specify any 'enlightened' agricultural practices. The message of this and other records of the demesne farms of the Lower Richelieu seems to be that the seigneurs of the region took no active interest in agriculture; rather a surprising finding about individuals who, to a large extent, drew their incomes indirectly from the soil and who often liked to think of themselves as country gentlemen!

Neglecting the demesne which required investment and attention to bear fruit, Lower Richelieu seigneurs looked instead to the 'mouvance,' the territory allotted to habitants; with the spread of colonization this section took up an increasing proportion of every fief until it accounted for almost the entire surface by the early nineteenth century. From the seigneur's point of view, these lands put in the possession of peasant households had the advantage of producing revenues without requiring supervision of the process of production. Lots were conceded under terms which, in principle, made them the perpetual property of the recipient (usually, though not necessarily, a habitant), and they could be inherited, sold, or mortgaged; the seigneur, however, retained domain rights and an equally perpetual claim to annual dues, as well as certain monopolies and restrictions that will be outlined below. Seigneur and habitant therefore had, each of them, various rights over a farm in the mouvance, rights that in our own day are normally inseparable and vested in a single owner.

Now this is not so strange as it may appear on first sight since no one in any society can really 'own' land in the same way that they own genuinely personal property such as clothes or tools. Land is simply a delimited part of the earth's crust and it cannot be physically appropriated or otherwise removed from its natural and social context. Even today, when reified land is, in the dominant view, simply a commodity, the state restricts the rights of property owners with zoning by-laws, rent controls, and so on. It seems fair then to regard private property in land as conferring on owners, not a thing, but, as E.P. Thompson puts it, a 'bundle of rights' to make use of a particular area in certain ways specified by social and legal convention.[11] One distinguishing feature of feudal tenure is the extreme ambiguity of ownership and the large number of parties enjoying different rights over a given territory and different claims on its produce. We have already noticed in discussing the communauté de biens and habitant inheritance practices that, even apart from seigneurial tenure, there was no absolute individual ownership of land, since family members each had some stake in their farms. To this should be added the distinct rights claimed by landlord and habitant family.

This ambiguity posed perplexing problems to medieval jurists, who resurrected Roman legal theory and attempted to apply it to a European society organized with such flagrant disregard for the basic Roman concept of absolute individual property. In England, the tendency was to regard landlords as proprietors since they were generally successful in imposing limited-term tenancies on the peasants, but French peasantries were more successful in defending heritable tenure and official opinion came increasingly to identify them as owners of the land.[12] Of course, in reality there was no ownership of land in the Roman sense on either side of the English Channel, but French peasants did enter the early modern period with a significant advantage over their English counterparts in theoretical and practical security of tenure. French-Canadian habitants benefited from this victory, more completely even than their French cousins whose rights of heritability were undermined in many areas by the expansion of seigneurial demesnes. Holding land in the mouvance of a seigneurie, they could not in theory be evicted and their tenure was therefore much more permanent and secure than, for example, that of an English copyholder. We might note in passing that this fundamental divergence in the bias of English and French land laws is essential to an understanding of the Lower Canadian debate over seigneurial tenure. Historians who portray the discussion as one pitting the champions of archaic feudalism against the forces of modern 'free' tenure fail to appreciate the centrality of the question of who was to benefit by any modification of the rules governing land ownership. Most English proponents of the 'abolition' of feudalism took it for granted that the seigneur was the rightful possessor of all the lands in his fief and they sought to end the ambiguities of seigneurialism basically at the expense of habitant rights.[13] It was against this position that middle-class liberals and their peasant allies waged their defensive struggle.

Nevertheless, the habitant was not absolute master of his land and though he had more proprietory rights and greater security than a copy-holder, he and his land were still subject to the authority of the seigneur in a number of respects which tended to make his permanent tenure less than perfectly secure. For example, the right to sell land was restricted by the seigneurs' right to expropriate lands which changed hands in this way on indemnifying the buyer for his purchase price plus expenses. This mechanism, called the 'retrait seigneurial,' had a contractual basis, being written into most concession deeds. It seems originally to have been designed to prevent habitants from cheating on mutation fines by reporting a purchase price lower than what they actually paid, but it was used in St Ours for quite different purposes. One eighteenth-century seigneur used his right of retrait to expropriate two farms occupying a space where he wished to found a village. In another case, he rescued a beleaguered peasant from a forced sale to a creditor, to the benefit of himself as well as the seller, who was able the next day to secure a much higher price, entailing double the mutation fine.[14] It is impossible to say how often the retrait seigneurial was exercised but it certainly made the seigneur of St Ours something more than a passive observer of land transactions in his mouvance.

Moreover, the seigneur did not have to wait for a sale in order to get his hands on habitant lands. The edict of 1711, designed to accelerate colonization, ordered all habitants to occupy and begin clearing their lands within a year of concession and permitted Canadian seigneurs to repossess vacant lots. Accordingly, St Ours seigneurs inserted a clause in concession deeds that held the recipient to 'tenir feu et lieu' but, an additional phrase reveals the motives behind this patriotic injunction: habitants must occupy and cultivate their land, 'en sorte que sur icelle les dits cens et rentes sy puissent aisement prendre.'[15] According to Cole Harris, seigneurs took advantage of the opportunity to revoke concessions not, as the law intended, to deal with habitants who neglected to develop their lots, but rather to get rid of those who failed to pay their dues.[16] Under the French régime evictions ostensibly for failure to occupy and develop lands required time-consuming and uncertain procedures. Seigneurs had to apply to the intendant at Quebec and this official generally issued official warnings to recalcitrants and allowed them a year or more grace period in which to pay their arrears and fulfil settlement duties before ordering repossession.[17] In keeping with the 'French' notion that land belonged to the peasants, eviction was clearly viewed as an exceptionally stern measure. Repossession became easier after the British Conquest however, as no official filled the functions of intendant and seigneurs seem to have proceeded on their own authority to evict negligent habitants. Moreover, they did not limit themselves to cases of non-occupation.[18] One final legal privilege, the seigneur's right to expropriate mill sites, added to the insecurity of habitant tenure.

The St Ours estate rolls indicate that many lots were taken away from their habitant possessors and re-granted to others in the late eighteenth and early nineteenth centuries, but the circumstances of most of these confiscations are not clear. Some may have been acquired through eviction supposedly for failure to occupy and develop, but others were likely the result of forced 'sales,' the seigneur threatening to sue a habitant for arrears of rent, then agreeing to accept his land in lieu of payment. This presumably is the explanation of the large number of St Ours concession deeds made out to different individuals at different dates for the same piece of land. Many deeds mention a previous owner and note that the property was 'rétrocédée.' A clear example of this sort of procedure is outlined in a letter from the seigneurial agent of Sorel, dated 1764:

J'ay été trouver Freniere Trempe possesseur en apparence de la terre de Pellerin dans le dessein de le produire en cause à la chambre d'audience de la valtrie, mais cet homme qui pour tout bien ne possède pas une cuiller, m'a fait comprendre que je serois duppe des fraix, et puisqu'il consent faire un abandon de la terre, son adieu suffit comme une condemnation, ainsy je luy ay fait declaré ce qui suit ...[19]

The seigneurs had no interest in acquiring farms in this way for their own sake; instead they usually turned around and re-granted them to another habitant. As we shall see, seigneurs had great difficulty extracting dues from habitants, who often simply lacked the means of paying and this was one strategy for maximizing revenues by weeding out the lazy and the stubborn who could not or would not pay and replacing them with more suitable candidates.

If a habitant family occupied land and cleared it, if they secured a proper concession deed, and if they paid their feudal rents with reasonable regularity, then they could feel quite secure in the possession of their property. Furthermore, their heirs, generation after generation, could also feel a similar security and so, for the most part, could anyone who purchased their land. Some seigneurial monopolies and restrictions (to be discussed below) limited what they could do with this land but, in most senses, it was theirs to use as they saw fit. As long as a specified amount of produce was turned over to him every year, the seigneur took little interest in the process of production or in the transfer of title. In this sense, one could almost say that the Lower Richelieu belonged to the peasants. On the other hand, habitant control was by no means complete. Individuals who proved to be liabilities rather than assets to their seigneurs, because of a failure to develop their lands or pay their rents, might be deprived of the property. The cases of seigneurial repossession and expropriation, even if they affected only a minority, show that habitant tenure was not entirely secure and that seigneurs retained a certain degree of proprietary control, a practical ability to rearrange the allotment of lands, in the mouvance as well as in the demesne and the unconceded domain. To that extent, the region belonged to the seigneurs.

THE SEIGNEUR'S AUTHORITY

Power over land implied power over people. The basic function of seigneurial tenure was to give to landlords some ability to command the labour of the peasantry. Although they worked unsupervised and according to their own judgment and on their own schedules, the habitants were nevertheless subject to the authority of a seigneur who had the power to restrict their activities and shape the contours of their local community. Obviously, we are a long way, in the eighteenth-century Lower Richelieu, from the severe coercion characteristic of the medieval heyday of European feudalism. Where serfdom prevailed, peasants were bound to the soil, restricted in such elementary personal rights as that of moving from place to place and that of choosing a spouse; moreover, lordly exactions could be more or less arbitrary and, at times, brutally enforced. In the early modern period, however, such degradation was generally confined to Eastern Europe, while, in the West, serfdom was gone, leaving in its place more subtle sorts of peasant unfreedom, 'a mere tributary relationship,' that still combined exploitation with extra-economic subjection. In this feature too, rural French Canada followed the pattern of Old Régime Europe.

The seigneurs' ascendancy over the people of the Lower Richelieu was manifested in a number of ways, most of them deriving from seigneurial control over the land, backed by the power of the state. Mention was made in the last chapter of the seigneurs' role in supervising and channelling the colonization that turned wilderness into rural civilization. Going a step further, seigneurial authority also provided the framework that helped to shape urban development in the Lower Richelieu. The seigneur did not always select the location for the establishment of 'villages' (really small towns of merchants, craftsmen, and professionals rather than the residence of agriculturalists) but, in other respects, he did shape the form of urban development. In the 1780s, one of the co-seigneurs of St Ours, following the example of his counterpart in St Denis, acquired two farms near the church and began laying out streets and building lots, which he granted to craftsmen and others under normal seigneurial conditions (rents, mutation fines, and so on).[20] In the absence of any municipal self-government before the mid-nineteenth century, the little town developed in accordance with regulations set down in the seigneurial concession deeds. St Ours villagers were thus required to fence their yards, install sidewalks, and maintain the street in front. Shingle roofing, clay fireplaces, and ovens without proper chimneys were prohibited because of the risk of fire; there were even rules against storing hay in rooms with an open fire.[21] All these were of course sensible regulations, but the fact that they were ordered by the seigneur shows that his authority could, in some cases, be virtually governmental.

Seigneurs were certainly not the only local figures vested with power and prestige in this period. Back in the days of Pierre de Sorel and Pierre de St Ours, the region's seigneurs had no rivals of any similar degree of local pre-eminence and their powers were limited primarily by the collective resistance of the habitant group. However, by the middle of the eighteenth century, the Catholic clergy had established a strong presence in the Canadian countryside. In St Ours there was a certain amount of friction for a time between seigneur and curé over the closing of a church,[22] but normally relations between the two figures were quite cordial. The Church, with a large number of fiefs of its own, was no enemy to seigneurial tenure and it tended to preach submission and respect for feudal obligations. Seigneurs in return were generous in offering material support for local churches, and in using their command over land to force parishioners to fulfil obligations towards the church. The bailiff of St Denis suggested in a 1767 letter to the seigneur that promised land concessions be denied to peasants who failed to do road work and to contribute to a new church.[23] The parish and the seigneurie could be complementary instruments of compulsion, and the priest and seigneur were often partners in a feudal ascendancy over the habitants. This was a paternalistic authority, however, and the two figures could be found interceding on behalf of 'their' peasants with a colonial government that did not welcome petitions directly from the lower classes.[24] In the special case of Sorel, on the other hand, owned by the government itself after 1781, seigneurial powers could be turned in the opposite direction and used to manipulate the population. There is clear evidence that pressure was exerted on censitaires to vote for government candidates for the colonial assembly.[25]

What about the militia captain, a local officer who levied fines, kept order locally and, according to a long-prevalent view, cut a far more imposing figure in rural New France than the powerless seigneurs? Some suggest that he was a rival authority who, in overshadowing the seigneur, proved that feudal domination was an empty shell, but this is like arguing that presidents of major corporations exercise little influence in modern society because, unlike policemen, they are not allowed to stop speeding motorists. Militia captains, as officers of the government obeying orders from the governor and intendant and answerable to them, exercised an authority that was entirely delegated and of a completely different order from that of a seigneur. The latter was no one's agent. Under the French régime, a large number of individuals were both seigneur and militia captain and therefore had different sorts of authority in their several capacities, but where habitants filled the military-administrative role, such as in the Lower Richelieu, there was no question of taking precedence over the seigneur. André Charbonnier dit Saint-Laurent, for example, 'capitaine de la milice bourgeoise de la seigneurie de Saint-Ours' in the 1730s, was not only a servant of the government but also a faithful agent of the St Ours family.[26]

The local pre-eminence of the seigneur was underlined by a number of rituals sanctioned by custom and law. In the church, he was entitled to a special pew at the front and to a position of respect in processions and other ceremonies. The Mayday celebration was a secular French-Canadian event that symbolized habitant deference towards the seigneur father-figure. Each year on the first of May a tall phallic tree trunk would be planted in front of the manor house. According to the conservative Philippe Aubert de Gaspé, this was followed by dancing, rejoicing, and the discharge of firearms, but one historian suggests that peasants resented having to perform this troublesome ceremony.[27] It is impossible to know how regularly the Maypole custom was observed in the seigneuries of the Lower Richelieu as our only source of information is concession deeds which occasionally list this as one of the obligations of a censitaire. The majority of deeds are silent on this point, which may mean that the ceremony was not normally performed or, more likely, that it was so common as to require no legal sanction. Supporting the second hypothesis is the fact that the few Maypole clauses discovered seem to be concerned more with laying down procedures than with ensuring that the event takes place. One insecure seigneur, for example, insisted that his pole thrust at least fifty feet into the air.[28]

What was the nature and basis of the seigneur's authority in early Canada? Some historians would have us believe that, except insofar as the seigneur acted as the local agent of the state, the connection between lord and peasant was strictly contractual.[29] This view tends to assimilate feudal relations with the landlord-tenant relationship characteristic of capitalist societies where the parties 'freely' enter into an arrangement, the duration and terms of which are clearly set out in advance. What gives this argument superficial appeal is the fact that concession deeds were quite common in French Canada and they constituted the legal foundation for a number of seigneurial exactions and privileges. However, these were not the most important dues; the seigneurial rents, mutation fines, and gristmill monopolies did not have to be set out in deeds to carry the force of law. The concession deed was, in any case, not a genuine contract but rather a document formalizing the habitant's possession of a lot and enumerating the seigneur's conditions. In the French period particularly, many habitants occupied lands for years, often for a lifetime, with the seigneur's permission, but without a deed, and they were subjected to exactly the same dues and restrictions as their neighbours. An estate roll drawn up for one of the sections of St Ours in 1751 mentions deeds for only seven of the forty-six farm-lots. Most of the remaining entries are labelled 'no contract [ie, deed]' and before the record of annual rents is written the phrase, 'in conformity with the contracts of the neighbouring lands.'[30] Once signed, concession 'contracts' supposedly determined the conditions of tenure for all eternity, but it would be a mistake to assume that seigneurs never allowed themselves to overstep the limits established by deeds in the distant past. We have already noted an evolution in the wording of deeds for newly conceded lands that tended to make privileges and monopolies more extensive and to undermine peasant proprietary rights. Now, in theory, if a clause, for example reserving to the seigneur commercial timber on mouvance lands was only introduced in the 1760s, the provision could not be enforced on lands granted before that time. In practice, however, it seems unlikely that seigneurs made such fine distinctions among the lands of their fiefs (that is, except as far as rents were concerned; these were set at the time of concession and never tampered with after that). The 'titre nouveau,' essentially the issuing of new title deeds (at the habitant's expense, naturally), could always be used to update old deeds and substitute more recent, more exacting wording of clauses.[31] This procedure makes the claim that terms of tenure were contractually set for all time difficult to accept.

Another common view sees the Canadian seigneur as deriving his power entirely from the state and as subject to the strict supervision of the state. According to this interpretation, government regulation as well as contractual agreement determined landlord-peasant relations, but the history of the Lower Richelieu seigneuries suggests otherwise. Ultimately of course, the colonial régimes of France and then Britain provided the power that guaranteed the seigneur's privileges. Thus it was to the king's officials and lawcourts that he applied for redress when habitants failed to pay their rents or bring their grain to the banal mill. This is only normal; preserving property rights of a certain sort is one of the prime functions of all states and the governments of early Canada were all ready to defend seigneurial rights even though they were not willing to permit 'abuses' and excessive exploitation of the peasantry. Unfortunately, historians have paid so much attention to expressions of official concern about the details of seigneurial tenure that they have often failed to notice the unspoken commitment to the defence of this feudal form of property. Furthermore, they often tend to ignore the great gap separating the aspirations of governors and intendants to regulate landlord-peasant relations and the limited achievements possible with the means at their disposal.

Although the seigneurs of the Lower Richelieu had recourse to the courts in more than one dispute with habitants, they were by no means entirely fettered by the law.[32] As we shall see, seigneurs had no hesitation about stretching the provisions of government directives or even contravening the law directly where such things as mill monopolies and timber reserves were concerned. They also raised rent scales in defiance of expressed state policy and added fees that had no legal basis. Moreover, as mentioned earlier, de facto evictions of doubtful legitimacy were not unheard of.

Other non-legal reserves and exactions should also be mentioned. One was speculation in undeveloped lands, strictly forbidden by the Edicts of Marly, which insist that seigneurs grant wilderness lands to settlers without requiring a purchase price. To avoid this restriction, while increasing the revenues of his estate, at least one St Ours co-seigneur took the course of granting large tracts to his own children under habitant tenure, then waiting for their value to rise with the development of adjoining lands and eventually selling them for a substantial sum.[33] Since this is the sort of 'abuse' often considered characteristic of the early nineteenth century, it should be noted that these nepotic concessions occurred in St Ours only in the 1750s. In later years, a variation on this theme was at least discussed by the manager of the seigneurie of Sorel; whether or not it was put into practice cannot be determined but the plan was to grant lots to a local accomplice who would then sell them to genuine settlers.[34]

More important than the points on which seigneurs were able to ignore or evade the law were the vast areas of landlord-peasant relations which were subject to no state regulation. When one of the co-seigneurs of St Ours summoned endebted habitants to appear before him and levied arbitrary fines on them (see below), he was breaking no law but he was certainly exercising power. The seigneurie was neither an institution of the state nor a minutely regulated set of rules; it was a species of property vested in an individual (or a body), backed in the last analysis by the state and subject, like all forms of property, to some government regulation that was limited in scope and only partially enforced. The nature of seigneurial property was such that it conferred, not only lucrative privileges, but also power and authority over lands and people. A seigneur did not dictate, as a modern factory owner or an ancient slave-master did, the details of productive activity to his 'subjects'; he did not control most aspects of peasant life, nor would he have any reason for wishing to do so; but he did have the means of making his influence felt in the community, of parlaying a command over lands into a more general authority.

A seigneur's powers were by no means unlimited. They were hedged in, not only by government regulations, but also, and probably more importantly, by peasant resistance, active, passive, and potential. Louise Dechêne has shown that, in seventeenth-century Montreal as in Europe, the nature and degree of feudal exploitation were set and revised as a result of unequal contests between landlords and habitants, the latter threatening rebellion or simply refusing to pay certain dues.[35] We know that similar struggles occurred in the early years of the Lower Richelieu settlement, for example over the attempt by Pierre de St Ours to force his peasants to live in a village. Later seigneurs probably had a clearer idea of just how far they could push their authority without provoking rebellion. The records they left signal few incidents of overt conflict after the early eighteenth century, but this does not mean that none occurred. The seigneurial archives of the Lower Richelieu have little in the way of letters and other narrative documents that would describe disputes. Judicial archives, on the other hand, are apparently full of litigation between seigneurs and habitants. Lawsuits were the seigneur's main weapon in dealing with opposition and it is therefore natural that any rent-strikes or attacks on property would have led to legal action. Since court records were not examined for the present study, the question of how and how often peasants fought back against their landlords and with what success will have to be left for other researchers. We shall see that the habitants were quite assertive in their dealings with the Church and so it seems reasonable to expect that they also found ways of combating their seigneurs.

A COLONIAL ARISTOCRACY: THE ST OURS FAMILY

Within the narrow world of the seigneurie, we have seen that the social order was based on the seigneur's domination and exploitation of the peasantry, however subtle and qualified that unequal relationship may have been. But who were these seigneurs who were so endowed by seigneurial institutions and what role did they play in the larger colonial community?

It so happens that two of our seigneuries, St Ours and St Denis, were originally granted to members of the nobility and they both remained in noble hands until the liquidation of seigneurial tenure almost 200 years later. Sorel had a more complicated history. First acquired by a Carignan officer of ambiguous and marginally noble status, it later passed through the hands of a Canadian noble family before being purchased in 1764 by an English merchant and later acquired by the colonial government. There is nothing extraordinary in the predominance of the nobility among the seigneurs of the Lower Richelieu. The 'privileged orders,' that is, nobles and ecclesiastical bodies, possessed by far the greatest part of seigneurial Canada throughout the French régime and into the early decades of British rule.[36] In this and other parts of the colony there were indeed seigneurs of bourgeois and even peasant origin, but this fact, while true, is scarcely as significant as some would have us believe. The presence in New France of seigneurs of humble origin is sometimes put forth as evidence of a social revolution accompanying the migration of Frenchmen to North America; here in the New World, it is claimed, traditional distinctions meant nothing since any peasant could join the ranks of the seigneurs. The emphasis in this interpretation is on the fact that it was theoretically possible for a habitant to acquire a fief; less prominence is accorded to the equally true fact that this happened only on very rare occasions. It was also possible, and much more common, for a rich merchant to achieve noble status, by purchase or by royal decree, and the acquisition of a seigneurie was often part of this ascent. Proponents of the North American uniqueness thesis seem to forget, however, that this sort of social mobility was common in Old Régime France as well as in New France. On this score, as on many others, the 'frontier interpretation' and its variants rest on a bogus comparison with Europe. The 'paysan parvenu' was a familiar figure in seventeenth- and eighteenth-century France and the purchase of seigneuries by members of the Third Estate was a phenomenon of massive proportions. On both sides of the Atlantic, the fief was nevertheless seen as a 'noble' form of tenure, appropriate for clerical bodies and lay aristocrats, and social realities tended to reflect this view even if the correspondence between seigneurial property and noble-clerical status was less than perfect.

The nobility of the Lower Richelieu seigneurs needs to be particularly stressed as a generation of historians has almost managed to write this class out of discussions of early Canadian society. As officially recognized nobles, and not as seigneurs, people like Claude de Ramezay and Pierre de St Ours could count on the benevolence of the state to provide legal privileges, preferment, and patronage.[37] Fiefs were the principle form of endowment, the basis of a solid independence, but when the agrarian economy was undeveloped they were worth little and the Crown found other means of favouring the colony's many nobles and of allowing them to maintain the semblance of an aristocratic life while awaiting the emergence of a substantial peasantry. The progress of the St Ours family from impecunious warriors to country gentry seems to illustrate the history of the Canadian seigneurial aristocracy.[38]

The patriarch Pierre de St Ours was, it will be recalled, a Carignan officer demobilized in New France and given a seigneurie in 1672 on the Iroquois frontier. He had difficulty providing for his large family on the paltry income provided by his insecure little community of soldier-settlers. The king came to his rescue, however, first with a cash gift, and later with other patronage. Through an influential relative in France, St Ours applied repeatedly for various favours and lucrative posts. In 1717, when the fur trade was severely restricted, he was awarded a trading licence which he likely sold at the prevailing rate of 1000 livres. In 1687, a regular colonial military force was formed in Canada and Pierre de St Ours received one of the first captain's commissions. Although the rank and file of the 'troupes de la marine' were filled by recruits from France, the officer corps quickly became the 'chasse gardée' of the Canadian nobility. When Pierre retired from the service in 1708, his eldest son, Jean-Baptiste (often called Deschaillons), took over his company, a step along the way to much more distinguished military positions. In fact, all the males of the St Ours family under the French régime pursued careers in the colonial forces and at least three of them were awarded the Cross of St Louis. The women tended to marry officers or to become nuns. Each military officer disposed of a basic income of 1000 livres or so, less than a fortune but more than the seigneurie provided in the first two generations.

Military positions were not entirely sinecures in bellicose New France. Like many Canadian officers and militiamen, the St Ours distinguished themselves as courageous fighters. Pierre, for example, commanded a battalion during the 1690 siege of Quebec and, sixty-nine years later, his grandson, François-Xavier, was killed in the Battle of the Plains of Abraham after participating in seventeen campaigns. Jean-Baptiste de St Ours Deschaillons began his military career at the age of nineteen

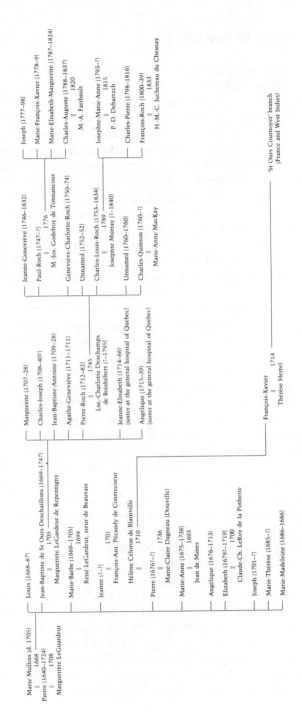

FIGURE 8

Partial genealogy of the St Ours family

and, rising through the ranks, attained in 1733 the position of King's Lieutenant at Quebec, second in command to the governor. As a young man, he led at least two expeditions against English settlements, including the 1708 attack on Haverhill, Massachusetts, one of the bloodiest raids in the long struggle for North America. Before being stationed at Quebec, Deschaillons spent about fifteen years in command of various posts in the northwest. His son, Pierre-Roch de St Ours, was the commander in charge of building the French forts at Beaubassin on the frontier of Nova Scotia from 1748 to 1751 and later he impressed Montcalm at Chouagouen and Carillon and led a brigade at Quebec in 1759.

Modest salaries were not the only reward that the St Ours men and the rest of the Canadian noblesse received for such devoted service to the king. The power these officers wielded, particularly when they commanded isolated posts, often provided the opportunity for enrichment by more or less illegitimate means. Pierre-Roch, for example, was charged with corrupt use of government supplies during the construction of the Beaubassin forts. His father, Jean-Baptiste, developed an even more lucrative enterprise preying on the Indians and fur traders of the upper Great Lakes when he served successively as commander at Niagara, Kaministiquia, and Detroit between 1717 and 1730. It was common practice at this time for officers to use their position to monopolize trade in the vicinity of their posts; unable to stop this abuse, the government sanctioned it and made fur trading a perquisite of the position. Jean-Baptiste de St Ours took full advantage of the privilege to build his fortunes, bringing thousands of livres worth of trade goods up the waterways every year, in partnership with merchants or on his own account, and returning bales of pelts to Montreal.

Although his father had accumulated three seigneuries, it was really Jean-Baptiste (Deschaillons) who established the St Ours family fortunes on a firm footing in the first half of the eighteenth century. Towards the end of his life, around 1740, Deschaillons enjoyed a handsome income: 1800 livres annually for the position of King's Lieutenant, which left him free for the greatest part of the year, a pension of 800 livres a year as chevalier de St Louis, additional *gratifications* of 400 livres every few years, all this from the royal treasury; he also had two houses in Montreal that brought in 800 livres annually. Next to this, the 400 livres he drew from his half of the seigneurie of St Ours seem paltry indeed.[39] The contrast is the more striking when we realize that the profits from earlier activities in the fur trade were likely huge, out of all proportion with these rents, salaries, and pensions.

Since Jean-Baptiste de St Ours drew the bulk of his wealth from the government and from commerce, one might almost think that in spite of his blue blood, he was no aristocrat, but rather a 'bourgeois-gentleman.' Certainly Cameron Nish would place him within an essentially bourgeois ruling class.[40] Nish's position is undermined, however, by his failure to define the term 'bourgeois' adequately. He tends to apply the word to anyone who, by virtue of wealth or political influence, could be considered part of a colonial élite and thus the argument that pre-Conquest Canada was dominated by a bourgeoisie appears to be wholly tautological. It is difficult indeed to make a bourgeois of Jean-Baptiste de St Ours, a man who owed his career and his riches almost entirely to the privileges of birth. He became an officer because he was a noble and he advanced through the ranks, as his fellow officers generally did, mainly on the basis of seniority. No doubt Jean-Baptiste was truly a 'brave soldier'; the traditionally aristocratic profession of arms was the continuing focus of his existence throughout his adult life. Fur-trading, by contrast, was a temporary means to an end and his activities in this field seem to have begun when he acquired a position of privileged monopoly and to have ceased when he moved to Quebec. This is not so much the way of the bourgeois as that of the robber baron, taking advantage of special privilege and armed might to exact tribute from merchants and native producers. In this light, it is scarcely an exaggeration to consider the wealth of Jean-Baptiste de St Ours as having a feudal origin, coming as it did through privilege and military power from the Indian trappers and tax-paying French peasants who actually produced it.

On the other hand, this was, for the most part, not income that came from the soil of Deschaillon's Canadian estates, not surprisingly since there was very little agricultural wealth to be made in the colony at that time. This seigneur only lived at St Ours as a child; instead he established his family at Montreal and later Quebec. His father, Pierre de St Ours, also lived in Montreal for twenty-three years when he served as captain in the colonial forces, but he did live in the manor house from 1672 to 1687 and again, after he retired, from 1710 to his death in 1724. Pierre-Roch de St Ours, the third seigneur, lived in Montreal and then in Quebec where his wife, Louise-Charlotte des Champs de Boishébert, held a salon that was a favourite with General Montcalm. After the British conquest ended his military career, Pierre-Roch moved to the country, though not to St Ours but to L'Assomption. With their families installed in the city, these three military men wandered much further from the Lower Richelieu on remote postings, and yet none of them really neglected the old family estate, even though it was no gold mine as the fur trade monopolies were. During their husbands' absences and after their deaths, it was often the women of the St Ours family who looked after the affairs of the seigneurie. There seem to have been periodic visits to the country, concession deeds were signed by the seigneurs or their local agents and, to some extent, revenue from outside sources was invested in the seigneurie, as when Jean-Baptiste and his brother each loaned their father 1000 livres to build a banal mill. What the first seigneurs of St Ours sought from their fiefs was not sudden riches, but security, prestige, and the hope of eventually enjoying a comfortable agrarian independence. 'Families can only keep up their position if they are backed by substantial properties in land,' said Colbert, the French minister who laid the foundations of rural Canada;[41] the nobles of New France seem to have heeded this advice, as did many of the colony's wealthy commoners, infected like Colbert himself with the aristocratic outlook.

After the Conquest there were some important changes in the position of the colonial noblesse, enough to make the de Ramezays of Sorel and many others leave Canada. The colonial troops were disbanded and with them went the secure military careers and the opportunity to exact tribute from the fur trade. Handouts from the royal treasury also all but disappeared, although Pierre-Roch de St Ours did manage to secure a pension during a visit to France in 1763. About the same time, however, the development of rural settlement and the opening of overseas grain markets were making L'Assomption and St Ours into valuable properties able to support a real landed gentry. In spite of the obstacles, the St Ours family long retained its military character. Pierre-Roch's youngest son, Quinson, though born in Canada under British rule, sold his share of the family estates, and left his home for Guadeloupe where he fought for France and met 'une mort glorieuse.'[42] Quinson's brother Charles served the British at the time of the American Revolution – captured at St Jean, he was held prisoner in the United States for two years – and remained an officer of the British army until 1796. François-Roch de St Ours, who inherited the fief from his father Charles in 1834, was the first principal seigneur of St Ours in 162 years who was not a professional soldier and who never led troops in combat; even so, he was at least a colonel of militia.

Charles de St Ours was not just a soldier, he was also a world traveller and man-about-town in his youth and, after his marriage at the age of thirty-six, he became a genuine country gentleman and a prominent figure in colonial politics. 'Le chevalier,' as he was known in the family, returned from imprisonment in the United States in 1777 and served as aide-de-camp to two successive governors of Canada and then to Prince William Henry, Queen Victoria's father, who visited North America in 1787. Charles had already been exposed to royalty two years earlier; on a tour of Europe he was presented at the courts of George III and Louis XVI, so the family chronicler asserts, and he even had an audience with Frederick the Great, a man whose pedigree was almost as thoroughly military as that of le chevalier himself. He married in 1789; shortly after that he gained control of the greatest part of the seigneurie of St Ours and settled there permanently with his family. Curiously, Charles was only the second son of Pierre-Roch and therefore not a favoured heir, but his oldest brother, Paul-Roch, always preferred L'Assomption and was content to leave St Ours and St Jean Deschaillons to his co-heirs. Since L'Assomption was a much more valuable property than the other two – with annual rents of 5086 livres plus 770 minots of wheat in 1795, compared to 2650 livres and 860 minots for St Ours – this arrangement was faithful to the noble inheritance custom of allowing half the feudal estates to the oldest son. Charles began with one-third of these two fiefs, but he bought out the shares of his sister and brother to acquire 80 per cent of the territory of each. The outcome of several intra-family transactions was that Paul-Roch and his heirs held L'Assomption while Charles passed along St Ours and St Jean Deschaillons to his son. Where fifty years earlier the three St Ours seigneuries would not support even one family of aristocrats, as of 1790 they began to support two separate lines.

Even if he did spend most of his time in the country, Charles de St Ours was a prominent figure in Lower Canada as well as locally. He was a militia colonel and, from 1808 on, a member of the colony's legislative council, following the examples of both his brother and his father. The St Ours family received more than its share of this sort of political patronage, benefiting from the early British policy of ruling the French Canadians by co-opting the aristocracy. Even so, Charles's political views seem to have been those of a conservative nationalist; he fought against the proposed union of Upper and Lower Canada in 1822 and he founded, about the same time, an organization to bolster the Canadian Catholic clergy by sponsoring seminarians from the Richelieu valley. His son, François-Roch, was elected to the House of Assembly on two occasions before the government in 1832 made him a lifelong Legislative Councillor like his father, grandfather, and uncle before him. During the political

TABLE 12
Annual Revenues, St Ours Seigneurie

1714	300 livres (St Ours, L'Assomption, St Jean)
1734	800 livres (St Ours, L'Assomption, St Jean)
c1765	2200 livres (St Ours only)
1795	4450 livres (St Ours only)
1810	16,566 livres (St Ours, rents only)
1813	12,450 livres (St. Ours, rents only)
1855–6	13,926 livres (St Ours, all revenues)

crisis of 1837 the governor appointed François-Roch Sherriff of Montreal and, when the latter accepted, he was spurned as a turncoat by the democratic-nationalist Patriotes, all the more so after the rebellion when his position involved jailing thousands of political prisoners.

Charles de St Ours and his family seem to have lived comfortably in the new manor house he had built on the banks of the Richelieu in 1792. This two-storey building was not an imposing structure but, with eight bedrooms, it could easily accommodate the family and servants. Here he lived, entertained guests, and managed the affairs of the seigneurie in all their details. Charles de St Ours was in fact the first truly resident seigneur and the first to take charge of the day-to-day affairs of the fief since the days of his great-grandfather, Pierre de St Ours, seventy years earlier. Documents from this period show the seigneur's own hand, not only signing deeds, but also noting each habitant's rent payments and listing requests for land grants. A large number of lands were in fact granted to habitants in the last decade of the eighteenth century and the first decade of the nineteenth; almost half the fief's territory, the 'rear' portion towards the Yamaska, was opened at this time. Charles de St Ours took the initiative in establishing new institutions and economic facilities for this section, eventually organized in 1822 as the parish of St Jude. The seigneur was instrumental in setting up this ecclesiastical institution and he also had a large mill erected on the Yamaska seven years earlier. In contrast to the contemporary seigneurs of Sorel and St Denis, Charles was a community-builder in the tradition of the seventeenth-century founders of Sorel and St Ours; and his efforts helped make his estate a much more valuable and lucrative property than it had been. The figures on St Ours seigneurial revenues shown in Table 12 indicate clearly that it was under Charles de St Ours, around the turn of the nineteenth century, that the most impressive gains were registered.[43] Subsequently, after 1810, there was stability or even decline (it is hard to say which on the basis of a few isolated figures) as there was no new land left to concede and as wheat prices entered a downward trend.

Charles de St Ours developed his seigneurie to its full economic potential (in the Canadian context at least) and left an estate that permitted his son to continue the leisurely life of a country gentleman, while participating intermittently in public affairs as Charles himself had done. But François-Roch died prematurely, only five years after his father. His funeral in 1839 was an elaborate public affair in the ancient style; 2000 printed invitations were distributed through the region and in Montreal; the domestic staff were all fitted out in mourning attire; a large contingent of habitants paid their last respects by discharging a musket volley (a nervous magistrate saw about 250 guns at the funeral) over the mahogany casket.[44] François-Roch left no male heir to continue the St Ours name, but his widow and four daughters kept the fief undivided until seigneurial tenure was liquidated in 1854. Long after this 'abolition,' however, Quebec habitants had to make annual payments to compensate the former seigneurs for their losses; these payments were still referred to generally as 'seigneurial rents' and, even in the twentieth century, local people were still handing over part of their surplus production to the descendants of Pierre de St Ours.

PRIEST AND PARISHIONER

Like the seigneurs, the clergymen of the Lower Richelieu enjoyed both authority and revenues. Clerics had some control over the private affairs of their flocks and over the collective life of the community. Moreover, they had a right to a share of all grain harvests through the tithe and they presided over parish institutions that exacted various other contributions from the habitants. Under the French and the British régimes, priests had the backing of the state – though in varying degrees – for their claims to part of the fruits of peasant labour and for certain forms of control over the private and collective life of the community. In addition to this secular sanction, however, they also claimed supernatural support for their privileges. Thus a bishop could often bring unruly laymen to obedience without recourse to secular courts simply by threatening to remove the local curé or close the parish church.

All indications are that throughout our period the habitants saw themselves as Catholics and accepted the spiritual authority of the Church. Babies were baptized promptly, usually the day of their birth and almost

TABLE 13
Interval between birth and baptism, Sorel 1740–79

Days between birth and baptism	No.	Cumul. per cent
0	606	45.9
1	542	87.0
2	76	92.8
3	31	95.1
4–6	38	98.0
7+	26	100.0
?	12	
total	1331	

never beyond the three-day limit set by the Church (see Table 13).[45] People attended mass regularly and performed their 'Easter duties' almost without exception. Of course there was a popular peasant religion that did not coincide precisely with official theology. Habitants often had recourse to magic potions, incantations, and other practices condemned by the Church as 'superstitious.' They were also inclined to enjoy themselves more on religious holidays than the churchmen would have liked and many of them tended to be rather boisterous during solemn ceremonies.[46] In other words, eighteenth-century peasants had their own religious outlook, one that was different from, but not in conscious rebellion against, that of the Church. Indeed, French-Canadian peasants seemed quite prepared to defer to the clergy in spiritual matters and to acknowledge a clerical monopoly in many rituals.

But the Church was an institution of this world as well as of the next. Where the secular and material aspects of parish life were concerned, relations between clergy and laity in the Lower Richelieu were not so harmonious. Curés and habitants were frequently at loggerheads over political and economic questions, such as the control and use of parish property and the weight of ecclesiastical exactions. A related source of strife was disagreements over where the boundary between spiritual (ie, clergy-controlled) and secular (lay-controlled) should be drawn. On several occasions in the eighteenth century, there were bitter disputes between priests and laymen over whether to rebuild or repair a church, over whether parishioners had a right to congregate in the rectory, over the allocation of pews and so on.[47] The issues sometimes seem petty but at stake was the shape of the community and the struggle for local leadership; accordingly passions often ran high. Although open conflict was occasional rather than continuous, it seems to have sprung from deep-seated tensions in the lay / cleric relationship. Given the economic connection between the two groups, this is hardly surprising.

The tithe was the most important of all clerical exactions. In Canada it was set by law at one twenty-sixth of all grain harvests, although in some cases other farm produce was also tithed.[48] Habitants in the Lower Richelieu seem to have had few complaints about the tithe, surprisingly in view of their assertiveness on other issues. For European peasants, by contrast, the tithe was often a source of profound resentment and violent anti-clericalism. Why the apparent acceptance of this levy in Quebec? First the rate was relatively moderate. Even so, it was a substantial burden, particularly for the poorer peasants, as we shall see below. A second peculiarity of the Canadian tithe may have been more important: it was levied at a uniform rate in all parishes of the colony and this no doubt gave it more the appearance of part of the divine order and less that of a vexatious human invention. Even more significant is the fact that tithes here were almost always given entirely to the local curé for his exclusive benefit. Compare this with Old-Régime France where tithes in many rural areas had long ago been alienated and where they were collected by impersonal agents for a distant monastery or an urban businessman. Here it took much more credibility than was demanded of the Lower Richelieu habitant to believe that the tithe was God's share of the harvest.

In a well-populated agricultural parish the tithe alone supplied a priest with a substantial revenue. In the 1780s, the tithes of St Ours for example were said to amount to about 1000 minots of wheat, 200 minots of oats, and 50 of peas annually. By 1831, after the parish had lost a portion of its territory, the average tithe was estimated at 600 minots of wheat, 400 minots of oats, 150 of peas, 12 of barley, and 30 of rye.[49] This much grain would have been sold by the curé of the 1780s for about 5 to 6 thousand livres; given the subsequent rise in prices, his successor would have received about the same amount in 1831. In addition to the tithe, parish priests received fees for funerals and for masses for souls in purgatory. Free lodging in the rectory was another important benefit.

For the habitants, the Church constituted an economic burden that was greater than simply the amount of the tithe. Collections, assessments, fees, and pew rents were all paid from household revenues for the support of the parish rather than for the curé personally. On these matters, the latent hostility of priest and parishioner came to the surface in more than one dispute. In all the battles, there were two distinct but related axes of conflict, one was the habitants' struggle to minimize the material burden on parishioners and the other was the contest between clerics and laity to control parish finances and buildings and to run the community itself. Vestries were the focus of many such controversies.

The vestry ('fabrique') was the body charged with administering the material affairs of a parish and it was made up, in theory, of all local Catholics. An executive board of three or four churchwardens ('marguilliers') actually handled the finances with the curé playing a role that could be quite substantial if his political position was strong. Vestry revenues came mainly from pew rentals, voluntary contributions, and a share of fees from special masses. Out of these funds, the parish had to pay for the routine upkeep of the church, the rectory and the cemetery; it also purchased the wine, oil, and other supplies needed for religious ceremonies as well as robes for the priest, paintings for the church, and silver sacramental vessels. In Old Régime France, the person or body collecting tithes ('décimateur') was usually responsible for the upkeep of part of the choir. Furthermore, rural vestries in that country often possessed landed endowments whose rents paid most of the remaining expenses.[50] In Canada, on the other hand, rural churches were maintained by the vestry alone and the burden of annual expenses rested squarely on the habitants.

Pew rentals, a major source of vestry revenue, were a chronic bone of contention in the eighteenth-century Lower Richelieu, dividing priests who sought to enhance parish income and habitants anxious to moderate annual payments. The disposal of pews offers a marvelous analogy to seigneurial property in land. Divided from the rest of the church by a solid enclosure, each pew was reserved for the exclusive use of a particular family for the lifetime of its head. Though it 'belonged to' an owner, it was obviously not his to do with exactly as he pleased; moreover, he had to pay a specified annual rent for its use. Ambiguous ownership, secure possession with an obligation to pay an annual rent – these were all conceptions of property that would have been quite familiar to Canadian habitants. There were even ways in which patterns of social reproduction were reflected in the allotment of pews. When a new balcony was added to the church of St Ours, the curé, like a seigneur opening a new row of lots, was approached by men wishing to secure a second pew to be kept for a son until he married and needed a place of his own in the church.[51]

Theoretically, the procedures for renting pews were set down in the 1720s by ordinances of the colonial government.[52] Pews were supposed to be conceded at the annual rent offered by the highest bidder in a public auction; at the death of the occupant or of his widow, the place would be put on the block once more, but a clause similar to the 'retrait lignager' of land law allowed an heir of the deceased to claim it for the same rate as the highest bid. The basic aim of this legislation was to preserve family attachment to a particular pew while ensuring maximum revenues for the parish through the use of competitive auctions. But the habitants of the eighteenth-century Lower Richelieu had no desire to see rentals forced up and they knew that any truly competitive system would put all the choice pews into the hands of rich villagers, leaving them the unreserved space at the back of the church. Accordingly, they used their control over the vestry, such as it was, to avoid any application of the auction rule. Pews were rented at a fixed rate (usually three livres a year), more or less in defiance of the law and of the express wishes of priests and bishops. Eventually, towards the end of the century, the clerics managed to impose the competitive system but, even so, parishioners sometimes maintained enough cohesion to rig auctions so that no one offered more than the traditional rate. By the early nineteenth century, however, real competition was normal; annual rents of 1.5 to 76 livres for an average of 27.5 livres were offered in twenty-five auctions in Sorel between 1809 and 1819.[53]

Vestry funds were only for the decoration and routine maintenance of the church. When major repairs were required or when a church or rectory was to be built, funds had to be raised by other means. Special assessments for this purpose were a particularly heavy burden for Canadian parishioners because, in the absence of a European system of ecclesiastical patronage, the rich were not inclined to shoulder the expense. Furthermore, construction projects were rather frequent in the eighteenth century when structures were not always built to last and when the rapidly expanding population required an ever larger space. Between 1740 and 1840, the church at Sorel was torn down and a new one built on two occasions, while the rectory was rebuilt four times; each of the buildings also received major alterations or repairs twice during this period. St Ours built one new church and two new rectories and St Denis three churches and two rectories during the century. This construction work became more and more expensive over the years as the size and magnificence of the edifices increased. Sorel's second church was built in 1750 at a cost of 3377 livres, but 3600 livres were spent to repair it fifty years later; the bill for the massive structure erected in the 1820s was at least 54,050 livres, though even this did not compare to the 80,250 livres spent earlier, at the turn of the century, on St Denis's ambitious temple.[54]

The initiative for these construction projects invariably came from the clergy, either the local curé or the bishop on a pastoral visit. The interest of a priest in a new or enlarged rectory is obvious enough but the clerics also had a keen desire to see their churches built on as large and impressive a scale as possible. Not only was majestic architecture fitting in a building devoted to the worship of the Lord, it was also enhanced the prestige of the curé who 'built' it. Parishioners too took some satisfaction and pride from stately churches and rectories but, as the ones who actually paid for them, they were much more modest in their ambitions than were the clergymen. This often made for friction, for example in Sorel in 1755. Despite an intendant's ordinance and a bishop's 'mandement,' the assembled population staunchly refused to replace their tumbledown rectory with a new stone one, 'ne voulant entendre parler d'aucune batisse alleguant pour raisons qu'il leur en couteroit beaucoup pour batir un presbiter en pierre.' It was only eleven years later, and after more orders and exhortations from the ecclesiastical authorities, that the parishioners agreed to build a rectory, but only of logs. The new building cannot have been a sturdy one, however, for it was badly deteriorated in 1780 when another curé renewed the call for a stone rectory. It went unheeded and within a few years he had moderated his demands, asking only for a new wooden house. In the end, he had to be content with a commitment to repair the old structure.[55]

Construction projects were supposed to be financed by an official assessment approved by majority vote of the parishioners. This amounted to a temporary annual tax for a specified number of years and, since it was levied in proportion to land holdings, habitants always paid almost the entire amount. In the nineteenth century, assessments were normally a cash exaction but in early periods material and labour were often contributed instead. As a means of lightening what could often be a considerable burden, parishioners were often anxious to dip into the vestry treasury to help pay for construction but the priests and bishops opposed this, preferring to keep these funds for vestments and ornaments. This too could become a point of bitter controversy as in 1779 when the people of St Ours insisted quite vehemently on using vestry funds to save them from an assessment. Shocked by their rebellious tone, Mgr Briand wrote to his flock:

En verité Mrs les canadiens vous devriez vous faire instruire avant de parler si haut et de prendre contre votre Eveque un ton si peu mesuré mais vous ne respectez personne ni roy ni prince, ni magistrats, ni loix ni prestres ni Evêques ni religion, ni puissance seculaire, ni autorité sacrée.[56]

Once a church or rectory was finished, the peasants who had paid for it had a natural tendency to regard it as their own collective property, but this attitude was at odds with that of the clergy, who saw parish buildings as belonging to God or His earthly representatives. Eighteenth-century rectories always had a 'salle des habitants' where men would gather to discuss parish affairs and to socialize generally. A St Ours curé might well announce, 'que le presbytère entier étant la demeure du curé,' but this was clearly not the case until the nineteenth century when priests did generally manage to make their houses into private residences.[57] And yet even then one finds traces of the old conception of lay ownership, for example in the words of a Sorel habitant who, angry about something or other, stormed into the rectory: 'En jurant et blasphemant, il a dit quil étoit aussi maitre qu'aucune personne dans la maison.'[58]

Tensions between the clergy and rural laity seem to have been a constant in rural Quebec, but the balance of power between the two groups changed considerably from the eighteenth century to the nineteenth century. In the Lower Richelieu and in other parts of the province, the period around the turn of the century saw developments on a number of fronts that favoured the priests and foreshadowed the establishment of real clerical control in the years following 1840.[59] Curés came to exercise more and more control over vestry affairs as churchwardens ceased to be democratically elected. In parish after parish, clerics managed to have these vestry executives selected by co-optation so as to make them independent of the mass of parishioners and more responsive to clerical direction. Around the same time the clergy won several victories on the pew front which greatly increased vestry revenue from pew rentals. This change had political as well as economic implications since it meant that the relative importance of voluntary contributions through collections such as the 'quête de l'enfant jésus' declined and consequently so did the vestry's dependence on the goodwill of parishioners.[60] There was a parallel evolution in the system of financing church construction by which legal assessments replaced voluntary donations of labour, material, and money. Thus the victories of the clergy were at the same time economic and political in their thrust and they had the effect of reducing lay influence over the parish community while increasing the material burden of ecclesiastical exactions.

This shift in the relative power of clergy and laity seems to have been a general phenomenon throughout rural Lower Canada around the turn of the nineteenth century, but it is not easy to explain. There does not seem to have been any shift in clerical ideology or strategy; whether 'gallican,' 'ultramontain,' or 'Jansenist,' clergymen seem naturally to have assumed that they should play a leading role in parish affairs. They were simply unable to do so, except within fairly narrow limits, because of the power of the laity in early periods. Nor does the relative force of numbers hold the key. The number of ecclesiastics in relation to the population at large was in fact at its lowest ebb in the history of Quebec around 1800.[61] On the other hand, the eighteenth-century agrarian expansion had increased tithes considerably and given country curés an ample and reliable income which they lacked in earlier periods. Consider the contrasting material positions of two rural priests, Charles Dufaux de la Jimerais, curé of Verchères, who died in 1750, and Jean-François Hébert of St Ours, who died in 1831.[62] The inventory of the eighteenth-century pastor suggests a standard of living resembling that of a moderately well-off habitant. He had a 30-arpent farm, the normal peasant outfit of livestock and agricultural implements (Did he farm himself or rent his land to a tenant?) and modest furnishings worth 1022 livres altogether, excluding the real estate. The only possessions that distinguish Father Dufaux's inventory from that of an habitant are a picture of the virgin, a statuette of Christ, a modest library of twenty-seven religious works, and a good supply of wine and eau-de-vie. A more striking feature of his material position was the overwhelming burden of debt. Dufaux owed 3272 livres, mostly to local merchants, and this likely outweighed the value of all his assets, including the little farm. Father Hébert, who died eighty years later, was incomparably better off. Among his possessions were a house in the village, a large farm, and a separate woodlot in the country, eighteen head of cattle, eleven sheep, three horses, a sleigh, two carriages, a silver snuff-box, a silver statuette of Christ, and four annuities totalling 4302 livres per year and representing a capital of 71,689 livres. Riches of this magnitude would have left the curé of St Ours with no reason to envy any of his neighbours, including the merchants, notaries, and seigneurs. Admittedly, he seems to have been an exceptionally rich priest, but even his less fortunate colleagues lived at a level that was far superior to that of the peasantry. Besides being richer, clergymen were rather less mobile, more firmly attached to a particular parish by the turn of the century than they had been earlier; this would have given them greater experience with local politics and, presumably, more influence than their predecessors enjoyed. These factors must have increased the power of curés but they are perhaps less significant than other developments which reduced the laity's power of resistance.

In the middle of the eighteenth century, the parishes of the Lower Richelieu were still made up overwhelmingly of habitants. This peasantry was fairly homogeneous and this favoured the formation of a solid front of parishioners when disputes arose with the priest or the bishop. But developments in the late eighteenth century tended to produce a more complex local society thereby undermining the bases of lay solidarity. Although there was still rough economic equality within the peasantry and although habitants still constituted the largest class in the Lower Richelieu, we shall see below that other groups – artisans, day-labourers, professionals, and so on – grew to form a significant proportion of the region's Catholic population. As a result of this diversity, it must have been much harder than in the past to achieve a consensus among laymen and to organize opposition to clerical domination. The spirit of habitant self-government was certainly not crushed – for example, in 1837 the parishioners of St Denis defied curé and bishop in insisting that vestry funds be used to purchase arms for the rebellion[63] – but the clergy found it much easier to pursue a policy of divide and rule than they had in the past.

It should be clear now that the parish and the seigneurie were political institutions in a significant sense. Within their confines, habitant interests came into conflict with clerical and seigneurial interests and the two contended for power. Obviously there was very little open warfare between the classes – no society can survive deadly civil strife for long. Instead superiors and inferiors had to do as classes do in most societies, that is, come to some sort of accomodation that laid the basis of civil equilibrium. Given the conflicting interests of the parties, this had to be a somewhat uneasy balance and it rested on an unequal distribution of power. The peasants had little choice but to accept the pre-eminence of the clergy and seigneurs – particularly since religion, science, and their own long experience taught them that all men and women were not equal. And yet, the habitants naturally understood the rights and duties of superior and inferior in a way favourable to their own interests. Thus 'class struggle' remained a feature of peasant-aristocrat relations even through the relatively stable and thoroughly non-revolutionary times that concern us here. The various disputes over the management of parish affairs illustrate beautifully the way in which the peasantry could profess a sincere commitment to the leadership of the clergy and yet fight quite effectively for its own interests.

Thus when we argue that the clergy and nobility dominated the Lower Richelieu, this should not be taken to mean that these classes enjoyed total control, or anything like it, over the inhabitants of the region. As in all relationships of domination, the subordinates could never surrender their will entirely to their superiors even if they wanted to. Indeed, Canadian habitants disposed of a very wide margin of autonomy (particularly in areas where the material interests of the aristocracy were not at stake). Still, they were the weaker party in a largely masked, but nevertheless continuous, power struggle. And the economic stakes were well worth fighting for.

5

The feudal burden

Were seigneurial and ecclesiastical exactions nothing more than a minor nuisance to the early Canadian peasantry? How exactly was wealth transferred from the agricultural producers to the dominant classes? Was the basis of appropriation fixed or was it at all changeable or arbitrary? Finally, how significant an impact did these feudal dues have on the habitant family economy? In attempting to answer these questions, I shall continue to concentrate on the more problematic seigneurial economy.

SEIGNEURIAL DUES

The most important mechanism of transfer in most Canadian seigneuries was the 'cens et rentes,' an annual payment in money, produce, or labour, exacted on all lands in the 'mouvance' at a rate proportional to the size of each lot. The cens alone was a small payment, considered a token of the 'commoners'' form of tenure, which carried with it subjection to a number of dues, such as the 'lods et ventes,' outlined in the Custom of Paris. Rente was a lucrative charge added to and deliberately confused with the cens in order to subject the inhabitant to the penalties prescribed by law for late payment of the latter.[1] The term 'rent' will be used here in the feudal sense, as it was in the past, to refer to the total of these two charges.

The annual rent on each lot was established at the time of concession and it could not legally be altered, although variations in the value of money and grain had the effect of changing the effective burden of this charge. The edict of 1711 moreover, in ordering seigneurs to make new concessions at the prevailing rates of cens et rentes, implied that a standard rate should apply in each seigneurie, if not throughout the colony, on lands granted at any time after that date. A legalistic bias has led some historians to assume that rents on new concessions therefore remained stable during the French régime and only rose after the Conquest when a French government was replaced by a British one less sympathetic to the habitants. In fact, a clear pattern of ever-increasing rent scales on newly settled sections of the mouvance is evident in seventeenth-century Montreal.[2] Similarly, in St Ours, new rents rose steadily throughout the French régime, but remained stable after the 1750s, just the opposite of the pattern suggested by the traditional view. Apparently, the development of the region's agricultural productivity led seigneurs to insist on a proper share of the expanding peasant surplus.

But how did the seigneurs of St Ours manage to defy official policy in this way? An examination of St Ours concession deeds suggests that the rise was the outcome of a subtle policy of altering the combination of cash, produce, and livestock in the annual rents, substituting pseudo-equivalents so as to change the value of payments while appearing to alter only their form. Cash was substituted for capons, and then wheat was put in the place of the money; also area measurements were substituted for linear frontage. The switch to payments largely in wheat in the years after 1720 was partly a reflection of the emergence of an agricultural economy in the Lower Richelieu, but it was also a clever hedge against erosion of fixed money rents. The seigneurs' imposition of altered rates made a mockery of legislation intended to protect the peasantry; the eighteenth-century rise in grain prices, joined to biased alterations in the form of payment were such that, at early nineteenth-century wheat prices, a ninety-arpent farm conceded in the seventeenth century would owe about six livres per year, while one conceded after 1754 (this included the majority of St Ours farms) would owe twenty-seven livres.[3] The trouble that the French régime seigneurs of St Ours took to adjust their rent scales suggests that they did not regard these revenues as 'token payments.'

Less is known about the evolution of cens et rentes in Sorel and St Denis. Towards the end of the French régime, the charge seems to have been a roughly equivalent combination of money and wheat to that exacted in St Ours, although every lot in Sorel owed an additional levy of one day's corvée labour.[4] (Note that corvée was simply a form of payment, labour rather than money or produce, and not a separate variety of seigneurial exaction, as many have suggested. The corvée in mid-eighteenth-century Sorel seems to have been an element of the cens et rentes, whereas Pierre de St Ours exacted a day's work from the habitants for use of a common pasture.) However, the seigneurs of Sorel and St Denis, both of them absentees probably anxious to simplify accounts and collection procedures, converted all charges in labour and kind to a single annual cash exaction. This change occurred around 1770 in Sorel and probably much earlier in St Denis, with the effect that rents there were greatly devalued by the long-term inflation of the eighteenth century. In the early nineteenth century, a ninety-arpent farm was charged about 13.5 livres in St Denis, 18 livres in Sorel, and between 16 and 32 livres in St Ours, depending on the price of wheat.[5] The seigneurs of St Ours tended to benefit in the long run by their adherence to rents in kind. The relative advantage of seigneur and habitant in each seigneurie changed, in opposite directions, with fluctuating grain prices. Moreover, the positions of the two parties reverse as one moves from St Ours to Sorel or St Denis; that is, a rise in wheat prices favoured St Ours seigneurs and Sorel habitants, while a price decline tended to favour Sorel seigneurs and St Ours habitants.

In addition to the cens et rentes, Canadian seigneurs benefited from a variety of lucrative charges, including the lods et ventes, a mutation fine amounting to one-twelfth of the purchase price owed by the buyer of land in the mouvance. In France, and in some Canadian seigneuries, purchasers who paid promptly were charged a third or a quarter less than the legal rate, but this discount was not universal and St Ours seigneurs invariably demanded the full amount.[6] They even pursued habitants who acquired farms by deed of gift from an unrelated donor (transactions within a family were exempt from lods et ventes), although this entailed estimating a cash value for every element in an elaborate pension alimentaire, converting the total annual value into the capital it represented at 5 or 6 per cent interest, and finally determining the one-twelfth mutation fine on this sum.[7] To realize its full value, the right of lods et ventes required that a seigneur be aware of the details of land transactions in his fief and it was therefore closely tied, in its practical application, to the various official and unofficial aspects of his control over people and lands. In addition to his role as the main repository of land title records, the seigneur disposed of the retrait seigneurial to guarantee the proper reporting of prices. Of course the co-operation of the local notary, who officiated at transactions and kept their records, was invaluable, but what notary could risk offending the seigneur, normally his most important client?

Several minor exactions were added to the basic feudal rent and mutation fines. One of these was the annual fee for admission to the common pasture; such 'droit de commune' was demanded of all Sorel habitants until the late eighteenth century and of the residents of the St Lawrence section of St Ours until the end of seigneurial tenure. The situation here was not what it was in Old Régime France, where commons were generally controlled by peasant communities whose possession was only partially usurped by aggressive seigneurial offensives.[8] Far from having to fight for one-third of the commons ('triage'), the seigneurs of Sorel and St Ours began with full control of pastures that were simply reserved sections of the demesne. The Sorel commons were an island in the river but, in the neighbouring fief, Pierre de St Ours forced his habitants – after a bitter struggle that required the intervention of the intendant of New France – to bear the full burden of fencing in the shoreline pasture.[9] Those holding land nearby were then charged one day's corvée per year, later converted to a money payment of 3 livres, to graze their beasts there.

Although they profited through the above-mentioned exactions from habitant grain-growing, livestock raising, and property sales, the seigneurs of the Lower Richelieu were not prepared to let even minor ancillary productions go untaxed. In Sorel, there was a levy on maple sugar-making as well as a fishing fee. In the eighteenth century, choice locations on islands in the St Lawrence were farmed out to habitants for seventy-eight livres annually, as much as the rents of a dozen farms. A document dated 1809 mentions an exaction of two fish from each netful of shad caught.[10] There was no basis in law for this 'droit de pêche,' but this seems to have escaped the seigneurs' notice.

Seigneurs benefited, not only from these direct exactions, but also from various monopolies, above all the 'banalité' (grist mill monopoly), which will be discussed later. These privileges are quite different from the dues mentioned so far in that they were not lucrative in themselves, even though they could be used to enrich the seigneur at the habitants' expense. The banal mill was a protected enterprise with a captive market, but it did provide a service; the milling toll was therefore unlike the almost entirely parasitic cens et rentes as it went partly to defray expenses. Only a portion of this fee was profit for the seigneur and only part of that could be attributed to the effects of protection from competition.[11] Collecting the milling toll was a simple matter of withholding one-fourteenth of the grain processed, whereas seigneurs experienced considerable difficulty in securing payment of annual dues and mutation fines.

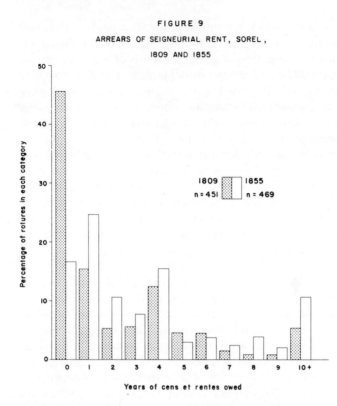

FIGURE 9

ARREARS OF SEIGNEURIAL RENT, SOREL,

1809 AND 1855

1809 n = 451   1855 n = 469

Percentage of roltures in each category

Years of cens et rentes owed

PAYMENT

Seigneurial dues were notoriously difficult to collect (frontier or no frontier, Canada was exactly like France in this respect).[12] Most habitants
were a few years in arrears on occasion and many fell behind more
seriously and were never able to get out of debt. Behind this backlog
was probably a combination of inability to pay, unwillingness to pay,
and a calculated postponement based on the knowledge that it was not
worthwhile for the seigneur to take action to recover small debts. Some
habitants lived so close to the edge of subsistence that chronic debt to
the seigneur must have been almost unavoidable; whereas others, normally able to pay regularly, must have experienced temporary distress
that put them slightly in arrears now and then. Most likely, there was
also a certain amount of passive resistance to seigneurial exploitation
expressed in the failure to pay promptly. Figure 9 shows that only 15

TABLE 14
Seigneurial rents and arrears paid, Sorel 1798–1805

Year	Annual rent due	Rent and arrears received	Percentage
1798	2643	1817	69
1799	2787	1988	71
1800	2874	2268	79
1801	2930	1523	52
1802	2942	2572	87
1803	3407	3564	105
1804	3407	2213	65
1805	3407	2493	73

per cent of Sorel's lands had rent arrears of more than four years in 1809. By 1855, however, this figure had risen to 25 per cent, reflecting the general distress of the seigneurie's habitants in the period when fur-trade employment had disappeared.[13] Accumulated arrears seem to have been disproportionately great in recently conceded lands, probably because many of them were not fully cleared and productive for several years. In Sorel, and presumably in other seigneuries, payments of current and overdue rents fluctuated from year to year with the harvests, the general economic situation, and the varying pressure exerted by the seigneur (see Table 14).[14]

Arrears of lods et ventes were more common and of much longer duration than arrears of rents. The former charge usually amounted to a relatively substantial sum due all at once, and many habitants found themselves unable to pay it for years, or even generations, even if they could make the more moderate rent payments year by year. 'Quitte excepté les lods' is a recurrent phrase in the St Ours estate rolls. From the seigneur's point of view then, the actual revenue in any one year was never even close to the total value of the dues to which he was legally entitled. By about 1840 the censitaires of Sorel and St Ours owed their seigneurs at least 92,000 and 71,158 livres respectively. Of course many of these arrears would never be paid at all. The notaries who drew up the inventory of 1841 following the death of François Roch de St Ours judged that one-third of the arrears of the seigneurie should simply be written off since they were owed on uncleared lots of very little value.[15]

Extracting payments of arrears from indebted habitants was a delicate task requiring, on the part of the seigneur or his agent, a thorough acquaintance with the individuals and the productive capacities of their lands. If the seigneur was convinced that the debtor would never pay, he would generally take steps to have him removed so that the land could be turned over to a more promising candidate. This sometimes required an expensive and time-consuming lawsuit to obtain a judicial seizure.[16] Seigneurs naturally preferred the various procedures mentioned above – repossession for failure to develop and 'voluntary' abandonment – that weeded out undesirables with much less inconvenience. For less serious cases, they were inclined to show a certain amount of patience in the hopes of eventually recovering overdue rents. Paternalistic attitudes may have had something to do with it, but there were also more practical motives for forbearance. Since habitant agriculture was often quite unproductive and short harvests were common, rigid insistence on immediate payment would clearly be unreasonable and self-defeating in many cases. As long as a habitant made a visible effort to make good back dues and as long as his farm was valuable enough to bear the debt, he could usually feel safe. In the end, a seigneur could take advantage of his position as legally privileged creditor to claim arrears from the estate when his debtor died. Prompter payment was certainly preferable, however, and seigneurs used a variety of strategies, threating, cajoling, setting deadlines, and accepting payments in unusual forms, in order to wring as much as possible out of peasants who had the slimmest of surpluses and who were disinclined to part with them. Always it was the threat, implied or stated, of being deprived of their homes and livelihood that encouraged such marginal cases to turn over what they could.

Scraps of paper in the estate roll of one St Ours sub-fief tell the story of the dealings between the seigneur, François-Xavier Malhiot, and some of his habitants between 1818 and 1829.[17] When lods et ventes or rents were unpaid for several years, Malhiot would often send for the offender, who had to go to the seigneur's home at Verchères, twenty to fifty kilometres away, to be presented with a bill for the arrears as well as an extra four or five livres 'pour l'avoir fait sommer.' The habitant often said he had no money to give but would sometimes promise to produce money or some item of value by a certain date or 'next year.' If no such promise were made, Malhiot might specify a precise schedule of payments, perhaps offering to reduce the debt in return for punctual payment, or, in some cases, threatening legal action. Insofar as these destitute peasants paid off their debts, they usually did so by working and Malhiot credited their accounts in accordance with certificates signed by his correspondents in St Ours attesting that a particular man had built or repaired roads, fences, or ditches.

Documents from other sections of St Ours suggest that seigneurial dues were acquitted in a great variety of forms. There were always a large number of habitants who apparently paid punctually and in the money and wheat specified in their title deeds but, for poorer censitaires, these commodities were only accounting abstractions. Products offered for rents and lods et ventes between the 1790s and the 1840s include oats, barley, peas, lumber, firewood, maple sugar, hay, cattle, and homespun cloth. Labour was also a common means of payment, even though officially there was no corvée in St Ours after about 1720. The estate rolls show that censitaires received a certain amount of credit for each day spent working on roads and fences or on the construction of a mill. When a gristmill on the Yamaska River was planned in 1814, the contract with the seigneur required the builder to employ, as far as possible, St Ours habitants who would be paid half their wages in cash and the other half in coupons to be applied to their accounts with the seigneur.[18] Once again it seems clear that the form in which feudal dues were officially set down was of no essential importance; what was appropriated was the surplus labour of the peasant, either in its raw form, or as agricultural produce or as produce converted into cash.

SEIGNEURIAL MONOPOLIES

As an outgrowth of seigneurial judicial powers, Canadian landlords enjoyed certain privileges and monopolies over the territories of their estates and the people who lived there; long after they had ceased to act as local judges, the seigneurs of Sorel, St Ours, and St Denis continued to insist on the lucrative perquisites of the position. The most important of these was the gristmill monopoly and it was more widespread and more stringent in Canada than it was in most parts of Old Régime France.[19] Here, it was often an important source of seigneurial revenues, and a real inconvenience to habitants. The Custom of Paris only allowed seigneurs to require their vassals to grind the wheat they needed for domestic consumption at the seigneurial watermill and only in cases where the right was sanctioned by written titles or ancient custom. A royal edict of 1686 enlarged the Canadian seigneur's rights in this regard by declaring banal every mill, whether water- or wind-driven, and without any need for stipulation in title deeds.[20]

Nevertheless, every St Ours deed mentioned the mill monopoly, in order to spell out the habitant's obligations and to specify penalties for infractions. The trend over the course of the eighteenth century was towards more extensive obligations and more stringent penalties. In the seventeenth century, only grain used for home consumption had to be ground at the seigneur's mill and the fine for processing flour elsewhere was the equivalent of the milling toll on the amount of grain. By the 1790s, the formula in concession deeds subjected all grain grown to the banalité, whether it was consumed at home or sent abroad, and piled penalty on top of penalty: not only would a fine equal to the milling toll be exacted, the illicit flour could also be seized and additional arbitrary fines imposed. This evolution in title deed clauses seems to reflect a wider trend towards a more careful and exacting style of estate management. Note, however, that, right from the beginning, the seigneurs of St Ours assumed the right to subject all varieties of grain to their monopoly even though the law of the land limited the banalité to wheat alone, and only to the amount needed for domestic consumption.[21]

There is a long-established myth in Canadian historiography to the effect that the law of 1686 giving all seigneurial mills monopoly privileges was as much a burden for the seigneurs as it was for the habitants, since it also forced the former to build mills within a year or forever forfeit their right of banalité.[22] In fact, many seigneurs easily retained their privileges even though they only opened a mill long after that date. Pierre de Sorel had a mill built in 1670, no doubt as much to contribute to the development of his estate as in anticipation of future profits, but Pierre de St Ours waited until twenty years after the law of 1686 before erecting a windmill, and his banal privileges were never revoked. Worse still, the absentee seigneurs of St Denis left their peasants with no mill until after the Conquest, noting all the same in concession deeds that granted lands would be, 'sujette au moulin de ladte. seigneurie lorsqu'il y en aura un de construit.'[23] Two small seigneurial mills, one wind-driven and the other water-driven, were eventually built in the late eighteenth century, but the seigneurs of St Denis found they did not even have to bother investing in milling facilities to profit from their banalité. Between 1817 and 1837, they leased out the privilege of operating gristmills to five different millers, who took on full responsibility for building and operating the mills.[24] This earned the seigneur ninety-two minots of wheat per year (worth about 600 livres in the 1830s) without requiring any risk or investment. Elsewhere in Quebec, seigneurs struck even more advantageous agreements, temporarily waiving their monopoly and granting permission to entrepreneurs to build and operate a gristmill on condition that they be given possession of the mill after a specified number of years.[25] Regardless of the law, the banalité could be a very lucrative privilege under favourable economic circumstances.

After a period of severely fragmented ownership around the middle of the eighteenth century, the seigneurs of St Ours showed a greater willingness than their neighbours to establish their own mills and profit directly from the monopoly. This was partly because the fief was well supplied with good hydraulic sites, but also because the seigneurs generally lived on the estate for at least part of the year and took a personal hand in managing it. In addition to Pierre de St Ours's old windmill on the St Lawrence, there was a water-driven mill on the Richelieu, built in 1773 and, following the development of the rear sections of the seigneurie, another watermill was established in 1815, this one on the Yamaska River. This last mill was the largest in St Ours and it contained three pairs of stones with bolts, as well as a fulling mill; in 1842 the building and machinery were insured for 10,000 livres.[26]

The milling toll in early Quebec was set by law at one-fourteenth of the grain ground but of course expenses claimed a considerable portion of the gross revenue. Mills were always leased out to a miller, either for a set annual rent or, more commonly, for a proportion of the proceeds; in various contracts this amounted to one-half, one-third, or one-quarter of the revenues.[27] The seigneur also had to pay for major repairs and for a portion of the operating expenses. This left, according to one optimistic estimate, about two-thirds of the milling tolls, or 4.8 per cent of all the grain processed, as the seigneur's net profit.[28] In Sorel, badly served by two decrepit windmills, net profits were only 160 minots of wheat (worth 480 livres) in 1782–3, but the big gristmills of St Ours were worth 1500 minots of grain (value about 3000–7000 livres) annually to their seigneur around 1840.[29]

Much of this can be seen simply as return on an industrial investment and so the question remains, how much of the mill revenue actually stemmed from the monopoly conferred by the banalité? This was a question that the commissioners charged with liquidating the seigneurial régime in Quebec had to face in 1860. Within five years of the 'abolition' of 1854, they found, two new gristmills were established in St Ours to compete with those of the seigneur and the revenues of the latter dropped by more than one-third. Estimating the number of habitants who would find it more convenient to take their grain to one of the new mills or to a gristmill outside the seigneurie, the commissioners judged the monopoly to be worth 2450 livres per year.[30]

A source of revenue to the seigneur, the banalité appeared from the habitant's point of view as a double restriction, preventing him both from having his grain ground where he wished and from establishing a gristmill of his own. In practice, it was the latter restriction that was most effectively enforced and economically most important. Although they always insisted on their right to prevent habitants from taking unground grain outside the fief, seigneurs were unable to police movements of this sort; contraventions seem to have been common.[31] On the other hand, it was impossible for interlopers to build unauthorized gristmills and escape detection. Two St Denis residents built mills on their own land but the seigneur promptly sued them and, in an out-of-court settlement, imposed the annual tribute mentioned earlier as the price of allowing them to continue operations; a less accommodating seigneur might have had the offending mills razed, with the full backing of the law. The lack of competition did not affect the cost of services to the habitant, since this was set by law at a moderate rate. On the other hand, the quality of flour and the regularity of service may have suffered. More serious was the inconvenience of having to carry grain to seigneurial mills that were, for many users, far from home. In France, only peasants within a certain distance, usually one league, were subject to the mill monopoly but, in Canadian seigneuries, which were generally quite vast, there was no such limit and farmers had to transport their grain many leagues to the banal mill. In St Ours between 1815 and 1845, habitants south of the Richelieu had a return journey of up to thirty kilometres to the banal mill.[32]

Although the gristmill monopoly was well established in the Custom of Paris and colonial legislation, Canadian seigneurs arrogated some additional privileges which had no such legal basis. After the Conquest, for example, concession deeds in Sorel and St Ours often referred to a seigneurial sawmill monopoly.[33] Moreover, in order to exploit banal and pseudo-banal rights, seigneurs also insisted on being able to take possession of any land they might require in the mouvance to build a mill. According to the legal expert Cugnet, French Régime law allowed seigneurs to take up to ten arpents from their censitaires, with indemnification, to construct a banal gristmill,[34] but the St Ours concession deeds broadened this privilege to include both sawmills and flourmills and they expressly denied the need to provide an indemnity. Of course, a sawmill is useless without wood and, as unconceded domains dwindled, seigneurs tended increasingly to press their claim to cut timber on land possessed by habitants in the mouvance. In concession deeds, this amounted to a gradual extension of clauses, inserted at the instigation of the French Régime government, reserving oak timber for use in building the king's ships. The intendants of New France objected to any timber reserve for the seigneur's own profit but pre-Conquest deeds in

St Ours nevertheless permitted seigneurs to cut wood on censitaires' lands for the construction of 'public' buildings, namely churches, rectories, mills, and manor houses.[35] Limitations on seigneurial timber reserves tended to disappear over the course of the eighteenth century, particularly after the British Conquest. Concession deeds then confidently began to speak of the seigneur's right to cut trees on habitant lands, even for commercial manufacturing, 'afin que si led. Sieur seigneur voulait dans la suitte faire batir des moulins à scie, il puisse aisement trouvé (sic) tous les matériaux qui luy seront necessaire.'[36] Monsieur de St Ours did acquire a sawmill in 1793,[37] but it is impossible to know the extent to which he actually exercised this pretended right to all the timber in his fief.

It was not absolutely impossible for anyone but a seigneur to establish a sawmill or a gristmill in the Lower Richelieu. Exemptions could sometimes be secured but, on the whole, the increasingly extensive conception of monopolies and reserves set out in concession deeds, tended to discourage quite effectively any impulse habitants may have had to found industrial enterprises on their 'own' land. If they did purchase exemption from banal or pseudo-banal monopolies, the annual tribute to the seigneur would of course cut into their profits and limit capital formation. In an agrarian economy of this sort, flour and lumber manufacturing in fact offered important opportunities for non-agricultural investment and they might have been a vehicle by which some peasants propelled themselves to bourgeois status.

FEUDAL EXACTIONS AND THE PEASANT HOUSEHOLD
ECONOMY

If we add the ecclesiastical payments discussed in the last chapter to the seigneurial dues enumerated here, it becomes clear that eighteenth-century habitants were subject to a diverse array of rents, tithes, fees, and fines. And yet, according to many historians, these all added up to an aggregate 'feudal burden' that was paltry indeed.[38] The people of the Lower Richelieu, on the other hand, were more inclined to take these matters seriously. We have seen the heated disputes that often arose between priests and parishioners over pew rents and assessments for construction projects. Think also of the great pains that seigneurs took to adjust rent scales and to levy the full mutation fine on every imaginable transaction, and of the risks that many habitants ran in allowing backrents to accumulate even when they were in danger of losing their farms. These exactions mattered both to exploiters and to exploited because the wealth at stake was significant.

What exactly was the material weight of feudalism on the peasantry? This is a question that has bedeviled historians of both Canada and Europe; many have attempted estimates but results have always been controversial and generally unsatisfactory.[39] Source deficiencies – the absence of reliable figures on agricultural production and aristocratic revenues – are only part of the problem. More serious are a number of thorny conceptual issues, many of them connected to the diversity of the forms of feudal exactions. It is very difficult to construct a single index out of the various dues when some were paid in cash, some in kind, and others in labour. Furthermore, some – tithes, pew rents, and seigneurial rents, for example – were due on a regular annual basis, while others – mutation fines and ecclesiastical assessments, for instance – had to be paid only on certain occasions. A further problem has to do with the fact that many payments to priests and seigneurs were at least partially compensation for a genuine service. Mill tolls fall into this category since only part of the fee can be attributed to the seigneur's privileged position. Finally, there is the question of whether the demands of the state – taxes, military service, road work – should be counted as part of the feudal burden. All this makes it next to impossible to measure the feudal economy with any precision or to make meaningful comparisons between different periods or between different countries.

Beyond these methodological dilemmas loom some options more theoretical than technical. Researchers wishing to determine the economic importance of feudalism must consider the questions, important for whom? and according to what criteria? The tendency is often to ignore the distinctions between capitalist and precapitalist economies and treat seigneurs and habitants as though they were landowners and agricultural entrepreneurs. From this point of view it makes sense to divide seigneurial revenues by the area of the censive to find a rate of seigneurial exactions amounting to so many livres per arpent. A similar procedure consists of estimating peasant agricultural income and dividing by the total of seigneurial and ecclesiastical revenues; this gives a percentage figure representing the proportion of habitant harvests absorbed by the feudal classes. This would be fine if the agriculturalists in question were genuine farmers engaged in a profit-making enterprise, selling all or most of what they grew and paying ground-rent as one of the expenses of doing business. Eighteenth-century habitants were of course nothing of the sort; they were peasants and their economy centred on production for domestic consumption. Thus there was a fairly inflexible minimum supply of many crops that habitant families needed to survive and to reproduce themselves. Ignoring this basic characteristic of pre-capitalist agrarian society allows one to conclude that 'seigneurial dues ... were very low, representing 10 percent of the produce of their concessions,'[40] but it does not tell us much about the realities of the feudal economy since the 'produce' of peasant lands remains an abstract quantity. In fact, the figure of 10 per cent does not seem so low, especially when we realize that it does not include the tithe or other ecclesiastical dues, but that is not the point. The problem with this approach is that we do not know what the loss of 10 per cent of its harvest would mean for an habitant family, whether, for example, this would simply leave it with a little less wheat to sell or whether it would threaten its very survival by cutting into the stock needed for seed and for subsistence.

A better way of evaluating feudal exactions is therefore to consider them in relation to habitant *surpluses*. This requires estimating, not only how much peasants grew annually, but also how much they needed to retain in order to last the year. Because of the methodological and source difficulties mentioned above, I am not in a position to set up a complete 'model' of the habitant economy in the eighteenth century but I do have enough information to make a rough estimate of production, surplus, and exactions for wheat alone. Thus, only one aspect of Lower Richelieu agriculture is covered, although wheat was surely the most important element. In Chapter 2, I used figures from the 1765 census on grain sown to estimate how much wheat Théophile Allaire and Felicité Audet probably harvested. Data from this same source can now be used to estimate the wheat production of all the habitants of St Ours. Census figures on the population of adults and children, along with information from deeds of gift on flour consumption, allow us then to calculate roughly the amount of wheat needed for home consumption. Taking the difference between production and consumption gives the estimated wheat surplus of each habitant family in the parish. It is then a simple matter to evaluate the impact on this surplus of the tithe and the wheat portion of seigneurial rents (see Table 15).[41]

According to this model then, almost half (45 per cent) of the wheat grown by the habitants of St Ours in 1765, beyond what was needed to maintain the growers, would have been owed to the local seigneur and curé just to pay those feudal exactions that were set down in terms of wheat. This of course does not give us a complete picture of the relationship between peasant surpluses and aristocratic exploitation. Habi-

TABLE 15
Habitant surpluses and feudal exactions, wheat only, St Ours 1765

'habitant' households		99
Production		
(a) grain sown	2098 minots	
(b) wheat sown (2/3 a)	1399 minots	
(c) yield per seed	5.8	
(d) wheat harvested (b × c)	8112 minots	8112 minots
Deductions		
(e) wheat seed for next year	− 1399 minots	
(f) mill toll (1/13)	− 385 minots	
(g) total	− 1784 minots	− 1784 minots
Domestic consumption		
(h) adult population	238	
(i) boys under 15	158	
(j) 'girls'	134	
(k) adult rations (h + i/2 + 3j/4)	417.5	
(l) consumption (12k)	5010 minots	− 5010 minots
(m) surplus (d − g − l)		1318 minots
Exactions		
(n) wheat portion seign. rent	276 minots	
(o) wheat tithe (d/26)	312 minots	
(p) total	588 minots	588 minots
Feudal exactions = 588/1232 = 45% of habitant wheat surplus		

tants raised many products other than wheat, but most of these were exclusively for domestic use and therefore not part of a saleable surplus. On the other hand, many important feudal dues – mutation fines, pew rents, church assessments, and the cash portion of seigneurial rents, to name a few – do not enter into our calculations. If anything therefore, this partial estimate underestimates the feudal burden.

It should be noted that this is a 'model' and not a detailed description of reality. In fact, harvests varied greatly from year to year, and so therefore did the relative weight of fixed dues; the seed-yield figure of 1: 5.8 is simply one historian's estimate of the 'normal' return. Also, some families no doubt ate more wheat than others and thus the twelve-minot ration would not have been strictly uniform. The Allaires, for example, did not grow quite enough to allow everyone this much wheat once the tithe and rent had been paid. Other families, the deeds of gift suggest, were able to provide as much as fifteen minots per adult and still make ends meet. I shall examine the different experiences of rich

TABLE 16
Proportion of wheat surplus devoted to tithe and seigneurial rent (wheat only) by
habitant household, St Ours 1765

	Households	Per cent
No surplus left after exactions	48	48
Exactions require 0–10% of surplus	2	2
" " 10–20% " "	21	21
" " 20–30% " "	11	11
" " 30–50% " "	11	11
" " 50–100% " "	4	4
" " 100% + " "	2	2
Total	99	99

and poor habitants below but, for the moment it is important to recognize
that, imprecise and partial though this aggregate model may be, it does
indicate that feudal dues deprived the Lower Richelieu peasantry of a
substantial portion – probably more than half – of its agricultural surpluses.

Beyond this 'average' experience, individual returns from the 1765
census make it clear that the production, surplus, and feudal burden
varied greatly from one St Ours household to the next. For half the cases
it is impossible to compute the percentage of wheat surpluses drained
by tithe and seigneurial rent, since forty-eight of the families had no
surplus at all once the exactions were subtracted. Of these households,
eleven grew less than five minots of wheat per 'adult equivalent'; evidently marginal grain-growers, these families may have been artisans
or day-labourers. The other thirty-seven who apparently lacked a wheat
surplus must have had to scramble to get by, perhaps making do with
less bread than their neighbours or earning a little money as hired hands
at harvest time. These are no doubt the habitants who let their rents go
unpaid for long stretches and who paid the seigneur, when they could,
in lumber, cloth, and labour. Feudal dues must have been a serious
problem for these families, but also for those, slightly better off, who
grew enough in good years to retain a small surplus after they had paid
the landlord and the curé. Table 16 shows that the wealthier half of the
St Ours peasantry generally owed a substantial portion of their excess
wheat to the aristocrats. Only two paid less than 10 per cent, whereas
twenty-eight paid more than 30 per cent of their surplus, some losing
their entire surplus to feudal dues. For a handful of the richest peasants,
on the other hand, tithes and rents were a much less significant drain.

The three largest producers had a net wheat surplus after deductions, exactions and consumption of 110, 122, and 122 minots respectively. After them came ten others with fifty to one hundred minots surplus. Feudal dues did not exceed 20 per cent of the excess of any of these thirteen prosperous families. They normally had substantial quantities of grain to sell and were the section of the community that grain dealers were most interested in.

This 'model' of wheat surpluses by household demonstrates, not only the differing impact of feudal exactions, but also the variety of economic positions within the Lower Richelieu peasantry. As to the economic impact of feudal dues, it seems fair to conclude that they were an obstacle to the accumulation of capital in peasant hands. Certainly tithes, rents and assessments did not absolutely prevent a habitant from amassing wealth, but generally they were a significant drain and particularly so for modest habitants like the Allaires who had a good deal of trouble in keeping above the subsistence line.

If extra-economic exactions and a prevalence of subsistence agriculture are the two primary characteristics of the feudal economy, here then is one connection between them. The first feature tended to reinforce the second by depriving peasants of part of the fruits of their labour. Seigneurial and ecclesiastical dues helped prevent the formation of an agrarian bourgeoisie by working against the accumulation of capital in habitant hands. Instead, a large portion of the agricultural surplus was delivered to priests and landlords who showed little inclination to invest their revenues in the land. Farms therefore remained relatively small and unproductive. Obviously feudal exploitation was not the only factor responsible for this state of affairs. The limited market for agricultural produce in the early years of the Lower Richelieu settlement also discouraged investment and egalitarian inheritance customs counteracted any long-term concentration of property. Moreover, the limitations on peasant ownership inherent in seigneurial tenure could be an obstacle to enterprise in some cases. Thus, although it would be an exaggeration to say that tithes, rents, and so on by themselves prevented the development of agriculture, it is nevertheless clear that they were a real burden for the habitant household, one that added its influence to other factors in making large-scale market-oriented production unlikely.

In other words, many of the basic characteristics of Lower Richelieu social and economic life were mutually reinforcing. The habitant majority lived and worked in family units, with household production organized mainly around the direct satisfaction of household consumption needs.

This self-sufficient peasantry found a significant portion of its surplus drained off to support local priests and seigneurs, the latter constituting a local aristocracy whose political ascendancy guaranteed its economic privileges. This combination of peasant self-sufficiency, together with aristocratic appropriation through extra-economic compulsion, is the basically 'feudal' configuration that is essential to an understanding of this rural society.

6

The country merchant

But seigneurs, clergymen, and habitants are not the only classes to be found in the eighteenth-century Richelieu valley and these 'feudal' aspects are not the only social and economic realities of rural life there. Money, buying, selling, renting, and hiring can all be found from the earliest European settlement. Indeed, a small merchant community began to emerge as a significant force in the region about the middle of the century. How did this growing bourgeois presence affect the peasantry? More generally, how did it affect the whole 'feudal nexus' described so far? Was merchant capital a force fundamentally at odds with the existing configuration of Canadian society? In the next two chapters, I shall look at the mercantile element as it entered the Lower Richelieu in two quite different guises, first as a seller of merchandise and buyer of grain and second as an employer of labour.

A WANDERING JEW COMES TO ST DENIS

While rural Canada developed initially under feudal auspices and in isolation from the commercial world of Montreal, Quebec, and the fur-producing hinterland, the eighteenth century saw urban capital looking increasingly for profits to the agrarian regions of the St Lawrence lowlands. From about the 1720s on, the development of Louisbourg and the international trend towards higher prices began to provide a modest but growing market for Canadian wheat and, at the same time, the expansion of agricultural colonization produced ever larger surpluses, including both the grain that passed through the hands of priests and seigneurs and that left to the peasants. Import-export merchants, anxious to secure returns to pay for European purchases and to fill ships' holds after the relatively compact fur exports had been loaded, sought to purchase wheat and other agricultural products.[1] At first, they depended on habitants bringing their produce to town and on travelling agents who toured the countryside buying grain from rentiers and direct producers, but eventually merchants began settling permanently in the countryside, drawn by the increasing concentration of population there, population that appeared as so many potential customers who could pay for their purchases if they could sell excess wheat. Rural merchants were still quite rare when François Bailly de Messein set up shop at Varennes in 1730, but by 1741 there were enough to annoy the businessmen of Quebec City who petitioned the government to have them outlawed.[2]

At this time the Richelieu valley was still in the early stages of settlement and habitants with something to buy or sell had to go as far as Montreal or Quebec. Even so the market for agricultural produce was limited and uncertain; the vestry of Sorel was left in 1743 with a quantity of wheat that had been donated to the parish but simply could not be converted into cash.[3] Within a decade, however, the region had acquired a reputation – one it would retain for almost a century – as the most productive grain-growing area in the colony and several individuals soon arrived to set up shops here in the early 1750s.[4] There was, for example, Jean LeRoux dit Provençal, an innkeeper who began retailing dry goods as well as beverages and purchasing produce at his house between the rectory and the manor at the 'fort of Sorel.'[5] From his base at the mouth of the Richelieu, he engaged in the grain trade but his location proved to be a handicap in competing with other dealers living upriver, nearer the heart of the new producing area. Illiterate and apparently a rustic native of Sorel, Provençal is a very rare example of a habitant who entered the business world. Other early merchants were much more clearly outsiders in the feudal Lower Richelieu. Marin Jehanne, for example, was from a town in Brittany and came to St Denis around 1750 after living in Quebec City for a time; shortly after the Conquest he abandoned commerce and became the local notary. In all, six merchants are known to have operated in the region before 1760, one each in Sorel and St Ours and the rest in St Denis. Joseph Paradis, who moved frequently between St Denis and St Antoine, made a small fortune supplying the French forces during the Seven Years' War; according to one contemporary, his success was largely due to corruption.[6] In 1763 he found himself holding French government notes worth 83,689 livres, more than anyone in the colony except for one other merchant.[7] This was an illusory fortune since most of this paper was redeemed several years later at only 15 per cent of face value, but it nevertheless gives an indication of the scale of Paradis' business. Under English rule, Paradis remained an important figure in the regional grain trade for many years.

Historians may well debate the overall significance of the British Conquest in Canadian history but there can be little doubt that this event immediately had an important effect on the colony's business community. Not only was overseas trade shifted into new channels leading to England and her other colonies, but a sudden influx of English-speaking traders occurred right after the French defeat. This event is usually seen primarily in ethnic terms, as the beginning of anglophone business ascendancy in Quebec, the newcomers benefiting from their connections with metropolitan traders. There is certainly something in this view, although the decline of the French-Canadian commercial bourgeoisie was more gradual than many suggest. Besides the ethnic aspect, however, there is another way of looking at the impact of the Conquest on Canadian business, one that focuses on the quantitative change in the number of merchants and the amount of capital. A local study of the Richelieu valley is no place to explore this topic properly but, even on the surface, it seems clear that the sudden arrival of some 200 entrepreneurs in a colony that cannot have had much more than that number before the war must have had a substantial impact.[8] Even if some French businessmen left the colony at the cession, immigration more than compensated for the loss. Many of the new arrivals came from the thirteen colonies and the economic situation at the time explains their migration. British military expenditures during the war contributed to a rapid accumulation of capital in the hands of American traders who must have been looking for investment opportunities, particularly after the conclusion of hostilities when the boom came to an end.[9] Just at this time, Canada was brought into the British Empire, its economy in ruins after several years of blockade and famine. Thus it was no time at all before the commercial sharks moved in to make a killing, even though ordinary American settlers, contrary to official expectations, showed no interest in the northern colony. It was not long before supernumeraries were leaving the overcrowded urban business communities and setting up shops in the countryside.

One of the earliest merchant-immigrants of the new régime was Samuel Jacobs, who arrived at Quebec in 1759 as a supplier to General Wolfe's army. During the following nine years he explored a wide range of potentially profitable sectors of the Canadian economy. Meeting with indifferent success, he eventually settled at St Denis where he was a key figure in the region's retail commerce and grain trade until his death in 1786. A voluminous collection of his correspondence and business records provides an unparalleled opportunity to examine the structure of rural commerce in the eighteenth century and to watch the encounter between merchant capital and the self-sufficient peasant economy.[10]

Samuel Jacobs was a German Jew who had seen a good bit of the world before coming to Canada. No precise details about his early life are known but passing references in his correspondence suggest that, since leaving Europe, he had lived in Britain, the West Indies, and continental British America. His position, a common one in an age when military forces did not usually have centralized supply services, was that of private supplier to a regiment of the British army and he followed one unit from about 1747 until the Battle of the Plains of Abraham. Although he spoke four languages and was able to write Hebrew, his written English with its phonetic spelling and awkward penmanship was virtually unintelligible and consequently he had to dictate all his business letters to a French or an English clerk, depending on the language of his correspondent. Jacobs was certainly not an uneducated man, however, as his copies of Racine's memoirs and Montesquieu's *Persian Letters* prove. He had a gruff but engaging character and a colourful style of speaking that was larded with military metaphors, the legacy of a long association with the army and highly appropriate for the cut-throat atmosphere of early Canadian business. Passionate and hot-tempered, Jacobs was nevertheless a sociable man who enjoyed nothing better than a plate of oysters and a bowl of punch in good company. He never formally married in Canada but he formed unions with two French-Canadian women in succession; he shared a fairly normal domestic life with the second, Marie-Josette Audet dit Lapointe, and always referred to her as his wife. Jacobs retained his Jewish identity to the point of adding the Hebrew version of his name in the flourish of his signature, but he seems to have been indifferent to religion. He sent two daughters to a convent school but gave his eldest son a protestant education. Although concerned with the material welfare and education of his seven children, he was inclined to be a stern and aloof father, vindictive when disobeyed and generally untouched by the new sensibility that was beginning to transform middle-class attitudes towards children in the second half of the eighteenth century. Shortly before his death, Jacobs disowned one of his daughters for marrying against his wishes, cutting her out of his will and forbidding her mother to offer her any support on pain of losing her own inheritance.[11]

This was the man then who followed the advancing British forces in the Seven Years' War, first in 1758 to Fort Cumberland, Nova Scotia, where he set up a store and speculated in land. He was also a partner in a Louisbourg brewery about this time. The next year he arrived at Quebec within a month of the battle there, bought a load of dried fish, and was about to set off with it to Portugal when his schooner was suddenly commandeered for military transport. With little choice but to stay in the city, Jacobs opened a retail store catering primarily to the clientele he knew best, the British officer corps. He also carried on an important import-export trade, primarily it seems with the other British colonies in North America. Initially, he relied heavily on contacts with other Jewish merchants in New York and Boston, as well as in Canada, for supplies and information but after about 1763 he had wide connections in the gentile business community and dealings with his coreligionists became rare. Meanwhile, Jacobs resumed his restless search for further commercial opportunities, always maintaining his Quebec City shop as a base of operations. He was at Montreal more than once and set up a short-lived shop at Trois-Rivières in the early 1760s. Furs were one of the commodities he brought back from both these places but he seems to have obtained them from up-country traders rather than through expeditions of his own to the northwest. While so many of his colleagues were throwing themselves into the fur trade however, Jacobs soon ceased even his minor and indirect involvement: 'I look upon it worse than being concern'd in fitting out privateers,' he once observed, expressing not so much moral scruples as a keen sense of the risks involved in transporting goods by canoe and in granting credit to 'a parcell of savages.'[12] Instead, in 1761 he joined in a distillery enterprise and, at the same time, true to his calling as purveyor to the army, he established a store at the Lake Champlain fort of Crown Point. Jacobs' idea was to take advantage of the St Lawrence-Richelieu waterway to ship goods to this isolated post more cheaply than New York traders could do so. He maintained a junior partner there for three years but the rapids of the upper Richelieu turned out to be a greater obstacle than he had expected and the enterprise was liquidated in 1764.

Apparently it was the Crown Point venture that brought Samuel Jacobs to St Denis. On his way up the Richelieu in 1761 he bought or rented a building there and installed Charles Curtius, a German soldier recently demobilized from the British army, as the salaried manager. The original intention seems to have been to use this as an intermediate warehouse on the long route between Quebec and Crown Point but Jacobs also intended his clerk to cater to any military officers stationed in the area. Wine, brandy, figs, snuff, flour, butter, cheese, shoes, and shirts went to Curtius but little of it sold except for the liquor bought for cash by British soldiers and 'Frenchmen.' After a few months Jacobs began to realize that the 'Frenchmen' of St Denis might constitute a worthwhile market although he was so contemptuous of these potential customers as to send up sour wine and shopworn textiles that could not be sold at his Quebec store. His instructions to Curtius were to dispose of these goods for cash and furs or, if necessary, to accept grain. Here was a merchant who had much to learn about the rural economy! Fortunately for Jacobs, Curtius had enough sense to save the business while informing his master of the inescapable conditions attached to dealing with the peasants of the Lower Richelieu. Grain would have to be accepted in payment and short-term credit until the threshing season would have to be granted. 'I am obliged to geave at credit to the inhabitants,' explained the German, 'till to the month of february and march, at which time they sell theire corn and other grains.'[13] Furthermore, a more appropriate selection of merchandise would be needed and good quality would be essential, 'because the Inhabitants up heer are not such a fools as a menny thinks.'[14] Curtius even managed to get his hands on some furs by going abroad, probably to the Montreal area.

At first, Curtius' business was largely wholesale: 'I fournish too all the Tabern-keepers in the River Chambly [ie, Richelieu] the liquor they wanths,' he wrote.[15] This, together with sales to priests and to the 'little merchants' of the region predominated; the latter were mostly traders left over from the French Régime who, with the exception of Provençal, operated on a much smaller scale than Curtius. In the fall of 1761, however, as Quebec City continued to suffer from food shortages, Jacobs began showing more interest in the habitants and the wheat that was their main product. 'I mentioned in my last about some corn,' he wrote, 'I would have you buy what you can get either in exchange for rum, dry goods and even if you was to give some cash as likewise purchase Furrs ...' Two weeks later, at the end of November, Jacobs was more pressing, though clearly he was interested in wheat as a one-shot speculation rather than to carry on a regular business. 'As nobody is for buying corn there but yourself I would not seem eager at it but for all that would have you purchase as large as you possibly can even to 10000 bushels or more as much as you can get ... and I'll tell you something in the spring will make your heart glad.'[16] As it turned out, no hearts were gladdened on this score for the monopoly was illusory; high demand brought buyers to the Richelieu from Quebec and the price of wheat went higher than Curtius dared offer. This was just as well since his employer was short of funds in the spring and resumed his call for the cash and furs needed to purchase supplies. Long after this initial failure, Jacobs continued to cherish the hope of cornering the Richelieu wheat supply, but in the meantime he realized that he would have to accept a share of the region's harvest every year as a necessary condition of carrying on trade in an area that had nothing but agricultural produce to offer in exchange for purchases.

Although Samuel Jacobs originally viewed the grain trade simply as a means to enable him to sell imported goods, he did have to pursue it with some vigour to secure amounts of wheat that would make it worthwhile. This meant that, aside from sending the produce collected from his Lower Richelieu customers, Curtius often had to scour the countryside purchasing additional quantities. Between 1762 and 1764 when he left Jacobs' employ, the German storekeeper went as far upriver as Chambly and back down to Sorel, up the St Lawrence to Varennes and across to L'Assomption, obtaining in all 8594 minots in two years, about half of it from priests, small merchants, and innkeepers.[17] The value of this grain (20,000 livres) still covered only one-quarter of the merchandise sold in the same period (80,740 livres): cash returns (21,200 livres) and outstanding debts (19,160 livres) accounted for roughly similar sums.[18] The large amount of cash returns suggests that some of Curtius' customers were selling their produce to other dealers and his correspondence confirms the fact that competition was brisk in the grain trade; Provençal, Paradis, and a few others, active since the 1750s, vied for the region's surplus, as did John Grant, a newcomer with a store at St Ours as of 1763.

Competition was only one of the problems Charles Curtius had to contend with in the grain and retail trades. Both these enterprises were regulated by the British military government (1760–4) in a measure designed to prevent speculation in vital foodstuffs. General Gage, governor of Montreal, went so far as to order all rural merchants out of the country in late 1761 but Curtius travelled to the city and managed to procure a tavern licence from an official named Mathurin. Although this gave him the right only to sell drinks for consumption on the premises, the merchant simply continued his practice of supplying barrels of wine wholesale to the genuine innkeepers while prudently serving out small quantities to any 'strangers, officers or gentlemen' who might pass through St Denis. Violating the law himself, Curtius tried to use the licensing system as a weapon against smaller competitors, particularly the French Canadians who had been trading in the region for a decade already.

I was since at Montreal and spoak to Mr Maturin who promised me the licence of St Charles, if the other fellow, who was here now, deed not come in a months time. I am shoor he is not able to pay for the licence, and so if it is your pleasure I shall set up a men there ... It is a good and riche parrish, where there is no marchand or any drye goods, 6 miles from St Denis.[19]

Jacobs readily agreed to the proposal and urged his assistant to get licences for Sorel and Chambly as well. It was also necessary in 1763 to secure government permission to transport wheat out of the district of Montreal. This too required subterfuge to avoid giving the authorities the impression of a massive export. 'You'll please to try to get Liberty to send down some corn [wrote Jacobs]. I suppose you know how this must be managed. Get the liberty in your own name and don't ask permition for all at once.'[20] Curtius did indeed know how to handle the affair; he began with a pass for 2000 minots but ended up shipping almost twice that much.

In 1764 Charles Curtius struck out on his own account in business at St Denis with his former employer acting as his supplier from Quebec City. His luck was bad, however; the next two harvests were poor and, as the habitants could not pay him, he could not pay his creditors and he soon went bankrupt. Samuel Jacobs, as principal creditor, thus re-acquired the St Denis store and he was once more directly involved in the Richelieu trade, for a time in partnership with John Grant of St Ours. Since 1761 in fact he had never ceased to be the most important merchant in the region and, while he remained a resident of Quebec and active in a variety of enterprises, he was a frequent visitor to St Denis. In 1768, however, he decided that his best prospects lay in the Richelieu valley; in the autumn of that year he moved with his family to St Denis, 'a place in the Country well established a pleasant situation and flourishing in Regard to Trade.'[21] By then he had been in Canada nine years, engaging in every sort of money-making venture. After settling on the Richelieu he concentrated on retail commerce and the wheat trade, but even then this restless businessman could never limit himself entirely to a single line.

IRONS IN THE FIRE

For Samuel Jacobs, as for most eighteenth-century merchants, business was not so much a continuous process as a series of discrete 'adventures.'[22] Moreover, in Canada, the absence of banks and of corporate organizations meant that financing was often a matter of special arrangements among entrepreneurs and the association of capital came only in the form of more or less temporary partnerships. It is true that in the last years of his life, the important fur merchants of the colony joined together in a single enterprise, the Northwest Company. Even so, this was quite a loose federation of capital. Nevertheless, the independent Jacobs was just as representative of his times as were the 'Nor'Westers.' Without the benefit of any sort of limited liability, he invested now and then in a number of joint enterprises in a variety of fields. To a large extent, his strategy was to diversify his holdings to avoid disastrous failures and he was indeed able to weather several storms, including the one that ruined Charles Curtius, thanks to this tactic.

In the earliest years of the British Régime, as we have seen, Jacobs was active in the trade to Crown Point and the Richelieu valley, as well as importing and exporting through Quebec and carrying on retail trade in the capital. There was more to his business than that, however. In 1761, just when he was establishing Charles Curtius at St Denis, Jacobs also joined in a 'distillery company' with two other merchants, Benjamin Price and John Hays. The partners purchased a building near the old Intendant's Palace but they produced no liquor for several years. Instead the company apparently used the building as a granary and Jacobs sent much of the Richelieu wheat there to be stored and later sold, mostly in large quantities to local millers. Years later distilling equipment was set up, a distiller brought in from overseas and a certain amount of rum was made from imported molasses, but the enterprise was plagued by problems and was never really a success. The first distiller was incompetent, supplies of molasses ran out, and then a rival distillery began operations in 1769. Just at this point one of the partners died and the other one decided to withdraw, but Jacobs wanted to press on alone, convinced that

A distillery well managed here must do well, getting their molasses from the West Indies and making that into Rum, would ingross the best part of the trading cash in Canada. This would enable the Person to purchase peltries and grain, as there is a great advantage to be made by cash in a country which is as poor of it as this is and it would knock up the New England trade here ...[23]

But his capital was not equal to his speculative ambitions and he had to abandon the field to his competitor.

Before the demise of the distillery Samuel Jacobs had become a partner in another pioneering industrial enterprise, this time a potash works at Quebec. One of his partners, James Stewart, was in charge of technical operations but the main force in the venture was the Quebec import-export merchant, George Allsopp.[24] The company was formed in 1766 and the following year the works were ready and efforts were made to collect wood ashes in the rural communities up and down the St Lawrence. Like the distillery, this effort too met with indifferent success, partly because Stewart did not know his business very well, but certainly a shortage of operating funds was also to blame. Jacobs in particular seems to have failed to contribute his share to the undertaking, especially in the late 1760s when his Richelieu trade was experiencing difficulties. In 1770 he withdrew from the company having invested little and lost little, except for the friendship of George Allsopp.

After 1770, Jacobs generally confined his attentions to the Richelieu valley, where he lived most of the year. Although this was primarily a matter of retail sales and grain trafficking, he also looked for other opportunities, particularly in years of agricultural distress. The forest resources of the region and of the upper Richelieu-Lake Champlain area helped him meet payments on more than one occasion. In 1768, for example, with the backing of a larger Quebec merchant, he ran a stave-cutting operation on Lake Champlain and realized 'a genteel profit.' He also floated rafts of squared timber down to Quebec, but not on a regular basis. Once at least, he even entered the ship-building business.

Jacobs' various schemes such as the distillery and the potash works were all good ideas in themselves but they were never entirely successful for him, partly because he would not give adequate attention to any one of them and partly because he was always short of working capital. The two problems in fact were related for, as Jacobs himself observed once, 'by Woefull experience, [I] find a Rowling stone does not gether moss.'[25] On the other hand, the diversity of his investments probably saved him from bankruptcy more than once when successes in one sector compensated for disasters in others. Still, Jacobs eventually realized that the life of a rural shopkeeper was the only secure one for a merchant of his means. 'The trade in the country does not require pompous living nor large house rent,' he reflected, 'neither is there any grate debts made that can be hurtfull risks if bad debts.'[26] By the early 1770s, his business was entirely centred on the Richelieu region and his only assets elsewhere were three houses that he rented in Quebec City.

For most of the period after Jacobs moved to the valley, he had branches run by salaried clerks in St Charles and St Ours; there was also a short-lived store at Sorel that closed in 1770. St Denis was always his head-quarters and he had a large wooden house there that apparently served as living quarters and shop, with space for some of the bulky merchandise in the basement and the attic. There were also two 'hangars' nearby that were used mainly to store grain. As for employees, there seem to have been two clerks at St Denis to deal with the public, care for stocks, and keep the books. Jacobs did not pay his clerks handsomely – one surviving contract for a man hired to manage the entire business before Jacobs moved to St Denis specified a salary of fifty livres plus two minots of wheat per month[27] – but he provided the training and experience that allowed more than one of them later to set up shop on their own. Henri Laparre, for example, the son of a Quebec surgeon, came to Jacobs as an apprentice to learn 'the trade or mystery of bookkeeping in the trade of the country,'[28] and became one of the largest traders in St Denis after his master's death. Although Jacobs was more comfortable speaking English than French, the majority of his clerks (six out of nine recorded names) were French Canadian and they used their native language when communicating with their employer; the other clerks of course had to know some French to deal with their unilingual customers (hence the linguistic confusion of English-speaking clerks, such as the man who explained that bad wheat had been stored on top of good grain, 'owing to the people versen leur poche on it').[29] All the clerks, judging by their names, seem to have been strangers to the region, just as the merchant community in general was an 'outsider' in this rural society. Jacobs did hire local habitants, however, on a temporary basis to load and unload boats, to tend his garden and to make leather moccasins.

The duties of the clerks at St Denis and the branches were various. They tended to customers and kept track of their debts, drawing up annual statements of each customer's account when it came time to 'settle.' Once a year, they also took an inventory of stock on hand to guide Jacobs in purchasing supplies. Buying wheat was another pre-occupation at certain times of the year and often a clerk would have to roam the countryside beyond his own parish in search of supplies to purchase. Jacobs kept up a steady correspondence with his representatives at St Ours and St Charles, telling them how much grain to buy and at what price but, on the whole, he allowed them considerable freedom. Letter-writing was an important activity in the St Denis office, since continuous communication with the traders of Quebec was a vital source of information on prices and quantities of imported goods and on overseas demand for Canadian grain. There was no regular postal service up the Richelieu until 1815 and so, in Jacobs' day, letters had to be sent with river schooners during navigation season or taken by special messenger down the Richelieu and across the St Lawrence to Berthier where they could be picked up by the weekly Montreal-Quebec mail.[30]

Jacobs and his clerks seem to have done an adequate job of keeping records of the retail trade and consumer credit but, at another level, there was something woefully deficient in the accounting of the business. In the mass of documents preserved in the Jacobs papers, nothing resembling a balance sheet or an income statement can be found and the implication is that Samuel Jacobs never knew what he was worth and he never knew precisely what his profit was, overall or on any particular enterprise. Obviously he must have had some idea of whether or not he was making money in a given endeavour, but he does not seem to have had the precise information needed for rational capitalist calculation. His central preoccupation was instead the short-term problem of making payments.

Although his assets were considerable, Jacobs was faced with a chronic 'crisis of liquidity.' Canada's unfavourable balance of payments at the time was such that colonial traders were invariably endebted to British suppliers and stymied by the problem of paying for imports. The situation was so much the worse for Samuel Jacobs, at one remove from the Quebec traders and frequently overextended. It was therefore the struggle to keep his business afloat by securing enough marketable assets to meet payments each year that captured all of the merchant's attention; there were dreams too of speculative windfalls, but little in the way of routine attention to profit and loss. In bad years, he was simply unable to extract enough from his own debtors to satisfy his creditors and had to depend on the forebearance of the latter. On one buying trip to the capital, it was reported that Jacobs had to flee his creditors and lock himself in his house, daring to emerge only on Sundays.[31] This was in 1770, after a disastrous season when wheat was more scarce and imported merchandise more plentiful than the merchant had expected. The following years were more prosperous and Jacobs managed to pay off most of his debts and re-establish his credit after a difficult period when he could only secure supplies by barter for wheat. Even so, when he drew up a will in 1775, he left only his house and lands in the Richelieu valley to his wife and children, hoping, without very much apparent confidence, that his creditors would be satisfied out of his other effects.

And yet Samuel Jacobs died a rich man with a net worth of 413,763 livres only eleven years later (see Table 17).[32] What was the secret of his

TABLE 17
The Jacobs fortune, September 1786 (in livres)

Business worth		
Assets		
Real property (mainly 12 farms in the Richelieu valley and 18 houses in the villages of St Ours and St Denis)	49,950	
Accounts receivable (100% of 'good debts' (298,343) + 50% of 'doubtful debts' (3381) + 0% of 'bad debts' (10,212))	300,034	
Merchandise	28,445	
Livestock and farm equipment	1516	
Cash	720	
Total assets		380,665
Liabilities		
Debts	5463	
Total liabilities		5463
Net worth		375,202
Personal worth		
From sale of household effects	39,922	
Minus funeral expenses	1361	
Personal wealth		38,561
Total, business and personal wealth		413,763

success? Jacobs was lucky enough to have been blessed with another war at just the right stage in his career. Although the War of the American Revolution began badly for the merchant, it eventually brought him extremely lucrative military supply contracts. For St Denis, the drama opened with the American attempt in 1775 to conquer Canada, invading by way of the Richelieu. The valley was occupied for almost a year and, though the invaders were well received by the habitants, they did not endear themselves to Jacobs. They seized a boat he was having built at St Charles and then commandeered another of his schooners at Quebec City, this one loaded with merchandise. To make matters worse, several customers took advantage of the temporary breakdown of the judicial system and refused to pay their debts to the merchant. It was no doubt the general affront it inadvertently delivered to the established authorities and mechanisms of exploitation that explains the enthusiastic response accorded to the American army by the rural masses of the region. This same undermining of the established order would, along with the seizure of the two vessels, account for the hostility of Jacobs, who otherwise should have had more reason to sympathize with the 'bastonnais' than his French-Canadian neighbours. There is an intriguing document in the Jacobs papers written in a strange combination of Hebrew characters and English phonetics that seems to be the shopkeeper's secret diary of the period of American occupation. It is almost unintelligible but one philologist extracted this much sense from it: 'It is obvious that Jacobs, even when threatened by his aroused neighbours, was determined to raise his cup to the king alone, while the enthusiastic peasants, embittered against seigneurs and clergy, were equally determined to dedicate their toasts to liberty and to the American Continental Congress.'[33] How much the habitants cared about the Continental Congress and how much Samuel Jacobs cared about the king is debatable, but it is certainly clear that there were serious tensions between the merchant and the populace and these likely had their roots in the fundamentally antagonistic nature of their relationship. In any case, it was not long before Jacobs' loyalty was appropriately rewarded.

A British force of 10,000 men arrived at Quebec to relieve the siege in the spring of 1776 and the Americans quickly left the colony for good. By fall a sizeable portion of the British troops were stationed in the Richelieu, guarding the strategic entry to Canada. It was from the Lower Richelieu that General Burgoyne launched his unsuccessful assault against New York in 1777 but, before and after that event, from October 1776 until the end of the war, the region was an armed camp with every parish, particularly Sorel, the headquarters, hosting hundreds of soldiers. Here was Samuel Jacobs' golden opportunity. He immediately sent for 4000 gallons of rum. 'At present there is about five hundred Germans to be distributed here and at St Charles. I have the Charge to furnish them, with bread and fresh provisions and if that fails, have pork and beef etc for that purpose, If I had not had so many irons in the fire, might have supplied a great part of the army with liquors etc. ...'[34]

Perhaps because he was the most substantial merchant in the area, or because he had experience as a military supplier, or even because he was neither 'disloyal' nor French, Jacobs was appointed assistant commissary-general with the responsibility of victualling the troops stationed in the area. Although it carried a salary of about 2000 livres per year, this was not a position that required full-time attention and he was therefore able to continue his regular business with the local population; in fact, it thrived as never before. The salary was only a small part of the benefits Jacobs derived from his official appointment. For example, he collected 123,000 vouchers for spruce beer from the soldiers – exchanged for stronger beverages most likely – and disposed of these for 10,000 livres. He also took advantage of his access to military transport facilities to have his own merchandise brought up from Quebec, thus gaining a significant edge over his competitors at a time when all the boats in the colony had been requisitioned for the king's service. The flour Jacobs handled as commissary was furnished by another merchant who had a contract for all the forces in Canada, but Jacobs did provide thousands of pounds of fresh beef from oxen purchased locally and he was able to sell this meat at an attractive price. In addition to all these more or less legal forms of profiteering, it does not seem unjust to suspect that the merchant-commissary may have even rerouted some of the king's supplies into his own storehouse. Certainly corruption of this sort was not uncommon during the American War,[35] and the striking rise of Jacobs' fortunes over the course of the conflict suggests that foul means as well as fair were employed. A few months before the peace treaty was signed in Paris, he expressed his gratitude in a letter to his patron, the commissary-general: 'Your kind attention and benefit received from your bounty has enabled me to give a Genteel education to my helpless children, and provide a little against misery, for a tender mother and a good wife to me.' Of course the lady in question was not really his wife and the 'little against misery' amounted to a tidy sum, but Jacobs was by now an old man in failing health, genuinely anxious about the future of his dependents, and so he can be excused some sentimental excesses. He goes on to discuss his plans to retire gradually from business. 'This I will do while God spare me, settle my affairs, with every one, make my trade less, and what I can recover, from my debts etc. will lay it out in some security to bring up my little children.'[36]

After the war Jacobs lived in comfort and security such as he had not known previously. He could now afford to hire a tutor for his children at St Denis, as well as a drawing master and a dancing instructor. Quebec merchants were now asking him for loans instead of the other way round. Jacobs had ideas of moving back to the capital where he could spend more time enjoying the company of old friends at the coffee house but it was neither quick nor easy to liquidate a rural business like his when the assets were largely in the form of debts owed by impecunious habitants. He did close down the branch stores, but at St Denis he continued his retail and wheat-buying business, if only to make it easier to collect his debts. At the same time, he began acquiring a number of farms in the region, probably through judicial seizures for debt. Previously the merchant had shown no inclination to keep possession of real estate obtained this way but in the 1780s he rented many farms out to tenant-farmers, no doubt in an effort to accumulate secure investments that did not require his personal attention but that would provide an annual income for his family. Samuel Jacobs died in 1786, leaving to his survivors an estate that was still made up largely of unpaid accounts. For several years after this, the executors of his will continued to run the St Denis store as this seemed the best way to get revenues for the widow and children. Even in 1804 there were many habitants in the Lower Richelieu who still owed money to the Jacobs estate.[37]

RETAIL SALES

The sale of imported goods from the general stores at St Denis, St Ours, and St Charles was the foundation of Samuel Jacobs' business during most of his sojourn in Canada. Records of his purchases and sales are not complete enough to enable us to see what he made from this but there is a passing reference in one of his letters to sales at 100 per cent mark-up as being 'to good proffitt.'[38] This suggests that retail sales were far more profitable to him than grain trafficking (if indeed one can separate these two aspects of rural commerce); they seem also to have been a more reliable source of gain than the uncertain wheat trade. For most commodities, prices seem to have been stable and uniform in all the competing stores of the Lower Richelieu. The problem, however, was not so much one of selling goods at an advantageous price, but of getting customers to pay for their purchases. There were some cash sales but, by and large, habitants (and other customers as well) required credit, at least for several months, but often for much longer than that. Consequently there was nothing impersonal about shopping at a rural store; the clerks would only grant credit to people they knew and they made a rule of refusing to serve 'volontaires' (labourers) unless their employers guaranteed the debts.[39] Activities at the sales counters had pronounced seasonal and weekly rhythms. Sundays and holidays were particularly busy as habitants from the remote parts of the parishes converged on the villages for religious services, socializing, and shopping. The yearly peak was in the autumn when Jacobs returned from Quebec with new stocks of merchandise. He always did his best to maintain a full 'assortment' as rural customers liked to find everything they wanted in one shop.

After his initial foray into the Richelieu in 1761 with all the wrong merchandise, Jacobs quickly learned about the needs of the local population. Charles Curtius at St Denis gave him instructions about the var-

TABLE 18
Inventories of Samuel Jacobs' store at St Denis

Types of merchandise	May 1764 value*	%	June 1775 value	%	Sept 1786 value	%
Cloth, blankets	12,762	51.8	13,765	30.5	15,548	54.7
Sewing supplies	1729	7.0	2880	6.4	1684	5.9
Clothing, shoes	4088	16.6	1882	4.2	1513	5.3
Personal accessories	1327	5.4	2402	5.3	1534	5.4
Domestic utensils	592	2.4	2404	5.3	1188	4.2
Tools, building supplies	474	1.9	1097	2.4	1376	4.8
Agricultural implements	0	0	1218	2.7	1143	4.0
Guns, fishhooks, etc.	6	0	164	0.4	28	0.1
Iron, steel, stoves	267	1.1	291	0.6	1244	4.4
Non-food consumables	932	3.8	2877	6.4	1860	6.5
Foodstuffs	918	3.7	358	0.8	150	0.5
Wine, liquor	984	4.0	12,585	27.9	33	0.1
Miscellaneous	328	1.3	3080	6.8	746	2.6
Unidentified	227	0.9	121	0.3	398	1.4
Total	24,636	99.9	45,125	100.0	28,444	99.9

* All values are in livres.

ious types of cloth that could be expected to sell and, in addition, he recommended salt, alum, burning oil and candles, window glass, women's shoes and stockings, ribbons, hats, blankets, and wine. Other items were soon added to the list and the merchant always did his best to send appropriate quantities of each up from Quebec. Year in, year out, the range of goods demanded by rural customers remained remarkably stable. Consumer demand was rather inelastic as it was dominated by the real needs of the population, mostly habitants. Jacobs had to explain this situation to a Quebec City importer who wished to get rid of an oversupply of salt by consigning a large quantity to St Denis: 'The country trade cannot be forced tho' you should sell for half the value it cost, the inhabitants buy no more than they realy stand in need of.'[40]

Inventories of the St Denis store from 1764, 1775, and 1786 show that, apart from the exceptionally large supply of rum at the time of the second inventory, the value of the total stock and the proportions of the various types of merchandise remained roughly unchanged (see Table 18).[41] Textile products generally accounted for more than half the store's value. These ranged from cheap Irish linens to fine silks and included a variety of taffetas, camblets, callicoes, velvets, serges, moltons, muslins, and gauzes. In a related category, 'sewing supplies' comprised needles, thread, patterns, bordering, buttons, buckles, and so on. Much of this material was probably used by habitants making Sunday finery; clothing for everyday use was made mainly from homespun. Certainly readymade clothes made up a small proportion of Jacobs' stock, particularly after 1764. There were hats, stockings, ladies' shoes, and some 'red capps,' but most items in the habitant costume were not available at all. 'Personal accessories' include large quantities of ribbon and handkerchiefs as well as looking glasses, combs, and inexpensive jewellery. Jacobs also carried a supply of pots, pans, and other 'domestic utensils.' His store had few tools (mainly axes) but substantial quantities of nails as well as some paint and window glass. 'Agricultural implements' were also quite limited and consisted almost entirely of harnesses, scythes, sickles, and ploughshares. Jacobs retailed stoves from the St Maurice Forges and apparently supplied local blacksmiths with bar iron and steel. 'Non-food consumables' are salt, an important staple import, as well as soap, alum, candles, and lamp oil. Food products (rice, cheese, chocolate) made up a small part of the stock and one which decreased over the years. In the 'miscellaneous' category can be found such items as ice skates and leather brought in from Quebec City tanneries. Many of the things offered for sale at Samuel Jacobs' store – needles, salt, and stoves, for example – would have been required by almost all the inhabitants of St Denis but many others, perhaps the largest number, were intended to widen the selection of merchandise for a minority of village dignitaries and rich peasants. Some of the fancy yardgoods therefore remained on the shelves for years.

If customer demand was basically stable and if prices on most commodities were not subject to competition, how could a rural merchant hope to expand his share of the retail business in a given territory? In Jacobs' day, cheap rum seems to have been the most important vehicle of growth. From the trader's point of view, the advantage of liquor was its elastic demand and he used it as a battering-ram to break into the habitant's self-sufficient household economy. Certainly Jacobs did not introduce rum to a population that had never before tasted alcohol. Wine and brandy were available under the French Régime and constituted a major element in Canada's trade with the mother country then,[42] but these were rather expensive commodities. Lower Richelieu merchants always brought in a certain amount of wine and liquor from the continent of Europe to supply local priests, aristocrats, and professionals and for the habitants, who bought small quantities for feasts and for 'medicinal purposes.' It was rum, however, imported at low prices from New England and the British West Indies, that quickly became the liquor of mass consumption in the Canadian countryside after the Conquest. An English official wrote of the French Canadians in 1772: 'Many of the Lower Class begin to be dram Drinkers, since the great innundations of a poisonous firey stuff from New England, called rum, which sells cheap because it pays no Duties.'[43] Samuel Jacobs sold large quantities to inn-keepers and to habitants for home consumption, though this is not immediately apparent from the store inventories which record stock on hand, not amounts sold. However, we do know from the merchant's correspondence and from the bills of lading of his shipments from Quebec that alcoholic beverages, above all rum, made up a large proportion of his sales.[44]

The trade in rum, unlike other aspects of Jacobs' retail business, was fiercely competitive. Sales were potentially limitless but supplies were quite finite as they generally arrived from abroad only once for the entire year. Merchants at Quebec and in the Richelieu valley therefore strug-gled at times to engross the rum,[45] not only for the sake of windfall profits, but also because this article played a key role in attracting and keeping a regular clientele. It might have been different if the French Canadians had developed a taste for whiskey; then there might have been rural distilleries in Quebec as there were later in Upper Canada to absorb the peasants' barley and rye and to compete with the rum im-porters in quenching their thirst. But the habitants insisted on imported spirits – or at least ones made from imported materials – and thus they were deprived of a market for non-wheat grains and also delivered into the hands of the rum merchants. This is why Samuel Jacobs was so interested in the Quebec distillery, especially in the 1760s when he had an eye on the role of alcohol in the fur trade as well as in the grain trade. When he limited his ambitions and adjusted his sights from in-ternational commerce to the Richelieu regional trade, Jacobs still viewed rum as the essential key. For example, he once proposed a joint venture with William Grant, one of the big Quebec merchants, to corner the entire Richelieu wheat crop; all he required of his partner for half the profits was a copious supply of New England rum.[46] Small wonder then that the habitants of Quebec, blessed as of 1760 with the benefits of British civilization and trade, soon gained a reputation as drinkers.[47]

For each merchant, rum was an important arm in the struggle with his competitors but, for the merchants as a class, liquor was just as important as a vehicle for making contact with the peasant economy and for expanding their foothold in the precapitalist world of rural French Canada. While Jacobs and the others were flooding the Richelieu in a tide of cheap rum, other Canadian merchants were finding alcohol just as useful in securing a share of the fur trade with the interior Indians, and for similar reasons. Native trappers and peasants obviously had quite dissimilar economic organizations but what they shared from the trader's point of view was a deplorably limited capacity to absorb imported commodities. Hence the recourse to liquor with its marvelous property of creating an escalating demand. British merchants in the Orient later found that opium answered their purposes even better. The general pattern found in much of the world, rural Quebec included, is one of commercial capital introducing a worthless or harmful habit of consumption as a means of initiating or increasing trade with a population whose life is not already organized around buying and selling.[48] In the specific case of the Lower Richelieu, rum served the function, not of initiating commercial exchanges – those had always existed; in fact, the habitant way of life was impossible without a certain number of imported supplies – but of providing the flexible element that could absorb any extra peasant surpluses that escaped the curé and the seigneur.

Samuel Jacobs may have obtained some rum from his own distillery but that operation was never very successful and so most of his supply had to come from Jamaica and, before the American Revolution, from New England. The West Indian variety was superior in quality and commanded a higher price. Except for some St Maurice stoves and leather and harnesses from Quebec, most of the other products sold in the St Denis store seem to have been imported from Europe. Inventories mention 'German serge,' 'Spanish red wine,' and 'Irish linen,' but we can only guess at the origin of most items; the salt probably came from France or Spain but almost everything else was likely of British manufacture. Almost all of this came to Canada from England and was landed every summer at the port of Quebec.

The winter freeze-up of the St Lawrence combined with the peculiar schedules of the fur and grain trades to impose a rigid seasonal pattern on Canadian business. Accordingly, Jacobs travelled down to Quebec every summer to spend August and September purchasing supplies for the stores, selling his wheat, and meeting his fellow businessmen at the city's coffee house. Normally he patronized the import-export merchants, often the same ones who bought his grain. He could have secured better prices dealing directly with a British supplier but, living at St Denis, this would be inconvenient; besides Jacobs never disposed of enough liquid assets to offer advance payment and he was too small a fish to get trans-Atlantic credit. He did once manage to place an order with Watson, Olive and Rashleigh of London and was granted credit as a special favour because Brook Watson, the senior partner, had known him in Nova Scotia. Unfortunately he took on this obligation in 1769, a year of disastrous crop failure and the debt hung over his head for five years, with the British firm hounding him all the while through their Quebec correspondent, George Allsopp. After this there was no further question of direct importing; Jacobs had enough difficulty getting Quebec merchants to supply him on credit. The latter were his main source, although when he had a little money he was often a buyer at 'vendus,' auctions of a ship's cargo or of a bankrupt merchant's stock, held at the coffee house. Short-term credit was vital to eighteenth-century business and it was credit that kept Samuel Jacobs in his proper place in the hierarchy, under the thumb of importers who were themselves dominated by metropolitan suppliers.[49]

It was mentioned earlier that credit was also a necessary element in Jacobs' dealings with his own Lower Richelieu customers. This was partly because the seasonal cycle of agriculture only allowed habitants to pay the merchant once a year, or even less frequently in times of crop failure. There was very little cash in this part of the eighteenth-century world. Between two-thirds and three-quarters of the habitant estate inventories from the 1740–69 period list no money at all and in the remaining cases much of the 'cash' is next-to-worthless government notes left over from the French régime (see Appendix 4).[50] Samuel Jacobs himself was very often without hard currency. When he did have money, it came in a variety of forms, gold and silver, of English, French, Portuguese, Spanish, and Spanish-American origin; the coin mentioned most often in the merchant's correspondence was a Portuguese gold piece worth 48 livres that Jacobs referred to as a 'half-Joe' and his French-speaking clerk called a 'portugaise.'[51] In any case, cash transactions played a minor part in the rural merchant's dealings with customers and suppliers. Often money seemed to be not so much a medium of exchange as an imported commodity that the merchant supplied to favoured habitants wishing to purchase land, hire labourers, or pay seigneurial dues.[52] In addition to granting routine consumer credit therefore, Jacobs also acted as a local banker when he had funds to advance and confidence in the borrower's ability to repay. He did not seek out this role, however – until the last years of his life, Jacobs was invariably short of cash – but instead felt obliged to make small loans as a means of attaching habitants to himself as retail customers and as wheat suppliers.[53] Like other merchants of the period, Jacobs made his profits from retail sales but to sell imports he had to provide 'returns' and this required him to take an active role in the grain trade.

THE GRAIN TRADE

Writing in 1769, Samuel Jacobs estimated that the Richelieu valley normally produced a surplus of about 60,000 minots of wheat, a plausible figure confirming the impression that this region was the breadbasket of eighteenth-century Canada.[54] A certain amount of this grain was consumed by the colony's urban population and its military garrison, but in all but the worst years there was plenty left over for export. With Canada now in the British imperial trading system, there was an acceleration of the growing tendency, evident in the last decades of French rule, for overseas markets to absorb this surplus. When Jacobs was first active in this business the West Indies were the most important purchaser but, by the end of his career, an industrializing Great Britain had assumed the position she would long hold as the main outlet for colonial wheat. The Iberian peninsula, Nova Scotia, and Newfoundland were also important markets.[55]

Foreign demand certainly varied from year to year and, along with occasional shortages of ships and government orders prohibiting export, this made it difficult for the rural merchant to know in advance how much wheat he could sell and at what price. Uncertainties of this sort were a normal part of pre-industrial commerce and they made the exchange of market information between merchants in distant ports a crucial business activity.[56] Canada was especially handicapped by the annual freeze-up which hindered communications with potential markets as well as imposing a rigid seasonal schedule on the movement of goods. In other words, foreign demand was somewhat unstable and Canadian knowledge of that demand was imperfect; furthermore, Jacobs, up the Richelieu at St Denis, was even more uncertain about market prospects than were the import-export merchants of Quebec. And yet, demand was not so unreliable that the rural merchant ever willingly abstained from the grain trade altogether. In many years he had misgivings about the price he should offer producers but he always bought significant quantities, except when he was unable to, either because of a deficient harvest or because the supply had been engrossed by speculators. Table 19 shows the amounts of recorded shipments by Jacobs from the Richelieu; each figure represents a minimum since additional

TABLE 19
Wheat shipped by Samuel Jacobs from the Richelieu 1762–73

Year	Minots of wheat
1762	0
1763	3878
1764	5755
1765	1000
1766	1897
1767	7974
1768	4366
1769	543
1770	10,061
1771	11,711
1772	?
1773	13,227

quantities might have been sent that do not appear in the documents.[57] The year-to-year fluctuations nicely follow the changing fortunes of Quebec agriculture: poor harvests in 1765 and 1766 and the 'disette' of 1769 are followed by the bumper crops of the early 1770s.[58]

In the early 1760s Jacobs disposed of most of his grain through the 'distillery company' at Quebec which sold wheat to millers and merchants. He also chartered a ship on occasion and sent his grain overseas directly. For the most part, however, particularly after he moved from the port city to St Denis, Jacobs took no direct part in the international grain trade and instead sold his wheat to the import-export merchants of Quebec. The latter group were of course the same men who supplied the country merchant with imported merchandise and the grain was offered to pay for these supplies, either directly when Jacobs sold to the same merchant he bought from, or indirectly when he sold to one merchant and used the proceeds to pay his debts to another. Jacobs naturally valued his freedom to sell to any of the competing exporters in order to secure as high a price as possible for his produce, but when he was short of cash and credit, as he often was before the American War, he might have to sell hastily at whatever price he could get in order to keep up his credit and secure supplies for the following year. It was easy for the country shopkeeper to fall into a dependent relationship with one import-export house. This was Jacobs' fate more than once. In 1773, for example, he relied on John Welles of Quebec to advance him merchandise and cash and to buy his wheat at current rates or, failing that, to store it and sell it on consignment to a third party. There was some security for the rural trader in an arrangement of this sort but Jacobs shunned such commitments when he could to allow himself room to manoeuvre.

In 'normal' years Jacobs could make a modest profit acting as the intermediary between Lower Richelieu producers and the millers and exporters of Quebec city. Under these conditions, wheat was sought out more as a medium of payment than for any profits that might arise from the traffic. On the other hand, there was sometimes the hope of making huge gains by monopolizing an entire year's harvest and then forcing the price to soar. Jacobs himself was periodically seized by the urge to corner the market in this way but usually he was concerned mainly with seeing that his customers turned over grain for what they owed him and that he acquired enough to buy supplies and meet his obligations at Quebec. Therefore, every year in January or early February, when the habitants were finishing their threshing and when the sleighs could easily move goods over the snow and ice, the shopkeeper would have announcements published in front of the churches of the region inviting his customers to deliver their wheat and settle their accounts. A period of bargaining would then ensue until the price 'broke' when one of the area's merchants agreed on a price per minot with one of his customers and other traders and peasants followed the lead. Theoretically, Jacobs' debtors would then settle their accounts and bring any wheat they could spare once subsistence needs, tithes, and seigneurial rents were taken care of. Depending on the year, many habitants would not have any surplus wheat, or at least not enough to cover their debt, while others would have large amounts worth more than their retail debts. Jacobs bought from these wealthy peasants, whether or not they were customers, as well as from priests and small shopkeepers in the region.

Grain was carried to the 'hangar' at St Denis in February and March before the roads became impassable with the spring thaw. For want of storage space, some sellers might be asked to keep the grain – now the merchant's property – at home until the river boats came to take it away. The storage of this perishable commodity required some care; the mass had to be 'turned' or stirred periodically to keep out moisture and to prevent spoilage. From Jacobs' granary wheat was transported to Quebec or, far less frequently, to Montreal on a schedule dictated by both geography and market conditions. For most of the bateaux, sloops, and schooners that plied the inland waterways of Canada, the rapids on the Richelieu just above the village of St Ours presented a barrier except at the high-water season of late April and May when small vessels of 1000 to 1500 minots capacity could reach the storehouses of St Denis and St Charles. However, boats carrying up to 2100 minots were loaded at St Ours all summer long with carts and rowboats bringing the grain from the upriver parishes. Although some merchants owned their own vessels, most shipping was done by independent masters who sailed their own boats with crews of two or three, charging five sols per minot of wheat for the trip to Quebec. Captain and merchant sometimes had difficulty agreeing on which 'demi-minot' would be used to measure the wheat as it was loaded into the hold. At the destination, it had to be measured again and, if it was to be exported, the exporter would have to see that it was stored, cleaned, and loaded onto the ships, usually in the late summer or early fall. These final arrangements did not normally concern Jacobs as most of his sales were f.o.b. the Richelieu, with the purchaser assuming the risks and expense of transport to Quebec.

In principle, there was a fairly orderly pattern to the marketing of grain, with wheat passing down the St Lawrence and up the mercantile hierarchy to offset the flow of imported goods in the opposite direction. The realities of this commerce were rather more chaotic. The Canadian grain trade of the eighteenth century was in fact quite disorganized, fiercely competitive, and subject to speculative disruption, as a closer look at Samuel Jacobs' activities will show.

One might expect that the country merchant would be in a strong position, thanks to the retail sales that made him creditor to hundreds of peasants, to command a substantial share of the local harvest, regardless of market conditions. Indeed, one historian has written of rural traders as though they were local economic dictators, deciding to buy hundreds of minots of wheat from a local habitant one year and leaving him with useless surpluses in years of inadequate overseas demand.[59] This view, in line with the thesis stressing demand factors as the determinant of Lower Canadian agriculture, has to be rejected in the light of what we know from Samuel Jacobs' correspondance. The country shopkeeper simply did not have that sort of power over the peasantry and when he did not buy wheat from a surplus-producing habitant, we may be quite certain that it was because the habitant simply sold to another buyer, not because the merchant scorned his product.

How is it that Jacobs' position as retail creditor did not give him complete control over the local grain supply? A number of factors tended to undermine his powers in this regard. First, as one merchant among many competing for the lucrative local retail trade, Jacobs could not afford to risk alienating customers by insisting too strongly on prompt deliveries of wheat.⁶⁰ Second, there were years of crop failure when habitants really had no surplus to give, when even a lawsuit could not squeeze blood from a stone, and Jacobs had to carry a great many retail debts over to the next years. Third, the endebted peasants over whom he exercised the greatest leverage were precisely the poor and marginal ones like Théophile Allaire who had little enough to offer even in the best of years. Even if they did form a majority of the local population, Jacobs could not collect enough grain from these smaller producers to pay his bills to the Quebec exporters. The key to the Richelieu wheat · trade was the 50 to 100 'rich' habitants who could not be bullied as they normally produced wheat worth much more than what they owed the merchant each year. Jacobs referred once to the 'middling sort' who usually sold 150 to 200 minots but he clearly meant 'middling' in the context of substantial producers well above the average for all habitant households.⁶¹ These were the chosen quarry of the resident traders and itinerant buyers who stalked the Richelieu valley, their numbers and tactics varying with the changing prospects for profitable export. Jacobs was particularly vulnerable in bargaining with the habitants in this category, as well as with the local priests and innkeepers, because he seldom had the cash to pay for all their wheat; he could sometimes offer a cash advance, but he had to ask for credit until he sold the grain in the fall. Jacobs' position then as creditor to a large section of the region's agrarian population was an asset in his grain-buying activities, but it was not one that freed him from the need to struggle hard with competing purchasers.

To secure an adequate share in each year's harvest the merchant had to offer several services to producers, particularly the larger ones, but even to endebted habitants. He would, for example, store grain free of charge during the months between winter threshing and the springtime shipping season for habitants who remained free to sell it to another merchant if they wished. Another arrangement that also relieved the peasant of the need to store and care for wheat, while allowing him to benefit by any late-season price rise was the purchase 'prix pas fixé en avance' by which the merchant took possession of grain agreeing to pay for it at the price current when it was shipped later in the year. To secure the wheat of a large producer, Jacobs would often agree to accept some peas as well or to take damaged or sprouted wheat along with the good. At times of heavy demand, he might also offer a cash advance or a few gallons of rum 'par-dessus le marché' on striking a bargain.

Price was, of course, the central issue in the Richelieu grain trade;

even though very little cash changed hands, all transactions were expressed in the language of livres per minot. To play the game to best advantage all parties had to take stock as best they could of prospective overseas demand, the magnitude of Canadian supply, and the financial strength of the various dealers; naturally the merchants were in a better position to gauge these factors than were the habitants. Price rates were established through a war of nerves on two fronts. First there was the struggle pitting the habitants as a group against the buyers as a group, the former anxious to hold out for as high a price as possible but restrained in some cases by a need to pay retail debts and in general by the spectre of pricing themselves out of the market. The merchants, for their part, had to hide their desire to secure a supply of grain under a mask of indifference to avoid giving any hint of high demand. The result was usually a stand-off in the early months of the year, with each side hoping, in Jacobs' word, to 'outwind' the other, before the price finally 'broke' with the first transaction. 'It seems we lye all on our oars at present in Regard to purchasing Grain, and the inhabitants more sensible, waits till we begin first which they call Les [sic: laisse] Enrager les Marchandes pour Trouvais un bon prix.'[62] Sometimes, as in 1775, Jacobs squirmed with anxiety as he waited, still affecting outward nonchalance, to see what he would have to offer for badly needed wheat.

This year I believe they do not Incline to brake the price till the Traders goes to jail for the debts they owe them, and the vessels that comes obliged to go without their loads. Even this year succeeds with them and they force a high price from the Traders, which necessity may oblige them to give, which just answers their Expectation for the longer they keep it on hand the better price they get.[63]

The first to settle were usually the habitants who needed to pay off retail debts or other obligations but, once the price broke, the solid fronts on both sides broke as well and individual sales took place over the course of the spring and summer while prices continued to evolve. Jacobs' attention then had to shift to the second front in the war for grain as he struggled against his fellow merchants to secure as large a share as possible of the finite supply of wheat. A shared class interest induced him to pursue this goal as quietly as possible to avoid strengthening the habitants' hand by an open display of competitive bidding, but he could not afford to be too casual for fear of missing his chance to buy. In 1775 Jacobs was indeed injured when he baulked at the 'extravagent prices' demanded by producers who counted on the effects of that year's poor harvest. In January he reported that, 'the good inhabitants are not for fixing a price at all as yet therefore I lie as coole as they.' He was rather too cool as it turned out for, in May, prices at Quebec rose suddenly, sending 'speculators' rushing to the Richelieu to buy up every available grain. 'While I lay still,' Jacobs later lamented, 'the wheat was purchased up even from them that owed me the best part of it, though I keep their custom, have neither their grain nor debts paid.'[64]

To avoid disasters of this sort, Jacobs tried to keep a watch on the activities of his competitors, monitoring the amounts purchased, the price and terms, while keeping his own cards close to his chest. The merchant's correspondence with his clerks at St Ours and St Charles in the early 1770s tells a fascinating story of espionage and intrigue aimed at discovering this vital information. In periods of high demand and volatile prices particularly, merchants would have one another followed constantly and they would send spies to competitors' stores. Here, to take one example among many, are Jacobs' instructions to his man at St Charles:

There is so many lis [sic] going forward that you can hardly rely on them. I heard Dugan, Levitre and Grant gave four livres. They did so the devil got into them the other day and they gave cash down for it at that price. I sent a person down to them which they could not suspect to sell them three or four hundred minots for the cash at that price. He offered it, if they could get credit that insures me the wheat is four livres and it cant be much higher. I would have you make no great show in it and the same time buy all you can from those inhabitants which you know that does want to sell to pay their debts (at four livres) payable part at embarkment or all then if it is necessary ...[65]

Another favourite trick was to spread rumours to the effect that a rival merchant was in financial difficulty, this in the hopes that large producers would hesitate to grant him credit for their grain.

Contending with five or six other Lower Richelieu merchants was bad enough, but what really caused trouble for Samuel Jacobs were the 'coureurs des côtes,' travelling agents sent by impatient Quebec exporters to buy wheat from the habitants. Not only did these interlopers bypass the established commercial network, they made their offers loudly and openly, giving clear signals to the peasants that demand was high and prices likely to rise. This always sent Jacobs into a rage. 'The speculators hunts down the wheat here as a press-gang does a run-away sailor ... if they would not make such a hubbub and wait with patience till the grain got down they could buy it cheaper and turn out more to the sellers advantage ...'[66] The merchant clearly felt that habitants had no business knowing that their wheat was in demand and therefore he tended to blame the buyers unfairly for market conditions that were not their fault. On the other hand, one can certainly sympathize with Jacobs' dismay at being abruptly squeezed out of the normal chain of wheat marketing.

The price of wheat broke pretty well from fifty five sols to three livers per Minot, and so it might have continued had the devil not got into the exporters again, for the stroling imps, and the people employed by them, have no other interest in it than to rise the price of grain on the Countrey traders, for the Sake of Commision or being allowed so much per Minot, how happy would a Countrey Trader be coud he live quite in his Territories, he coud sell his grain even delivered at quebec, get a good Proffit for the same these imps buys at, to show themselfs of Consequence and satisfy the ambition of their employers, Hoppey Kickeys gang Part of them are like saylors, who have Received three months advance pay, distributes it in all their pockets to make a show ...[67]

At times, he complained, commission agents would sign a contract with him to supply so many thousand minots and then turn around and begin buying up additional quantities from the local peasants he himself counted on to fill his obligation. On at least one occasion, the resident merchants of the Richelieu valley attempted to join together to combat the agents, agreeing to raise the price of wheat until they drove out the interlopers, only to let it drop again after they left. This strategy could not work though as the local traders did not have enough capital to hold out against the big exporters; moreover, many of them – Jacobs was not among these – themselves operated from time to time as agents for a Quebec merchant.

The disorganization of the eighteenth-century grain market was at the same time the cause and the result of speculation. Fluctuations of supply and demand, the seasonal isolation of the colony, and the financial weakness of so many of its traders made Canada particularly tempting prey for an alert merchant, armed with liquid capital and advance information about overseas shortages or the dispatch of troops, to gain control of the entire wheat surplus. Jacobs tried to secure financial backing more than once for engrossing ventures of this sort but his plans and those of his competitors were generally frustrated. The only spectacularly successful coup in his day occurred in 1779 when Jacob Jordan and his associates cornered the wheat supply and made huge profits by selling later at very high prices. The key to Jordan's success was his position as deputy paymaster general to His Majesty's forces, which gave him control of large sums of public monies for long enough to make the necessary purchases when he heard of the 'amazing price of wheat and flour in other parts of America.'[68] Although there was nothing under the English régime to rival the enormous corruption of François Bigot's years as the last intendant of New France, the distinction between private and state funds remained unclear after the Conquest and hence also the opportunity to make a private fortune by investing money held in trust for the king.[69] Without such special privileges, merchants like Jacobs were unable to gain command of a single commodity, but this did not prevent them from trying and their speculative mania exacerbated the instability of the already disorderly Canadian grain trade.

This impulse in a businessman to gamble for the big stakes might seem rather archaic in the age of Adam Smith and the physiocrats, although it is perfectly understandable when one takes account of the disorganized commercial environment. The economic theorists of the day could regard the 'laws of the marketplace' with serenity but, for a merchant like Jacobs, the operations of the market were not always impersonal or mechanical and, when they worked to his disadvantage, they were scarcely legitimate. When not himself attempting to engross wheat supplies, he would rail against 'the covetousness of the inhabitants and the ambitiousness of the traders.'[70] Business, for Jacobs, was not simply a matter of manipulating abstract values, it was combat with human beings who were morally responsible for their actions. 'A few days past the Traders commenced hostilities,' he would write; 'Mr Stuart attacks this trade sword in hand ... ,' betraying by his choice of metaphors, not only his military background, but also his personalized and passionate conception of commerce.[71] We tend to think of resistance to the despotism of market forces in this period of historic transition as a monopoly of the 'lower orders' who were its main victims; but even a merchant like Samuel Jacobs was not prepared to give up the concept of a 'moral economy.'[72]

While Jacobs seems old-fashioned in his economic views, this sketch of the grain trade reveals the habitants to be sharp bargainers quite out of keeping with any image of peasants as bumpkins bewildered by the market economy. Those who had a surplus beyond the requirements of feudal dues and retail debts knew how to get the most for their wheat by gauging demand, playing off one purchaser against the other, and waiting for the right moment to conclude a deal. On the other hand, we must remember that producers in this position were generally a minority of the region's habitants and that their numbers shrank to a handful in some years of bad harvests. Most habitants tended in the long run to purchase more than they could pay for with their own produce and they sank into the position of permanent debtors. Their fate was not determined primarily by any 'unfair' disadvantage in the market sphere; they knew how to bargain effectively and they were not unduly coerced by the merchant, even when they owed him money. The problem was instead the larger social and economic structures to which these peasants were subjected, structures that were in many respects reinforced rather than challenged by the likes of Samuel Jacobs.

COMMERCE AND AGRICULTURE

All this commercial activity was not without its effects on the peasant tilling his field. As early as 1741, when merchants were first beginning to become numerous in the New France countryside, the governor and intendant welcomed this trend as a stimulus to agricultural production. 'L'habitant n'ayant aucun impôt à payer, le luxe est necessaire pour l'exciter au travail, il convient donc de le mettre dans l'occasion de beaucoup consommer.'[73] The installation of country traders selling rum and other products in the Lower Richelieu, together with the opening of overseas markets, particularly after the Conquest, must indeed have contributed in some degree to the striking growth of marketable wheat surpluses. If Samuel Jacobs captured a roughly constant proportion of the region's produce, then the figures in Table 19 would suggest a rapid expansion between 1762 and 1773. Census data indicate a similar trend; the amount of grain sown in St Denis climbed from 1211 minots in 1765 to 4416 in 1784, while in St Ours the figure jumped from 2031 to 4012 minots. On the other hand, it would be a mistake to suppose that each habitant family in the region therefore must have doubled or tripled its production. In fact these figures on planting and exports reflect an increase in the number of producers more than a growth in average output. Dividing the amounts sown by the number of households in each parish, we find a much more moderate rise from 1765 to 1784 of 20.9 minots per household to 23.9 in St Denis and of 19.0 to 25.4 minots per household in St Ours.

Moreover, there is every reason to suspect that the increase in average seedings was mainly due to the disproportionate gains registered by the largest peasants, gains which more than compensated for the stagnation of the majority. We only have detailed records of individual grain purchases for the period before 1764 when Charles Curtius handled Jacobs' affairs at St Denis. At that time, habitants sold only small amounts of wheat; 130 transactions in 1763 brought the shopkeeper only 3878 minots for an average of 29.8 minots per purchase. Only a handful of sales were for more than 100 minots and most of these involved priests and other merchants rather than direct producers.[74] Within ten years however, as noted in the previous section, Jacobs was relying heavily on habitants able to sell 150 to 200 minots, and as much as 300 and 400 minots in years of good harvests. Precise data are still lacking but it does appear that the rapid growth of Canada's wheat surplus in the second half of the eighteenth century was largely the work of a minority of comparatively rich peasants, who simply cleared new ground and expanded the arable portions of their farms.

Even if the expansion of wheat-growing was a general phenomenon affecting all the peasants of the Lower Richelieu – and this seems very unlikely – it still should not be seen as anything resembling an 'agricultural revolution.' There was no abandonment of the pattern of production for subsistence, no technical improvements, and no adoption of new commercial crops. Instead, the importance of wheat, the principal crop in the traditional subsistence scheme, was reinforced. Samuel Jacobs and the other merchants showed almost no interest in other products or potential products of this rich farming region; a few head of cattle were shipped down to Quebec but peas and oats were only purchased reluctantly as a favour to insistent habitants. By way of contrast, Yankee merchants in the Connecticut valley at this time gladly accepted a wide range of produce from their rural customers, including corn, oats, rye, butter, cheese, flaxseed, vegetables, apples, wax, fish, pork, beef, wood, and potash.[75] Of course, the New Englanders were in a different position with large urban markets fairly close at hand, but the indifference of the Richelieu merchants to everything but wheat is nevertheless striking. There were indeed various attempts on the part of merchants and government officials before and after the British conquest to encourage the cultivation of hemp, but these met with little success since hemp, unlike wheat, was a strictly commercial crop with no value outside the market. As such it could have little place in an agrarian economy organized around household self-sufficiency and feudal exactions. The reinforcement of wheat monoculture is therefore not simply a result of personal failings on the part of the merchants. The point is that the grain-trading activities of Samuel Jacobs and his colleagues did not alter or even challenge existing rural structures but rather depended on and profited by the traditional order.

Jacobs was no revolutionary; he was not even an agricultural 'improver' after the model of the European gentlemen-agronomists of his day, such as Duhamel du Monceau and Arthur Young. For a man so active in the grain trade, this merchant took remarkably little interest in agriculture. Other than occasional comments about the current prospects for a good harvest and one isolated complaint about the way the habitants threshed flaxseed, there is nothing in his voluminous correspondence about systems of cultivation. Never did he betray any desire to alter the unenlightened farming methods of his neighbours in the interests of greater productivity. Furthermore, he never took any apparent notice of feudal exactions or of seigneurial tenure as an obstacle to agrarian development. This businessman made his money from the exchange of commodities; the forces and relations of production left him indifferent. This seems all the more surprising in view of Jacobs' activities outside the commercial realm in potash and rum manufacturing, and yet it makes perfect sense when one remembers that he originally came to the Richelieu to sell rather than to buy. Military supply work apart, retail sales seem always to have been Jacobs' principal source of profits throughout his career in Canada, and this point requires some emphasis in view of the 'staples thesis' stranglehold over Canadian economic history which has led to excessive preoccupation with the outflow of colonial products.

Of course the country trader acted as a channel both for imported goods coming into the region and for grain leaving it; it may therefore appear a quibble to stress one aspect of this commerce when the two were really inseparable. And yet there was a hierarchy; wheat was a medium of payment, a means to an end, and this subordination to retail commerce shaped Jacobs' attitudes toward local productivity. Almost all the schemes for agricultural reform current in his day called for the formation of large land holdings to permit greater efficiency in crop rotation and livestock management.[76] These schemes would imply a reduced human population in a given territory and to Jacobs that would mean a reduced pool of potential customers. It is true that large agrarian enterprises might still require large numbers of hired labourers but the effect still would be negative for the shopkeeper since rural proletarians, lacking landed security for their debts, made poor customers. As vendors of imported goods then, Samuel Jacobs and others in his position had an interest, not in increasing agricultural productivity, but in keeping the number of productive units high. On the other hand, there was no good multiplying farms through the subdivision of holdings as this might jeopardize the marketable surpluses needed to pay for purchases at the store. Thus, the rural merchant required agrarian structures featuring peasant possession of the land (to guarantee debts), and a predominance of holdings large enough to produce a wheat surplus beyond subsistence and rent needs but small enough to leave room for as many farming families as possible. This is just the situation Samuel Jacobs found in St Denis and it is quite understandable that he made no effort to alter it.

The result was inevitably an unbalanced commercial system. In the long run, wheat shipments fell short of imports and, accordingly, more and more of Jacobs' expanding capital was tied up in credit extended to his habitant-customers. The debtors' lands provided some security – limited nevertheless by seigneurial priority, the douaire, and other privileged debts – but securing payments could be extremely difficult even on accounts that were years overdue. This tendency toward long-term debt was partly a result of the merchant's emphasis on retail sales, as well as the competitive nature of Lower Richelieu trade which forced him to be indulgent with debt-ridden customers for fear they might take their business elsewhere. The vagaries of Old Régime agriculture were a further cause of debt; even habitants who could sell enough wheat to cover purchases in normal years would be unable to pay for needed supplies in times of crop failure. A third cause of debt, though not usually to the merchant except insofar as he acted as local banker, was the system of social reproduction which required some peasants to pay compensation to siblings who ceded shares in land inheritance. Finally, there were the feudal exactions of priest and seigneur which tended to raise the annual threshold at which rural households could begin paying retail debts. As a result of all these factors, most of Jacobs' customers fell into debt at some time and some of them became deeply endebted; other studies show that this was the pattern elsewhere in rural Quebec in the eighteenth century.[77]

Three inventories of debts owed to branch stores taken not long after Samuel Jacobs settled at St Denis suggest that, on the whole, customers had not gone very far into the red at that time.[78]

Store	Date	Number of debtors	Total due	Mean debt
St Ours	25/4/1768	219	11,070	50.5
Sorel	4/7/1770	87	5,271	60.6
St Charles	30/7/1773	394	17,479	44.4

Nevertheless, these are not negligible amounts; all three lists were drawn up after the season of settling accounts but before the fall purchases and therefore they represent real debt and not just short-term retail credit. By the time Jacobs died some fifteen years later, hundreds of customers were in his debt very deeply indeed. Leaving aside the large sum he was owed by the exporter who bought his annual supply of wheat, the merchant had 519 debtors who owed an average of 496 livres each. This inventory of debts, unlike the three earlier ones, was taken in September and so it may include a certain amount of short-term consumer credit, but the larger debts formalized in bonds and promissory notes were certainly not of this sort. Following the example of other eighteenth-century merchants, Jacobs allowed debts to accumulate in his account books up to a certain point but, beyond that, he required customers to sign a promissory note for the amount due plus 6 per cent interest. For the largest debts, a notary was called in to draw up a bond ('obligation') which specified interest and a mortgage on the debtor's land (Table 20). The years following Samuel Jacobs' death were not a time of agricultural prosperity and, despite the best efforts of the executors of his will to collect overdue accounts, most of the old customers fell deeper into debt as their payments in wheat, cash, and livestock failed to match the inexhorable accumulation of interest.[79]

Whether debts were covered by 'hypothèques spéciales' or not, land was always Jacobs' security and consequently he could not avoid some involvement in farms and agriculture. Debtors who failed to demonstrate a serious effort to pay something every year were likely to be sued and have their property seized and auctioned off. Jacobs undertook lawsuits as much to frighten others into paying as to recover the sums owed by the defendents. It was simpler in many cases to 'buy' the land of an endebted habitant for the balance owing, thus avoiding the trouble and expense of legal procedures.[80] Normally he sold farms acquired in this way but, in the last years of his life, Jacobs began to keep them, perhaps with a view to providing for his retirement. He had twelve farms in various locations from Beloeil to Sorel when he died, as well as a number of house lots in the villages of the region. Most of the farms were rented

TABLE 20
Debts to Samuel Jacobs estate 1786

	Less than 100 livres	100–499 livres	500 livres or more	Unspecified	Total
By book debit	151	65	9	16	241
By promissory note	29	70	19	2	120
By bond ('obligation')	0	49	105	1	155
Other	1	3	0	0	4
Total	181	187	133	19	520

to tenants – often the former owners – either under sharecropping arrangements for half the harvest or for a fixed rent of so many minots of wheat per year. Leases were for one to six years and at the end of the term they might be renewed or the tenant might be evicted.[81] Copies of some of Jacobs' contracts with his tenants survive and their conditions give no hint of any particular concern for technical improvements. Whereas many contemporary leases prescribe certain forms of crop rotation, manuring, and fencing, Jacobs settled for the vague minimum requirement, 'd'avoir soin de la dte. terre en bon père de famille et comme si elle lui appartenoit.' The tools and equipment listed in one lease are clearly those acquired from the former owner, with no trace of 'improvement.' Moreover, Jacobs' interest in wheat to the exclusion of other crops led him to insert a special clause directing his farmer to sow the land with 'bleds.'[82]

Here we have the merchant beginning to settle down as a rentier at the end of a busy life of commerce. As landlord and as trader, Samuel Jacobs took the world essentially as he found it, endeavouring to extract 'a genteel profit' from a society of self-sufficient peasant households and feudal overlords. He did, however, make some contribution to the expansion of the agrarian economy of the Richelieu, but without undermining existing structures. His activities in the region therefore were not those of a genuine 'entrepreneur' in Schumpeter's sense, and the process in which he participated in rural Quebec was economic *growth* rather than *development*.[83] In all this Jacobs was a typical merchant of the era before the advent of capitalist society. Confined for the most part within the 'sphere of circulation' where goods are not made but only exchanged, traders acted as parasitic intermediaries between productive systems over which they exercised little control. Merchant's capital, amassed through the process of buying cheap and selling dear, is a necessary prerequisite for the emergence of capitalist production but, 'its development ... is incapable by itself of promoting and explaining the transition from one mode of production to another.'[84] This is not to say that commerce has no impact on the producing societies with which it deals. As we shall see, the enterprises of Samuel Jacobs and his eighteenth-century colleagues, joined with the internal dynamics of the feudal Lower Richelieu, fostered some hesitant beginnings of industry and urbanization in the region. Because the feudal order was left essentially intact, however, the impulse in the direction of economic development and the establishment of a full-blown capitalist society was strangled in the cradle.

But, before discussing the results of this encounter between feudal and mercantile forces, we must examine the peculiar experience of Sorel in the late eighteenth century. Largely neglected by Samuel Jacobs and the grain merchants of his day, this habitant community nevertheless found its destiny shaped by businessmen of a different sort.

7

Habitant-voyageurs

Though they seldom set foot in Sorel, it was the Canadian fur barons, operating from their isolated northern posts and their mansions in Montreal, who eventually played a leading part in shaping the destiny of that parish's peasantry.[1] This was in the late eighteenth century. Earlier, a commercial trail had been blazed into the mouth of the Richelieu by country traders such as Jean LeRoux dit Provençal, who had his headquarters there at the middle of the eighteenth century, and Samuel Jacobs himself, who had a store in the parish for a short time in the 1760s. By the time the Northwest Company began hiring local men as voyageurs around 1790 then, the habitants of Sorel had been integrated into the international trading system to the same limited extent as the peasants of St Ours or St Denis.

What distinguished them from their neighbours to the south in the years preceding their massive involvement in the fur trade was their general inability to grow sizeable quantities of surplus grain. On the whole, the soil of Sorel is rather sandy and it became clear by the second half of the eighteenth century, when its initial fertility had been exhausted, that it would not be a centre of the wheat trade. Around 1784, more oats were grown here than wheat, whereas St Denis habitants, blessed with comparatively rich soil, still concentrated on wheat, Canada's main export crop, and grew about twice as much of it per capita as Sorel habitants. The decline of wheat continued in Sorel, much to the chagrin of the local priest who saw his tithe slowly disappearing. In 1790, he described the contrast between agriculture in his parish and that practised in neighbouring communities where

le blé et autres Grains y venant abondament. Mais icy tres mauvaise terre ou le blé vient à peine, pois et avoines. [sic] Les habitants industrieux connoissant leur terre en employent la meilleur partie qui est proche de leurs Batiments en encorre y metant L'engrais qu'il faudroit, sur leur terre en Blé dinde, feves, patates et tabac en quoi ils réusissent fort bien.[2]

The substitute crops mentioned here – oats, corn, beans, potatoes, and tobacco – may have been exchanged locally for wheat but, in Lower Canada in the 1790s, they were not marketable commodities and, no matter how well they grew, they could scarcely be of use except for the subsistence of the local population. Thus the habitants here came to require some exotic goods but they had a great deal of difficulty paying for them since they were less likely to have wheat to sell than were the peasants of St Ours and St Denis. This presumably is why Jacobs had to close his Sorel shop sometime before 1770, making his customers liquidate their unpaid debts by providing him with timber to be shipped to Quebec.[3]

Although Sorel's forests might provide enough timber to take care of retail debts on one occasion, they were a shrinking resource that offered no hope for long-term revenues. It is conceivable that a reorientation of agriculture in the direction of cattle- or sheep-raising might have made the parish prosperous in spite of its sandy soil, but this probably would have required the formation of larger farms and some modification of the traditional scheme of household self-sufficiency. Influences from outside the Lower Richelieu did not favour such an alteration of the local agrarian economy, however. On the contrary, the fur-trading enterprises that came seeking cheap seasonal labour had an interest in maintaining a Sorel peopled by poor small-holders engaged in subsistence agriculture. With the arrival of Northwest Company recruiters in the late eighteenth century, wages from temporary work as voyageurs began to take the place of missing grain surpluses for the peasantry of Sorel.

How did Sorel become a 'voyageur parish' and what effect did this have on the local society and economy? These are questions that will be taken up below, but first a background sketch of the labour history of the Canadian fur trade is required.

TRANSPORT LABOUR IN THE FUR TRADE

In the early Canadian fur trade, the job of trapping the animals and treating the skins was almost always performed by native Indians who then bartered the furs to Canadian or European traders. The production of pelts was therefore the work of 'independent' workers and the connection between producer and merchant was normally a strictly commercial one. Except in the early years of the French colony, this processing of skins and their exchange for imported goods took place in the interior of the continent, thousands of trackless kilometres from seaports and European settlements. Thus the transportation of furs and trade goods across the wilderness between Montreal and the hinterland was a significant expense for traders and an important component of the value of export-ready pelts. Unlike the collecting and treating of skins, this equally vital work of transportation was performed mainly by French Canadians, under conditions that evolved over the centuries, essentially in the direction of capitalist enterprise.

In the early years, around the middle of the seventeenth century, the organization of the Indian trade was fairly simple; the trade was more or less open to all and most settlers at Montreal obtained a few pelts from visiting Indians. Specialized merchants gradually emerged and, as the Indians ceased making the trip down to Montreal, Canadian 'coureurs des bois' began making trading journeys to the Great Lakes region. These coureurs des bois, or 'voyageurs' as they were called after about 1680, depended on the merchants for backing but they operated their trading expeditions quite independently, generally forming partnerships of three or four men to complete the crew of a canoe. The first appearance of the 'engagé' was late in the seventeenth century. Engagés had no interest in the canoe, the cargo, or the profits of an expedition; instead they worked for a voyageur or a merchant in return for a contractually specified salary. The tendency in the first half of the eighteenth century was for the engagés to become more numerous as the voyageur category disappeared, a few of the more successful voyageurs joining the ranks of the merchants while the rest found themselves reduced to the status of wage labourers. By the late eighteenth century, if not earlier, the fur brigades were manned entirely by engagés.[4] Voyageurs (in this narrow sense of the term – often engagés were referred to as 'voyageurs' in later years) occupied a position similar to that of a pre-industrial artisan: 'independent' yet subjected to merchant capital through debt. And they were even less successful in maintaining their ownership of the means of making a livelihood in the face of advancing capitalism; the eighteenth century saw, 'la prolétarisation progressive du personnel de la traite.'[5]

Labour and ownership were separated and control of the Canadian fur trade was eventually concentrated in a single merchant enterprise.

After the British conquest, large partnerships were formed until, in 1779, the Northwest Company united all the major traders in a loose coalition that grew more solid with the passage of time. This process of consolidation was partly connected to the increasing cost of competing transportation lines as the trade moved into more distant territories, but it also owed much to government policies, such as the requirement of posting bonds, and to the merchants' ruthless methods in combating independent traders.

In the early eighteenth century, the majority of voyageurs and engagés came from the immediate vicinity of Montreal and, to a lesser extent, Trois-Rivières, the traditional bases of the Indian trade,[6] but, as the trade was rationalized along capitalist lines, merchants increasingly cultivated a rural workforce. Those then who cite late eighteenth-century evidence to suggest that fur-trade labourers always came mainly from the countryside fail to notice that patterns of recruitment changed greatly over the course of the century.[7] With the advent of the Northwest Company and the expensive lengthening of transportation routes into the most remote regions of the continent, efforts were made to control costs by adopting more efficient boats and by recruiting cheap and docile labour from country parishes. Instead of remaining in Montreal and competing with other urban employers for the services of men who had come to town looking for work, fur traders sent agents out into the countryside in an active attempt to develop new sources of manpower. Even after the demise of the Northwest Company, its recruiting traditions were followed by the Hudson's Bay Company, whose agents hiring men in Lower Canada were 'carefully excluding those who are brought up in the neighbourhood of Towns ...'[8]

Rural areas, particularly poor communities, were admirably suited to filling the labour needs of the Northwest Company. Since the demand for canoemen fluctuated from year to year and since a large number of seasonal workers was always needed, there was little place in the fur trade for a genuine proletariat. Instead, traders found they were best served by land-owning peasants who could sustain themselves between stints in the northwest. Employers could then draw on a reservoir of experienced workers to suit their requirements without having to worry about paying a 'living wage' for year-round subsistence. Dispersed through the countryside much of the time, peasant-workers were unlikely to form 'combinations' against the traders' interests and, as their possession of land protected them from complete indigence, they did not represent the same sort of social danger that, for example, unemployed sailors did.[9]

TABLE 21
Fur-trade engagements: Sorel, St Ours, and St Denis 1790–9

	Sorel	St Ours	St Denis
Engagements	128	48	11
individuals	106	40	10
adult males*	316	389	418
proportion of adult males involved (%)	33.5	10.3	2.4

* Men aged 16–60 according to 1790 census

THE NORTHWEST COMPANY DISCOVERS SOREL

The bourgeois 'Nor'Westers' are celebrated in the textbooks for their explorations and discoveries in Western Canada, but their discovery of a cheap rural labour force in the heart of old Quebec was just as critical to their commercial success. Sorel was one of the rural parishes particularly favoured by McTavish and Frobisher, the partnership at the core of the Northwest Company. After hiring large numbers of men there throughout the 1790s, McTavish and Frobisher even engaged a local notary and a local habitant-voyageur in 1797 to recruit Sorel men and process their *engagement* contracts on the spot.[10] Located about seventy kilometres from Montreal, Sorel was not too distant from the city, yet far enough away to be untouched by the urban labour market and other unsettling influences. A local priest suggested that men from Sorel rather than Lachine engagés be hired for a missionary expedition to Red River as they were experienced, honest, polite, and, above all, inexpensive.[11]

Through most of the eighteenth century, comparatively few men from this area served as engagés,[12] but by the end of the century, that is, from about the time the Northwest Company was formed, unusually large numbers of local men were departing with the western fur brigades. An exhaustive examination of the files of notaries practising in Sorel and nearby parishes, together with a search through an inventory of *engagements* signed in Montreal, suggests that employment contracts can be traced in the 1790–9 period for one-third of Sorel's adult male population (see Table 21).[13] This is certainly an underestimate of the actual numbers involved since a great many engagés served without signing a notarized *engagement* for the benefit of future historians.[14] Moreover, since work of this sort was mainly a young man's occupation,[15] the proportion of Sorel males in their twenties mentioned in these contracts must have been much greater than 33.5 per cent, even leaving aside source deficiencies. These figures then only represent a minimum estimate of fur-trade participation, but they show a clear contrast between Sorel, where it would hardly be an exaggeration to suggest that a majority of young men worked as engagés at some time in the decade, and St Denis, thirty kilometres up the Richelieu, which was almost untouched by the fur trade.

For the majority, work in the fur trade was seasonal, but many signed on for a few years at a time. The main distinction, in the eighteenth century, was between 'winterers' and 'Montreal men' or 'porkeaters.' The former remained in the northwest for terms of three years or more, subsisting for long stretches on pemmican, and transporting furs and supplies between the remote posts and a Great Lakes rendez-vous. There they met the seasonal engagés whom they sneered at as 'mangeurs de lard.' The latter were the more numerous group, however. They paddled the large canoes that left Lachine early in May for the Grand Portage or some other advance base, returning late in August. The sources do not always make it clear whether an individual signed on for only a summer's trip or as a winterer, but some idea of the relative numbers involved in each group can be inferred from the destinations mentioned in the *engagements*. Ninety-nine of the 106 contracts involving Sorel engagés between 1790 and 1799 specify the destination and, of these, fifty-two were for trips to Grand Portage and another thirteen for trips to other Great Lakes bases. In other words, about two-thirds of the departures from Sorel in the 1790s were for seasonal work only.

Certainly some of the men who left Sorel to serve several years as winterers never returned to their homes, either because they died prematurely or because they spent the rest of their lives in the West. At least ten engagés brought Métis children they had fathered to be baptized at the church in Sorel between 1795 and 1827. (The dates give a rough indication of the period of maximum local participation in the fur trade.) Since the children were six to twelve years old when christened, it seems likely that their fathers had settled more or less permanently in the West. Any attempt to determine precisely how many engagés returned and how many were lost to Sorel forever is doomed to failure by the absence of nominal censuses between 1681 and 1851 (censuses for the intervening period give only aggregate local figures or, at best, list heads of households. How many engagés were household heads?) and by the problem of namesakes, which would make it impossible to link names appearing without additional personal information on *engagement* contracts to any listing of inhabitants. Nevertheless, rough indicators suggest strongly that most men involved in the fur trade were only temporarily absent from Sorel. For one thing, the parish's rapid demographic growth argues against any notion that the western trade was a significant drain on population. There is the additional fact, mentioned earlier, that a substantial majority of the voyages from Sorel were seasonal and the pork-eaters involved were in little danger of deserting Lower Canada during a four-month trip to Lake Superior.

The Canadian fur trade was at a peak of activity in the 1790s but, even as it declined in later years, Sorel remained a favourite source of temporary labour. In the first half of the nineteenth century, the American Fur Company recruited engagés here, as did the Hudson's Bay Company.[16] A study of Hudson's Bay Company personnel records for the period 1823-48 shows that, of employees whose Lower-Canadian origins could be traced, more were from Sorel than any other community with the exception of Montreal; not one man was from St Denis.[17] This local concentration was not accidental; Governor Simpson's instructions to recruiters in 1840 were quite specific: 'The engagements of the Recruits to be for a term of 3 to 5 years, all to be taken from the Voyageur parishes ... and as many of the favorite names, LaVallée, L'Esperances, Felixes, Convoyées, (sic: Cournoyers) etc. as possible.'[18] Three of these four 'favorite names' belong to long-established Sorel clans. Since there were no more summer voyages between Montreal and Lake Superior after the demise of the Northwest Company in 1821, work for the Hudson's Bay and American companies meant longer absenses with a greater likelihood of definitive emigration. The numbers involved seem to have been proportionally much smaller than in the 1790s. Thus the fur trade was presumably less important to Sorel's rural economy in the later period than it was between 1790 and 1821. Nevertheless, it does seem clear that, since the end of the eighteenth century, Sorel had established itself as a 'voyageur parish.'

At the time of the Northwest Company, the engagés do not seem to have been a group apart in Sorel. Instead, temporary or seasonal work in the fur trade was a normal part of a local habitant's life. Wage-labour of this sort was not the preserve of seasoned professionals. The 128 *engagement* contracts from the 1790s mention 106 different names; eighty-six men (81 per cent) went on only one trip in the decade, while only eighteen (17 per cent) signed on twice and two (2 per cent) went three times. Although the Hudson's Bay Company may have directed recruiting efforts in 1840 toward 'favorite names,' there was hardly a concentration of engagés within particular family groups in the earlier period, when summer employment was common. Few family names recur in

TABLE 22
Family concentration among Sorel engagés 1790–9

Engagés with the same family name	Families number	per cent	engagés
1	48	73	48
2	10	15	20
3	1	2	3
4	2	3	8
5	3	4	15
6	2	3	12
Total	66	100	106

the collection of Sorel contracts, which is all the more striking in view of the large number of individuals in the population at large sharing some of Sorel's more common surnames (see Table 22). Three-quarters of the families involved had only one representative in the sample. A century earlier, work in the fur trade tended to be dominated by particular families and by town-based 'professionals' who made this commerce their career.[19] This pattern had changed completely by the 1790s so that service as an engagé was occasional and hardly a specialist's activity in Sorel. Nor does it seem to have been the mark of low status: eleven of the 106 engagés in this sample were eventually elected churchwardens of Sorel, the highest lay office in the community.[20] Anything but marginal figures, veterans of the fur trade were well integrated into a community whose economy was based on a mutually supporting system of subsistence agriculture and temporary wage labour.

THE FORMATION OF A SEMI-PROLETARIAT

It seems clear that the voyageurs of Sorel were land-owning peasants who subsisted, at least part of the time, on the produce of their own farms. Data on the land-holdings of individual engagés are not available but the general prevalence of peasant proprietorship in the parish suggests that men who departed for the west either had a farm or would soon acquire one. To the extent that voyageurs could satisfy their needs from their own property between periods of salaried employment, the fur-trade work-force was not proletarian; on the other hand, insofar as the local peasantry as a whole required injections of cash from Northwest Company salaries, then this group was not a set of genuinely independent agriculturalists either. Here too, hard evidence on individual cases is lacking, but all indications are that the habitant community of Sorel did indeed occupy a position in between that of a peasantry and that of a working class. Agriculture here at the turn of the nineteenth century was generally a matter of growing basic foodstuffs, with little surplus for sale. This might feed voyageurs' families, but it would not pay seigneurial rents, nor would it permit purchases of necessary imported goods or help to finance the reproducton of habitant households for succeeding generations. This is where fur-trade earnings tended to play a role,[21] in fact, the very role played by wheat sales in genuinely agricultural parishes like St Denis. It is no doubt for this reason that fur-trade *engagements* were usually signed, and an advance of pay given, in the months of January and February, that is, in the threshing season when rural merchants pressed their customers to deliver their grain and settle their annual accounts.[22] In this respect, engagé earnings were a direct substitute for agricultural sales.

During the first decade of mass participation in the fur trade these earnings seem to have more than made up for the deficiencies of Sorel's agriculture. An analysis of the estate inventory sample suggests that the habitants of the fur-trade community were far better off in the 1790s than they were forty years earlier or forty years later (see Table 23). Land is not assigned a money value in Lower-Canadian estate inventories but the total value of moveable property (such as furniture, implements, and livestock) gives a rough indication of an individual's standard of living. The average value of such property was high among Sorel habitants in the 1790s, not only relative to other periods, but also in comparison with habitants of the agriculturally prosperous communities of St Ours and St Denis. Moreover, it was only at this time, when Northwest Company recruitment was at a peak, that residents of Sorel included in the sample were not heavily in debt; in fact, slightly more money was owed to them, on the whole, than was owed by them. Accordingly, the 'net worth' of Sorel habitants (that is, moveable property plus cash minus debts) was at a maximum in the 1790s when it was much higher than in the other parishes.

One of the more prosperous individuals whose possessions were evaluated – he ranked fourth out of twenty-seven in the 1790s – was Pierre Letendre of Sorel, 'décedé dans les pays d'en haut' in 1795.[23] At his death this engagé left quite a small farm (fifty arpents, half the area still wooded) on the St Lawrence, but he had moveable possessions worth 1274 livres, including the usual complement of farm animals and agricultural implements, as well as a moose and a caribou hide. The

TABLE 23
Average wealth from habitant inventories 1740–1839 (in livres)

	Uncorrected means			
	Sorel		St Ours-St Denis	
	mean	S.D.	mean	S.D.
1740–69				
number of inventories	15		16	
moveable property	856	478	764	414
cash	22	51	20	58
balance of debt	−367	708	−415	752
net worth (excl. land)	512	1087	369	717
1790–9				
number of inventories	15		21	
moveable property	1278	882	765	581
cash	41	87	36	106
balance of debt	38	553	−374	458
net worth (excl. land)	1358	1417	427	749
1830–9				
number of inventories	11		17	
moveable property	922	636	1465	571
cash	2	5	139	377
balance of debt	−476	405	−159	2262
net worth (excl. land)	448	728	1444	2566

	Corrected means*			
	Sorel		St Ours-St Denis	
	mean	S.D.	mean	S.D.
1740–69 (correction factor 1.72)				
number of inventories	15		16	
moveable property	1472	822	1314	713
cash	38	88	34	88
balance of debt	−631	1218	−714	1293
net worth (excl. land)	881	1870	635	1233
1790–9 (correction factor 1)				
number of inventories	15		21	
moveable property	1278	882	765	581
cash	41	87	36	106
balance of debt	38	553	−374	458
net worth (excl. land)	1358	1417	427	749
1830–9 (correction factor 0.90)				
number of inventories	11		17	
moveable property	830	572	1318	514
cash	2	2	125	339
balance of debt	−428	364	−143	2036
net worth (excl. land)	403	655	1300	2309

* In order to counteract the effects of inflation, a correction factor was calculated on the basis of local wheat prices. Wheat sold on the average at about 3.2 livres per minot between 1740 and 1769 (excluding the war crisis) at about 5.5 livres in the 1790s and 6.1 livres in the 1830s. Taking 1790–9 as the base period, the correction factor is then

signs of comparative prosperity included 'un criste d'argent,' a bag full of French and Spanish coins worth 281 livres, and an absence of debts. Indeed, various individuals owed Letendre's estate a total of 119 livres.

Even if it did bring prosperity at first, the fur trade was a Trojan Horse with ultimately disastrous consequences for rural Sorel. The wages that probably appeared initially as a windfall soon became a necessity as Sorel's economic structures were shaped in the early nineteenth century by a dependence on this form of non-agricultural income. As we shall see below, population expanded, holdings were subdivided and an already poor agriculture deteriorated further. The upshot was generalized poverty in the parish and this was made much worse after 1821 by the collapse of the Montreal-based fur trade. Employment was still available in later years with the Hudson's Bay and the American Fur companies but only on three-year contracts; the summer run to Lake Superior, once the most common way for Sorel habitants to make some money, ended with the demise of the Northwest Company.

As a result of these changes, the standard of living of the Sorel semi-proletariat plummeted after the boom years of the 1790s. The average net worth of habitant households in the inventory sample fell to 448 livres in the 1830s. Now that seasonal fur-trade employment was gone, Sorel habitants incurred massive debts that made their estates worth far less than those of the generation of the 1790s. Even before the collapse of the Montreal trade, however, there were signs that the pressures accompanying a dependence on wages had produced general impoverishment. Visitors to Sorel in the early nineteenth century were struck by the poverty of its inhabitants, but they generally mistook its cause. Governor Dalhousie spent several summers here and wrote in his diary in 1820: 'The more I walk about here, the more I see of poverty, idleness, and loose disolute habits – mean unblushing beggary ...'[24] Although the governor blamed this poverty on moral deficiencies of the population, another British visitor, John Lambert, pointed to the effects of the fur trade.

The country people in the vicinity are mostly employed as voyageurs in the North-west fur-trade, and the cultivation of their farms is left to their wives and children. When they return home, they seldom bring more than enough to support them during the winter. The soil is thus neglected, and the town is badly supplied with provisions.[25]

Like Lambert, many historians have argued that the fur trade was

detrimental to Quebec's agricultural development and they too emphasize the diversion of labour from the fields to the woods.[26] There is no
real evidence, however, that Sorel's agriculture suffered primarily from
a shortage of manpower. The problem should some day be studied at
the family level, since it may be that engagés tended to come from
households with enough other adult males that their help could easly
be dispensed with. It is true that in the fur trade, unlike the timber trade,
seasonal employment was in the summer when men were most needed
in the fields, but the porkeaters did return home in time for the grain
harvest. Rural Sorel was at a peak of prosperity in the 1790s just when
summer departures for the west were most common and it was most
distressed in the 1830s when able-bodied men were superabundant. It
was not so much a shortage of hands that impoverished Sorel; rather it
was the combination of poor soil and socio-economic structures fostered
by a general dependence on occasional wage-labour.

LAND AND POPULATION

One way of gauging the effects of fur-trade employment is to compare
Sorel with St Denis, a parish that was scarcely touched by semi-
proletarization. The census of 1831 is the most appropriate instrument
for a comparative examination of patterns of agriculture, demography,
and land ownership in the two communities. At that date, ten years
after the demise of the Northwest Company, the régime of seasonal
employment had had thirty years in which to shape Sorel's social and
economic structures.

The census figures suggest, first of all, that while habitants in the
two parishes grew crops for home consumption, those in St Denis grew
additional quantities, of wheat particularly, for sale (see Table 24). This
is not simply because the soil was better in St Denis; it results from the
larger surfaces under cultivation in the farms of that parish. The mean
size of cleared arable was seventy-nine arpents for St Denis in 1831,
compared to thirty arpents for Sorel farms. The latter figure is exactly
the average cleared area found fifty years later in the Saguenay community of Hébertville where subsistence agriculture was combined with
seasonal work in the forest.[27] Not only were the fields of Sorel quite
small on the average, they tended to be fairly uniform in size (see
Table 25).[28] The majority had cultivated areas of between ten and thirty-
nine arpents; very few were larger than forty arpents. In St Denis, on
the other hand, arable size varied over a much wider range.

TABLE 24
Agricultural production (in minots) per farming household, Sorel and St Denis 1831

	Sorel		St Denis	
	N	per hhld	N	per hhld
Farming households	445		261	
Wheat	19,796	44.5	35,803	137.2
Peas	2981	6.7	7594	29.1
Oats	25,873	58.1	21,592	82.7
Barley	666	1.5	4920	18.8
Rye	6205	13.9	1045	4.0
Corn	681	1.5	621	2.4
Potatoes	66,703	149.9	43,273	165.8
Buckwheat	1221	2.7	0	0

TABLE 25
Extent of cultivated land in habitant farms, Sorel and St Denis 1831

Arpents cultivated	Sorel		St Denis	
	number	per cent	number	per cent
0–9	82	19.0	3	1.5
10–19	115	26.6	4	2.0
20–39	146	33.8	32	15.9
40–59	61	14.1	52	25.9
60–79	15	3.5	53	26.4
80–99	4	0.9	28	13.9
100–49	4	0.9	20	9.9
150+	0	0	9	4.5
Unspecified	5	1.2	0	0
Total habitant farms	432	100	201	100

Relying largely on wages for all but the food needs of their house-holds, Sorel habitants had little reason to maintain extensive land holdings. Farms in Sorel always tended to be smaller than those of St Denis, partly because original concessions by the local seigneur were small; sixty arpents each was the rule from the 1760s. Between 1765 and 1831, however, average holdings declined in size here. There was a decline in St Denis also, but individual holdings in this wheat-growing parish were still much larger than they were in Sorel by 1831 (see Table 26).[29] Before speaking too hastily of the effects of partible inheritance systems and of 'fragmentation of holdings,' we should recall that censuses give figures on the total landholdings of individuals and this often included two or more farm-lots, some of them located outside the parish where

TABLE 26
Habitant land holdings, Sorel and St Denis 1765–1831

	Sorel			St Denis		
Arpents	1765	1831	change	1765	1831	change
0–19	3%	5%	+2%	2%	1%	−1%
20–39	5	13	+8	0	1	+1
40–59	9	14	+5	2	7	+5
60–79	38	33	−5	8	17	+9
80–99	20	12	−8	16	31	+15
100–49	17	14	−3	34	18	−16
150–249	8	6	−2	32	19	−13
250+	0	1	+1	6	6	0
Unspecified	0	1		0	0	
	100%	99%		100%	100%	
N	130	432		50	201	

the owner lived. Also, many new concessions were made between 1765 and 1831, most of them for smaller lots than had been granted earlier. Thus, average holdings in a community could decline in size without any farm being subdivided.

Unfortunately, the sorts of land records ('terriers,' 'aveux et dénombrements') that would make it possible to determine whether fragmentation occurred in St Denis are not available. Studies of other similar grain-growing localities, however, have indicated a complete absense of any lasting subdivision over the course of two centuries and more.[30] In Sorel, on the other hand, farms were definitely split into smaller units in the late eighteenth and early nineteenth century. By 1831, about one-third of the parish's habitants held less than sixty arpents, the normal size of a seigneurial concession here. One row of lots, the 'rang du chénal du moine,' was divided among fifteen habitants in 1724; by 1861, the same area had been subdivided to the point where there were fifty-two lots owned by forty-five individuals.[31] An additional, though very rough, indication of the prevalence of subdivision through inheritance is the fact that, in the 1831 census, 24 per cent of Sorel's habitants lived next to a neighbour with the same family name; in St Denis the figure was only 10 per cent. The subdivision of holdings, often presented as the inevitable result of the inheritance laws of the Custom of Paris or of the French-Canadian habitant's mentality, seems then to have been a local, not a universal phenomenon, and one connected with specific economic circumstances.

TABLE 27
Migratory balance, Catholic populations of Sorel and St Denis 1739–1831

Year	Population	Increase	Natural growth	Net migration
		Sorel		
1739	342			
1765	670	328	287*	41
1784	934	264	510*	−246
1822	3521	2587	1957	630
1831	4804	1283	1183	100
		St Denis		
1770	996			
1790	1694	698	955	−257
1801	2197	503	806	−303
1822	2906	709	1415	−706
1831	3074	168	813	−645

* Interpolation to cover gap in birth and death registration

By altering the local economy and encouraging the profusion of miniscule holdings, the intrusion of the wage system also had a profound effect on Sorel's demography. During the period when men from Sorel were most active in the fur trade, the parish's population grew enormously. Between 1790 and 1831, the annual rate of growth here was 3.5 per cent, while the rate for Lower Canada as a whole was 2.6 per cent and for St Denis 1.4 per cent.[32] These different growth rates were connected, above all, with different patterns of in- and out-migration. The wheat farms of St Denis could only be kept intact at the cost of a net emigration; that is, more people left the parish than entered it from the last quarter of the eighteenth century on (see Table 27).[33] Sorel too suffered from a negative migratory balance before the advent of the Northwest Company but, from 1784 to 1822, there were substantially more immigrants than emigrants.

As a result of this rapid growth, Sorel's population density came to exceed that of St Denis even though the engagé parish had a much larger area. Excluding the 'urban' (or village) portion of each community, there were 12.1 arpents of land for every rural inhabitant of St Denis in 1831 and only 10.1 arpents for each man, woman, and child living in rural Sorel. If these were Malthusian populations, their size controlled by the food-producing capabilities of the lands they occupied, we would expect to find the richer soils of St Denis supporting larger numbers on every square mile of territory. Reality was just the opposite in the Lower Richelieu, largely, it seems, because fur-trade earnings enabled Sorel habitants to get by on small holdings that would not otherwise have been viable agricultural units.

Marriage patterns in Sorel were also unusual. Figures from the 1825 census suggest that males tended to marry at a younger age here than in St Denis (the census does not give any indication of female marriage practices).[34] It was less difficult for young people in Sorel to establish new households in their home parish – perhaps by buying or inheriting part of an existing farm – when they did not require more than a basic food supply from the land. Furthermore, service in the fur trade may have allowed some local habitants' sons to accumulate the capital needed to marry and raise a family earlier than they could have hoped to inherit their parents' property. Thus the average age at first marriage did not increase in Sorel during the fur-trade period as it did in many other pre-industrial populations faced with incipient overpopulation.[35] The parish registers suggest that, on the contrary, the ages of newlyweds tended to decline in the long run, though the changes are probably not significant (see Table 7). Missing then was a mechanism which elsewhere had the effect of redressing the balance between land and population by limiting fertility. Sorel's overcrowding instead worsened as people continued to marry young and fertility remained high. The best explanation of this unusual pattern is the local economic system combining subsistence agriculture and part-time wage labour. The introduction of domestic industry into agrarian households in eighteenth-century Europe had a similar effect: population grew, holdings were subdivided, and overcrowding became severe.[36] All this suggests that Eric Wolf may have confused cause and effect when he argued that partible inheritance 'favored the introduction of small industry and contributed to rural poverty.'[37]

The results of this semi-proletarization may not have been happy for the peasantry of Sorel, but they were rather favourable for the fur traders. The very characteristics that attracted the Northwest Company recruiters to the parish tended to be reinforced and exaggerated by the system of part-time wage-work. Small holders able to feed themselves from their own land but unable to produce a saleable surplus were just what the fur merchants were looking for and they found them in Sorel in ever-larger numbers as the availability of salaries encouraged the subdivision of farms and the growth of population density without undermining the habitants' control of the land. This seems to be a case of a capitalist enterprise making profitable use of labour from a pre-capitalist social formation in such a way as to prevent rather than to encourage the development of its productive forces. Later in the nineteenth century, the timber industry, another employer of semi-proletarians, played a similar role in many parts of rural Quebec.[38] Today, this process continues apace on the 'Third World' frontiers of capitalism with far more tragic consequences.

For all their differences, Sorel and St Denis still had a great deal in common. In the early nineteenth century, these were still primarily agrarian communities peopled mainly by peasants who fed themselves with the produce of their own land and labour. They also lost some of what they grew to feudal exactions. Finally, the two habitant communities found themselves tributary to a local merchant class which siphoned off much of any remaining surplus through retail trade. The contrast comes in at this point, that is, in the transfer of peasant surpluses outside the basic 'feudal' network of subsistence and aristocratic appropriation. Insofar as habitants disposed of a surplus, those in St Denis tended to sell grain, the fruits of their labour, while those in Sorel generally sold their labour power itself. This, in conjunction with differences in soil quality, seems to account for the different agrarian structures of the two parishes.

8

Turning the nineteenth century: development or crisis?

A 'feudal' peasant society? The expansion of capital and the commercialization of agriculture? Merchant economic offensives and habitant resistance? The topics broached so far bear upon many of the current preoccupations of Lower-Canadian historiography. Debate has raged passionately over the vagaries of the rural economy, and it has focused on the decades around 1800 when French-Canadian nationalist movements first made their appearance, in an atmosphere of crisis according to some, in a context of prosperity according to others. Most parties to the dispute seem to agree that rural life changed drastically about this time but their views on the nature and causes of the transformation have clashed dramatically. Some argue that commercial expansion resulted in prosperity and economic modernization while others assert that demographic pressure and peasant traditionalism defeated the forces of progress and caused a major agrarian crisis.

The time has come then to see what light the annals of the Lower Richelieu can shed on this debate. We have determined that local socioeconomic structures were originally feudal. It is also evident that, by the early nineteenth century, merchants had been at work for several decades, selling goods, buying grain, and hiring voyageurs in an accelerating scramble for profits. Now a mercantile frontier, the region was no longer a frontier of settlement as most of the wilderness land had already been colonized. Population growth and the penetration of merchant capital were two of the fundamental dynamics of the Lower Richelieu's socio-economic development in this period. But how profoundly was the social order and the economy affected by these changes. Did the region enter the stage of the 'market economy'? Did urban settlements and non-agricultural production play a significant role? What about habitant agriculture; did it become increasingly mired in out-dated routines? And did the peasantry lose the rough homogeneity of an earlier age? Did population growth and 'commercialization' lead to class cleavages? In sum, was there a tragic crisis, a euphoric 'take-off' or no significant transition at all?

URBAN AND INDUSTRIAL DEVELOPMENT

The Lower Richelieu was never completely rural or entirely agricultural. Samuel Jacobs' store at the time of the American Revolution was situated near the church and the rectory, surrounded by the shops of blacksmiths, potters, and cabinetmakers and by the houses of the local notary and the doctor in a cluster of buildings known as the 'village of St Denis.' Long after this merchant's death, St Denis continued to be a commercial centre with several shopkeepers and wholesalers. An observer writing in 1815 counted about eighty houses in the little town and found it a 'favourable specimen of picturesque beauty' when viewed from across the Richelieu. 'Between the main street and the river are some capacious storehouses, chiefly used as granaries, and wherein large quantities of corn are collected from adjacent seigniories for exportation; as the lands for many leagues about this part are considered the most productive in grain of the whole district of Montreal.'[1] The village of St Ours, though slightly smaller, had the same vocation as agrarian entrepôt in the early nineteenth century.

On the right bank of the Richelieu is the village of St Ours, of about sixty houses, many of them substantially and well constructed of stone; in the centre of it is a handsome church and parsonage-house, and at a little distance the manor-house: besides traders and artizans, many persons of considerable property reside here, who are corn-dealers, and make large purchases of grain of all kinds, that is produced in abundance throughout this and the adjoining seigniories, which is put on board large river craft in the Richelieu and Yamaska, and sent to Quebec for exportation.[2]

There were always little proto-urban settlements around the churches and manor-houses of Sorel, St Ours, and St Denis, but it was in the second half of the eighteenth century, when a considerable wheat trade developed, that the three villages became sizeable. In St Denis the seigneur had small building lots laid out near the church after securing official permission to found a village in 1758. The town quickly outgrew

TABLE 28
Urban growth, village of St Denis 1758–
1840

Date	Houses	Population
1758	7	
1770	13	64
1789	38	169
1801	63	347
1809	70	
1831	108	567
1840	123	

its territory and new areas had to be subdivided in 1780, 1797, and 1800.[3] This geographic expansion simply mirrors the demographic growth apparent in Table 28.[4] In all periods, the population of the village grew faster than that of the rural part of St Denis, but this expansion was not quite as rapid after 1801 as it was in the eighteenth century.

The term 'village' is a rather misleading label for the concentrated settlements of the Lower Richelieu for they were not generally inhabited by peasants, or even, in the pre-1840 period, by retired habitants who had left their farms to the younger generation. In the second half of the nineteenth century, it was common for farming couples to move into the nearest village after they ceded their land by *donation*, but this practice was more recent than some observers believe.[5] Earlier, most donateurs still remained in their old homes sharing quarters with their successors. The 'villages' were really small towns with genuinely urban functions of commerce, administration, and industry. Occupational data from the census of 1831, the first to provide information of this sort, demonstrates this characteristic quite forcefully (see Table 29). Whereas the heads of rural households were almost all habitants or agricultural labourers, the 'urban' dwellers were merchants, notaries, seigneurs, craftsmen, transport workers, and so on. On the other hand, almost all the urban occupations mentioned in the census were ones that catered primarily to the agrarian majority. The 'professionals' (clergy, notaries, surveyors, doctors) did most of their business with habitants as did the merchants, teachers, and innkeepers. The 'manufacturers' were mostly millers and the artisans generally practised trades (blacksmith, carpenter, butcher, etc.) that met local consumer needs.

The potteries first established in the village of St Denis about 1780 by an Acadian refugee, were the only important handicraft industry that catered to a wider market beyond the region.[6] Through informal

TABLE 29
Occupations of heads of households, Sorel, St Ours, St Denis 1831

Occupation	Urban areas		Rural areas		Total	
	N	%	N	%	N	%
Rentiers	19	4.6	5	0.3	24	1.2
Professionals	13	3.2	0	0	13	0.7
Merchants	27	6.5	1	0.1	28	1.4
Teachers	8	1.9	11	0.7	19	1.0
Innkeepers	12	2.9	4	0.3	16	0.8
Manufacturers	2	0.5	13	0.8	15	0.8
Artisans	119	28.9	63	4.0	182	9.2
Sailors	40	9.7	18	1.1	58	2.9
Carters	14	3.4	0	0	14	0.7
Beggars	1	0.2	8	0.5	9	0.5
Farmers	6	1.5	941	60.1	947	47.9
Tenant-farmers	1	0.2	87	5.6	88	4.4
Retired farmers	4	1.0	38	2.4	42	2.1
Labourers	108	26.2	364	23.3	472	23.9
Other	38	9.2	12	0.8	50	2.5
Total	412	100	1565	100	1977	100

apprenticeship arrangements and a strong tendency to transmit the trade along family lines, the potters grew in number through the late eighteenth and early nineteenth centuries. There were at least seventeen potters in St Denis in 1831, just before their numbers appear to have declined. These artisans specialized in rough ceramic vessels that were used mainly to store and prepare food in the countryside. Their products were sold locally or distributed throughout Lower Canada. This industry probably became established at St Denis because the parish was near the centre of a rich agricultural region in the late eighteenth century and because the grain trade had already provided it with a transportation and commercial network.

Besides these artisans with their hand-tools, there were also real industrial establishments using wind, water, or steam power and sometimes employing several hands. For the most part, these too catered to the needs of the local population. First among them in priority and importance were the region's gristmills. That these mills were designed to serve local consumers is shown by the fact that grain sold to outside buyers was shipped unground. In the eighteenth century there were also sawmills in Sorel and St Ours. In the first part of the following century the region had, at various times, fulling and carding mills (adjuncts to the domestic manufacture of woolens), linseed oil mills, a brewery, and a brick-kiln.[7] The region's first distillery – one of the earliest in rural French Canada – was built in St Denis at some time between 1831 and 1836. Little is known about relations between employees and owners in these industrial enterprises. On the other hand, it is clear that sawmilling and gristmilling, the principal industrial undertakings in the eighteenth century at least, were subject to the banalité entailing, in some cases, a real seigneurial monopoly or, in others, a seigneurial appropriation of a share of the profits.

In the early period, wood and tar were important non-agricultural products of the Richelieu valley used to supply the shipyards at Quebec and, to some extent, at Sorel itself. Close to supplies of raw materials, with ready access to the St Lawrence, but protected from the ice floes of that river, Sorel was well situated for the construction of small river boats as well as larger craft. Ships were built here under the French régime, beginning as early as 1730 and including one vessel of 192 tons made for export to the West Indies.[8] A real boom in local ship-building occurred later, in the 1790s. Isaac Weld visited Sorel then and declared: 'The chief business carried on here is that of shipbuilding; there are several vessels annually launched from fifty to two hundred tons burthen; these are floated down to Quebec, and there rigged.'[9] The records of a local notary show that vessels of various sorts were built at this time, from small bateaux to schooners, brigs, and even a 250-ton square-stern ship.[10] Sorel's shipbuilding industry declined in the last years of the eighteenth century, although there were attempts to revive it early in the nineteenth.

The most striking characteristic of Sorel's shipbuilding industry before 1840 is that it seems to have been carried on largely without the participation of the local (permanent) population. Among the financial backers who can be identified, those from the French régime lived in Quebec and those from the later periods were all Englishmen or Loyalists. Many of the capitalists of the late eighteenth century apparently left the town when the boom of the 1790s came to an end; certainly Moses Hart, one of the most active financiers, followed this course. The skilled workmen from this period also seem to have been newcomers or transients. Many, like George Lane, were obviously English or American. Others (perhaps half) had French names but none of them are recognizable as belonging to Sorel families. Most likely these shipwrights came from the shipyards of Quebec City. Lower Richelieu habitants may have worked as casual labourers in the shipyards of Sorel, but if so no trace of this has been found in the historical records.

The fortunes of the town of William Henry (Sorel) mirror those of the local shipbuilding industry with its spectacular growth followed by an equally rapid decline. The seigneurie of Sorel was purchased by the crown during the American Revolution for military-strategic reasons and, at the end of the war, Governor Frederick Haldimand founded a town on the site of the old 'fort de Sorel' to accommodate some of the thousands of Loyalist refugees who had flocked to the area during the conflict. The town, soon known as William Henry, was an artificial creation, established almost overnight by the decree of a central authority. It was laid out on an ambitious plan with straight, wide streets and a large central square. Haldimand was confident that its situation, at the confluence of the St Lawrence and the Richelieu, would soon make it a thriving commercial centre.

For it is observable numbers are aiming at possessions on that spot, the great advantages of which are now conspicuous to everybody, particularly that of affording a secure wintering place for all vessels who can cross Lake St Peter, where there is 16 Feet of water in the Spring and 11 or 12 in the autumn, an advantage not to be found in equal perfection in any part of the River St Lawrence.[11]

For a decade or so, William Henry did indeed prosper. Its shipyards were busy in the 1790s. There was also the military establishment and an 'asylum' for destitute veterans of the Revolutionary War which helped to support a number of merchants and artisans. The influx of population and the very process of building the town probably accounted to a large degree for its initial spurt of economic activity. The prosperity was short-lived, however. According to one prominent resident, Christopher Carter, there were only seventy-five houses on the town's 180 lots in 1798 and fourteen of these were empty. His view of the situation was quite gloomy:

Many of the original proprietors that found from experience that they could not support their Families in the place sold their property, and moved to different parts of the World, by which some persons are become possessed of a number of Lots and most of the buildings are upon the Lots so purchased, about twenty families have left the place within these two years past ... It is certain that business is as dull in the place as in any Country parish in Canada – There are only three or four denominations of persons that can make a living, and they would have a difficulty of doing it were they restricted by Law from taking undue advantages of the public. There was a time when there was a considerable number of Troops and Invalid Loyalists in the place which added something to the Trading part of the Community, but that support is now much diminished, the prospect of Shipbuilding has also failed and indeed every prospect of the place seems to vanish.

The land in and near Sorel is in general very poor so that nothing can be expected from it in bringing forward the place, that it is a general saying among the people that if they could sell their Buildings for one half of what they cost them they would leave the place ...

It is the Halfpay Officers, Pensioners and persons employed in Government service that give a miserable support to the few miserable Inhabitants ...[12]

Two factors help to explain William Henry's turn-of-the-century crisis. First, there was the problem of seigneurial tenure which aroused the hostility of some of the business-minded Loyalists. For many years, there was confusion and misunderstanding about the tenure under which land would be held in the new town but, when it became clear that the government (as seigneur) would demand the customary feudal dues, there were angry meetings, petitions, and an exodus of people and capital. 'We beg leave to assure your Excellency, that if the cens et rents and lods et vents, etc. be enforced upon us, it will prevent many valuable members of society from settling among us, and in the end reduce the present flourishing Borough of William Henry to an obscure and ordinary Canadian village.'[13] Colonial officials felt unable to grant land on terms different from those applying to other lands in the seigneurie of Sorel, but the Loyalists responded that 'every seignior may dispose of his Property as he pleases.' Thus, ironically, the English tradition of landlord-as-proprietor was invoked in the interests of tenants! The English-speaking burghers of William Henry adamantly refused to accept seigneurial deeds for their lands and eventually many of them left the town. They left, not only because of the land tenure question, but also because of economic difficulties unconnected with seigneurial exactions.

In the context of pre-industrial Lower Canada in the early nineteenth century, William Henry's location was a poor one. It was not a natural terminus for the fur or timber trades and it was not at the centre of a prosperous farming region as, for example, St Denis was. The rural section of Sorel was not only infertile, as Christopher Carter observed, it was also home to a burgeoning semi-proletariat increasingly impoverished as a result of its connection with the Northwest Company. As such, it was badly suited for supplying urban food needs and, more important, it constituted a poor market for William Henry's wares and an unattractive outlet for investment. Thus the 'capitalist underdevelopment' of the Sorel countryside had an adverse effect on the town at the mouth of the Richelieu.

William Henry's fortunes only revived in the 1820s when it became part of a transportation network that freed it from any need to rely on rural Sorel. With the advent of steam navigation on the St Lawrence, the town emerged as an important fueling and maintenance depot on the route between Montreal and Quebec. Large numbers of immigrants from Britain were soon passing through the town and many of them landed there to begin the overland journey to the Eastern Townships. Governor Dalhousie, who spent his summers here between 1820 and 1827, observed with pleasure the construction of a number of houses and wharves; he was somewhat less enthusiastic the day his Sunday rest was disturbed by the arrival of 400 Irish immigrants who, transborded from their ship to a riverboat at Quebec, touched dry land for the first time at William Henry and ran about 'hooping, hollowing, jumping and frisking.'[14] Once again the boom was short-lived. A certain amount of shipbuilding and maintenance kept the town going but, in the second half of the nineteenth century, William Henry (once again called Sorel) experienced sluggish economic and demographic growth.[15]

The point about urban-industrial development in the Lower Richelieu is that it was neither extensive nor lasting in its effects. St Denis and St Ours developed as minor commercial centres with the growth of the Richelieu grain trade in the second half of the eighteenth century. Tied as they were to the agricultural economy, these two towns experienced stagnation and relative decline after the 1830s when the region ceased to be a major exporter of wheat. William Henry began life with much fanfare and extravagant ambitions but its growth was even more uncertain and disappointing than that of the other two towns. An exotic plant grafted onto the Lower Richelieu landscape, it was initially peopled by foreigners and experienced a brief but artificial prosperity before sinking back into mediocrity in the nineteenth century. Its periods of prosperity were connected to its shipbuilding industry and to its role as a staging point for immigrants, two activities that had almost no connection to the habitant world of rural Sorel. The industrial and urban growth of St Ours and St Denis, on the other hand, grew out of the region's agricultural development. This was not 'self-sustaining growth,' however, nor was it development that was capable of transforming the socio-economic structures of the surrounding countryside. The towns of Sorel, St Ours, and St Denis, like the merchants who inhabited them, flourished in the feudal Lower Richelieu without disturbing the existing order of things. Meanwhile, in the surrounding countryside, self-sufficiency remained the basic rule.

A COMMERCIAL ECONOMY?

The expansion of population and the development of the grain trade fostered a degree of urban-industrial growth, but agriculture remained central to the Lower Richelieu economy in the early nineteenth century. Obviously there would have been no export of wheat unless peasants grew amounts in excess of their own needs and of the feudal dues they had to pay. Merchants like Samuel Jacobs had made it their business to attach habitants to the international market by getting them in the habit of buying a certain amount of imported merchandise. The result was that, in places like St Denis, grain to pay the merchant took its place beside grain to pay the seigneur and the priest and grain for subsistence as a necessary part of the annual production of habitant families. What was the impact of this connection to the market on the region's agrarian economy? We have already seen that the most important trader of the eighteenth-century Lower Richelieu had no particular interest in altering the existing economic, social, and, technical order but, could it be that, regardless of Samuel Jacobs' outlook or intentions, the transforming powers of the market-place changed Quebec's agriculture?

This is certainly what followers of Adam Smith would expect. It will be recalled that, for Smith, productivity and opulence are primarily the result of division of labour, but specialization is limited always by 'the extent of the market.' Trade therefore plays the vital role of unleashing the innate human 'propensity to truck, barter, and exchange,' thus permitting people to supply their needs through purchases while directing their efforts towards production for sale. 'Every man thus lives by exchanging, or becomes in some measure a merchant, and the society itself grows to be what is properly a commercial society.'[16] One of the criticisms frequently levelled at this aspect of Adam Smith's theory is that it presupposes a capitalist society in which labour is 'free' and mobile and land a purchasable commodity, so that 'factors of production' can be marshalled in response to market demand.[17] The Smithian interpretation, stressing the revolutionary effects of expanding commerce is nevertheless at the root of much contemporary scholarship in the economic history of Lower Canada. For some, the surge of imports and exports at the beginning of the nineteenth century ushered in a full-blown 'market economy' and constituted the decisive step in the direction of a

'modern' economic order.[18] Another interpretation speaks of the 'commercialization of agriculture' in the late eighteenth century, a movement
that did not lead, as it 'should' have, to a real 'commercial society'
because of the stubborn traditionalism of a bewildered French-Canadian
peasantry; it was followed in the early nineteenth century by a retreat
from the market.[19] Within the parameters of this trade-centred approach,
there has been much heated debate over the chronology of commercialization, over its extent and over the economic 'rationality' of the
habitants, but there is a common tendency to view the subject from
Adam Smith's perspective.[20] All parties in the discussion seem to accept
the notion that 'the silent and insensible operation of foreign commerce'
should (barring pathological reactions) bring market orientation and
specialized production; they also agree that the grain trade resulted in
'commercialized agriculture' in rural Lower Canada, at least for a time.

This is not the place to discuss the theoretical presuppositions of the
Smithian model, but it is worth noting that empirical evidence from the
Lower Richelieu, a major centre of Canadian grain production, provides
no support to the claim that trade alone engenders specialization, market
production, or economic development. On the contrary, the rural economy of the region remained one essentially of household self-sufficiency,
with no fundamental change either late in the eighteenth century or
early in the nineteenth. As in earlier periods, habitant families produced
most of their own food and other necessities while turning over some
of their surplus produce as feudal rent and as payment for goods and
services they could not provide for themselves. The peasants of the
Richelieu were, of course, never allergic to economic transactions, nor
were they indifferent to money or to other forms of wealth; Samuel
Jacobs could certainly testify to their bargaining shrewdness! This is
perfectly normal after all; all peasants have some dealings with the market, as Daniel Thorner points out quite forcefully in his article on peasant
economy.

In a peasant economy the first concern of the productive units is to grow food
crops to feed themselves. But this cannot be their sole concern. By definition,
they live in a State and are linked with urban areas. They must willy-nilly sustain
the State, the towns, the local lords ... We should be careful not to slip into the
trap of imagining a 'pure' type of peasant household which consumes practically
everything it produces and practically nothing else, as distinct from an 'impure'
type which produces for a market as well as for its own immediate needs. The
latter is historically more common and more characteristic ...

We are sure to go astray if we try to conceive of peasant economies as exclusively 'subsistence' oriented and to suspect capitalism wherever the peasants show evidence of being 'market' oriented. It is much sounder to take it for granted, as a starting point, that for ages peasant economies have had a double orientation towards both. In this way, much fruitless discussion about the nature of so-called 'subsistence' economies can be avoided.[21]

And yet much of the discussion of the rural economy of Lower Canada does seem to rest on an implied equation of subsistence agriculture and complete autarchy, every habitant sale or purchase appearing as evidence of commercialization and emergent capitalism.[22] The discussion is fruitless in that it begins with a misconceived dichotomy, with 'pure' subsistence on one side and 'commercial agriculture' on the other, and no room in between for a typical peasant economy based on household self-sufficiency plus some production for sale. If we wish to categorize the economy of rural Quebec in the early nineteenth century, we should therefore abandon this radical polarity and ask instead whether there was, to use Karl Polanyi's terminology, a 'market economy' in which production was primarily for gain or whether the economy was dominated by 'production for use' with 'accessory production for the market.'[23]

Gilles Paquet and Jean-Pierre Wallot invoke Polanyi's model on several occasions, but they seem to be confused about the distinction between a market and a pre-market economy. In support of their argument that Lower Canada became a market economy at the beginning of the nineteenth century, they cite evidence that the habitants of that period sold produce, bought imported goods, and knew the value of money.[24] This may prove that rural Lower Canada did not adhere to a régime of strict autarchy, but that is not the issue. Habitant economic organization, with family production filling *most* family consumption needs, corresponds nicely to what Polanyi calls the 'principle of householding,' an arrangement characteristic of a pre-market economy. As if to cover the kind of transactions that Paquet and Wallot bring up, this author adds:

Accessory production for the market need not ... destroy the self-sufficiency of the household as long as the cash crop would also otherwise be raised on the farm for sustenance, as cattle or grain; the sale of surpluses need not destroy the basis of householding ... as long as markets and money were mere accessories to an otherwise self-sufficient household, the principle of production for use could operate.[25]

The available data on crops give no indication that Lower Richelieu habitants ever abandoned products intended for their own consumption in favour of crops grown primarily for sale. The emphasis in 1830 as in 1730 was on grain crops – wheat, peas, and oats – to feed humans and livestock and, if there was any left over once household need was met, for sale (see Appendix 6). The only significant change in the later period was the expansion of potato production, which took the place of grain, to some degree, in human diets and as animal feed. In feeding their families potatoes instead of bread, habitants were able to divert a larger proportion of their wheat crops to the merchant. This change was therefore a response of sorts to market opportunities, but it was one that brought a decline in one aspect of peasant living conditions; moreover, it entailed no abandonment of the traditional practice of satisfying family needs directly from the produce of the family farm. Overseas demand and rising prices in the late eighteenth century may well have prompted those habitants who could to plant more of the wheat they had always grown for bread and to cut down on home consumption in the interests of increased sales, but it did not make them turn to non-food crops such as hemp and flaxseed.[26] Products like these might have fetched high prices, but any habitant who concentrated on them ran the risk of going hungry if demand suddenly plummeted. The safety-first peasant economy therefore required that dependence on the market be avoided. In the 1790s and in the 1810s, as in the 1740s, harvests were first a source of food and only secondarily a commodity for sale.

Figures on farm animals show a similarly constant orientation toward use-value rather than any market-oriented specialization (see Appendix 5). On the whole, herds were small and quite uniform from one farm to the next. Whether one looks at the middle of the eighteenth century, the 1790s or the 1830s, one tends to find two horses, a pair of oxen, two to four cows, half a dozen sheep, and a few pigs. There were differences between Sorel and St Denis and there were some changes over the course of the century – for example, horses became more numerous as the habitants relied on them increasingly to take the place of oxen – but the basic rough uniformity remained unchanged. Obviously there was some variation in the size of herds, since some families were larger and some more prosperous than others, but there is no more evidence of large-scale stock-raising for the market in the later periods than in the earlier ones. Out of 110 estate inventories, none listed more than five horses, more than six oxen, or more than six cows. There were admittedly a few with large numbers of sheep and swine – four had more than twenty sheep and four had more than ten pigs – but these cases occurred in the mid-eighteenth century as well as in the 1830s. Again there is no real evidence of growing commercialization. Apart from a few enterprising sheep- and hog-raisers, the habitants of the Lower Richelieu seem always to have had herds whose size was determined, not by market considerations, but by domestic needs.

Evidence on habitant consumption patterns generally confirms this image of continuing household self-sufficiency in the early nineteenth century. Our source here is the deeds of gift in which parents set out the *pensions alimentaires* to be paid by the children to whom they ceded their farms. The list of supplies required annually by Paul Paquin and his wife is typical of those demanded by well-off St Denis habitants of the 1830s:[27]

15 minots wheat
1-1/2 minots white peas
150 pounds salt pork
12 pounds lard
40 pounds beef
3 *pots* rum
1 pound green tea
20 pounds [maple] sugar
12 pounds good candles
1/2 pound pepper
12 pounds good quality soap
8 dozen eggs
15 minots potatoes
150 onions
50 medium cabbages
20 pounds good quality smoking tobacco
1-1/2 minots salt
1 *pot* molasses
1 chopine vinegar
1 *pot* lamp-oil
15 cords firewood
3-1/2 yards good checked cloth, grey or black
1 pair cowhide moccasins
1 hat
1 pair squirrel or moosehide mittens
76 livres in place of handkerchief, collar, summer clothes, and a servant girl
use of a horse, a milk-cow, and a ewe

Like many deeds of gift from this period, the Paquins' contains a long and detailed list of supplies. Moreover, it includes several 'store-bought' items (rum, tea, salt, pepper, molasses, oil, cloth, hat, and possibly tobacco); there is even an annual money payment. All this suggests a more comfortable standard of living than what one finds reflected in most eighteenth-century *pensions alimentaires*, but it does not indicate any essential abandonment of the peasant economy of household self-sufficiency. All the basic elements of the food supply (such as wheat, potatoes, meat, vegetables, and eggs) are still home-grown and, to underline this, the document even specifies a schedule of delivery in line with the agricultural seasons (pork, 'dans le temps des boucheries d'automne'; wheat, part at Michelmas, part in February, and so on). The deeds of gift of poorer habitants generally mention the same range of domestically produced provisions, but without the exotic luxuries listed above.[28] Since the Paquins only purchased articles that their neighbours managed to do without, it would hardly be fair to say that the local peasantry was oriented toward or dependent upon the market in any fundamental way.

Estate inventories listing all the possessions of deceased habitants give no more evidence than the other sources of any turn-of-the-century rupture with the past. Houses described in inventories from the 1830s are, on the whole, slightly larger than those of earlier periods, but their design was essentially unchanged; pièce-sur-pièce log construction remained the rule until the second half of the nineteenth century. Inside the houses and barns, the furniture, utensils, and personal effects seem to be a little more plentiful and varied, but essentially similar to those described in the eighteenth century, with a continuing predominance of rough, home-made wooden furniture. Money may have been found in more of the habitant inventories from the nineteenth century, but this was only a quantitative change – 23 per cent still listed no money – and a geographically limited one (see Appendix 4). While St Ours and St Denis showed 'progress' in this regard, Sorel's habitants were less likely to have cash in the 1830s than in the eighteenth century. In the more agricultural parishes, many habitants were liable to accumulate a little bag of coins, at least temporarily, but does this mean that their economic life was ruled by money?

A superficial look at the notarial records by which habitants formalized land sales, leases, inheritance settlements, loans, and so on would indeed suggest that money was the medium of exchange for the habitants of the early nineteenth century. The historical documents of the period certainly speak the currency idiom of the market-place, but then so do the records of earlier centuries. In all the periods studied however, the language of livres and sols seems to mask an economic reality in which barter predominated. We have already seen that debts expressed in monetary terms were paid to merchants and seigneurs in goods and labour. An additional indication of the importance of barter exchanges comes from the household accounts that a St Ours notary left scribbled in the margins of his official records in the 1830s. The notary recorded his debts to various habitants for work and for supplies of hay, oats, and butter; payment for these debts was more often in bread, salt, pork, fish, and potatoes than in cash.[29]

In sum, there was no changeover in the Lower Richelieu to 'commercial agriculture' or to a 'market economy' at any time before 1840; hence there was no subsequent 'retreat from the market' either. Instead the structure of the agrarian economy remained basically stable despite the rise and fall of the export grain trade. This is really not a very startling conclusion when one takes into account the profound transformations that would have been required of a peasantry like that of early French Canada in order to make agricultural production respond to the needs of the market. Cultivators would need a secure food supply to assure them the flexibility to experiment and to specialize in the crops currently most profitable. They might require, for example, when stock-raising was indicated, extensive land holdings and substantial capital to compete successfully with the most efficient operations. Any large-scale farming enterprise would also require a wage-labour force. Furthermore, the ability to respond to changing market stimuli implies an agricultural entrepreneur with full control over the use of his land, control that was not normally possible under seigneurial tenure. In other words, an agrarian economy in which production for the market was dominant and not an accessory to subsistence, implies the prior reorganization of society along capitalist lines. This sort of transformation was beyond the powers of commerce unaided.

In the Adam Smith tradition, one might view the opening of markets for Lower-Canadian agricultural produce as an 'opportunity' to which habitants responded positively or negatively. One might argue that they took advantage of every possibility to enrich themselves and conclude that they were 'rational,' or one might suggest that, on the contrary, habitants neglected these opportunities because they were 'traditional.' The problem with this approach is that it takes too little notice of the complex social, economic, political and cultural web that narrowed the range of options open to the peasant. Instead, it presents the economic attitudes of the peasantry as the key to the success or failure of economic development. The habitants certainly had an outlook that might be described as 'traditional' – so too did merchants like Samuel Jacobs, for that matter – but their mentality should not be separated from other aspects of their historical situation and treated as an autonomous causal factor. Concentrating on the habitant mentality has the effect of emphasizing the supposed choices open to this class and of providing retrospectively a collective scapegoat for the problems of the Lower-Canadian economy. It should be noted, moreover, that there is nothing unusual in the Lower-Canadian habitants' inability and unwillingness to enter fully into a market economy. Peasants the world over have reacted in much the same way to 'opportunities for profit.'[30] There is no need therefore to invoke any specifically French-Canadian 'hardening of mentalities' to explain quite normal attitudes and behaviour.

If the grain trade did not make the habitants of the Lower Richelieu into 'profit maximizers,' did it at least make them better farmers? Even though they continued to produce primarily for home consumption, their need for a certain amount of 'store-bought' merchandise must have provided some incentive to seek a better return for the efforts they invested in cultivating the soil. Or were they indifferent husbandmen, as many scholars have argued, stubbornly rejecting technical improvements as their outmoded methods eventually led to disastrous agricultural failures?

AGRICULTURAL PRODUCTIVITY

Habitant agricultural practices of the first half of the nineteenth century have certainly had a bad press. In the St Lawrence valley as in other parts of North America, there were occasional critiques of the scandalously wasteful New World farming habits in earlier periods, but it is only after about 1800 that the historian encounters a deafening chorus of denunciation from visitors, journalists, officials, and businessmen concerned about the technical backwardness of French-Canadian agriculture. Ploughing was too shallow, it was claimed, fertilizer unknown, crop rotation was defective, and weeds choked the fields.[31] Since this same period saw the precipitous decline of the export trade in Lower Canadian wheat, it is tempting to adopt the perspective of these writers – naturally, none of them were habitants – and conclude that something had gone wrong with the province's agriculture. On the other hand, it may have been the perceptions and preoccupations of the observers that changed, rather than the agriculture they discussed. It so happens that the turn of the nineteenth century was a time when Canada had taken its place as a fairly important supplier of wheat to the British market, one that appeared all the more important to patriotic Englishmen in view of the wars with France. Moreover, in Lower Canada itself, the relative decline of the fur trade led merchants to take a greater interest in the productive potential of the rural areas of the province at about the same time. Was there an economic crisis then within the Quebec peasantry or was it the commercial bourgeoisie that entered the nineteenth century in bewilderment and disarray?

Apart from Sorel, where the intrusion of the Northwest Company made itself felt, the Lower Richelieu does not seem to have experienced an agricultural decline in the early nineteenth century. Farming methods improved slightly over those of earlier periods, although they did not change in any fundamental way. Some of these minor changes can be perceived in the descriptions of agricultural equipment found in habitant estate inventories. There are, for example, far more ploughs mentioned in the 1830s sample than in those of earlier periods; there was more than one plough per inventory in the last period, whereas 42 per cent of the mid-eighteenth-century inventories mentioned only parts of a plough or no plough at all. Moreover, 'English ploughs' make their first appearance in the 1830–9 sample; these were present in one-quarter of the habitant estates. Harrows too became much more common. Four-fifths of the nineteenth-century lists included them, but only a minority of the eighteenth-century inventories. Also, a majority of the harrows had iron teeth in the 1830s (fourteen out of twenty-three), whereas crude wooden pegs were the rule in the 1790s.

Farm leases give some indication of agricultural practices, or at least of the norms and ideals of a particular period. The majority of the surviving contracts are strictly habitant affairs, reflecting arrangements between peasants for the temporary rental of land, usually the property of orphaned children. Of interest here are the clauses by which the lessee agrees to take proper care of the farm. An impressionistic survey of a few dozen leases suggests that some of the charges levelled against French-Canadian agriculture were quite unfair. Lease after lease from the late eighteenth and early nineteenth centuries directs tenants to spread manure over the fields. Were these stipulations simply empty formulae inserted by zealous notaries? The detailed instructions in René Guertin's contract with Jacques Codère implies that they were not: 'sera tenu ledit preneur de charrier sur laditte terre tous les fumiers tant devant que dedans les batiments ...'[32] Now it is true that, given the relatively large fields and small herds of the Lower Richelieu, proper fertilizing of the entire arable was out of the question. Manure seems to have been limited mainly to gardens and potato patches and it would therefore have contributed little to the bounty of grain harvests. None the less, it does seem clear that habitants did not think of it as something to be dumped in the river.

Weeds were another common bugbear for habitants drawing up leases. Tenants commonly agreed to, 'cercler les mauvaises herbes dans le meilleur tems de manière à les empecher de produire leur graine ...'[33] Again, this stipulation seems to have represented more than a pious wish: one St Antoine peasant renting land to a neighbour insisted that the lessee destroy weeds on the farm, 'ainsi qu'il fait sur sa propre terre ...'[34] Other clauses dealt with the upkeep of roads, fences, and ditches.

All this suggests that habitant farming techniques were not as unenlightened in the early nineteenth century as some have claimed. They were essentially similar to those practised in the previous century, although in some respects there had been improvements by the 1830s. And yet, studies of the international grain trade clearly show that Lower Canada ceased, some time before 1840, to be a reliable exporter of wheat. Unable to grow a surplus except in exceptional years, the province became a net importer of grain during the first half of the century. According to Fernand Ouellet, the decline set in around 1803 and was due, partly to the onset of rural overpopulation and partly to a disastrous decline in crop yields caused in turn by bad farming methods which sapped the fertility of the soil.[35] This historian therefore characterizes the first four decades of the nineteenth century as a period of 'Agricultural Crisis,' during which agrarian malaise bred social and political tensions that culminated in the nationalist risings of 1837–8.

A major element of the Agricultural Crisis, it is claimed, was the precipitous decline in habitant wheat production but, in the Lower Richelieu, problems of this sort do not fit easily into Ouellet's chronology. In Sorel, wheat was relegated to the status of a secondary crop in the second half of the eighteenth century, just when Quebec agriculture was supposed to have been thriving. Up the Richelieu in St Denis, by contrast, wheat seems to have held its own until the 1830s when crops were ravaged by insect pests. Now there are indeed ways of looking at agricultural data that would give the impression that St Denis wheat production collapsed much earlier than 1830. One could calculate the proportion that wheat contributed to total harvest figures for different dates and the result would suggest a rapid drop in the early nineteenth

TABLE 30
Grain production per farm (in minots), Sorel and St Denis 1765 and 1831

	1765	1831
Sorel		
Farm households (owned and rented)	130	445
Grain sown	1669	
Grain harvested	9680*	57,423
Grain harvested per farm	74.5*	129.0
Wheat harvested	6453*	19,796
Wheat per farm	49.6*	44.5
St Denis		
Farm households (owned and rented)	50	261
Grain sown	1231	
Grain harvested	7140*	71,575
Grain harvested per farm	142.8*	274.2
Wheat harvested	4760*	35,803
Wheat per farm	95.2*	137.2

* Estimate

century. Tithe and census data reveal that wheat accounted for 75 per cent of the parish's crops in the early 1780s, but only 29 per cent in the mid-1820s and 2 per cent in 1844.[36] Figures of this sort give a misleading impression of the fortunes of wheat production however. Instead of reflecting simply the decline of wheat, these figures are indicative mainly of an increase in the production of oats and potatoes. These crops were grown in increasing quantities to feed the parish's growing populations of horses and pigs, besides contributing to the human diet as well. Moreover, the apparent decline of wheat is exaggerated by the use of volume measurements; a minot of potatoes is not comparable to a minot of wheat in nutritional value, in market price, or in the land and effort required to grow it.

A more straightforward way of gauging changes in agricultural production is through direct diachronic comparisons such as that outlined in Table 30.[37] Data from the censuses of 1765 and 1831 suggest that, on the average, farms in Sorel and St Denis produced more grain at the later date. Moreover, average wheat production also rose substantially in St Denis, though it fell slightly in the other parish. It is true that the crop recorded in the 1831 census was an exceptionally good one for the period, but the comparison is still a fair one as the production figures for 1765 were estimated from seeding statistics on the assumption of a good seed-yield ratio (1: 5.8). In calculating grain harvests in terms of farming households, these data have the advantage of isolating agricultural productivity from the effects of changing social structure. The approach which analyses per capita production for a given community tends to give distorted results where the effects of agricultural change are mixed with the effects of the growth of a non-agricultural population.

What about crop yields? Was there a decline in the early nineteenth century in the amount reaped for each minot of grain sown? Given the sources available for the Lower Richelieu and for Lower Canada generally, it is simply impossible to answer this question. The census of 1851 is the earliest one to provide statistics on both areas planted and volumes harvested. A few fragmentary figures for individual farms can be found for periods before that date and historians have fallen back on guesses and crude estimates. Fernand Ouellet tends to rely on the casual and contradictory estimates of contemporaries who testified before the Agriculture Committee of the Lower Canadian House of Assembly.[38] It is not clear, however, what the qualifications of these 'experts' were nor how wide their knowledge of the different regions of the province. David Anderson, the witness Ouellet seems to prefer, was actually quite vague:

The quantity of wheat per acre, produced in this province may be estimated at from 4 to 40 bushels [!] ... Some time ago I was led to believe that the average produce of wheat in Lower Canada, might be estimated about 10 or 11 bushels per acre. From further enquiries and observations however, I am convinced that it does not exceed 8 or 9.[39]

Ouellet's other main authority, William Mieklejohn, who appeared before the Assembly in 1823, based his estimate, not on personal experience, but on a bizarre series of manipulations of outdated statistics. Starting with figures from the 1784 census, Mieklejohn guessed at the changes the province had undergone in forty years ('I consider the Population now quadrupled, the encrease of bestial not doubled ...'). Combining this with guesses about Lower Canada's grain exports and the subsistence needs of the population, he calculated an overall grain yield of six minots to the acre.[40] Clearly the game here is 'Pick a number, any number.' Ouellet's choice is a wheat yield figure of ten to twelve minots to the arpent, which is probably as good a guess as any, corresponding as it does to seventeenth-century crop yields.[41] What is most disconcerting about Ouellet's procedure is the fact that he inexplicably assigns this figure, not to the period when the 'evidence' upon which it is based was collected, but to the second half of the eighteenth century, long before Anderson and Mieklejohn ever set foot in Canada! If these two witnesses could be relied upon and if the ten to twelve minots per arpent figure accurately summarizes their testimony, then the conclusion would seem to follow that wheat yields remained stable from the early settlement of New France until 1816 or 1823. Such an interpretation is certainly at odds with Fernand Ouellet's chronology of agrarian crisis, but then it rests on the same defective foundations as Ouellet's own observations. Really the only safe conclusion is that crop yields for the period before 1851 are unknown and unknowable with the evidence presently available.

All this seems to cast doubt on the idea that there was an agricultural catastrophe early in the nineteenth century. This is not to deny that there were years of crop failure after 1800 – in 1806 for example – but these were essentially similar to earlier failures, and indeed less severe than the worst of the eighteenth-century disettes. Nor is it to question the gradual decline of wheat production indicated by tithe figures for a number of Lower Canadian parishes in the decades before 1830.[42] However, in all this there is no evidence of any dramatic or decisive change deserving the term 'crisis.' Neither is there any indication that soil exhaustion or poor farming techniques played a role.

If there was a wheat crisis in agricultural communities like St Denis, it occurred in the 1830s, just when an earlier generation of historians dated it.[43] In this decade, wheat crops really did fail, and not just occasionally, but year after year. The cause of this collapse seems to have been insect pests: the same wheat midge that devastated neighbouring New England caused severe damage to Richelieu crops in 1834, 1835, 1836, and 1839, destroying vast quantities of wheat and other grains. We see this reflected in a dispute in 1839 between a St Denis sharecropper and his landlady, disappointed with her portion of the annual produce and evidently suspecting fraud. Witnesses were called on and one of them testified that he had worked the land in question from 1836 to 1838, harvesting only pitiful amounts of damaged grain, 'depuis plusieurs années vu le fléau.' Sowing nine minots of wheat, eight minots of peas, and twelve minots of oats, the former tenant had reaped only twenty-two, eighteen, and sixty-four minots of the respective crops. This implies a seed-yield ratio of only 1: 2.4 for wheat, 1: 2.2 for peas, and 1: 5.3 for oats.[44] The accounts of another St Denis farm rented on a sharecropping arrangement point to similar difficulties with grain crops after 1833 (see Table 31). Revenues for this farm – and probably for many

TABLE 31
Revenues of a St Denis farm 1831–7

	1831	1832	1833	1834	1835	1836	1837
Wheat (vol. in minots)	36	56	19	—	10	16	4
Wheat (value in livres)	229.5	229.5	114	—	67.5	96	28
Peas (vol. in minots)	22	22	4	1	4	2.5	—
Peas (value in livres)	99	99	13	4	24	20	—
Oats (vol. in minots)	98.5	59.5	140	42	20	—	14
Oats (value in livres)	256	149	280	50	36	—	28
Barley (vol. in minots)	24	—	—	—	20	10	6
Barley (value in livres)	75.5	—	—	—	60	36	24
Hay (bales)	225	250	50	175	160	100	100
Hay (value in livres)	78	84	9	52.5	18	31.5	24
Butter and eggs (livres)	—	—	—	4	16	18	—
Wool (livres)	—	—	—	32	12	—	—
Total value (livres)	738	561.5	416	143	235.5	201.5	104

other farms in the region – were partially saved only by increased sales of butter, poultry, wool, and livestock.[45]

For all of its difficulties, the agricultural economy of the Richelieu did not collapse completely in the 1830s. Even during the worst years of infestation, there is no indication that land-owning habitants went hungry; most likely they relied more heavily than previously on potatoes and other non-cereal foodstuffs. There are even signs of continuing prosperity in this decade. St Ours and St Denis were still exporting substantial quantities of wheat just before the wheat midge struck. A Montreal businessman later recalled his early activities in the Richelieu grain trade at this time.

The crops of wheat over all the flat country between Laprairie and St John's and down the valley of the Chambly [ie, Richelieu] river on both sides, were at that time very large. The country merchants in the different villages bought it up from the *habitants* during the winter with money furnished by the merchants in Montreal, who sent barges up the Chambly river in the spring for it. I was generally sent over in the month of April to ship the lots purchased by Mr Miller ... There were other operators besides Mr Miller, but in each of the years 1831 and 1832 I shipped for him alone about 100,000 bushels of wheat out of the Chambly River and 50,000 from the villages on the north shore.[46]

Even during this disastrous decade, the farmers of St Denis present every appearance of relative prosperity. Their revenues may have been failing, but the habitants covered by our estate inventory sample for the 1830s had nevertheless accumulated possessions and credits that gave them an average net worth that was much higher than the group from the 1790s, even when monetary values are deflated to offset the effects of rising prices (see Table 30).[47] This finding certainly seems to be at odds with the crisis interpretation of early nineteenth-century agriculture. Does this mean that the period was a prosperous one for the rural masses of the Lower Richelieu? Not quite. The collection of 'habitant' inventories includes only land-owning agriculturalists and, although these families were apparently better off than their eighteenth-century ancestors, they were no longer the only sizeable class in the region by the 1830s. The fur trade had helped produce a semi-proletariat in Sorel that had indeed experienced impoverishment, as the inventory sample indicates. Moreover, as we shall see below, the lands of St Denis could not provide for all the sons and daughters of its rich peasantry.

There was dislocation and impoverishment in the Lower Richelieu in the early decades of the nineteenth century, but there was hardly an *agricultural* crisis. Population pressure and the intrusions of capital introduced tensions and changes in the structure of society, but agriculture, that is, the way in which the soil was cultivated and the resulting fruits of that effort, was not at issue. The equipment and techniques of farming seem to have changed little, except for some marginal improvements in the early nineteenth century. In St Denis, grain production per farm remained relatively high in this period, plummeting only with the arrival of the wheat midge in 1833. Habitant standards of living were also relatively comfortable. The term 'relatively' is used advisedly since the quarrel here is only with the notion of an agricultural downturn, not with the perfectly justified proposition that, organized differently, the region's agriculture could have been more productive.

French-Canadian agriculture was clearly less productive and less technically advanced than that of northwestern Europe, both in the first half of the nineteenth century and in earlier periods.[48] In England particularly, capitalist agriculture made an early appearance, with large tracts of land worked by wage labour under the direction of farmer-entrepreneurs producing primarily for the market and with a high degree of efficiency. The Lower-Canadian bourgeoisie often seemed to have had in mind such an arrangement when they criticized the peasant agriculture of their province. For example, one expert witness testifying before the agriculture committee of the House of Assembly in 1816 suggested as the ideal system of cultivation a ten-course crop rotation scheme suitable for a 750-acre farm with fifteen workers, twenty-five horses, eleven ploughs, and so on.[49] Lord Dalhousie, the governor of Lower Canada, was another gentleman-farmer who hoped to improve the colony's agricultural performance by demonstrating to the 'ignorant habitants' the value of enlightened farming methods. When Dalhousie spent his summers at Sorel in the 1820s, he had the use of the seigneurial demesne there. He began with what he called a 'little flock of sheep' (consisting of 120 animals!) but he also attempted to grow wheat using tried and true English techniques. The grain crop, unfortunately, was completely ruined by the dry summer and the governor, who did not depend on it for his daily bread, nevertheless considered this a worthwhile experiment and concentrated for the future on livestock.[50]

Obviously a habitant family could not afford to experiment in this way with crops it needed for food, nor could it procure the land, capital, and labour needed for some of the more elaborate systems of cultivation. The habitants of the Lower Richelieu were not stubbornly opposed to all change, as their adoption of improved ploughs and harrows in the early nineteenth century proves, but they could hardly be expected to adopt more drastic changes requiring the liquidation of their way of life. Except within a narrow range, technical improvement, like market orientation, required a drastic reorganization of the social order. This is why the efforts of the agricultural societies to 'educate' the habitants about the virtues of turnips and marling were so futile. It was not information that was lacking so much as a different configuration of society, one that permitted one section of society freely to marshal the human and physical factors of production in the interests of optimum efficiency and one that gave the spur to technical innovation through the discipline of the competitive market. To duplicate the achievements of English agriculture, the basic self-sufficiency of the peasant household would have to be broken, as it had been in Britain, and a capitalist class structure of entrepreneurs and workers established in its place.[51] The pressures of commercial and demographic expansion were in fact producing a growing landless element within the Lower Richelieu habitant community of the early nineteenth century. Did the gradual emergence of this proletariat herald the advent of agrarian capitalism?

DIVISIONS WITHIN THE PEASANTRY?

We have already seen that, whereas once the Lower Richelieu was inhabited almost exclusively by land-owning peasants, population growth and the grain trade tended to produce, by the late eighteenth century, some substantial non-agricultural classes. Artisans, merchants, and 'professionals' generally lived in the small towns that grew up along the edge of the river in this period, but, even out in the countryside and within the agrarian mass, social cleavages began to appear. In the early nineteenth century there were rich habitants and poor ones; there were some who owned land, some who rented it, and others who, lacking land entirely, could only eke out a precarious living by selling their own labour. This differentiation might at first suggest the emergence of classes within the peasantry and an agrarian capitalism with property owners enriching themselves by exploiting rural proletarians. However, a closer look at evolving social structures reveals that these divisions were still quite limited. There were obstacles to the accumulation of capital that precluded the development of any radical distinction between owners and workers. Thus the economic equality of the Richelieu peasantry was threatened in the early nineteenth century, but it was not destroyed.

Even though their data are quite inconsistent, the censuses of 1765 and 1831 give some indication of the process of social differentiation that took place in sixty-six years. Whereas land-owning peasants were apparently at the head of 87 per cent of the region's households in 1765, they accounted for only about half the households in the Lower Richelieu by the later date (see Table 29). Even outside the little towns of St Denis, St Ours, and William Henry, there were large numbers of families who could not support themselves from the produce of their own farms. The process of differentiation was furthest advanced in St Denis, the parish most strongly affected by the wheat trade and the one least touched by the Northwest Company. In the strictly rural portion of this parish, less than half the heads of household (48 per cent) were peasant proprietors. What about the other rural folk of St Denis? A few were retired farmers ('donateurs') and others were artisans, millers, schoolteachers, and the like who happened to live outside the town. More significant are the genuinely agrarian groups lacking land: the tenant-farmers and day-labourers who constituted 14 and 24 per cent respectively of the rural householders of the parish.

Tenant-farmers were probably more numerous in St Denis in 1831 than they had been in the eighteenth century, although this cannot be established with any certainty. Most were share-croppers who turned over half their annual harvest in rent along with, in most cases, a certain quantity of eggs and butter and a portion of the proceeds of any sale of livestock. The rate of rent and other particulars were normally set out in a notarized lease which gave the tenant tenure for a specified period, often as short as one year. This sort of arrangement was quite onerous for the tenant but, on the other hand, it does not seem to have been very profitable for the owner; consequently, Lower Richelieu farms did not attract a great many urban investors anxious to become capitalist landlords. A search through the files of one St Denis notary between 1832 and 1839 unearthed eighteen farm leases.[52] Four of these involved farms owned by a local shopkeeper, Joseph Thibodeau, and one belonged to a man who styled himself 'bourgeois of St Denis.' The other properties belonged to eight habitants, two artisans, and two 'widows.' Most likely the lands of the habitants and widows were rented temporarily as part of an inheritance settlement. Far from representing any fundamental departure from the norm of peasant proprietorship, these arrangements were probably part of a traditional mechanism for supporting young orphans until they were old enough to take charge of the family farm. There were indeed 'capitalist landlords' like Joseph Thibodeau and Samuel Jacobs in the last years of his life but, if this sample of leases is any indication, they owned less than half the rented land in St Denis.

More numerous than tenant-farmers were the day labourers of St Denis. There had always been some rural proletarians in the region, but in the eighteenth century, they seem to have been mainly young people who would later obtain a farm of their own. By the 1830s, however, wage labour was becoming for some a permanent way of life and not just an episode in the life cycle. Marie Mercure and her husband, Pierre Fortier, are an example of a labouring family that never achieved the independence that comes with possessing a farm. Pierre's parents had been peasant proprietors, living in St Denis at a time when land was more readily available. Nevertheless, his mother had been reduced to a state of indigence after the death of her husband and Pierre and three of his brothers agreed in 1808 to support the widow with supplies of wheat and firewood. Marie Mercure seems also to have come from an habitant background, but a rather more comfortable one than Pierre for, when they married in 1811, she brought to the marriage comunity 1200 livres inherited from her father. Our next glimpse of this couple is twenty years later when the census lists Pierre as a 'journalier.' He and Marie by this time had three children; they owned no house – though they did have a cow – and presumably lived in rented lodgings in the town of St Denis. It was just after the census of 1831 that the family managed to acquire their own home, a rather run-down cabin in the town. The purchase price was lent to them by a local blacksmith and friend; they were only able to pay off this debt when Marie's mother, who apparently lived with them, came to the rescue. Marie Mercure died in 1839, leaving her husband with four children and rather dismal economic prospects. The estate inventory drawn up that year shows a crushing burden of debt: 899 livres against assets of 201 livres. The little house was sold (for a mere 112 livres), as were all the moveable possessions, to pay a small part of the debt. Land and house aside, the family's wealth was evaluated at 89 livres in all, about one-fifteenth the average moveable wealth of St Denis habitants of this period. Gone now was the cow mentioned eight years earlier. There were a few pots and dishes, a wooden table and some chairs, a feather bed, a spinning wheel, some other small household items, and one characteristically Lower-Canadian luxury, a cast-iron stove. This was little enough but, with the settling of the estate and of its debts, it was all gone, leaving Pierre Fortier and his children completely indigent; likely they found shelter with the widower's in-laws for one of his daughters was married at St Denis two years later.[53] A sizeable portion of the population of the parish shared the miserable and precarious existence of the Fortiers in the first half of the nineteenth century, but an even larger group, the land-owning habitants, were much better off.

Even in the bad years of the 1830s many habitant families, including that of the local militia captain, Jean-Baptiste Lussier, were indeed quite comfortable. No estate inventory could be found for Lussier and his wife, Marie-Joseph Gaudet, but, even if one were located, it would not tell the full story of the couple's wealth, which expanded and contracted over the years as they acquired land and reallocated it to grown-up children. Jean-Baptiste was sixty-seven years old, a grandfather just on the point of retiring, at the time of the 1831 census. His farm then was in the best part of St Denis and, though not a particularly large property (eighty-one arpents), it produced 250 minots of wheat as well as other grains and 200 minots of potatoes that year and was well stocked with seventeen head of cattle, four horses, fifteen sheep, and four pigs. Since this land was entirely under the plough, a small lot in the gravelly section of St Ours supplied the household with firewood. By this time, however, the Lussiers had already provided farms for two of their sons, though there were still seven more children at home. Their large family of five sons and four daughters was, to an important extent, the source of the Lussiers' wealth, as well as the motive spurring them to accumulate property.

Jean-Baptiste and Marie-Joseph were married in 1792. They began life with some advantages that the Fortiers never enjoyed, but they clearly owed their success to hard work as well. Where they lived and what they did in the first nineteen years of their marriage is unknown – they may have been labourers or, more likely, they had a farm in a remote section of the region – but their opportunity came in 1811 when Jean-Baptiste's parents decided to retire and cede the family farm to them. The property was quite small, only fifty arpents, but it was on the ruisseau Amiot (second *rang*), probably the richest soil in the Lower Richelieu. The senior Lussiers had qualms about giving their farm to only one of their seven children, but they explained their reasons in the deed of gift:

Lesquels se trouvant dans un âge avancé qui les rendroit incapables de faire valoir par euxmême le peu de biens qui leur reste, Désireroient partager entre leur sept enfans le seul lopin de terre qui leur resteroit, mais considérant combien il est désavantageuse et préjudiciable de sous diviser en tant de part un si petit terrain et ayant convenu avec Jean Bte Lussier un de leur enfans de lui faire cession en entier dudit lopin, à la charge pour lui de remettre une certaine somme pour ses frères et soeurs pour leur tenir lieu de leur part et portion dans le susdit lopin ...[54]

This 'gift' (really a sale) required of the junior Lussiers annual payments of 150 livres to the parents in place of the usual *pension alimentaire*, plus a lump sum of 1800 livres to be distributed to the non-inheriting brothers and sisters. The 1800 livres were loaned by a local merchant at 6 per cent interest and the Lussiers managed to repay the debt within three years.

Making good use of this base and of the strong arms of their teen-age sons, Jean-Baptiste and Marie-Joseph apparently sold a good deal of grain and soon they were able to expand their holdings. In 1817 they purchased a large farm of 160 arpents in the third *rang*, directly behind their land. The price was 8000 livres and this was paid, with interest, over the course of ten years. Most of that sum was secured when the Lussiers sold two small sections of their original farm to a local hat-maker (the property may have been located close to the town and therefore coveted for urban overflow). Not content with real estate specula-tion, Jean-Baptiste even dabbled in finance, paying 450 livres to an impatient St Ours habitant for the right to collect a debt for twice that amount to be paid five years later.[55] These are quite considerable sums of money and the Lussiers' activities sound rather entrepreneurial for peasants living in an essentially feudal society.

It would be a mistake to view Lussier as an agrarian capitalist, however. No doubt he employed day labourers for occasional tasks such as harvesting, but the 1831 census shows that there were no hired hands living in his house. Why should he throw away good money on wages, after all, with nine children, most of them fully grown? The efforts of all the Lussiers were aimed first at satisfying family needs directly by growing potatoes, wheat, peas, and oats, by caring for horses, cows, and pigs, by weaving, knitting, cooking, and gardening. Family labour to provide for family subsistence: the basic rule of the peasant economy applied to the rich Lussiers just as much as it did to the poor Allaires of an earlier generation. And yet, the former clearly strove, with some success, to produce more than they needed in order to sell wheat and other marketable commodities to make as much money as possible. That Jean-Baptiste and his family were hard-working, enterprising, and acquisitive there can be little doubt, but they were still peasants, as evidenced not only by their reliance on family labour and by their self-sufficiency, but also by the use to which they put their accumulated property. Jean-Baptiste and Marie-Joseph did not use their wealth to live in luxury; they did not invest in non-agricultural enterprises; nor did they attempt to found a dynasty by passing on their gains intact to one son or daughter. Instead, they divided up their little empire and they did so in order to 'establish' as many of their children as possible with the means to support a family in modest habitant style.

In 1825 they divided the big lot they had purchased in the third *rang* into two medium-sized farms of eighty arpents each and gave them by deeds of gift to two of their sons, Florentin and Pierre. Florentin had already been married for six years by this time and so it seems likely that the transaction merely formalized his occupation of the land. The two contracts were virtually identical and they stipulated burdens for the brothers that were so onerous as to make the term 'donation' seem rather ironical. Each was to turn over to his parents twenty minots of wheat, five minots of peas, five minots of oats, and five cords of firewood every January for the rest of their lives. This was a normal enough *pension alimentaire*, though somewhat redundant when the older Lussiers still had a farm of their own to provide their subsistence. In addition to the annual supply of produce however, Jean-Baptiste and his wife demanded a payment of 1000 livres to be paid in five yearly instalments of 200 livres. Florentin and Pierre in fact found these terms impossible to fulfil and their parents finally agreed after six years to revise them, eliminating the cash requirement and cutting the wheat supply by half. In return for these concessions, however, they did require larger annual tributes in peas and oats as well as an undertaking to pay for masses after the deaths of the mother and father. At the same time (1831), the old Lussiers settled on arrangements to turn over their original farm on the Amiot to a third son, Jean-Baptiste fils. Though he acquired the choicest property, along with the house, furniture, livestock, and agricultural implements, young Jean-Baptiste also had to shoulder an even heavier burden than his brothers. By the terms of the deed of gift, he had to pay his parents' debts and allow them to live with him; furthermore, he owed them very substantial quantities of peas, oats, hay, salt pork, beef, tallow, tea, salt, pepper, maple sugar, soap, West India rum, wine, eggs, chickens, and firewood.[56]

By these three deeds of 'gift,' Jean-Baptiste senior and Marie-Joseph provided farms for three of their sons, enabling each to support a family, though only through hard work and self-denial, given the heavy tributes they would have to turn over for an unknown number of years. In the process, the old folks assured themselves of a legal claim to revenues that would leave them wanting for nothing in their declining years. Their six non-inheriting children were not forgotten, however. While they were at the notary's arranging the deeds of gift in 1831, Jean-Baptiste and Marie-Joseph also had separate but identical wills drawn up to which they affixed their marks.[57] To each of their two younger sons they left a horse and a pair of oxen as well as half the St Ours woodlot. The five daughters who were still at home were to receive, when they married, the same household items (probably a cow, a spinning wheel, and a bed at a minimum) that their married sisters had already been given. Five other boys were named in the wills – they may have been grandsons – and they were to have any property that remained, though this would not have amounted to much.

We have already noted the tendency for habitant inheritance settlements to become less and less egalitarian and increasingly dominated by parents as one moves from the early eighteenth century to the nineteenth (see above, p 80). The Lussier family is a good illustration of the culmination of that development. Instead of leaving the distribution of property for a legally constituted 'family council' to handle after they died, Jean-Baptiste and Marie-Joseph took steps to allocate land and other wealth while they were still alive. Like many of their contemporaries, they even went so far as to draw up a will – something that would not have occurred to earlier generations of peasants – to assign the little that was left to them according to their own lights. Nowhere in the legal documents is there any indication that the family as a whole was given the opportunity to ratify these proceedings as they often did in the eighteenth century. Towards the three sons who were their principle heirs the Lussiers were quite exacting, demanding more than ample supplies of foodstuffs, money, and even personal services. There was favouritism too in this estate settlement; some of the children were given prosperous farms while others got next to nothing, in defiance of the concept of légitime, so important to the Custom of Paris. The inequality is more pronounced in the inheritance schemes of poorer habitants in this period: commonly everything was given by deed of gift (confirmed in many cases by a will) to one child, leaving the rest to fend for themselves.

What lay behind the Lussiers' decision to impose on their family a particular plan for the devolution of their property? One preoccupation obviously was to safeguard their own standard of living in their old age, but this goal could have been served almost as well by a variety of arrangements involving either greater fragmentation or greater concentration of the land holdings. The actual distribution seems to have been dictated by less selfish concerns, much the same as those that actuated Paul Hue and Etienne Allaire a century earlier. Like those Richelieu pioneers who occupied large tracts in the hope that they could be divided up after their deaths into farms for their children, the Lussiers seemed intent on providing viable farms for as many of their offspring (or at least of their sons) as possible, without completely neglecting the others. More than three peasant families might conceivably have eked out a bare subsistence from the 240 arpents of good soil that constituted the Lussier estate, but life for a St Denis habitant in the 1830s required more than just a basic food supply. There were annual dues to be paid to priest and seigneur, as well as some necessary purchases from the general store. Thus, a 'viable farm' meant something fairly large. The Lussiers' dilemma was the same one faced by Jean-Baptiste's parents twenty years earlier: how to provide for their large brood while avoiding uneconomic subdivision. Their compromise was more satisfactory than the arrangement that most of their contemporaries had to face – preserving the viability of their farms by leaving everything to only one heir – and bore a resemblance to the settlements of an earlier period when vacant land was still available close at hand.

Contrary to what many historians suggest, the habitants of agricultural areas like St Denis were not so foolish as to destroy the basis of their way of life by subdividing their land excessively. However, they were moved by an egalitarian attitude that effectively counteracted any long-term accumulation of property, even if it did not produce perfectly partible inheritance settlements. As long as couples who, like the Lussiers, were fortunate and industrious enough to amass large holdings, redistributed their lands before they died, there was little likelihood of a peasant bourgeoisie emerging. Thus, in spite of the opportunities for enrichment offered by the grain trade, the St Denis peasantry preserved a high degree of economic homogeneity even in the 1830s. Figures on net worth taken from our sample of estate inventories of habitants from St Ours and St Denis give a 'coefficient of variation' – a measure of the degree to which data vary from their norms – of 178 per cent, 1830–9; 175 per cent, 1790–9; and 207 per cent, 1740–69. This implies that differences in wealth from one peasant family to the next was about the same in Lussier's day as it was in the 1790s and a bit less than it had been in the middle of the eighteenth century. The grain trade does not seem to have had the effect of widening the gap between rich and poor peasants; at least not among those who owned their own land.

This is not to deny that there were economic disparities within the habitant class. Data from a census or any other survey of land holdings or crop production at a particular point in time will always show considerable variations from one household to the next. Lenin was one of many scholars to conclude hastily that inequality in census-type listings betokens the emergence of rural capitalism. In *The Development of Capitalism in Russia*, he argues that there was a growing class division within the peasantry of late nineteenth-century Russia; a widening gulf separated rich and poor as the less fortunate were forced to turn over their land and sell their labour to a growing peasant bourgeoisie.[58] The problem with an analysis of this sort, it has been claimed, is that it ignores the 'developmental cycle' that is so important a feature of the rustic household economy.[59] Unlike the collection of estate inventories discussed above, which includes mainly mature couples, censuses list all households: the struggling newlyweds, the satisfied middle-aged families, and the old retired folks. Insofar as holdings increased and production expanded over the years – of course not all habitants were able to do this, despite the pressures of a growing family – a listing of this sort would reflect the different stages households had reached in their quest for more land as much as any incipient class cleavages. The history of the Lussier family illustrates the dangers of studying social structure on the basis of census figures on landholding. When the census-taker visited St Denis in the summer of 1831, he discovered that Jean-Baptiste and Marie-Joseph owned 111 arpents of land, eighty-one in their farm and another thirty in the St Ours woodlot. If the census had been taken three months later, after the couple had turned their farm over to Jean-Baptiste fils, they would have had thirty arpents listed in the land column. On the other hand, a census taken six years earlier would have attributed to them 271 arpents since they had not at that time formalized *donations* to any of their sons. Some habitants certainly prospered more than others but, among those who owned farms, there was not as much variation as census data seem to imply.

Of course not everyone living in the parish was a habitant-proprietor and the Fortiers are a case in point. If we were to consider all those born in St Denis in the early nineteenth century, those who left the village as well as those who stayed, then the number who, like the three Lussier sons, acquired their own farms, would likely appear as a fortunate minority. Since all the lands of St Denis had been occupied by the late eighteenth century and since there was a need to keep farms comparatively large, it was inevitable that many sons and daughters of local habitants would have to leave the parish or find some other way of earning a living at home. With territory limited, every gain for expansionists like the Lussiers was likely to mean a loss for another local family who might see all their children banished from the area. Emigration from long-settled regions was normal enough in all parts of pre-industrial North America and so there is no reason to consider this phenomenon as peculiarly French-Canadian or as evidence of a rural crisis. In any case, this was not nascent capitalism, the relative opulence of the land-owners supported and advanced by the wage labour of the dispossessed.

Despite the appearance of a fairly substantial rural proletariat in the early nineteenth century, this group does not seem to have played a central role in the agriculture of St Denis. As in earlier periods, there was no doubt a certain number of households that employed a 'servant' because of some 'abnormality' – no grown children or too many men and not enough women, or the reverse – that forced them to rely on the help of an outsider. Many other families would be glad to employ a hand for a few weeks at haying time or during the harvest. Otherwise, labourers likely found work in the small town, digging clay for a potter or unloading a boat for a merchant, and perhaps depending on charity from time to time. Although they took advantage of the availability of landless labourers on some occasions, the habitants did not generally need this help in order to exist as a class. However numerous they may have been, day labourers were therefore marginal in the local agrarian economy. Agriculture was still predominantly a family matter in St Denis; the formation of a fairly large class of landless workers, the inevitable result of a 'full' territory and an agrarian economy requiring both subsistence and surplus, did not work in the interests of the peasant proprietors to any significant degree as the latter were not really an employing class. Even in the 1830s, there were no real 'kulaks' in the Lower Richelieu, and it was just this relative equality that made rural French Canada appear so backward in the eyes of a perceptive – and thoroughly bourgeois – Englishman like Lord Durham.[60]

CONCLUSIONS

Between the middle of the eighteenth century and the 1830s there were a number of important changes in the society and economy of the Lower Richelieu. As a result of continuous and vigorous demographic growth and of the colonizing efforts of succeeding generations of habitants, all the territory in the region capable of growing crops had been cleared and occupied. The 'frontier stage' had ended locally and, as natural increase continued unabated, emigration and overcrowding made their appearance. By the early nineteenth century, it was no longer possible for the majority of young adults to acquire farms in their home parishes or in the immediate vicinity.

Another important change was the development of rural commerce over the course of the eighteenth century. Samuel Jacobs and other merchants helped to accustom local habitants to a certain number of imported goods, including alcoholic beverages. To pay for their purchases and to finance the reproduction process by which new farms were established for every generation of peasants, habitants did their best to raise some grain for sale. This meant growing surplus wheat in addition to what was needed for family subsistence and for clerical and seigneurial exactions. Not all habitants had the land, the labour power, and the equipment to produce such quantities, particularly in years of bad harvest, but many did and they soon made the Richelieu valley a major exporter of wheat. No fundamental reorganization of the peasant household economy was required in this limited commercial expansion; habitants simply grew more of what they had always grown. The range of crops grown, the size and composition of livestock herds, and the ways in which the soil was cultivated remained essentially unchanged.

The growth of commerce, along with the growth of population, was not without its effects on habitant society. Particularly in St Denis, a centre of the grain trade, the partible inheritance customs of an earlier age had to be modified. There had always been a concern to avoid excessive fragmentation of holdings and to maintain farms of a reasonable size, but now the requirement of a saleable surplus tended to keep the minimum viable farm size relatively large. This combined with the fact that fathers could no longer obtain nearby wilderness land for their children meant that it was more difficult than ever to provide for all the offspring of a habitant family. Consequently parents, unless they were exceptionally rich, would leave all or most of their property to one child, usually a son.

Demographic and commercial expansion altered the structure of rural society in other respects. A significant non-agricultural element appeared in the Lower Richelieu in the latter part of the eighteenth century as the habitant clientele for goods and services became numerous enough and rich enough to support it. Small towns grew up around the churches in Sorel, St Ours, and St Denis and they were populated by doctors, notaries, merchants, craftsmen, and so on. Specialized artisans pursued handicraft industries of a sort not practised by most farming families. There was even some production (at the shipyards of Sorel, for instance) that brought together a number of workmen and catered to distant markets. The region's economy and society certainly became more complex over the course of our period, but only to a limited extent; even in the early nineteenth century, the urban and industrial sectors remained largely dependent on the agrarian base.

At various times that agricultural foundation experienced difficulties. The pre-modern agriculture practised here before 1840 was quite vulnerable to natural calamities and therefore it was subject to occasional short-falls. Furthermore, there were more serious and lasting problems with the region's wheat production. Wheat collapsed in Sorel about the time of the American Revolution as a result of that parish's poor soil. In St Ours and St Denis the definitive decline seems to have occurred only at the time of the wheat midge infestation of the 1830s. Before that there were certainly signs of distress among the peasantries of these two communities, but it was primarily demographic and social rather than agricultural. Given the limited supply of land and the requirements of the grain trade, the reproduction and multiplication of farm households could not keep pace with the burgeoning population and the result was long-distance emigration and the growth of a landless proletariat.

In the early nineteenth century, when the traditional pattern of step-by-step colonization could no longer work, the different parishes of the Lower Richelieu embarked on divergent courses. Dependent upon seasonal and temporary work in the fur trade, the peasantry of Sorel was generally reduced to a semi-proletariat. Accordingly, farms were subdivided and population density increased as the population turned to agriculture for food supplies only, while relying on wages to cover other expenses. In St Denis, on the other hand, farms remained fairly large and population growth levelled off, thanks mainly to massive emigration. Land-owning peasants made up a smaller proportion of the population in St Denis than in Sorel in 1831, but they were far more prosperous than the part-time cultivators of the voyageur parish.

What does the contrast between Sorel and St Denis tell us about Lower Canada generally? At the moment, we are in no position to say how far the experience of one parish or the other was 'typical,' but that is not really the purpose of the comparative analysis. Tracing the divergent paths of the voyageur community and the farming community in the early nineteenth century does suggest quite strongly that diversity was an important characteristic of the Lower Richelieu and a fortiori of rural French Canada. Moreover, Sorel and St Denis were different because they were subject to different forces and pressures. Again the larger implication is that conditions of habitant life varied in Lower Canada because the mechanisms of change were diverse. This suggests for the researcher, not necessarily a retreat into parochial studies, but at least a sensitivity to the variety of developments that may be encountered in the different parts of the St Lawrence valley. In the past, scholars who noted local and regional variations generally emphasized distinctions based on ethnic differences (the French seigneuries and the English townships) or environmental contrasts (the St Lawrence valley and the Shield).[61] Within the predominantly French St Lawrence valley, however, local diversity has been viewed as different symptoms of a single disease. The Agricultural Crisis, it is claimed, struck some parishes earlier than others, affected some localities severely and others less so, but it remained monolithic and the essential experience of all of rural French Canada.[62] Applied to the Lower Richelieu, this approach yields nonsensical results. Did 'the' crisis arrive earlier in Sorel than in St Denis? Was 'it' more severe there? One needs only pose these questions to realize that they cannot be answered, since they presuppose essentially similar experiences with essentially similar causes in the two parishes.

Close scrutiny of the mechanisms of change in Sorel and St Denis makes it difficult to accept any one-dimensional analysis of Lower Canada's agrarian problems. Demographic growth, inheritance customs, agricultural techniques, traditional mentalities, all these possible culprits explain nothing by themselves and they clearly produced quite contradictory results in the two parishes. For example, throughout the region, natural population growth was high, but in St Denis this led to emigration, whereas in Sorel it produced overcrowding. Laws and attitudes concerning inheritance were also a 'constant,' but in the northern community there was subdivision of holdings while, to the south, farms remained more or less intact. What seems to explain these differences is an intrusive factor so often ignored in studies of rural Quebec, namely merchant capital in its various forms. This is not to say that the workings of fur traders and grain merchants were the unique determinant of agrarian change any more than demography or mentalities. Rather it was the interplay between mercantile forces and existing feudal structures that, within certain limits, constantly shaped the rural world of the Lower Richelieu. In opposition at times, but also in harmony, these two factors constantly reinforced or modified one another, producing quite different conditions of life for the habitants of Sorel and St Denis.

Although there were some important changes in the society and economy of the Lower Richelieu between 1740 and 1840 – changes that took Sorel and St Denis down different paths – there was also a fundamental continuity over the course of the century in the structures of rural life. The habitant family household remained the basic unit of this society. Peasant families continued to satisfy their material needs primarily through their own efforts using their own land and equipment; the hiring of outside labour was occasional rather than normal. There was always a rough economic equality among the habitants (or at least among those who possessed their own land). In other words, the peasantry formed a class, not a collection of classes, even in the early nineteenth century when the grain trade could have been the vehicle by which a habitant bourgeoisie raised itself above the mass in St Ours and St Denis. Instead of accumulating land and capital to found a lasting and growing fortune, however, the richer peasants apparently dissipated their wealth by dividing it among as many of their children as possible. In so doing, they not only carried out their duties as good parents, but also assured themselves a handsome revenue in their old age from the various *pensions alimentaires*. More research is needed on Lower-Canadian inheritance practices but, for the moment, the behaviour of the Lussier family suggests that, insofar as there was exploitation *within* the peasantry, it was more a matter of generations than of classes.

Exploitation of the peasantry as a whole was of course another phenomenon that continued well past the turn of the century. Through rents, tithes, and profits, the habitants continued to turn over their surplus production to support the seigneurs, priests, and merchants of the Lower Richelieu. The fact that inheritance customs preserved an agrarian configuration of small, peasant-owned farms only served the interests of these over-classes since it kept the number of rent-payers and customers at a maximum. On the other hand, larger agricultural units worked by wage-labourers and producing primarily for the market would have been more conducive to technical improvement and increased efficiency. Heightened productivity, however, was not compatible with the feudal organization of the Lower-Canadian countryside and, despite the rhetoric of the 'Montreal merchants,' commercial development did not contribute to any breakthrough. It would be some decades more into the nineteenth century before forces more powerful than merchant capital would shake this old edifice to its foundations; seigneurial tenure would be done away with, schooling would become universal, railroads would connect the region to distant cities, and the peasants of the Lower Richelieu would stream to the factories of Lowell, Biddeford, and Montreal. By 1840 these genuinely revolutionary changes had hardly begun.

Appendix 1

Population by census: Sorel, St Ours, and St Denis 1681–1844

Year	Sorel	St Ours	St Denis
1681	117	87	0
1695	87	66	0
1698	59	79	0
1706	104	65	0
1739	342		
1765	670	786	310
1784	1158	1265	981
1790	1208	1606	1694
1801			2197
1822	3711	3268	2906
1825	4471	3529*	3102
1831	5063	3559	3074
1844		3002	2915

* Parish of St Ours reduced in size in 1822, after the census of that year
Sources: 1681, 1695, 1698, 1706, 1739 – Archives des colonies, G1, vol. 460, recensements du Canada (PAC microfilm)
    1765 – *RAPQ*, 1936–7, pp 1–121
    1784 – PAC, Haldimand Papers, Add. Mss 21885–2, pp 259–60
    1790 – Canada, Department of Agriculture, *Census of Canada, 1870–71* 5 vols (Ottawa: I.B. Taylor 1873–8) 4: 75–80
    1801 – ACESH, 'Chronique de la Paroisse de St-Denis, Rivière Chambly,' by Isidore Desnoyers, 2 vols, 2: 92
    1822 – *JHALC*, 1821–2, app. N
    1825 – *JHALC*, 1826, app. Q
    1831 – *JHALC*, 1831–2, app. OO
    1844 – *JLAC*, 1846, app. D
Manuscript returns for the censuses of 1825 and 1831 were also consulted (PAC, microfilm C–717 and C–722).

A NOTE ON THE CENSUSES

Before 1851, censuses were taken in Quebec at irregular intervals and without any standard procedure or set of categories. Only the returns for the census of 1681 have separate entries for every man, woman, and child in the colony. Returns listing the names of household heads and enumerating other inhabitants have been preserved for the censuses of 1765, 1825, and 1831. For the other censuses (1695, 1698, 1706, 1739, 1784, 1790, 1801, and 1822) all that is available are parish aggregate figures, although these are broken down into age and sex categories. Figures provided by these censuses cannot be considered perfectly accurate and many of them are clearly distorted by mistakes in the location of local boundaries, by underenumeration, and by arithmetic errors. Some attempt was made to identify and correct these inaccuracies in drawing up the table above, but the result is still a series of estimates.[1]

Appendix 2

Habitant estate inventories

One of the main sources for this book is a number of habitant estate inventories ('inventaires-après-décès'), inheritance documents drawn up on the occasion of the dissolution of a communauté de biens, normally after the death of a married man or woman, but often several years after the death (see Chapter 3). In theory, all the possessions of the couple were listed and, except where land is concerned, their money value was estimated. In Canada, unlike some parts of France where notaries assigned purely conventional values to property, every effort seems to have been made to provide heirs with a true indication of the worth of an estate. Furthermore, it appears that French Canadians of our period were more likely than their French contemporaries to have an inventory drawn up. Do data from estate inventories give an accurate indication of the wealth and material culture of the community at large? After examining more than a hundred inventories, and finding that pathetically poor habitants as well as relatively rich ones are represented, I am confident that a good-sized sample does indeed give a reasonable picture of the peasantry as a whole. Comparisons with other sources seem to bear this out. For example, figures on livestock holdings from the 1765 census correspond quite closely to those derived from local inventories from the same decade.[2] On the other hand, it would be foolhardy to suggest that estate inventories can provide a precise and accurate image of the distribution of property at a particular time. The people covered by these documents tended, no doubt, to be rather old. Also, many inventories were, in practice, less than complete as surviving spouses could sometimes keep valuable objects out of the estate by arguing that these were 'personal' possessions reserved to them by the terms of a marriage contract. Still, for all their imperfections, the estate inventories of pre-industrial Quebec are far more numerous, detailed, and reliable than the probate records that have been studied so assiduously by researchers in other parts of the world. Certainly they are by far our best source of information on the material environment and economic position of the habitants of the eighteenth and nineteenth centuries.[3]

Actually using the inventories can be a tedious job as they lie scattered through the files of local notaries. It was only possible to collect and analyse a small fraction of the hundreds of inventories compiled for Lower Richelieu residents between 1740 and 1840 and so the list below constitutes a 'sample.' Only three periods, 1740–69, 1790–9, and 1830–9, were considered and only the inventories of 'habitants' possessing land, agricultural implements, and livestock were selected. I went through the files of most local notaries practising during the three periods, as well as one Verchères notary (Jacques Duvernay) who served many St Denis residents in the 1740s. Otherwise, Lower Richelieu inventories that happened to be drawn up by notaries from neighbouring villages would not find their way into this list. Other inventories were left out deliberately in order to preserve a rough balance in coverage over the three periods and between the two subsections of the region, Sorel on one side and St Ours and St Denis on the other. Accordingly, every second habitant inventory in two of the larger notarial collections (Michaud, Mignault) was left out.

This left me with a total of 110 habitant inventories, but not all of them were of equal value. A few seem to have been incomplete and others came from the economically troubled war years from 1757 to 1762; in both cases, it seemed unwise to include their economic data in the period averages. Even if only ninety-five inventories had useful wealth data however, the rest were valuable for the non-statistical information they provided on such things as farming and material culture.

| | | | | | Data on: | | |
No. Husband	Wife	Date	Notary	wealth	cash	livestock
Sorel 1740–69						
1 Paul Heu	M-Rose Deguire	29-10-43	1	x	x	x
2 Gabriel Bérard	M-Thérèse Chevalier	30-6-46	1	x	x	x
3 Pierre Carré	Marie Cochon	30-8-51	1	x	x	x
4 Antoine Heu	Marianne Bissonnet	23-3-52	1	x	x	x
5 J-Bte Massé	M-Ursule Heu	27-3-53	1	x	x	x
6 Joseph Chevallier	Marthe Collin	14-3-54	1	x	x	x

No. Husband	Wife	Date	Notary	Data on: wealth	cash	livestock
7 Pierre Tessier	Catherine Laguerche	10-3-55	1	x	x	x
8 Germain LeRoux	M-Louise Mandeville	5-7-55	1	x	x	x
9 Antoine Dutremble	Marianne St-Yves	10-7-55	1	x	x	x
10 J-François Dusault	Charlotte Pilotte	2-3-63	2	x	x	x
11 Antoine Heu Millet	Ursule Laguerche	26-4-63	2	x	x	x
12 Joseph Loiseau	M-Magdeleine Belaire	16-1-64	2		x	x
13 Pierre Peltier		12-2-65	3	x	x	x
14 Pierre Lamy Desfonds	Catherine Salvaye	13-5-65	4	x	x	x
15 Gabriel Bérard	Celeste Drinville	16-8-68	4	x	x	x
16 Pierre Hus Paul	Genevieve Bruneau	29-3-69	5		x	
17 Pierre Peltier	Charlotte Mandeville	1-4-69	4	x	x	x

St Ours and St Denis 1740–69

No. Husband	Wife	Date	Notary	wealth	cash	livestock
18 Charles Maheu	M-Joseph Dudevoir	12-10-48	6	x	x	x
19 Pierre Vaine	Marianne Roy	20-3-54	1	x	x	x
20 Séraphin Bourgard	Angélique Brunette	18-6-54	1	x	x	x
21 Pierre Ledoux	Charlotte Quintal	17-1-57	6		x	x
22 Pierre Harpin	Margueritte Truchon	26-11-57	6		x	x
23 J-Baptiste Martin	Marianne Desloriers	4-11-61	7		x	x
24 Pierre Duval	M-Françoise Belval	2-2-62	7		x	x
25 Théophil Alère	M-Amable Ménard	4-2-62	7		x	x
26 Pierre Ménard	M-Charlotte Vel	10-2-63	2		x	x
27 André Guay Dragon	M-Catherine Allard	23-1-64	2	x	x	x
28 Jean-Louis Hemery	M-Magdeleine Royé	4-6-64	2	x	x	x
29 Pierre Ledoux	Josephte Lacoste	26-6-64	3	x	x	x
30 François Lamoureux	M-Angélique Chapdelaine	18-7-64	3	x	x	x
31 J-Bte Guay Dragon	Thérese Goulet	24-6-65	2	x	x	x
32 Charles Bousquet	M-Judith Bousquet	24-2-66	2	x	x	x
33 François Ménard	M-Mag. Lamoureux	5-3-66	2	x	x	x
34 J-Bte Laporte	Marianne Audet	25-2-67	2	x	x	x
35 Etienne Ledoux	M-Josephte Bourgot	7-3-67	2	x	x	x
36 Théofil Alaire	C-Félicité Audet	9-3-67	2	x	x	x
37 François Messié	M-Catherine Champigny	3-2-69	8	x	x	x
38 Joseph Sénécal	Archange Chapû	10-7-69	8	x	x	x
39 Gabriel Lefebvre	Charlotte Vel	28-12-69	8	x	x	x

Sorel 1790–9

No. Husband	Wife	Date	Notary	wealth	cash	livestock
40 Joseph Heut Paul	Geneviève Drinville	20-6-90	5	x	x	x
41 Alexis Vilandré	Marianne Desorcy	18-7-91	5	x	x	x
42 Michel Desorsy	M-Josephte Désy	20-7-91	5	x	x	x
43 J-Baptiste Cardin	Janne Carie	17-9-91	5	x	x	x

No. Husband	Wife	Date	Notary	Data on: wealth	cash	livestock
44 François Poirier	M-Louise Laguersse	2-1-93	5	x	x	x
45 Charles Arteneau	Anathasie Leblanc	18-3-93	9			x
46 Germain LeRoux	Agathe Mandeville	27-6-93	5	x	x	x
47 Charles Milliet	Charlotte Mandeville	11-3-94	5	x	x	x
48 J-Baptiste Dufeau	Josette Ragotte	29-9-94	5		x	x
49 Joseph Chevalier	Ursule Cournoyer	28-1-95	5	x	x	x
50 Pierre Letendre	Catherine Pelletier	25-10-95	5	x	x	x
51 Pierre Plante	Thérèse Dargy	16-3-96	10	x	x	x
52 François Félix	Agathe Blette	18-7-96	10	x	x	x
53 Joseph Cournoyer	Agathe Thibert	30-1-97	10	x	x	x
54 Pierre Ethier	Magdelaine Landry	19-1-98	10	x	x	x
55 Louis de Rinville	Catherine Plante	4-7-99	10	x	x	x
56 Pierre Arseneau	Marie Lefaivre	22-7-99	10	x	x	x

St Ours and St Denis 1790–9

No. Husband	Wife	Date	Notary	wealth	cash	livestock
57 Pierre Emery Codère	M-Marguerite Plouf	2-2-90	11	x	x	x
58 J-Baptiste Bousquet	M-Louise Archambault	19-4-90	11		x	x
59 J-Marie d'Allaire	M-Marguerite Cochon	31-7-90	11	x	x	x
60 Jacques Bourg	M-Marguerite Cormier	23-2-91	11	x	x	x
61 Pierre Boudrau	M-Ursule Alaire	14-3-91	11	x	x	x
62 Joseph Chaillé	Marie Bargevin	21-3-91	9	x	x	x
63 Michel Larivière	Cecile Lapierre	14-4-91	9	x	x	x
64 André Larivière	Lisette Payant	17-9-91	9	x	x	x
65 Amable Gaudet	Elizabeth Benoit	21-9-91	9	x	x	x
66 Charles Godet	Marguerite Faneuf	11-11-91	11	x	x	x
67 Alexis Lafrenaye	Amable Avare	13-12-92	9	x	x	x
68 Antoine Meunier	M-Marguerite Allaire	15-6-93	9	x	x	x
69 Louis Jonson	Josephte Baron	5-7-93	11	x	x	x
70 Louis Duval	Marguerite Bouvier	10-12-93	9	x	x	x
71 Bazil Cloutier	M-Magdelaine Peltier	25-2-94	11	x	x	x
72 René Neau	Véronique Mathieu	12-11-94	9	x	x	x
73 Jacques Daigle	Angélique Chapdelaine	28-7-95	9	x	x	x
74 Antoine Benoist	Catherine Neau	8-3-96	9	x	x	x
75 Antoine Dufaux	Françoise Dumas	1-10-96	9	x	x	x
76 Louis Ledoux	M-Jeanne Roy	19-10-96	11	x	x	x
77 François Piché	Angélique Paul-Hus	26-7-97	10		x	x
78 Joseph Carpentier	M-Louise Leblanc	8-4-99	11	x	x	x
79 Joseph Bourgeois	M-Séraphine Leblanc	26-7-99	11	x	x	x

No. Husband	Wife	Date	Notary	Data on: wealth	cash	livestock

Sorel 1830–9

No. Husband	Wife	Date	Notary	wealth	cash	livestock
80 Barthelemy Cournoyer	Marie St-Martin	21-6-30	10	x	x	x
81 Joseph Cartier	Marie Leclaire	2-2-31	12	x	x	x
82 Augustin Lavallé	Catherine Peloquin	9-1-32	10	x	x	x
83 Charles Delard	Catherine Antaya	24-10-32	10	x	x	x
84 Joseph Forcier	Catherine Desorcy	24-11-32	10	x	x	x
85 François Paul	Pélagie Pagé	16-12-33	13	x	x	x
86 Joseph Poirier	M-Madelaine Milhiet	14-7-34	13	x	x	x
87 J-Bte Lavallé	Archange Chapdelaine	2-3-35	14	x	x	x
88 Louis Thibeau	Agathe Etier	2-6-35	10	x	x	x
89 Denis Lavallé	Marie Roi	13-4-36	14	x	x	x
90 Frs-Pierre Jolie	Pélagie Dusseault	3-10-36	14		x	x
91 Pierre Aussant	Josephte Peltier	5-11-38	14	x	x	x
92 J-Baptiste Tessier	Angélique Lavallée	20-3-39	13		x	x

St Ours and St Denis 1830–9

No. Husband	Wife	Date	Notary	wealth	cash	livestock
93 Michel Dufault	Catherine Jalbert	23-2-30	15	x	x	x
94 Gabriel Ledoux	Agathe Coté	21-9-30	15	x	x	x
95 Alexis Giard	Agathe Daigle	23-3-31	12	x	x	x
96 J-Bte Bourgeois	Agathe Leblanc	6-9-31	15		x	x
97 J-Bte Baudreau	Magdelaine Denis	2-10-32	16	x	x	x
98 J-Louis Gadu	M-Josephte Laroche	25-2-33	15	x	x	x
99 Joseph Bellanger	Judithe Dudevoir	2-4-33	16	x	x	x
100 François Larue	Magdelaine Pataine	8-4-33	15	x	x	x
101 Charles Allard	M-Magdelaine Lussier	15-4-33	16	x	x	x
102 François Emery	M-Julie Vigeant	18-9-33	15	x		x
103 François Martin	Marie LeBrodeur	2-10-33	16	x	x	x
104 Pierre Chatelle	Marie Gazaille	10-9-34	16	x	x	x
105 Joseph Fredette	Geneviève Bonier	9-3-35	15	x	x	x
106 Pierre Leblanc	Barbe Allard	23-9-35	15	x	x	x
107 Paul Paquin	Marguerite Mandeville	29-3-37	15	x	x	x
108 Louis Martin	Josephte Bousquet	2-3-38	15	x	x	x
109 Jean Archambault	Marguerite Cordeau	23-7-38	15	x	x	x
110 Joseph Kimineur	Monique Benoit	29-3-39	15	x	x	x

Notaries

1 Cyr de Montmerque (M)	9 Louis Bonnet (M)
2 L.S. Frichet (S)	10 Henry Crebassa (S)
3 L.L. de Courville (M)	11 Christophe Michaud (M)
4 Bart. Faribault (S)	12 A.C. LeNoblet Duplessis (M)
5 Antoine Robin (S)	13 Moise LeNoblet Duplessis (M)
6 Jacques C. Duvernay (M)	14 Narcissse-D. Crebassa (S)
7 Charles Deguire (M)	15 Joseph-E. Mignault (M)
8 Marin Jehanne (M)	16 Louis Bourdages (M)

M = Archives Nationales du Québec, dépôt de Montréal
S = Archives judiciaires de Sorel

Appendix 3

Economic data from habitant inventories (in livres)

Inv. no.	Moveables	Cash	Balance of debt	Net worth
		Sorel 1740–69		
1	1458.8	0	− 164.8	1294.0
2	1049.0	0	− 54.4	994.6
3	295.9	0	− 149.5	146.0
4	1297.4	0	− 77.5	1219.9
5	1812.9	0	962.5	2775.4
6	1004.7	0	− 26.0	978.7
7	847.1	0	− 29.0	818.1
8	559.6	0	− 301.1	258.5
9	575.0	0	− 975.5	− 400.5
10	1207.2	189.1	29.0	1425.3
11	439.0	63.0	− 88.0	414.0
13	256.7	0	− 770.5	− 513.8
14	295.5	60.0	− 2200.0	− 1844.5
15	1202.3	19.5	− 512.9	708.9
17	546.0	0	− 1146.2	− 600.2
		St Ours and St Denis 1740–69		
18	839.9	0	− 488.3	351.6
19	1216.7	58.5	− 329.5	945.7
20	96.3	0	− 95.0	1.3
21	548.0	37.5	− 226.4	359.1
28	1184.0	0	155.0	1339.0
29	1160.0	221.1	116.5	1497.6
30	757.0	0	− 37.5	719.5
31	483.0	0	− 158.7	324.3
32	1280.5	0	91.0	1371.5
33	666.5	0	− 139.9	526.6
34	275.6	0	− 322.4	− 46.8

Inv. no.	Moveables	Cash	Balance of debt	Net worth
35	1139.7	0	− 1474.0	− 334.3
36	470.0	0	− 224.5	246.0
37	1463.3	0	− 2967.0	− 1503.7
38	228.9	0	− 255.9	− 27.0
39	422.6	0	− 283.9	138.7
		Sorel 1790–9		
40	1956.3	74.9	351.2	2382.4
41	904.3	0	− 126.8	777.5
42	1636.0	27.3	101.0	1764.3
43	1028.2	0	− 728.9	299.3
44	787.6	0	− 78.0	709.6
46	377.0	0	− 450.8	− 73.8
47	718.6	0	− 200.0	518.6
49	2028.6	0	3.0	2031.6
50	1274.0	281.0	117.5	1672.5
51	377.9	0	− 106.5	271.4
52	1759.4	12.0	− 96.0	1675.8
53	392.8	0	0	392.8
54	1762.0	0	0	1762.0
55	3635.9	212.6	1825.2	5673.7
56	536.1	8.0	− 36.0	508.1
		St Ours and St Denis 1790–9		
57	88.5	0	− 204.2	− 115.7
59	774.0	0	− 538.7	235.3
60	121.3	0	− 679.0	− 557.7
61	1698.4	103.0	− 1707.8	93.6
62	539.8	0	246.9	786.7
63	974.4	0	− 866.2	108.2
64	767.2	0	− 241.5	525.7
65	153.7	0	− 85.5	68.2
66	618.7	0	− 265.5	353.2
67	181.6	0	− 190.4	− 8.8
68	531.1	0	− 573.0	− 41.9
69	210.9	0	− 339.7	− 128.8
70	936.0	0	86.0	1022.0
71	426.2	81.6	− 23.0	484.8
72	441.5	0	− 198.0	243.5
73	960.2	0	− 14.0	946.2
74	1215.3	19.3	− 108.3	1126.3.
75	2317.3	484.0	17.0	2818.3
76	752.8	0	− 1197.0	− 444.2
78	1714.7	36.0	− 353.1	1397.6
79	649.2	36.0	− 624.5	60.7

Inv. no.	Moveables	Cash	Balance of debt	Net worth
		Sorel 1830–9		
80	1151.4	0	− 621.8	529.6
81	474.7	1.1	− 354.8	121.0
82	1151.3	0	− 165.3	986.0
83	891.9	0.1	− 605.6	286.4
84	2458.3	0	− 807.2	1651.1
85	691.6	0	− 70.0	621.6
86	1429.7	16.1	− 270.0	1175.8
87	896.3	1.5	− 482.1	415.7
88	224.7	0	− 364.6	− 139.9
89	323.6	0	− 1459.8	− 1136.2
91	448.6	0	− 36.0	412.6
		St Denis and St Ours 1830–9		
93	1458.4	27.8	− 621.7	864.5
94	1099.8	6.3	− 530.8	575.3
95	2417.1	1506.7	3036.4	6960.2
97	1974.6	0	− 4851.5	− 2876.9
98	963.0	16.9	− 582.4	397.5
99	1409.6	0	− 600.4	809.2
100	2539.7	99.0	− 105.7	2533.0
101	1721.3	40.9	− 575.1	1187.1
102	526.4	0	− 385.4	141.0
103	1679.1	0	− 2114.3	− 435.2
104	2310.2	0	− 1098.4	1211.8
105	1245.5	1.5	115.1	1362.1
106	1022.6	0	− 1491.5	− 468.9
107	1274.0	25.0	− 460.9	838.1
108	851.4	21.2	449.5	1322.1
109	1203.8	558.9	6205.6	7967.3
110	1203.9	54.0	902.4	2160.3

PROCEDURE

As noted in Appendix 2, only ninety-five of the 110 habitant inventories in my sample were used in this table, the rest being eliminated because their economic data were incomplete or distorted. Land is always mentioned in estate inventories but, since it is not usually assigned a value, only the remaining elements in the fortunes of these ninety-five peasants can be quantified. The first major component is 'moveables,' the estimated value of all furniture, utensils, animals, and other property, land excepted. Second is 'money,' hard cash or paper; card money and 'ordinances' from the Bigot era are included here at 15 per cent of their face value, which is all that habitants were likely to receive for them.[4] The 'balance of debt' is the difference between sums owed *to* to the marriage community ('dettes actives') and amounts owed *by* the community ('dettes passives') at the time of dissolution. Finally, the 'net worth' of each couple represents the sum total of moveables, money, and balance of debt.

Appendix 4

Cash listed in habitant inventories

Cash listed per inventory (in 1790–9 equivalent livres)*	Sorel		St Ours-St Denis	
	N	%	N	%
1740–69				
0	11	65	16	73
1–9	1	6	0	0
10–99	1	6	4	18
100–999	4	23	2	9
1000+	0	0	0	0
	17	100	22	100
1790–9				
0	9	56	17	74
1–9	1	6	0	0
10–99	4	25	4	17
100–999	2	13	2	9
1000+	0	0	0	0
	16	100	23	100
1830–9				
0	8	62	5	29
1–9	4	31	2	12
10–99	1	8	7	41
100–999	0	0	2	12
1000+	0	0	1	6
	13	101	17	100

* Correction factors – 1.72 for 1740–69 and 0.90 for 1830s – were derived from wheat prices, as explained in Table 30.

Appendix 5

Livestock listed in habitant estate inventories

The following tables give figures for each of the five main animals raised by Lower Richelieu peasants. Only full-grown animals are included. Once again, Sorel is considered apart from St Ours and St Denis in each of the three periods covered by the inventory sample. The figures shown here represent the percentage of habitant inventories possessing the number of adult animals indicated at the head of each column. The total number of inventories considered was sixteen for Sorel, 1740–69; twenty-two for St Ours and St Denis in the same period; for 1790–9, seventeen Sorel and twenty-three St Ours-St Denis inventories were used; and for the 1830s, thirteen Sorel and eighteen St Ours-St Denis listings included information on livestock.

	cows				
	0	1	2	3–4	5–6
1740–69					
Sorel	6.2	12.5	50.0	12.5	18.8
St O.-St D.	4.5	18.2	31.8	36.4	9.1
1790–9					
Sorel	0	11.8	41.2	29.4	17.6
St O.-St D.	13.0	8.7	17.4	34.8	26.1
1830–9					
Sorel	7.7	23.1	38.5	30.8	0
St O.-St D.	11.1	16.7	5.5	61.1	5.5

SHEEP

	0	1–2	3–5	6–10	11–20	21+
1740–69						
Sorel	43.7	12.5	6.3	18.7	12.5	6.3
St O.-St D.	36.4	27.3	18.2	18.2	0	0
1790–9						
Sorel	11.8	11.8	23.5	23.5	23.5	5.9
St O.-St D.	8.7	8.7	34.8	39.1	8.7	0
1830–9						
Sorel	0	7.7	30.8	30.8	23.1	7.7
St O.-St D.	11.1	5.5	11.1	38.9	27.8	5.5

HORSES

	0	1	2	3	4	5
1740–69						
Sorel	12.5	31.2	37.5	12.5	6.2	0
St O.-St D.	9.1	50.0	27.3	13.6	0	0
1790–9						
Sorel	5.9	35.3	47.0	5.9	5.9	0
St O.-St D.	13.6	36.4	45.4	4.5	0	0
1830–9						
Sorel	7.7	38.5	30.8	23.1	0	0
St O.-St D.	16.7	11.1	50.0	16.7	0	5.5

OXEN

	0	1–2	3–4	5–6
1740–69				
Sorel	81.2	12.5	6.2	0
St O.-St D.	40.9	40.9	18.2	0
1790–9				
Sorel	76.5	17.6	5.9	0
St O.-St D.	40.9	45.4	9.1	4.5
1830–9				
Sorel	84.6	15.4	0	0
St O.-St D.	44.4	33.3	22.2	0

	PIGS				
	0	1–2	3–5	6–10	11+
1740–69					
Sorel	18.8	25.0	31.2	18.7	6.2
St O.-St D.	22.7	54.5	18.2	4.5	0
1790–9					
Sorel	11.8	23.5	41.2	23.5	0
St O.-St D.	43.5	21.7	30.4	4.3	0
1830–9					
Sorel	7.7	46.2	30.8	0	15.4
St O.-St D.	22.2	5.6	44.4	22.2	5.6

Appendix 6

Agricultural production (in minots) 1730–1830

	Sorel 1730	Sorel 1732	Sorel 1736	Sorel 1737	Sorel 1739
Source	1	1	1	1	1
Wheat	3500	3960	3380	1000	2600
Oats	1500	1780	1040	780	1000
Peas	620	710	536	300	200
Corn	300	360	150	150	80

	Sorel, Ile Dupas 1784	St Ours 1784	St Denis 1784	St Ours 1789
Source	2	2	2	3
Wheat	9490	19,500	15,600	17,654
Oats	11,830	5200	3900	7306
Peas	1430	2080	1300	1352
Barley	0	260	0	0

	Sorel 1830	St Ours 1830	St Denis 1830
Source	4	4	4
Wheat	19,796	27,906	35,803
Oats	25,873	22,071	21,592
Peas	2981	5539	7594
Rye	6205	4741	1045
Corn	681	691	621
Barley	666	942	4920
Buckwheat	1221	343	0
Potatoes	66,703	50,474	43,273

Sources: 1 Archives des colonies, G1, vol. 461, pp 26–32, recensement du Canada
2 Calculated from Bishop Briand's estimates of tithes, June 1784, quoted in Ivanhoe Caron, *La colonisation de la province de Québec* 2 vols (Quebec: L'Action Sociale 1923–7) 1: 275–80
3 Calculated from tithe figures reported in ACESH, C39, Boucher to bishop, 11 September 1790
4 Census of Lower Canada, 1831

Appendix 7

Units of measure and currency

A more or less uniform system of currency and measurements based on metropolitan French models was imposed on Canada in the seventeenth century. The British conquest introduced miles, acres, shillings, and pounds and, to complicate the monetary system further, the Halifax pound was substituted in 1777 for the New York pound, which had been the standard of currency since 1765. In the countryside, however, people continued to use the old French units, even in legal documents, throughout our period. In the few cases where the sources give data in British units, these have been convered to livres, arpents, etc. Rough evaluations are facilitated by the fact that the arpent (area) is approximately equal to an English acre, the minot is about a bushel, and the livre equals one shilling (Halifax currency). The arpent was both a linear measure and a unit of area equal to a square with sides one arpent in length.

1 arpent (lin.) = 10 perches = 192 feet = 58.4 metres
1 arpent (area) = 0.845 acres = 0.342 hectares
1 minot = 1.107 bushels = 39 litres
1 livre = 20 sols = 240 deniers = 1 shilling (Halifax)

Appendix 8

Settlement in the seigneurie of Sorel 1770

(SEE MAP OVERLEAF)

A PLAN

of the

SEIGNIORY *of* SORRELL

in the

Province OF *Quebec*

the Property of

Mess.ʳˢ Greenwood & Higginson

Merchants in London

Ysamore Bay

I's. Common

Date
1770

B. O

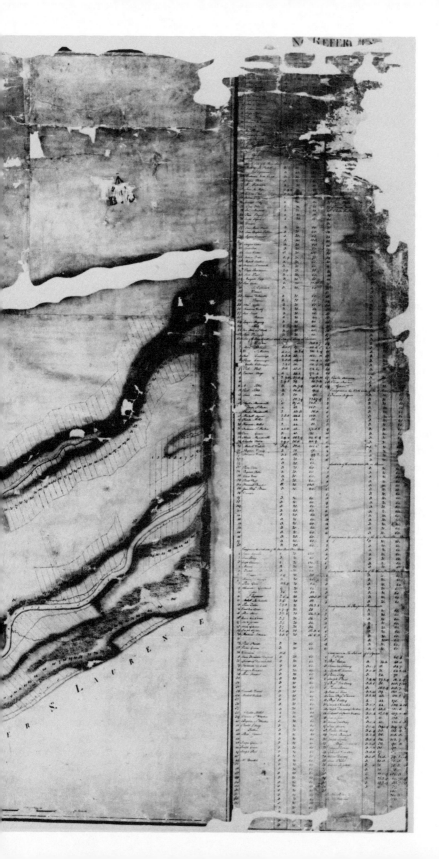

Notes

ABBREVIATIONS

ACESH Archives de la Chancellerie de l'Evêché de St Hyacinthe
AESC   Annales: économies, sociétés, civilisations
AJS   Archives judiciaires de Sorel
ANQ   Archives nationales du Québec
ANQM   Archives nationales du Québec, dépôt de Montréal
ASQ   Archives du séminaire de Québec
BRH   Bulletin des recherches historiques
CHR   Canadian Historical Review
HS-SH Histoire sociale-Social History
JHALC Journals of the House of Assembly of Lower Canada
PAC   Public Archives of Canada
RAPQ   Rapport de l'archiviste de la province de Québec
RHAF   Revue d'histoire de l'amérique française

PREFACE

1 See, for example, Normand Séguin, *La Conquête du sol au 19e siècle* (Sillery: Boréal Express 1977); Normand Séguin, ed., *Agriculture et colonisation au Québec: aspects historiques* (Montreal: Boréal Express 1980); Gérard Bouchard, 'Introduction à l'étude de la société saguenayenne aux xixe et xxe siècles,' *RHAF* 31 (June 1977) 3–27.

2 Louise Dechêne, *Habitants et marchands de Montréal au xviie siècle* (Paris and Montreal: Plon 1974)

3 Eric Wolf, *Peasants* (Englewood Cliffs: Prentice-Hall 1966); Teodor Shanin, *The Awkward Class: Political Sociology of Peasantry in a Developing Society: Russia 1910–1925* (Oxford: Clarendon Press 1972); Teodor Shanin, 'Introduction,' in *Peasants and Peasant Societies: Selected Readings*, ed. Shanin (Harmondsworth: Penguin Books 1971); Teodor Shanin, 'Defining Peasants: Conceptualizations and De-Conceptualizations Old and New in a Marxist Debate,' *Peasant Studies* 8 (Fall 1979) 38–60; R.H. Hilton, 'The Peasantry as a Class,' in *The English Peasantry in the Later Middle Ages* (Oxford: Clarendon Press 1975) 3–19.

For a different conception of peasantry, an essentially idealist and Weberian view and one that exerted a strong influence on students of French-Canadian rural society, see Robert Redfield, *Peasant Society and Culture* (Chicago: University of Chicago Press 1956).

4 See R.H. Hilton, 'Introduction,' in Paul Sweezy et al., *The Transition from Feudalism to Capitalism* (London: NLB 1976); Perry Anderson, *Passages from Antiquity to Feudalism* (London: NLB 1974) 147; Ernesto Laclau, 'Feudalism and Capitalism in Latin America,' *New Left Review* 67 (May-June 1971) 19–38; Alain Guerreau, *Le féodalisme: un horizon théorique* (Paris: le Sycomore 1980); Pierre Vilar, 'La transition du féodalisme au capitalisme,' in Centre d'Etudes et de Recherches Marxistes, *Sur le féodalisme* (Paris: Editions Sociales 1974) 35–48; Guy Lemarchand, 'Féodalisme et société rurale dans la France moderne,' in ibid. 86–105.

Marx himself did not write extensively about the feudal mode of production per se, partly because he was more interested in the capitalist mode of production. Moreover, he would have felt no need to define this term explicitly since, by 'feudal,' he meant more or less the same thing that his contemporaries – including conservatives like Tocqueville – did when they used the word (cf. Alexis de Tocqueville, *The Old Regime and the French Revolution*, ed. and trans. Stuart Gilbert [New York: Doubleday 1955] 31). Marx's conception of the essential features of the feudal mode of production can be found in *Capital: A Critique of Political Economy* 3 vols (Moscow: Progress Publishers 1954) vol. 3, ch. 47, 'Genesis of Capitalist Ground-Rent.'

5 Marc Bloch, *Feudal Society*, trans. L.A. Manyon (Chicago: University of Chicago Press 1961)

6 See J.Q.C. Mackrell, *The Attack on 'Feudalism' in Eighteenth-Century France* (London: Routledge and Kegan Paul 1973).

7 Rodney Hilton, 'Capitalism: What's in a Name?' in Sweezy et al., *The Transition from Feudalism to Capitalism* 148

8 See, for example, Fernand Ouellet, 'Libéré ou exploité! Le paysan québécois d'avant 1850,' *HS-SH* 13 (November 1980) 339–68. This article includes excellent discussions of seigneurial and ecclesiastical exactions, but about commercial and capitalist exploitation of the peasantry, not a word!

9 See, for example, Denis Monière, 'L'utilité du concept de mode de production des petits producteurs pour l'historiographie de la Nouvelle-France,' *RHAF* 29 (March 1976) 483–502.

10 D.E.C. Eversley, 'Population, Economy and Society,' in *Population in History: Essays in Historical Demography*, ed. D.V. Glass and D.E.C. Eversley (London: Edward Arnold 1965) 24

CHAPTER ONE: INTRODUCTION: SEVENTEENTH-CENTURY BEGINNINGS

1 Lucien Campeau, *Les Cent-Associés et le peuplement de la Nouvelle-France, 1633–1663* (Montreal: Bellarmin 1974)

2 W.J. Eccles makes this point in 'A Belated Review of Harold Adams Innis, *The Fur Trade in Canada*,' *CHR* 60 (December 1979) 420–4. For figures on French expenditures in Canada, see Guy Frégault, 'Essai sur les finances canadiennes,' in *Le XVIIIe siècle canadien: études* (Montreal: HMH 1970) 289–363.

3 One of the earliest works to make this case was Maurice Dobb, *Studies in the Development of Capitalism* (New York: International Publishers 1947).

4 John Merrington, 'Town and Country in the Transition to Capitalism,' *New Left Review* 93 (September-October 1975) 71–92

5 Louise Dechêne, *Habitants et marchands de Montréal au XVIIe siècle* (Paris and Montreal: Plon 1974) 481–90

6 Emile Salone, *La colonisation de la Nouvelle-France: étude sur les origines de la nation canadienne-française* (Paris: E. Guilmot 1905) 165–6, 189

7 Azarie Couillard-Desprès, *Histoire de Sorel, de ses origines à nos jours* (Montreal: Imprimerie des sourds-muets 1926) 41

8 'Mémoire de Gédéon de Catalogne sur les plans des seigneuries et habitations des gouvernements de Québec, les Trois-Rivières et Montréal,' *BRH* 10 (October 1915) 297. Cf. Georges Duby, *The Early Growth of the European Economy: Warriors and Peasants from the Seventh to the Twelfth Century* (Ithaca: Cornell University Press 1974) 21.

9 Aileen Anne Cobban and Robert M. Lithgow, 'A Regional Study of the Richelieu Valley' (MA thesis, McGill University 1952) 9

10 Ludger Beauregard, 'Les étapes de la mise en valeur agricole de la vallée du Richelieu,' *Cahiers de Géographie de Québec* 14 (September 1970) 193–4

11 Louise Dechêne, 'L'évolution du régime seigneurial au Canada: le cas de Montréal aux XVIIe et XVIIIe siècles,' *Recherches sociographiques* 12 (May-August 1971) 145

12 This is the view Sigmund Diamond presents in a study remarkable for its

fundamental confusion of social hierarchy and managerial subordination. To read this author one would think that seigneurs and habitants occupied different positions in the 'chain of command' of a modern corporation. Sigmund Diamond, 'An Experiment in "Feudalism": French Canada in the Seventeenth Century,' *William and Mary Quarterly* 3rd series, 18 (1961) 3–34.

13 'Les uns sont dédiés particulièrement au service de Dieu; les autres à conserver l'Estat par les armes; les autres à le nourir et le maintenir par les exercises de la paix.' Charles Loyseau, *Traité des Ordres et Simples Dignités* (1610), cited in Georges Duby, *Les trois ordres ou l'imaginaire du féodalisme* (Paris: Editions Gallimard 1978) 11

France was not the only colonial power whose land policies were dictated by an ideological aversion to a colonial society of free and independent small proprietors. In the first half of the nineteenth century, many British colonies (including Upper Canada) began selling wild lands at prices high enough to put them beyond the reach of poor immigrants. The inspiration for such policies was the theories of Edward Gibbon Wakefield, who insisted on the need to artificially restrict access to land in order to create the working class deemed vital to the (capitalist) development of a colony. The practical effects of these policies are not easy to gauge but, at the ideological level, we can see a middle-class England following the example of aristocratic France in remaking the New World society in its own image. Marx, *Capital*, vol. 1, ch. 33, 'The Modern Theory of Colonization'; Gilbert C. Patterson, 'Land Settlement in Upper Canada 1783–1840,' *Sixteenth Report of the Department of Archives for the Province of Ontario* (Toronto: King's Printer 1921) 146–8

14 PAC, St Ours seigneurie, vol. 1–1, concession by Jean Talon to Sieur de St Ours, 29 October 1672

15 Couillard-Despres, *Histoire de Sorel* 42–3

16 [Azarie Couillard-Despres], *Histoire de la seigneurie de St Ours* 2 vols (Montreal: Imprimerie de l'institution des sourds-muets, 1915–17) 1: 30–3

17 Ibid., 1: 72–3; Claude de Bonnault, 'Généalogie de la famille de Saint-Ours: Dauphiné et Canada,' *BRH* 55 (1949) 101–2. In an inventory drawn up in 1714, Pierre de St Ours stated his net income from the fief to be only 300 livres per year. PAC, St Ours seigneurie, vol. 5, estate inventory of Pierre de St Ours and Marie Mullois, 1 July 1714

18 See, for example, Jean-Pierre Wallot, 'Le régime seigneurial et son abolition au Canada,' in *Un Québec qui bougeait: trame socio-politique du Québec au tournant du XIXe siècle* (Sillery: Boréal Express 1973) 231.

19 France, archives des colonies, G1, vol. 460, recensement du Canada, 1681 (PAC microfilm copy).

20 The exact status of these 'servants' is rather difficult to pin down in some

cases. One of those listed as a 'domestique,' for example, was Gilles Danjou and his relationship with Pierre de Sorel was typically feudal in its ambiguity. Danjou apparently lived for some time in the manor house, but in some documents he is referred to as a tenant-farmer ('fermier'). He contracted to clear land and erect buildings for the seigneur and then to cultivate the newly cleared area, always paying a ground rent in addition to seigneurial dues; Danjou seems to have been deeply endebted to Monsieur de Sorel. The relationship between lord and servant obviously changed over the years, but it always remained one of subordination and dependence. Couillard-Desprès, *Histoire de Sorel* 54

21 Ibid.; PAC, MG8, A6, vol. 3, ordinance of Antoine-Denis Raudot, 7 July 1710; PAC, MG8, A6, vol. 4, ordinance of Michel Bégon, 14 July 1714

22 E-Z. Massicotte, 'Le tribunal seigneurial de Sorel et autres,' *BRH* 50 (1944) 13–14

23 H. Têtu and C-O. Gagnon, eds, *Mandements, lettres pastorales et circulaires des évêques de Québec* 8 vols (Quebec: Imprimerie générale A. Coté et Cie, 1887–93) 1: 115–28, 'Plan général de l'état des missions du Canada fait en l'année 1683'

24 In his will, the seigneur ordered that his body be buried in the building and that his cross of the military order of St Louis be attached to the holy sacrament. Couillard-Desprès, *Histoire de St-Ours* 1: 105–10

25 Ibid. 1: 107

26 Gédéon de Catalogne remarked on this in 1709. 'Mémoire de Gédéon de Catalogne' 296–7. Cf. de Bonnault, 'La famille de Saint-Ours' 104–6; PAC, St Ours seigneurie, 10: 6402–13, ordinance of Michel Bégon, 1 July 1714.

27 The frontier thesis rests too heavily on a certain parochialism that takes seriously only American realities when presenting contrasts with a superficially understood Europe.

28 Recensement du Canada, 1681. Most of these occupational labels obviously hark back to an earlier life in France, but several of the artisans (the carpenters and surgeons at least) continued to practise their crafts in the New World. ANQM, 'Inventaire des minutes du greffe Pierre Ménard, notaire du régime français à St Ours, Contrecoeur, et St Louis pour les années 1671 à 1693 conservées au palais de justice de la ville de Sorel,' by Gérald Ménard. On the early settlers of Canada generally, see Cole Harris, 'The French Background of Immigrants to Canada before 1700,' *Cahiers de géographie de Québec* 16 (September 1972) 313–24.

29 ANQM, inventaire du greffe Pierre Ménard, marché entre Jean Duval, mte. charpentier, et Jean Régeasse dit Laprade, 1 September 1675; ibid., obligation entre François Dubois dit LeBourbonnais et Mérie Herpin dit Poytevin, 15 January 1690; Couillard-Desprès, *Histoire de Sorel* 55–6

30 ANQM, inventaire du greffe Pierre Ménard. An important body of historical opinion takes mobility and 'freedom' of this sort to be evidence of laxity in the Canadian 'seigneurial system.' Partisans of this view, which might be called the 'hall monitor interpretation of feudalism,' seem to think that seigneurs occupied a position similar to that of the schoolchildren charged with policing the 'up' and 'down' stairways. (See, for example, Diamond, 'An Experiment in "Feudalism".') Seigneurs did indeed possess a certain ascendancy over their tenants and often played a leading role in community affairs, but they had virtually no control, in theory or in fact, over comings and goings. Like the post-medieval western European civilization it sprang from, French Canada had seigneurial institutions without the personal bondage associated with serfdom.

31 Claude-Charles Bacqueville de la Potherie, *Histoire de l'Amérique septentrionale* 4 vols (Paris: Jean-Luc Nion et François Didot, 1722) 1: 313–14

32 Ivanoe Caron, ed., 'Procès-verbaux du procureur-général Collet sur le district des paroisses de la Nouvelle-France,' *RAPQ*, 1921–2, pp 316–19

33 F.M. Montresor, 'Some Canadian Villages in 1760,' *CHR* 8 (December 1927) 307

34 Ludger Beauregard, 'Le peuplement du Richelieu,' *Revue de Géographie de Montréal* 19 (1965) 51

35 ANQM, 22RS4, Terrier de la seigneurie de St Denis, 31 August 1849.

36 See, for example, PAC, St Ours seigneurie, vol. 1–1, concession par François de Pécaudy à Marc Benoist, 19 March 1736.

37 Archives des colonies, G1, vol. 460, recensement du Canada, 1681 (PAC microfilm); PAC, MG8, A10, 1: 399–420, aveu et dénombrement, Sorel, 7 June 1724

38 ANQ, Aveux et dénombrements, régime français, cahier supplémentaire, aveu et dénombrement, St Ours, 15 May–4 June 1745; ibid., aveu et dénombrement, St Denis, 4 June 1745

CHAPTER TWO: THE PEASANT FAMILY HOUSEHOLD

1 Local differences are due mainly to the fact that the seigneurs of Sorel granted land in rather small lots while those who controlled St Denis were more generous. The returns of the 1765 census, with data listed by household, are published in *RAPQ*, 1936–7, pp 1–121. Parish totals found in this transcript are not reliable, but the individual entries seem to be accurate. The census lists 315 households in the parishes of Sorel, Petit St Ours, and St Denis. However, some of these were headed by priests, craftsmen, and other non-agriculturalists. In an effort to limit the analysis to 'habitants' only, the 40 households that had no land or that, according to the census, planted no

grain were eliminated. Two households with obviously deficient data (no men, women, children, or servants listed) were also set aside. This left 273 'habitant' households which are the basis for this table and for other figures presented below in this chapter.

2 A.V. Chayanov, 'Peasant Farm Organization,' in Daniel Thorner, Basile Kerblay, and R.E.F. Smith, eds, *A.V. Chayanov on the Theory of Peasant Economy* (Homewood, IL: American Economic Association 1966) 25–269

3 Total population of Sorel, St Denis, Grand St Ours, and Petit St Ours was 1766 in 1765 and 3404 in 1784; the number of servants was 72 and 123 respectively. The censuses which are the source of these data are discussed in Appendix 1.

4 See, for example, ANQM, gr. Bonnet, inventory of Jacques Daigle, 28 July 1795.

5 PAC, St Ours seigneurie, 11: 7719–21, petition of Joseph Graveline to 'les officiers de la chambre de justice du district de St-Antoine,' n.d. (clearly from the Military Régime 1760–4).

6 Louise Dechêne, *Habitants et marchands de Montréal au XVIIe siècle* (Paris and Montreal: Plon 1974) 312–14

7 PAC, Sorel seigneurie, vol. 11, estate roll, 1795, 2: 418. Cf. Rodolphe de Koninck, Anne-Marie Turcot, and André G. Zubrzycki, 'Les pâturaux communaux du Lac Saint-Pierre: de leur histoire et de leur actualité,' *Cahiers de géographie de Québec* 17 (September 1973) 322.

8 Abbé Cyprien Tanguay, *Dictionnaire généalogique des familles canadiennes depuis la fondation de la colonie jusqu'à nos jours* 7 vols (Montreal: E. Senécal 1871–90) 2: 11, 2: 15; J-Arthur Leboeuf, *Complément au dictionnaire généalogique Tanguay* 3 vols (Montreal: Publications de la Société généalogique canadienne-française 1957–64) 2: 3; abbé Azarie Couillard-Desprès, *Histoire de St-Ours* 1: 219–20, 237

9 ANQM, gr. Deguire, inventaire des biens de Théophile Alere veuf d'Amable Ménard, 4 February 1762; AJS, gr. Frichet, inventory of Claire Félicité Audet and Théophile Allaire, 9 March 1767

10 Dechêne, *Habitants et marchands* 265–6; R.C. Harris, *The Seigneurial System in Early Canada: A Geographical Study* (Madison: University of Wisconsin Press 1966) 119–21; Pierre Deffontaines, 'The *Rang*-Pattern of Rural Settlement in French Canada,' in *French Canadian Society*, vol. 1, ed. Marcel Rioux and Yves Martin (Toronto: McClelland and Stewart 1964) 11–12

11 Dechêne, *Habitants et marchands* 267

12 Of 38 developed farm lots in St Denis at the middle of the eighteenth century, 7 (18%) had only natural meadows, 16 (42%) had only artificial meadows, and the remaining 15 (39%) had some combination of the two. The mean

size of meadow area was 5.5 arpents per farm. ANQ, aveux et dénombrements, régime français, cahier supplémentaire, St Denis, 4 June 1745

13 The entire habitant inventory sample includes another 31 inventories from the 1830s as well. For more information on this collection, see Appendix 2.

14 John Lambert, *Travels through Canada and the United States of America in the Years 1806, 1807, and 1808* 2 vols (London: C. Cradock and W. Joy 1814) 1: 131

15 Robert-Lionel Séguin, *La civilisation traditionnelle de l''habitant' aux 17e et 18e siècles: Fonds Matériel* 2nd ed. (Montreal: Fides 1973) 597–609

16 A typical eighteenth-century farm lease specifies that the tenant must 'bucher deux cent perches de franc bois et les piquets seront plantés tous les ans en cloture sur ladte terre.' ANQM, gr. Jehanne, bail à ferme par René Guertin à Jacques Emery Godaire, 29 April 1781

17 ANQM, gr. Michaud, estate inventory of Pierre Boudrau and Marie Ursule Alaire, 14 March 1791

18 ANQM, gr. Jehanne, bail à ferme par J-B. Corbeille à Pierre Corbeil, 19 September 1778

19 William Evans, *A Treatise on the Theory and Practice of Agriculture* ... (Montreal: Fabre, Perrault and Co. 1835) 146

20 Ester Boserup, *The Conditions of Agricultural Growth* (London: George Allen and Unwin 1965). In attacking the Malthusian thesis that agricultural practices determine population growth, Boserup simply reversed the terms and argued that population determines cultivation systems. Although her argument is based on some valuable insights into the connections between labour, land, and fallowing systems, the conclusion, in reducing everything to population and agricultural practices, fails to transcend the terms of reference supplied by her Malthusian opponents. Since peasants are always part of a larger society and, by most definitions, subject to the domination of another class or classes, it is not surprising that changes in methods of cultivation are often imposed on them by other people and not by the forces of nature. The establishment of large sheep farms in early modern England and of plantations in tropical countries subjected to European imperialism are examples that come to mind.

21 Cf. Pierre de Sales Laterrière, *A Political and Historical Account of Lower Canada with Remarks on the Present Situation of the People, as Regards Their Manners, Character, Religion, etc. etc.* (London: William Marsh and Alfred Miller 1830) 123.

22 PAC, RG14, A1, vol. 3, Legislative Council, committee on Population, Agriculture and Crown Lands, 18 December 1786, 'Remarques et Observations que fait l'honnorable Lemoyne de Longueuil Ecuier.' Cf. Evans, *A Treatise* 113–15.

23 Joseph-François Perrault, *Traité d'agriculture pratique*, seconde partie; *De la grande et moyenne culture, adaptée au climat du Bas-Canada* (Quebec: Fréchette, 1831) 5

24 H.A. Innis, ed., *Select Documents in Canadian Economic History, 1497–1783* (Toronto: University of Toronto Press 1933) 297

25 For evidence that pensions alimentaires really were paid, see below, Chapter 3, pp 79–80.

26 ANQM, gr. Deguire, donation par la ve. Nicolas Thibault à Toussaint Thibault, 25 November 1760. Another deed of gift, published in its entirety, can be found in W. Stanford Reid, 'An Early French-Canadian Pension Agreement,' *CHR* 27 (September 1946) 291–4.

27 ANQM, gr. Bonnet, deed of gift by Joseph Blanchard and Marie Daigle to Joseph Blanchard fils, 4 October 1791

28 James T. Lemon, 'Household Consumption in Eighteenth-Century America and Its Relationship to Production and Trade: The Situation among Farmers in Southeastern Pennsylvania,' *Agricultural History* 41 (January 1967) 62; T.J.A. LeGoff, 'The Agricultural Crisis in Lower Canada, 1802–12: A Review of a Controversy,' *CHR* 55 (March 1974) 26. It also corresponds to the amount of wheat (13 minots) that eighteenth-century observers considered necessary for the three pounds of bread per day eaten in rural Quebec. Fernand Ouellet, *Le Bas-Canada 1791–1840: changements structuraux et crise* (Ottawa: Editions de l'université d'Ottawa 1976) 193; cf. Cameron Nish, *Les Bourgeois Gentilhommes de la Nouvelle-France, 1729–1748* (Montreal: Fides 1968) 121

29 Fernand Braudel, *Capitalism and Material Life 1400–1800*, trans. Miriam Kochan (New York: Harper and Row 1973) 94–5

30 Marvin L. Brown, ed., *Baroness von Riedesel and the American Revolution: Journal and Correspondence of a Tour of Duty 1776–1783* (Chapel Hill: University of North Carolina Press 1965) 207

31 Figures in Table 3 are from: Archives Nationales, Archives des colonies, G1, 461: 32, recensement général de la colonie de la Nouvelle-France, année 1739 (PAC microfilm); Ivanhoe Caron, *La colonisation de la province de Québec*, vol. 1: *Débuts du régime anglais 1760–1791* (Quebec: L'Action Sociale 1923) 275–80; ACESH, XVII, C39, Boucher to bishop, 11 September 1790.

32 Figures in Table 4 are from: ANQM, gr. Montmerque, inventory of Gabriel Bérard, 30 June 1746; ANQM, gr. Duvernay, inventory of Charles Maheu, 12 October 1748; ANQM, gr. Courville, inventory of Marie-Angélique Chapdelaine and François Lamoureux, 18 July 1764; ANQM, gr. Bonnet, inventory of Antoine Meunier dit Lapierre and Marie Marguerite Allaire, 15 June 1793; ANQM, gr. Bonnet, inventory of Angelique Chapdelaine and Jacques Daigle, 28 July 1795

33 Harris, *The Seigneurial System* 153. Louise Dechêne has called into question Harris' method of estimating crop yields in the absence of data on areas planted in grain. His figure should therefore be regarded more as a guess than as a precise measurement. Nevertheless, it seems a reasonable one and quite comparable to Dechêne's own estimate, based on different sources, of 1: 4.5 to 1: 6.5 for Montreal in the seventeenth century. Dechêne, *Habitants et marchands* 326–7

34 PAC, Jacobs Papers, 4: 51–2, Samuel Jacobs to Samuel Sills, 28 April 1784; ibid., Jacobs to William Grant, 28 April 1784. Jacobs' estimate of the normal level of tithes seems to be an exaggeration.

35 ACESH, XVII, C25, Gervais to Mgr Briand, 20 August 1769

36 Thus Fernand Ouellet's claim that habitant livestock holdings grew larger between 1765 and 1831 should be treated with some scepticism. *Economic and Social History* 349–53

37 This is not to say that habitants did not sell an ox now and then or a dozen eggs or some butter; in fact, sales of this sort, often requiring curtailed consumption at home, were probably quite important to families like the Allaires who did not always have wheat to sell. Nevertheless, selling was an incidental feature of Lower Richelieu animal husbandry, not its organizing motive.

38 'Les papiers La Pausse,' *RAPQ*, 1933–4, p 211

39 Peter N. Moogk, *Building a House in New France: An Account of the Perplexities of Client and Craftsmen in Early Canada* (Toronto: McClelland and Stewart 1977) 30

40 Mean floor area was 39 square metres from 1740 to 1769 (20 cases), 60 square metres from 1790 to 1799 (23 cases), and 70 square metres in the 1830s (6 cases).

41 Pierre Deffontaines, *L'homme et l'hiver au Canada* 8th ed. (Paris: Gallimard 1957) 69–70

42 Michel Terrisse, 'L'habitat en Suède aux temps modernes,' *Annales de démographie historique* (1975) 69–73

43 Brown, ed., *Baroness von Riedesel* 116

44 Séguin, *La civilisation traditionelle* 388–97

45 Lambert, *Travels through Canada* 1: 155

46 Braudel, *Capitalism and Material Life* 218–19; Marcel Moussette, 'Le chauffage domestique dans le Haut et le Bas-Canada (1759–1867)' (Ottawa: Ministère des Affaires Indiennes et du Nord 1973) 88–105

47 Deffontaines, *L'homme et l'hiver au Canada* 73–6; Marcel Moussette, 'Le chauffage domestique en Nouvelle-France' (Ottawa: Ministère des Affaires Indiennes et du Nord 1971) 99

48 Laterrière, *A Political and Historical Account*, 131–2

49 Lambert, *Travels through Canada* 1: 163; Hugh Gray, *Letters from Canada, Written during a Residence There in the Years 1806, 1807, and 1808; Shewing the Present State of Canada, Its Productions-Trade-Commercial Importance and Political Relations* (London: Longman, Hurst, Rees, and Orme 1809) 304–7; Moussette, 'Le chauffage domestique dans le Haut et le Bas-Canada' 88–105

CHAPTER THREE: GENERATIONS OF PEASANTS

1 One minor change from the seventeenth to the early nineteenth centuries in French Canada was the replacement of November by February as the most popular month for weddings. Raymond Roy, Yves Landry, and Hubert Charbonneau, 'Quelques comportements des canadiens au XVIIe siècle d'après les registres paroissiaux,' *RHAF* 31 (June 1977): 55; Etienne Gautier and Louis Henry, *La population de Crulai, paroisse normande: étude historique* (Paris: Presses universitaires de France 1958) 63; Jacques Houdaille, 'Un indicateur de pratique religieuse: la célébration saisonnière des mariages avant, pendant et après la révolution française (1740–1829),' *Population*, 33e année (March-April 1978) 367–80

2 Jean-Louis Flandrin, *Families in Former Times: Kinship, Household and Sexuality*, trans. Richard Southern (Cambridge: Cambridge University Press 1979) 19–23

3 J-M. Gouesse, 'Parenté, famille et mariage en Normandie aux XVIIe and XVIIIe siècles,' *AESC*, 27e année (July-October 1972) 1139–54

4 ACESH, XVII, c66, Joyer to Mgr Plessis, 14 December 1815; ibid., Kelly to Mgr Plessis, 29 April 1819

5 Ibid., c39, Hébert to Mgr Plessis, 10 May 1815; ibid., same to same, 10 April 1815

6 See below, p 143.

7 Daniel Scott Smith, 'The Demographic History of Colonial New England,' *Journal of Economic History* 32 (March 1972) 165–83. Cf. Jacques Houdaille, 'Démographie de la Nouvelle Angleterre aux XVIIe et XVIIIe siècles,' *Population*, 26e année (September-October 1971) 962–6.

8 J. Hajnal, 'European Marriage Patterns in Perspective,' in *Population in History: Essays in Historical Demography*, ed. David V. Glass and D.E.C. Eversley (London: Edward Arnold 1965) 101–43; Louis Henry and Altiva Pilatti Balhana, 'La population du Parana depuis le XVIIIe siècle,' *Population*, 30e année (November 1975) 173

9 Hubert Charbonneau, *Vie et mort de nos ancêtres: étude démographique* (Montreal: Presses de l'Université de Montréal 1975) 154–8

10 Jacques Henripin, *La population canadienne au début du XVIIIe siècle: nuptialité,*

fécondité, mortalité infantile (Paris: Presses universitaires de France 1954) 95; Charbonneau, *Vie et Mort* 184

11 The source for these figures and for other data on Sorel presented below is a typed summary, compiled under the direction of abbé Georges-Henri Cournoyer, of entries in the parish registers of Sorel (PAC, MG8, G59). A check with microfilms of the original registers showed this to be a perfectly accurate record of the parish's baptisms, marriages, and funerals.

The parish registers, and therefore this summary, seem to constitute a reliable record of the vital events occurring in Sorel. Under-registration is generally a problem in seventeenth-century Canada (Charbonneau, *Vie et mort* 86) but far less so, it seems, in the period under study here. Since neglect of infant deaths is the commonest form of under-registration, the relatively high levels of infant mortality found in Sorel (see below) encourage confidence in this source. Another potential difficulty with using parish registers for population studies is that, in Canada especially, the universe covered may change as parish boundaries are altered. Fortunately, however, the parish of St-Pierre-de-Sorel was not modified from the time it was established until 1843.

Using Cournoyer's transcript, I compiled monthly and yearly figures on births, deaths, and marriages for the period 1740–1839. I did not attempt full family reconstitution but I did link entries for some individuals in order to generate data on infant mortality and age at marriage. I also collected information on the marital status of brides and grooms. Details of this sort come from a sample of parish register entries only. Because the population of Sorel, and therefore the volume of its vital events, grew tremendously over the course of a century, I took different proportions of entries for different periods. Every entry in the 1740–79 period was included, while every second entry between 1780 and 1809 and every fifth entry from 1810 to 1839 went into the sample. As a result, the representation of each period in the sample was roughly equal, with an average of 57 acts per year from the first period, 60 from the second, and 62 from the third; in all, there were 5944 acts in the sample. This sampling procedure applied only to the examination of premarital conceptions, the sex of individuals baptized and buried and age and marital status at marriage; I at least counted every birth, death, and marriage in all three periods.

12 Charbonneau, *Vie et mort* 184

13 Studies of Old Régime peasantries of France suggest that widowers were much more successful in their pursuit of a new spouse than were widows. Given differential mortality, widowers were simply less numerous for one thing; a man who had lost his wife was therefore a rare fish and, since he

was normally older and perhaps better established economically than most bachelors, he was also a good catch. Widows, on the other hand, especially if they were encumbered with small children, were considered a second-best choice in this male-dominated society and widowers were therefore able, in many cases, to indulge their preference for a second virgin bride. Pierre Goubert, 'Les fondements démographiques,' in *Histoire économique et sociale de la France*, ed. Fernand Braudel and Ernest Labrousse, vol. 2 (Paris: Presses universitaires de France 1970) 30

14 François-Joseph Cugnet, *An Abstract of Those Parts of the Custom of the Viscounty and Provostship of Paris, which Were Received and Practised in the Province of Quebec, in the Time of the French Government* (London: C. Eyre and W. Strahan 1772) 56. Cf. Yves F. Zoltvany, 'Esquisse de la Coutume de Paris,' *RHAF* 25 (December 1971) 365–84. Although the Custom of Paris is essential reading for anyone wishing to understand early French-Canadian marriage and inheritance practices, this does not mean that nothing more is required. Habitant custom in this and all other matters evolved as a creative response to circumstance, not simply passive conformity to prescribed behaviour. Cf. Louise Dechêne, *Habitants et marchands de Montréal au XVIIe siècle* (Paris and Montreal: Plon 1974) 423.

15 Dechêne, *Habitants et marchands* 419

16 One might also mention the 'don mutuel,' a clause found in most habitant inventories, by which bride and groom gave one another all their possessions. In case one spouse died before any children were born, this ensured that the survivor would be allowed to keep all property brought to the marriage by the deceased; after the death of the widow or widower, any propres would return to the family whence they had come.

17 ANQM, gr. Deguire, mariage de Théophile Alaire et Claire Félicité Hodet, 30 March 1761

18 For another example, see AJS, gr. Faribault, séparation entre Joseph Letendre et Catherine Peloquin, 14 March 1767. In this case also the wife was a previously married widow and the husband was left in charge of the couple's only child.

19 ANQM, gr. Jehanne, séparation volontaire entre Etienne Ledoux père et Claire Félicité Audet, 8 June 1779

20 Ibid., vente par Claire Félicité Audet à Sr Louis Goulet, 18 June 1779; ibid., vente par J-Bte Ménard à Claire Félicité Audet, 5 July 1779

21 Jan Noel, 'Les femmes favorisées: Women of New France,' *Atlantis* 6 (Spring 1981) 80–98

22 ACESH, XVII, c66, Martel to bishop, n.d.; ibid., Bruneau to Mgr Plessis, 1 October 1814; ibid., same to same, 28 April 1815; ibid., c25, Kelly to Mgr

Plessis, 3 April 1817; ibid., Bédard to Mgr Plessis, 21 October 1818; ibid., c39; memorandum prepared for pastoral visit, May 1788
23 Cf. Sylvia Van Kirk, 'Many Tender Ties': Women in Fur-Trade Society in Western Canada (Winnipeg: Watson and Dwyer 1980).
24 More refined measures of illegitimacy than the overall ratio can eliminate purely demographic biases. Essentially this involves measuring the incidence of illegitimacy within particular age groups and in relation to the number of unmarried women only. Once again, full family reconstitution is required before this kind of analysis can be undertaken. Differences in the ratio of actual to reported illegitimate births could also distort comparisons between different populations. See Peter Laslett, Family Life and Illicit Love in Earlier Generations: Essays in Historical Sociology (Cambridge: Cambridge University Press 1977).
25 Cf. Edward Shorter, 'Illegitimacy, Sexual Revolution and Social Change in Modern Europe,' Journal of Interdisciplinary History 2 (August 1971) 237–72; Alain Molinier, 'Enfants trouvés, enfants abandonnés et enfants illégitimes en Languedoc aux xviie et xviiie siècles,' in Hommage à Marcel Reinhard: sur la population française au XVIIIe et au XIXe siècles (Paris: Société de démographie historique 1973) 445–73.
The illegitimacy rates presented here are much higher than those compiled by abbé Tanguay for Lower Canada as a whole in the same periods. Perhaps the presence of military garrisons throughout most of our period explains Sorel's apparently exceptional performance, although the absence of an unusual number of illegitimate births at the time of the American Revolution, when troops were very numerous, argues against this interpretation. Shortcomings in the provincial statistics are a more likely cause of the discrepancy in the figures. Tanguay does not make clear what criteria he required to count a birth as illegitimate, but his implausibly low figures suggest that he demanded the excessively limiting indication of an explicit mention of illegitimacy. See Cyprien Tanguay, Dictionnaire généalogique des familles canadiennes depuis la fondation de la colonie jusqu'à nos jours 7 vols (Montreal: E. Senécal 1871–90) 4: 607–8; cf. Jean-Pierre Wallot, 'Religion and French-Canadian Mores in the Early Nineteenth Century,' CHR 52 (March 1971) 85.
26 AJS, gr. H. Crebassa, déclaration de De. Marguerite Paul Hus, sage femme, 22 March 1838
27 William L. Langer, 'Infanticide: A Historical Survey,' History of Childhood Quarterly 1 (1974) 353–65
28 Innuendo about this sort of thing was at the root of an 1839 lawsuit over a public insult. One woman apparently had been heard to say of a neighbour, 'que la demanderesse Marguerite Mandeville marchait sur ses enfants morts

sans avoir reçu le baptême qui étoient enterrés dans sa cave, donnant par là à entendre que la Demanderesse avoit eu des enfans avant son mariage and qu'elle les avoit tués ...' AJS, gr. N-D. Crebassa, désistement de poursuite et réparation d'injures par Charlotte Gouin à Margueritte Mandeville, 18 November 1839

29 Cf. Charbonneau, *Vie et mort* 214; D.S. Smith and M.S. Hindus, 'Pre-Marital Pregnancy in America 1640–1971: An Overview and Interpretation,' *Journal of Interdisciplinary History* 5 (Spring 1975) 561–70.

30 Pierre de Sales Laterrière, *A Political and Historical Account of Lower Canada with Remarks on the Present Situation of the People, as Regards Their Manners, Characters, Religion etc. etc.* (Quebec: Fréchette 1831) 140. On the other hand, recent research in England suggests that there was a surprising lack of connection between illegitimacy and age at marriage. Laslett, *Family Life and Illicit Love* 106

31 ACESH, XVII, C25, Louis Edouard Hubert to bishop, 17 December 1832. It might be more correct to view this incident as an illustration of the rule that women must submit to the sexual impulses of their husbands.

32 See, for example, Georges Langlois, *Histoire de la population canadienne-française* 2nd ed. (Montreal: Editions Albert Lévesque 1935) 143–5.

33 Charbonneau, *Vie et mort*

34 Data on yearly numbers of births come from abbé Cournoyer's transcript of the Sorel parish registers, and from ACESH, 'Histoire de la Paroisse de St-Ours' by Isidore Desnoyers, pp 146–7 and ibid., 'Chronique de la Paroisse de St-Denis, Rivière Chambly' by Isidore Desnoyers, 2 vols, 2: 91–2. In France, the crude birth rate declined from 39.9 to 31.0 per thousand between 1740 and 1829. The contrast with the Lower Richelieu is slightly exaggerated by the fact that the French figures include urban as well as rural populations.

35 J. Potter, 'The Growth of Population in America, 1700–1860,' in *Population in History* 672; Henry and Pilatti Balhana, 'La population du Parana' 174

36 Cf. Pierre Goubert, *Beauvais et le Beauvaisis de 1600 à 1730: Contribution à l'histoire sociale de la France du XVIIe siècle* 2 vols (Paris: SEVPEN 1960) 1: 37, 1: 64; D.E.C. Eversley, 'A Survey of Population in an Area of Worcestershire from 1660 to 1850 on the basis of Parish Registers,' in *Population in History* 333; Louis Henry, 'The Population of France in the Eighteenth Century,' in *Population in History* 441; Philip J. Greven, *Four Generations: Population, Land, and Family in Colonial Andover, Massachusetts* (Ithaca and London: Cornell University Press 1970) 105

37 Greven, *Four Generations* 183; Kenneth A. Lockridge, 'The Population of Dedham, Massachusetts, 1636–1736,' *Economic History Review*, 2nd series, 19 (August 1966) 330

38 Jean Meuvret, 'Demographic Crisis in France from the Sixteenth to the Eighteenth Century,' in *Population in History* 507–22; Goubert, *Beauvais et le Beauvaisis*

39 Cf. Lockridge, 'The Population of Dedham.' Mortality peaks in North America occasionally slowed population growth but they did not bring net losses as they did in Europe, where populations actually dropped 10–15 per cent through mortality crises.

40 Pierre Goubert, 'La force du nombre,' in *Histoire économique et sociale de la France*, vol. 2, ed. Fernand Braudel and Ernest Labrousse (Paris: Presses universitaires de France 1970) 38–46

41 Fernand Ouellet, review of Hubert Charbonneau and André Larose, eds, *The Great Mortalities: Methodological Studies of Demographic Crises in the Past*, in *HS-SH* 14 (November 1981) 519–21

42 Richard Chabot, *Le curé de campagne et la contestation locale au Québec (de 1791 aux troubles de 1837–38)* (Montreal: Hurtubise HMH 1975) 103–4

43 ACESH, XVII, C25, Martin to Mgr Plessis, 15 November 1809

44 Geoffrey Bilson, 'The First Epidemic of Asiatic Cholera in Lower Canada, 1832,' *Medical History* 21 (October 1977) 428; Louise Dechêne and Jean-Claude Robert, 'Le choléra de 1832 dans le Bas-Canada: mesure des inégalités devant la mort,' in *The Great Mortalities: Methodological Studies of Demographic Crises in the Past*, ed. Hubert Charbonneau and André Larose (Liège: Ordina Editions, n.d.) 232–4

45 ACESH, XVII, C25, Gervais to Mgr Briand, 20 August 1769

46 Goubert, *Beauvais et le Beauvaisis* 1: 40

47 Ibid. 2: 64; Gérard Bouchard, *Le village immobile: Sennely-en-Sologne au XVIIIe siècle* (Paris: Plon 1972) 75; François Lebrun, *Les hommes et la mort en Anjou aux 17e et 18e siècles: essai de démographie et de psychologie historiques* (Paris: Mouton 1971) 189; Yves Blayo, 'La mortalité en France de 1740 à 1829,' *Population* 30e année (November 1975) 138–41

48 Charbonneau, *Vie et mort* 122; Henripin, *La population canadienne* 106; Jacques Dupâquier, 'Les caractères originaux de l'histoire démographique française au XVIIIe siècle,' *Revue d'histoire moderne et contemporaine* 23 (April-June 1976) 194–6; Gautier and Henry, *La population de Crulai* 162; Oiva Turpeinen, 'Infectious Diseases and Regional Differences in Finnish Death Rates, 1749–1773,' *Population Studies* 32 (November 1978) 525; E.A. Wrigley, 'Mortality in Pre-Industrial England: The Example of Colyton, Devon, over Three Centuries,' *Daedalus* 97 (Spring 1968) 570

49 Thomas McKeown and R.G. Brown, 'Medical Evidence Related to English Population Change in the Eighteenth Century,' in *Population in History* 294

50 PAC, Records of the Clerk of the Legislative Council, Quebec and Lower

Canada, vol. 3, submission of John Connor, MD, 19 January 1787. Connor's complaints about child delivery in Canada are almost exactly the same as those directed, about the same time, against midwives in France. Louise H. Tilly and Joan W. Scott, *Women, Work, and Family* (New York: Holt, Rinehart and Winston, 1978) 57

51 Jacques Gélis, 'Sages-femmes et accoucheurs: l'obstétrique populaire aux xviie et xviiie siècles,' *AESC*, 32e année (September-October 1977) 927-57

52 ANQM, gr. Duvernay, inventory of Pierre Harpin and Marguerite Truchon, 26 November 1757

53 Nicolas Gaspard Boucault, 'Etat présent du Canada,' *RAPQ*, 1920-1, p 16

54 Thomas McKeown, *The Modern Rise of Population* (London: Edward Arnold 1976)

55 PAC, Records of the Clerk of the Legislative Council, Quebec and Lower Canada, vol. 3, submission of Charles Blake, surgeon, 8 January 1787; Joseph-François Perrault, *Traité d'agriculture pratique*, seconde partie; *De la grande et moyenne culture, adaptée au climat du Bas-Canada* (Quebec: Fréchette 1831) 64, 92

56 ACESH, XVII, C25, Martin to Mgr Plessis, 17 December 1809; PAC, Jacobs Papers, 14: 1507, François Gatien to Samuel Jacobs, 6 March 1776

57 See Allan Greer, 'Habitants of the Lower Richelieu: Rural Society in Three Quebec Parishes, 1740-1840' (PH D thesis, York University 1980) 55-8.

58 See, for example, Bouchard, *Le village immobile* 109-20; Lebrun, *Les hommes et la mort* 261-9.

59 PAC, de Ramezay papers, p 2127, partage de la succession de Ramezay, n.d. (1752)

60 PAC, St Ours seigneurie, vol 5, partage de la succession de St Ours, 31 August 1734

61 Azarie Couillard-Desprès, *Histoire de la seigneurie de St-Ours* 2 vols (Montreal: Imprimerie de l'Institution des sourds-muets 1915-17) 1: 112-59

62 Emmanuel LeRoy Ladurie, 'Family Structures and Inheritance Customs in Sixteenth-Century France,' in *Family and Inheritance: Rural Society in Western Europe, 1200-1800*, ed. Jack Goody, Joan Thirsk, and E.P. Thompson (Cambridge: Cambridge University Press 1976) 41-51

63 Cugnet, *An Abstract* 114-15

64 Dechêne, *Habitants et marchands* 424-33

65 AJS, gr. Robin, inventory of J-Bte Cardin and feue Jeanne Carie, 17 September 1791

66 PAC, Sorel seigneurie, vol 10, 'concessions [sic] par Paul Heu, devant Petit Notr., 1727-1729'

67 ANQ, aveux et dénombrements, régime français, St Ours, 15 May-4 June 1745; ANQM, gr. Danré de Blanzy, dépôt d'accord entre Jean Ménard et Théophile

Alaire et uxor, 6 Feburary 1754; ANQM, gr. Duvernay, vente par Joseph Dufaux et sa femme et Jacques Allaire à Théophile Allaire, 26 March 1755; ibid., vente par les heritiers Allaire à François Dupré et Théophile Allaire, 10 April 1755.

68 PAC, records of the Clerk of the Legislative Council, Quebec and Lower Canada, vol. 3, submission of Alexandre Dumas to the committee on Population, Agriculture and Crown Lands, December 1786

69 Greven, *Four Generations* 72–99, 125–72; cf. Margaret Spufford, 'Peasant Inheritance Customs and Land Distribution in Cambridgeshire from the Sixteenth to the Eighteenth Centuries,' in *Family and Inheritance* 173.

70 AJS, gr. H. Crebassa, donation par Dame Magdelaine Landry veuve de Pierre Ethier à Demoiselle Marguerithe Ethier, 21 January 1798

71 ANQM, gr. Jehanne, donation par Marie Françoise Herpain veuve d'Antoine Lacoste dit Languedoc à Antoine Lacoste dit Languedoc son fils, 27 June 1769

72 ANQM, gr. Deguire, donation par Louis Poulin à Louis-Marie-Joseph Poulin, 28 November 1759. Note the way the section of the Custom of Paris that gives endowed heirs the option of keeping advantages or restoring them to the estate is blithely ignored!

73 AJS, gr. Faribault, donation de Pre. Plante et sa femme à Antoine leur fils, 23 February 1765.

74 ANQM, gr. Bourdages, donation par Louis Lefebvre et uxor à André Dupré et Marie Magdelaine Lefebvre sa femme, 8 October 1830

75 For a record of actual deliveries, see the account book of the estate of J-Bte Bourgeois and Agathe Leblanc, ANQM, gr. Migneault, 6 September 1831.

76 Theoretically, land received from parents was in fact a propre and consequently not part of the marriage community. The distinction between propres and conquêts, however, was one of those points in the Custom of Paris that French-Canadian habitants generally tended to ignore, and wives were therefore admitted to a share in the ownership of land their husbands acquired by deed of gift.

77 While generally upholding French civil law, the Quebec Act in fact proclaimed testamentary freedom, a provision completely at odds with the inheritance rules of the Custom of Paris. At the level of legal theory, the result was confusion and ambiguity (see André Morel, *Les limites de la liberté testamentaire dans le droit civil de la province de Québec* [Paris: Librairie de droit et de jurisprudence 1960] 22–3). In the countryside, on the other hand, this legislation produced no sudden profusion of wills; rather it seems to have passed unnoticed. If the English legal tradition had an influence here, it was subtle and gradual.

78 PAC, Map Division, John Collins, 'A Plan of the Seigniory of Sorrell in the

Province of Quebec the Property of Messr. Greenwood and Higginson Merchants in London,' 15 August 1770
79 Cf. Marcel Trudel, *The Seigneurial Regime* (Ottawa: Canadian Historical Association 1956) 5.
80 R.C. Harris, *The Seigneurial System in Early Canada: A Geographical Study* (Madison: University of Wisconsin Press 1966) 106. Cf. Guy Frégault, 'Le régime seigneurial et l'expansion de la colonisation dans le bassin du St-Laurent au dix-huitième siècle,' *Canadian Historical Association Report* (1944) 68–9.
81 See ASQ, fonds Verreau, carton 2, no. 96, J.A. Raymond to M. de Contrecoeur, 27 September 1763.
82 Some sample figures: concession deeds in St Ours cost 5.7 livres in 1736, 18 livres in 1817; survey fees were 7.5 livres in St Denis in 1763, 9 to 18 livres in St Ours in 1817. Ibid.; PAC, St Ours seigneurie, vol 1
83 By way of contrast, in the older sections, granted before 1770, only 35 (28%) out of 127 had been bought. PAC, Sorel seigneurie, vol. 11
84 Dechêne, *Habitants et marchands* 271–8
85 ANQM, gr. de Courville, inventory of Pierre Ledoux and Josephte Lacoste, 26 June 1764
86 AJS, gr. Frichet, inventory of Etienne Ledoux and the late Marie-Josephte Bourgot, 7 March 1767. Cf. ANQM, gr. Duvernay, inventory of Charles Maheu and late Marie-Josette Dudevoir, 12 October 1748; ANQM, gr. Montmerque, inventory of late Pierre Carré and Marie Cochon, 30 August 1751; ANQM, gr. Jehanne, inventory of François Messier dit St François and late Marie Catherine Champigny, 3 February 1769
87 Ivanoe Caron ed., 'Procès-verbaux du procureur-général Collet sur le district des paroisses de la Nouvelle-France,' *RAPQ* 1921–2, pp 316–19
88 J. Vallée, ed., *Tocqueville dans le Bas-Canada* (Montreal: Editions du Jour 1973) 86
89 Cf. Gérard Bouchard, 'Family Structures and Geographic Mobility at Laterrière, 1851–1935,' *Journal of Family History* 2 (December 1977) 350–69.
90 Ludger Beauregard, 'Le peuplement du Richelieu,' *Revue de géographie de Montréal* 19 (1965) 49–51
91 Greven, *Four Generations* 155
92 PAC, St Ours seigneurie, vol. 1, concession deeds, passim
93 Laterrière, *A Political and Historical Account* 120
94 For the 'independence' thesis, see Lionel Groulx, *Histoire du Canada français depuis la découverte*, 4th ed., 2 vols (Montreal: Fides 1960) 1: 287–92; A.L. Burt, *The Old Province of Quebec*, 2nd ed. (Toronto: McClelland and Stewart 1968) 1–2; W.J. Eccles, *France in America* (Vancouver: Fitzhenry and Whiteside 1972) 127–9; R. Cole Harris, 'The Extension of France into Rural Canada,' in

European Settlement and Development in North America: Essays on Geographical Change in Honour and Memory of Andrew Hill Clark, ed. J.R. Gibson (Toronto: University of Toronto Press 1978) 27–45.

Writings stressing the dependence of the habitants include: Francis Parkman, *The Old Régime in Canada* (London: Macmillan 1899) 304–25; G.M. Wrong, *The Rise and Fall of New France* (Toronto: Macmillan 1928) 397–416; Ouellet, 'Libéré ou exploité! Le paysan québécois d'avant 1850.'

CHAPTER FOUR: ARISTOCRATIC ASCENDANCY

1 A. Irving Hallowell, 'The Nature and Function of Property as a Social Institution,' in *Culture and Experience* (Philadelphia: University of Pennsylvania Press 1955) 246

2 Perry Anderson, *Passages from Antiquity to Feudalism* (London: NLB 1974) 148

3 R.C. Harris, *The Seigneurial System in Early Canada: A Geographical Study* (Madison: University of Wisconsin Press 1966) 107

4 A.J.E. Lunn, 'Economic Development in New France, 1713–1760' (PH D thesis, McGill University 1942) 220

5 See PAC, de Ramezay papers, p 1381, undated slip of paper (about 1760), listing names of eight Sorel habitants with the notation, 'ont busché du bois.'

6 Robert Forster, *The Nobility of Toulouse in the Eighteenth Century: A Social and Economic Study* (Baltimore: Johns Hopkins Press 1960) 88–94; Witold Kula, *An Economic Theory of the Feudal System: Towards a Model of the Polish Economy, 1500–1800* trans. Lawrence Garner (London: NLB 1976) 33–8

7 Marc Bloch, *French Rural History: An Essay on Its Basic Characteristics*, trans. Janet Sondheimer (Berkeley: University of California Press 1966) 126–49; Louis Merle, *La métairie et l'évolution agraire de la Gâtine poitevine de la fin du Moyen Age à la Révolution* (Paris: SEVPEN 1958)

8 For example, Merle, *La métairie*; Jean Meyer, *La noblesse bretonne au XVIIIe siècle* 2 vols (Paris: SEVPEN 1966) 2: 591–860. Cf. Dechêne, 'L'évolution du régime seigneurial au Canada: le cas de Montréal aux XVIIe et XVIIIe siècles,' *Recherches sociographiques* 12 (May-August 1971) 177–8.

9 The three demesnes measured respectively 302, 240, and 96 arpents according to the Lower-Canadian census of 1831.

10 PAC, de Ramezay papers, pp 684–91, lease by Mr de Ramezay to Joseph Mimaux, 29 January 1759; ibid., pp. 124–6, Dunoyet to Bellot, 17 April 1764. Gross production was 80 minots wheat, 10 minots peas, and 10 minots barley; seed and other deductions left the shares of landlord and tenant at 23.25 minots wheat, 3.5 minots peas, and 4 minots barley each.

11 E.P. Thompson, 'The Grid of Inheritance: A Comment,' in *Family and Inher-*

itance: Rural Society in Western Europe, 1200–1800, ed. Jack Goody, Joan Thirsk, and E.P. Thompson (Cambridge: Cambridge University Press 1976) 328–60; cf. V.G. Kiernan, 'Private Property in History,' in ibid. 361–98.

12 Marc Bloch, *French Rural History: An Essay on Its Basic Characteristics,* trans. J. Sondheimer (Berkeley: University of California Press, 1966) 126–9

13 See, for example, Fernand Ouellet, *Le Bas-Canada 1791–1840: Changements structuraux et crise* (Ottawa: Editions de l'Université d'Ottawa 1976) 233.

14 PAC, St Ours seigneurie, estate rolls of fief Laperrière, 1787; ANQM, gr. L. Bonnet, retrait by Louis Bonnet on Joseph Tarte, 19 October 1791; ibid., sale by Antoine Lamoureux to Jacques Laplante, 20 October 1791

15 For example, PAC, St Ours seigneurie, vol. 1, pt. 1, concession by M. de Léry to François-Marie Girard, 6 October 1753. Cf. Harris, *Seigneurial System* 129.

16 Harris, *Seigneurial System* 130. In principle, seigneurs could not evict censitaires for non-payment of dues alone; instead, their recourse was to a lawsuit which might, if they won their case, lead to the judicial seizure and sale of the debtor's property; still the land would not necessarily revert to the seigneur.

17 *Edits, ordonnances royaux, déclaration et Arrêts du Conseil d'état du Roi concernant le Canada* 3 vols (Quebec: E.R. Fréchette, 1854–6) 3: 397–8, 403–4; Pierre-Georges Roy, *Inventaire des Ordonnances des Intendants de la Nouvelle-France conservées aux Archives Provinciales de Québec* 4 vols (Beauceville: L'Eclaireur 1919) 2: 176; 3: 41

18 PAC, St Ours seigneurie, vol. 1, pt. 5, concession by the agent of the heirs St Ours Cournoyer to Jean-Baptiste Ledroit père, 17 May 1801. 'Ladte. terre presque toute en bois debout, n'ayant que le devant déserté sur la quel se trouve une petite maison en mauvais Etat occupée depuis huit années par la famille de defunt Larichardière qui a Toujours négligé de prendre titre ...'; ANQM, gr. L. Bonnet, vente par Charles de St Ours à Joseph Laroque, 30 October 1794

19 A statement by the indebted habitant follows, turning over his farm to the seigneur. The agent notes that this poor peasant also owed money to a local shopkeeper but adds that the latter would not intervene in the transaction, even though the land was his only guarantee of repayment. This was because the seigneur always had first priority as a creditor; if the merchant sued and won possession of the property he would find it burdened with a seigneurial debt that would then be his responsibility. Conditioned by a legal code biased in favour of the aristocracy, the outcome of this minor drama was that the merchant remained unpaid, the habitant lost his farm and the seigneur got possession of the property. PAC, de Ramezay papers, 1: 118–21, Dunoyet to Bellot, 19 May 1764. Cf. PAC, St Ours seigneurie, vol. 1, passim.

20 PAC, St Ours seigneurie, vol. 11, estate roll, fief Laperrière, 1787
21 Ibid., vol. 1, passim
22 Ibid., vol. 13. fols. 9169–70, déclaration par Marguerite de Repentigny, François de St Ours, Sr Courtemanche, Montreal, 4 March 1755
23 ASQ, fonds Verreau, carton 2, no. 100, Joseph LeBrodeur dt Lavigne to M. Contrecoeur, 12 June 1767 (PAC microfilm). Examples of seigneurial largesse towards local churches can be found in the vestry accounts of the parishes of St Ours and St Denis.
24 PAC, Haldimand papers, 47: 132–4, Cherrier and LaBruyère Montarville to Haldimand, 1 July 1783
25 Scottish Records Office, Dalhousie Papers, sec. 3, no. 177, J.K. Welles to Lord Dalhousie, 5 May 1828 (PAC microfilm); JHALC, 1825, pp 35–6, 78–80; ANQ, fonds Couillard-Desprès, Badeaux to T.A. Coffin, 22 January 1796
26 PAC, St Ours seigneurie, vol. 1, pt. 1, passim. Cf. Fernand Ouellet, 'Officiers de milice et structure sociale au Québec (1660–1815),' HS-SH 12 (May 1979) 46.
27 Harris, Seigneurial System 77
28 PAC, St Ours seigneurie, vol. 1, pt. 3, concession by Monsieur de Contrecoeur to Joseph and François Plouf, 10 March 1721.
29 Marcel Trudel, The Seigneurial Regime, Canadian Historical Association booklet 6 (Ottawa: CHA 1956) 17
30 PAC, St Ours seigneurie, vol. 11, estate roll, fief LaPotterie, 1751
31 Ibid., vol. 1, pt. 8, titres nouvels, fief Laperrière, 1846–7 and St Ours, 1854–5
32 Louise Dechêne has already made this point in relation to the seigneurie of Montreal. See 'L'évolution du régime seigneurial au Canada: le cas de Montréal aux XVIIe et XVIIIe siècles,' Recherches sociographiques 12 (May-August 1971) 143–83.
33 See, for example, PAC, St Ours seigneurie, vol. 2, pt. 1, vente par Monsieur de Contrecoeur pour Mlle sa fille au sr Joseph de Meulle, 19 March 1761. The sale was of a 120-arpent lot originally conceded by the seigneur to his daughter in 1756. The price was 2000 livres to be paid as an annuity at 100 livres per year (added to the normal seigneurial rents). There is no mention of any clearing or improvements in the deed. The buyer, a local shopkeeper, was probably willing to accept this arrangement because of the location of the land near the parish centre.
34 PAC, Sorel seigneurie, vol. 1, Théodore de Pincier to Robert Jones, 24 December 1805
35 Dechêne, 'L'évolution du régime seigneurial' 176–7
36 Fernand Ouellet, 'Propriété seigneuriale et groupes sociaux dans la vallée du Saint-Laurent (1663–1840),' in Mélanges d'histoire du Canada français offerts au

professeur Marcel Trudel (Ottawa: Editions de l'université d'Ottawa 1978) 183–213

37 Support was often given grudgingly by administrators who resented the idleness and arrogance of the excessively numerous Canadian noblesse, but it was given all the same. Dechêne, 'L'évolution du régime seigneurial' 383

38 The main sources for what follows are: Couillard-Desprès, *Histoire de St-Ours;* Claude de Bonnault, 'Généalogie de la famille de Saint-Ours: Dauphiné et Canada,' *Bulletin des recherches historiques* 55 (1949) 27–43, 97–110, 169–90, 228–44; 56 (1950) 17–32, 100–11; C.C.J. Bond, 'Pierre de Saint-Ours,' in *Dictionary of Canadian Biography* vol. 2 (Toronto: University of Toronto Press 1969) 592–3; C.J. Russ, 'Jean-Baptiste de Saint-Ours Deschaillons,' in ibid., vol. 3 (Toronto: University of Toronto Press, 1974): 578–9; PAC, St Ours-Dorion collection.

39 Cameron Nish, *Les Bourgeois-Gentilhommes de la Nouvelle-France, 1729–1748* (Montreal: Fides 1968) 150

40 Ibid.

41 Quoted in Bloch, *French Rural History* 138

42 Couillard-Desprès, *Histoire de St-Ours* 2: 34–5

43 Sources: Couillard-Desprès, *Histoire de St Ours* 1: 100–3; 1: 291; 2: 26–7; 2: 83; Nish, *Les bourgeois-gentilhommes* 150; PAC, St Ours seigneurie, 11: 7288, 7290, receipts of rents for Cournoyer heirs, 5 May 1811 and 1 February 1814. Some of these figures are estimates calculated from revenues of part of the seigneurie. The 1734 and 1795 entries are double the reported income of individuals who held half the fief's territory. The 1810 and 1813 figures are ten times the seigneurial rent paid to the 'Cournoyer heirs,' descendants of Pierre de St Ours II, who controlled one-tenth of the seigneurie. The raw data for the 1765 and 1795 estimates included wheat as well as cash; these were converted to money on the basis of current wheat prices, three livres and five livres to the minot respectively.

44 Total cost of the funeral and mourning was 11,080 livres. ANQ, fonds François-Roch de St Ours, estate inventory, 19 June 1841; ANQ, événements de 1837–8, T. Rainsford to Major Goldie, 3 October 1839

45 See Saint-Vallier, *Rituel du diocèse de Québec publié par l'ordre de Saint-Vallier, évêque de Québec* (Paris 1703) 14. Figures are from the parish register of Sorel from 1740 to 1779 (except September 1757–July 1761, missing). They suggest a population that was essentially obedient to ecclesiastical rules in this regard. Still, conformity was not perfect here as it was about this time in the strongly Catholic rural regions of western France. Cf. Yves Blayo and Louis Henry, 'Données démographiques sur la Bretagne et l'Anjou de 1740 à 1829,' *Annales de démographie historique* (1967) 91–171

46 H. Têtu and C-O. Gagnon, eds, *Mandements, lettres pastorales et circulaires des évêques de Québec* 8 vols (Quebec: Imprimerie Générale A. Coté et Cie 1887–93) 2: 457–9, 2: 35–6; *Mandements, lettres pastorales, circulaires et autres documents publiés dans le diocèse de Montréal depuis son érection* vol. 1 (Montreal: Le Nouveau Monde 1869) 46–52

47 For more details, see my article, 'L'habitant, la paroisse rurale et la politique locale au xviiie siècle: Quelques cas dans la Vallée du Richelieu,' Société canadienne d'histoire de l'église catholique, *Sessions d'études* 47 (1980) 19–33.

48 Curés often claimed the right to tithe other crops and, in Sorel, where non-cereal crops were relatively important, parishioners apparently delivered one 26th of their corn, beans, and potatoes. ACESH, XVII, C66, Martel to Mgr Hubert, 30 October 1790

49 Ibid., C39, memorandum prepared for pastoral visit to St Ours, May 1788; ibid., petition of parishioners of St Ours to Mgr Panet, 18 July 1831

50 Daniel Jousse, *Traité du gouvernement spirituel et temporel des paroisses ...* (Paris: Chez Debure père 1769) 13; Pierre Goubert, *The Ancien Régime: French Society 1600–1750*, trans. Steve Cox (London: Weidenfeld and Nicolson 1973) 88–9; Gérard Bouchard, *Le village immobile: Sennely-en-Sologne au XVIIIe siècle* (Paris: Plon 1971) 217

51 ACESH, XVII, C39, Hébert to Mgr Lartigue, 19 September 1826

52 Aurore Dupuis, 'Les contrats de bancs d'église à Montréal au xviiie siècle (1692–1760)' (mémoire de maîtrise, Université de Sherbrooke 1978) 67–74

53 Sorel parish archives, vestry accounts

54 These details come mainly from the old parish histories, written by clergymen and in which such matters feature prominently. Couillard-Desprès, *Histoire de Sorel*; idem, *Histoire de St-Ours*; Allaire, *Histoire de St-Denis*; Desnoyers, 'Histoire de St-Ours'; idem, 'Histoire de St-Denis,' passim

55 Sorel parish archives, minutes of parish meetings of 29 June 1755, 20 February 1780, and 6 January 1784

56 ACESH, XVII, C39, Mgr Briand aux habitants de St-Ours, 1779

57 St Ours parish archives, vestry deliberations and accounts, vol. 1, meeting of 11 October 1789

58 PAC, Sorel seigneurie, vol. 7, deposition of Sophie Kelly veuve Mignault before H. Crebassa, JP, 14 September 1826

59 Greer, 'L'habitant, la paroisse rurale'

60 In Sorel, St Ours, and St Denis, total vestry revenues rose considerably around the turn of the nineteenth century as pew rental replaced voluntary contributions as the largest source of income. Thus there is every reason for scepticism towards Gilles Paquet's and Jean-Pierre Wallot's claim that parish revenue figures constitute 'une mesure indirecte du bien-être des habitants.'

('Crise agricole et tensions socio-ethniques dans le Bas-Canada, 1802–1812: éléments pour une ré-interprétation,' *RHAF* 26 [September 1972] 227)
61 Louis-Edmond Hamelin, 'Evolution numérique séculaire du clergé catholique dans le Québec,' *Recherches sociographiques* 2 (April-June 1961) 189–242
62 ANQM, gr. J-C. Duvernay, inventory of Messire Charles Dufaux de la Jimerais, 23–4 March 1750; PAC, St Ours seigneurie, vol. 7 dépot du testament olographe de feu Messire Jean-Franc Hébert Prêtre, 13 September 1831
63 ACESH, XVII, C25, Demers to Mgr Lartigue, 17 November 1837

CHAPTER FIVE: THE FEUDAL BURDEN

1 Louise Dechêne, 'L'évolution du régime seigneurial au Canada: le cas de Montréal aux XVIIe et XVIIIe siècles,' *Recherches sociographiques* 12 (May-August 1971) 152
2 Ibid.; cf. William Bennett Munro, *Documents Relating to the Seigniorial Tenure in Canada, 1598–1854* (Toronto: Champlain Society 1908) 74.
3 The assumption here is that wheat is valued at 10 livres per minot and that the hypothetical farm measures 3 arpents frontage by 30 arpents depth. The earliest concessions were fixed at one sol per arpent of area plus one capon (value 10 sols in 1709) for each arpent of frontage. The rate applied from 1754 on was one sol per arpent plus one-half minot of wheat for each 20 arpents (PAC, St Ours seigneurie, vol. 1, concession deeds). The evolution of rents in the seigneurie of Longueuil was almost exactly parallel, except that the rise in rates occurred rather earlier. Louis Lemoine, 'Une société seigneuriale: Longueuil: méthode, sources, orientations' (Master's thesis, Université de Montréal 1975) 145
4 PAC, de Ramezay papers, pp 1532–42, estate roll, Sorel, n.d. (1761–3)
5 ANQM, St Denis seigneurie, 22RS7, list of arrears, 1840; PAC, Sorel seigneurie, vol. 11, estate roll, 1795
6 PAC, Sorel seigneurie, vol. 12, accounts of the seigneurie of Sorel, 1840–7. Cf. William Bennet Munro, *The Seigniorial System in Canada: A Study in French Colonial Policy* (Cambridge: Harvard University Press 1907) 96; Dechêne, 'L'évolution du régime seigneurial' 157–8.
7 See, for example, PAC, St Ours seigneurie vol. 1, pt. 6
8 Marc Bloch, *French Rural History: An Essay on Its Basic Characteristics*, trans. J. Sondheimer (Berkeley: University of California Press 1966) 180–9; Régine Robin, *La Société française en 1789: Sémur-en-Auxois* (Paris: Plon 1970) 153–4; Pierre de Saint-Jacob, *Les paysans de la Bourgogne du Nord au dernier siècle de l'ancien régime* (Paris: Université de Dijon 1960) 75–92, 377–80
9 PAC, MG8, A6, vol. 3, ordinance of Antoine-Denis Raudot, 7 July 1710

10 PAC, Haldimand papers, Add. Mss 21885, pt. 2, fols. 217–18; PAC, RG8, C, 278: 196–7, petition of Jean-Baptiste Veilleux, 22 July 1809

11 Louise Dechêne makes this point in 'L'évolution du régime seigneurial' 164. Other historians, on the other hand, include mill tolls, sometimes with operational expenses deducted, in lists of seigneurial revenues. This gives a misleading impression of the weight of seigneurial exactions. Habitants would have had to pay a charge to have their grain ground into flour even if there had been no seigneurial régime and it is difficult to say how much, if any, they would have saved had they not been subject to the banalité. Cf. Marcel Trudel, *The Seigneurial Régime* Canadian Historical Association booklet 6 (Ottawa: CHA 1956), 13; R.C. Harris *The Seigneurial System in Early Canada: A Geographical Study* (Madison: University of Wisconsin Press 1966) 78.

12 Cf. Jean Bastier, *La féodalité au siècle des lumières dans la région de Toulouse (1730–1790)* (Paris: Bibliothèque nationale 1975) 274–9

13 PAC, Sorel seigneurie, vol. 13, 'Rent Roll of His Majesty's Seigniory of Sorel for the year 1809,' 24 March 1810; ibid., 'Sorel Seigniory, abstract of arrears,' 31 March 1858

14 PAC, RG8, C, 279: 131, 'Report on the Accounts of Mr Robert Jones Agent of His Majestys Seigniory of Sorel' (amounts shown are in livres)

15 ANQ, AP.G.-288; PAC, MG11, Q, 240–1: 190–5

16 The disadvantages of this procedure did not stop the seigneur of St Ours from successfully suing ten habitants between 1839 and 1842. *Pièces et Documents relatifs à la tenure seigneurial, demandés par une adresse de l'Assemblée législative, 1851* (Quebec: E.R. Fréchette 1852) 150

17 PAC, St Ours seigneurie, vol. 11, estate roll, fief Laperrière, 1787

18 Ibid., agreement between Charles de St Ours and Bazile Bourg, 2 November 1815

19 Dechêne, 'L'évolution du régime seigneurial' 164

20 François-Joseph Cugnet, *Traité de la Loi des Fiefs* (Quebec: Guillaume Brown 1775) 36–7

21 Munro, *The Seigniorial System* 117–19

22 Trudel, *The Seigneurial Régime* 15; Harris, *The Seigneurial System* 72

23 ANQM, gr. Deguire, concession par M. de Contrecoeur à Jacques Coder, 8 December 1758

24 PAC, documents légaux des seigneuries, vol. 971, transaction between Louis Bourdages, proxy for co-seigneurs of St Denis, and Jean-Baptiste Masse and Alexis Chenette père, 2 April 1817; ibid., agreements dated 26 October 1820, 20 May 1817, and 19 June 1837; census of 1831

25 PAC, St Ours seigneurie, vol. 5, agreement between Charles de St Ours and J-E. Faribault, 6 September 1817; Mario Lalancette, 'La seigneurie de l'île aux

Coudres au xviiie siècle,' (unpublished paper, delivered at the annual meeting of the Institut d'histoire de l'amérique française, Ottawa 1979) 8

26 Couillard-Desprès, *Histoire de St-Ours* 1: 292–3; PAC, St Ours seigneurie, vol. 5, agreement between Charles de St Ours and Bazile Bourg dit Canic, 2 November 1815; ibid., vol. 10, Aetna Insurance Company, policy no. 3580, Mme R. de St Ours, 11 November 1842

27 ANQM, gr. Jehanne, lease by Monsieur de la Bruyère Montarville to Gabriel Chabot, 1 October 1779; ANQM, gr. Michaud, lease by Mr de la Bruère Montarville to Sr Joseph Bourque dit Canique, 21 October 1799; PAC, St Ours seigneurie, vol. 5, agreement between Charles de St Ours and Bazile Bourg dit Canic, 2 November 1815

28 PAC, Haldimand Papers, Add. Mss 21885, pt. 2, fol. 217–18, 'Etat actuel des rentes et autres revenues de la seigneurie de Sorel, suivant les deux dernières Recettes en 1782 et 1783'

29 Ibid.; ANQ, St Ours collection, estate inventory of François Roch de St Ours, 19 June 1841. The seigneur's cash revenues cannot be estimated with any precision since a variety of grains with different values were ground.

30 'Cadastre abrégé de la Seigneurie de St Ours,' in *Cadastres abrégés des seigneuries du District de Montréal* 3 vols (Quebec: Geo. Desbarats 1863) 3: 61; PAC, documents légaux des seigneuries, vol. 973, court of appeal, seigneurial act of 1854, petition of Dame Marie Catherine Juschereau Duchesnay and her daughters, seigneuresses of St Ours, 8 March 1860

31 *Edits, ordonnances, déclarations et arrêts relatifs à la tenure seigneuriale, demandés par une adresse de l'Assemblée Législative, 1851* (Quebec: E.R. Fréchette, 1852) 139–40; PAC, documents légaux des seigneuries, vol. 971, testimony of Joseph Mignault, 16 June 1860

32 PAC, documents légaux des seigneuries, vol. 971, testimony of Joseph Mignault, 16 June 1860

33 PAC, St Ours seigneurie, vol. 1, pt 2, concession by M. de St Ours to Noel Renaud, 30 March 1762; PAC, Sorel seigneurie, vol. 2, pt. 1, concession by Mr Harrison to René Trudelle, 3 September 1770

34 Cugnet, *Traité de la Loi des Fiefs* 52

35 Munro, *The Seigniorial System* 134–7

36 For example, PAC, St Ours seigneurie, vol. 1, pt. 3, concession by Roch de St Ours to Christophe Bousquet, 26 September 1765

37 AJS, gr. Frichet, donation par Joseph Demeule et son épouse à Hypolite Amelotte, 27 June 1765, with appendix dated 2 March 1793 renouncing the donation in favour of Charles de St Ours

38 See Fernand Ouellet's critical discussion of this position in two articles: 'Libéré ou exploité! Le paysan québécois d'avant 1850,' *HS-SH* 13 (November 1980)

339–68; 'La formation d'une société dans la vallée du Saint-Laurent: d'une société sans classes à une société de classes,' *CHR* 62 (December 1981) 407–50.

39 Harris, *Seigneurial System* 78; Lise Pilon-Lê, 'L'endettement des cultivateurs québécois: une analyse socio-historique de la rente foncière (1670–1904)' (PH D thesis, Université de Montréal 1978) 168–9; Guy Lemarchand, 'Féodalisme et société rurale dans la France moderne,' in *Sur le féodalisme* 86–105 (see also Jacques Dupâquier's comments in ibid. 107); Albert Soboul, 'Sur le prélèvement féodal,' in *Problèmes paysans de la révolution (1789–1848): études d'histoire révolutionnaire* (Paris: François Maspero 1976) 89–115; Bastier, *La féodalité au siècle des lumières* 258–9

40 W.J. Eccles, *France in America* (Vancouver: Fitzhenry and Whiteside 1973) 79

41 Only 99 of the 107 local households are included in this 'model,' the remaining 8 being eliminated either because data were evidently missing from their entries or because they had no land and were therefore apparently priests, artisans or labourers. The assumptions underlying this estimate are that two-thirds of the census-recorded grain sown was wheat, that the seed-yield ratio of wheat was 1: 5.8, that the 11,037 arpents held by these 99 families were subject to the prevailing rate of seigneurial rent which included a levy of 'one half minot of wheat for every 20 arpents,' that adults required 12 minots of wheat a year (the lowest individual ration commonly found in eighteenth-century pensions alimentaires), while children needed only half that amount and 'girls' (unmarried females not differentiated by age in the census) ate, on the average, three-quarters of an adult ration.

CHAPTER SIX: THE COUNTRY MERCHANT

1 Dale Miquelon, *Dugard of Rouen: French Trade to Canada and the West Indies, 1729–1770* (Montreal and London: McGill-Queen's University Press 1978) 82

2 Louis Michel, 'Un marchand rural en Nouvelle-France: François-Augustin Bailly de Messein, 1709–1771,' *RHAF* 33 (September 1979) 215–62; H.A. Innis, ed., *Select Documents in Canadian Economic History 1497–1783* (Toronto: University of Toronto Press 1929) 408–11

3 Sorel parish archives, vestry accounts, vol. 1

4 'Que les seigneuries le long de cette rivière [Richelieu] produisent beaucoup de grains, que c'est même l'un des cantons du Canada qui en produit davantage ...' [Louis Franquet], *Voyages et mémoires sur le Canada* (Quebec: Institut canadien 1889) 92

5 In 1752 LeRoux formed a partnership with Henry Marie Rustan of Berthier, across the St Lawrence. The partnership had a capital of 65,000 livres, to be

used 'dans le commerce des marchandises seches et liquides et autres qu'ils desirent faire l'un à Berthier et l'autre à Sorel ... pour etre les dt. marchandises converties en achats de grains tabac et autres denrees au proffit de ladt. société ...' ANQM, gr. Cyr de Montmerque, société entre sr Jean LeRoux et Sr Henry Marie Rustan, 20 October 1752

6 Réal Fortin, *Bateaux et épaves du Richelieu* (Saint-Jean: Editions Mille Roches 1978) 41

7 *RAPQ*, 1924–5, p 267

8 The governor and intendant estimated that Quebec City had 100 merchants in 1741 and they considered this twice as many as the town needed; perhaps there were an equal number in Montreal. Innis, ed., *Select Documents* 411

9 James A. Henretta, *The Evolution of American Society, 1700–1815: An Interdisciplinary Analysis* (Lexington, MA: D.C. Heath 1973) 141

10 PAC, MG 19, A2, series 3, vols 1–27, 59–71, 74–6, 95, 98, 101, 149–54, 156, 240, 247 (Jacobs Papers). Except where otherwise noted, the Jacobs Papers are the source of what follows in this chapter. A few of the letters in this collection are published in Innis, ed., *Select Documents* 521–9. The Jacobs Papers have been consulted by other historians to illustrate biographical works or discussions of Canadian trade. See, for example, Hilda Neatby, *Quebec: The Revolutionary Age 1760–1791* (Toronto: McClelland and Stewart 1966) passim; Jacob Rader Marcus, *Early American Jewry: The Jews of New York, New England and Canada, 1649–1794* 2 vols (Philadelphia: The Jewish Publication Society of America, 1951–3), 1: 204–71, passim; Denis Vaugeois, *Les juifs de la Nouvelle-France* (Trois-Rivières: Boréal Express 1968) 119–32. On Samuel Jacobs' life see, in addition, Vaugeois' article in the *Dictionary of Canadian Biography* (Toronto: University of Toronto Press 1979) 4: 384–6, quite useful despite a few errors of detail.

11 Jacobs Papers, 5: 67–76, Will, 15 October 1784. Cf. Philippe Ariès, *Centuries of Childhood: A Social History of Family Life* trans. Robert Baldick (New York: Vintage Books 1962); J.H. Plumb, 'The New World of Children in Eighteenth-Century England,' *Past and Present* 67 (May 1975) 64–95; Lawrence Stone, *The Family, Sex and Marriage in England, 1500–1800* (New York: Harper and Row 1979) 254–99.

12 Jacobs Papers, 10: 626–9, Jacobs to Watson, Olive and Rashleigh, 7 October 1769

13 Ibid. 7: 113, Curtius to Jacobs, n.d. [apparently fall 1762]

14 Ibid. 8: 46–9, Curtius to Jacobs, 18 November 1761

15 Ibid. 8: 45, Curtius to Jacobs, 13 November 1761

16 Ibid. 8: 43, Jacobs to Curtius, 13 November 1761; ibid. 8: 55, Jacobs to Curtius, 30 November 1761

17 Ibid. 62: 170, 'Account of all the corn purchased by Charles Curtius for Mr Samuel Jacobs Merchd. from April 24th 1762 to July 20th 1764.' The rest of the wheat was purchased in small quantities from what seem to be habitant-customers. Missing from the list of Curtius' suppliers are the region's seigneurs, presumably because those who drew rents in kind, like the co-seigneurs of St Ours, had their own means of getting their grain to an urban market where it would command higher prices.

18 Expenses accounted for 8320 livres, but this still left Curtius unaccountably short some 12,060 livres.

19 Jacobs Papers, 8: 105, Curtius to Jacobs, 24 August 1762

20 Ibid. 8: 126, Jacobs to Curtius, 8 June 1763

21 Ibid. 2: 3, Jacobs to W. Allan, ? August 1772

22 See Karl Polanyi, 'The Economy as Instituted Process,' in *Primitive, Archaic, and Modern Economies: Essays of Karl Polanyi*, ed. George Dalton (Boston: Beacon Press, 1968), p. 162.

23 Jacobs Papers, 10: 628, Jacobs to Watson, Olive and Rashleigh, 7 October 1769.

24 David Roberts, 'George Allsopp: Quebec Merchant, 1733–1805' (MA thesis, Queen's University 1974) 17–18, 46–8

25 Jacobs Papers, 14: 1669–72, Jacobs to Charles Grant, 26 October 1776

26 Ibid., 10: 629, Jacobs to Watson, Olive and Rashleigh, 7 October 1769

27 Ibid., 9: 303, Engagement of Louis Largeau to Jacobs, 26 August 1766

28 Ibid., 12: 1162, Engagement of Henry Laparre to Jacobs, 8 November 1774

29 Ibid., 25: 3293, Peter Burn to M. Cornud, 18 April 1788

30 Innis, ed., *Select Documents* 490; J.B.A. Allaire, *Histoire de St-Denis-sur-Richelieu, Canada* (St Hyacinthe: Imprimerie du Courrier de Saint-Hyacinthe 1905) 239–42

31 Jacobs Papers, 11: 831–2, Declaration of Paul Lamotte, 27 May 1771

32 Jacobs Papers, vols 149 and 240

33 Marcus, *Early American Jewry* 1: 249–50

34 Jacobs Papers 14: 1669–72, Jacobs to Charles Grant, 26 October 1776

35 Edward E. Curtis, *The Organization of the British Army in the American Revolution* (New Haven: Yale University Press 1926) 98–100

36 Jacobs Papers 21: 2850, Jacobs to Nathaniel Day, 23 January 1783

37 ANQM, gr. Dutalmé, 5 September 1804, inventaire des dettes de feu Samuel Jacobs

38 Jacobs Papers 8: 133–4, Jacobs to Curtius, 22 June 1763

39 'The bearer of this asked me for some goods,' wrote the clerk at St Denis to his counterpart at St Charles. 'As I did not know whether he was good or not sent him to you, believe it would be best to make him wait till Mr Jacobs

comes up. Do as you like I don't know him.' Ibid. 12: 1170, Thomas Connor to François Gatien, 12 November 1774

40 Ibid. 4: 158–9, Jacobs to R. Dalton, 18 May 1785

41 There are several partial inventories in the Jacobs collection, but these three are the only ones that include values and appear to be complete. One is from Jacobs' post-mortem estate inventory (1786), one was made at the conclusion of his partnership with Charles Curtius (1764), and one seems to have been a routine catalogue (1775). Jacobs Papers 63: 214; 65: 448, 149

42 Dale Miquelon, 'Havy and Lefebvre of Quebec: A Case Study of Metropolitan Participation in Canadian Trade, 1730–60,' *CHR* 56 (March 1975) 6

43 Anon., 'An Economic and Social Survey,' in *Select Documents*, ed. Innis 579

44 Note, however, that the entry for 1775 in Table 18 shows that, even at the end of a trading season, Jacobs' cellars could contain as much as 4195 gallons of rum, enough to account for one-quarter of his entire stock. On shipments, see the bills of lading in Jacobs Papers, vol. 76, 'Samuel Jacobs Shipment Book, 1762–1773.' Bills of lading record the number of pieces loaded onto a vessel (so many barrels of rum, so many bales of drygoods, and so on) and so they give a rough indication of the amounts of staple commodities but not their exact quantity or value. A passing reference in one of the merchant's letters suggests that he sold 1900 gallons of rum in less than a month. Jacobs Papers, 2: 9, Jacobs to ?, 25 August 1772.

45 'As Rum is a cash article and usually ingrossed in the fall by a few speculators I think it has Rose, for he that acts for Mr. Stuart one Cartier, endeavoured by a low plan to purchase mine, though he has twice as much as he can consume here till spring.' Ibid. 2: 27, Jacobs to John Welles, 14 November 1772

46 Ibid. 11: 861–2, Jacobs to William Grant, n.d. [Spring 1771]; cf. ibid. 2: 18–21, Jacobs to John Welles, 29 October 1772

47 'From an attentive examination and inquiry, it appeared to us that the same number of the Inhabitants of Lower Canada consume a far more considerable quantity of spirits perhaps double of what would be used by an equal number in this province. Instead of tea so generally used among us, a glass of rum and a crust of bread is the usual breakfast of the French Canadian; the rigor of their climate is alleged as the cause of their having frequent recourse to it at other times of the day – and their numerous holidays lead to such habits of idleness and dissipation as are very favorable to the consumption of rum.' R. Cartwright, John Munroe, and John MacDonell, 'Report of the Proceedings of the Commissioners for settling Duties ... in 1795,' cited in Leopold Lamontagne, 'Kingston's French Heritage,' *Ontario History* 45 (Summer 1953) 111. The Loyalists who wrote this report lived in Sorel for some time before moving to Upper Canada.

Lord Selkirk made similar observations in 1804: 'The Canadian peasantry were formerly remarkably sober, but are now much addicted to drink – even the women exceed – formerly it used to be disgraceful in any.' Quoted in H. Clare Pentland, *Labour and Capital in Canada, 1650–1860*, ed. Paul Phillips (Toronto: James Lorimer 1981) 65

48 Cf. Eric R. Wolf, *Europe and the People without History* (Berkeley: University of California Press 1982) 257–8.

49 Except for the change in colonial master, things were much the same in this regard in Jacobs' day as they had been under the French régime. In the first half of the eighteenth century, control of credit gave French suppliers ascendancy over Quebec importers who, in their turn, dominated the merchants of Montreal. Miquelon, *Dugard of Rouen* 160–1

50 There is little evidence here of the habitant's legendary tendency to hoard. Cf. for example, Neatby, *Quebec: The Revolutionary Age* 77: 'Every thrifty farmer had his bag of coins tucked away.'

51 An inventory of coins was taken in 1770 when the cash box was recovered from a clerk who had absconded with it. Of 773 livres 17 sols 4 deniers, more than half (528 livres) was in the form of portugaises, while the rest was made up of dollars, a guinea, a Louis d'or, and other French coins. Cf. Adam Shortt, 'Currency and Banking, 1760–1841,' in *Canada and Its Provinces: A History of the Canadian People and Their Institutions by One Hundred Associates*, ed. Adam Shortt and Arthur G. Doughty 23 vols (Toronto: Glasgow, Brook and Company 1914) 4: 599–636.

52 'The seignior arrived to collect his rents. My house is like a fair with those inhabitants whose custom I have. They request as usual to advance them to pay their Rents, which is from two to three dollars a piece ...' Jacobs Papers, 2: 48, Jacobs to Paterson and Hays, 3 March 1773. 'What little cash I had left advanced it to my customers to pay the people who helps them to get in their Recolte.' Ibid. 2: 9, Jacobs to Welles, 25 August 1772

53 'Mr. Tetro has been here and after he asked me for delay for what he owes me for which I received his note, still requests that I would advance him some cash that he might pay off the others who he owes to ... as I think there is no risque I have promised to lend him some as soon as I can get it from Montreal ... I rather do this then he should sell his wheat underhand which ought to clear his account with me.' Ibid. Jacobs to Gatien, 26 February 1775

54 Ibid. 10: 629, Jacobs to Watson, Olive and Rashleigh, 7 October 1769. A contemporary document suggests that the colony could export about 120,000 minots a year. Fernand Ouellet, *Economic and Social History of Quebec 1760–1850: Structures and Conjonctures* (Toronto: Gage 1980) 88

55 Ouellet, *Economic and Social History* 86–7

56 T.J.A. LeGoff, 'An Eighteenth-Century Grain Merchant: Ignace Advisse Des-
ruisseaux,' in *French Government and Society 1500–1850: Essays in Memory of
Alfred Cobban*, ed. J.F. Bosher (London: Athlone Press 1973) 94–122
57 These figures come from Jacobs Papers, vol. 76, 'Samuel Jacobs Shipment
Book, 1762–1773' (bills of lading), supplemented with scattered references in
the Jacobs correspondence.
58 Ouellet, *Economic and Social History* 85
59 Louis Michel, 'Le livre de compte (1784–1792) de Gaspard Massue, marchand
à Varennes,' *HS-SH* 13 (November 1980) 388
60 In a letter to his clerk at St Ours, Jacobs once suggested putting pressure on
debtors, but he obviously considered this an exceptionally stern measure:
> As I hear the Traders are beginning to Buy up wheat, I woud have you
> on receipt of this go round to your Customers, and fix with them, from
> three livres five to three livres ten ... Endeavour to buy up all you can
> from any one, but those who are indebted to you the most part of there
> Grain or more then it will come to, and wants to impose on me as usual
> by endeavouring to get a higher price then it is worth, tell them to fix or
> pay their accts. without being afraid of affronting any of them ...

Jacobs Papers, 14: 1564, Jacobs to Joseph Besançon, 20 July 1776
61 Ibid. 13: 1392, Jacobs to William Kay, 1 June 1775. In addition to this reference,
a series of bills of lading, 1770–3, identifies 48 of the biggest sellers, those
who had enough wheat that it was taken directly from their houses to the
river boats instead of being stored in the merchant's granary. The average
amount was 207 minots. A third indicator of the amounts sold by the larger
producers, a series of contracts signed in 1774 to supply wheat the following
year, also confirms the picture suggested by Jacobs' remark. The amounts
mentioned in the 38 contracts ranged from 12 to 900 minots with a mean of
180 minots. Ibid., vol. 76; ibid. 65: 449, 'A List of Wheat due by notes and
obligations to the store at St. Dennis taken the 9 July 1775'
62 Ibid. 2: 26, Jacobs to John Welles, 14 November 1772
63 Ibid. 13: 1302, Jacobs to Gatien, 18 March 1775
64 Ibid. 13: 1225–6, Jacobs to Gatien, 30 January 1775; ibid. 13: 1392, Jacobs to
William Kay, 1 June 1775. Clearly the habitants, or some of them at any rate,
had a good measure of freedom to bargain with a merchant so anxious to
'keep their custom,' even when they were endebted.
65 Ibid. 12: 1003, Jacobs to Gatien, 2 April 1774
66 Ibid. 4: 121, Jacobs to Melvin, Wills and Burn, 16 November 1784
67 Ibid. 2: 18–21, Jacobs to John Welles, 29 October 1772
68 A.J.H. Richardson, 'Jordan, Jacob,' *Dictionary of Canadian Biography* 4: 402–3
69 J.F. Bosher, 'Government and Private Interests in New France,' *Canadian
Public Administration* 10 (June 1967) 244–57

70 Jacobs Papers 13: 1292–3, Jacobs to Gatien, 14 March 1775. Compare the language of another Richelieu merchant, writing fifteen years later: 'Les marchands ne peuvent faire tollérer les habitans à un prix honnête ...' ANQ, AP-P, 1559, Jacques Cartier to Jean Painter, 26 January 1790

71 Jacobs Papers, 4: 174, Jacobs to R. Dalton, 18 June 1785; ibid. 2: 26, Jacobs to John Welles, 14 November 1772

72 See E.P. Thompson, 'The Moral Economy of the English Crowd in the Eighteenth Century,' *Past and Present* 50 (February 1971) 76–136.

73 Innis, ed., *Select Documents* 411

74 Jacobs Papers, 62: 170, 'Account of all the corn purchased by Charles Curtius for Mr. Samuel Jacobs Merchd. from April 24th to July 20th 1764'

75 Margaret E. Martin, *Merchants and Trade of the Connecticut River Valley, 1750–1820* (Northampton, MA: Department of History of Smith College 1939) 5–6, 164

76 André J. Bourde, *Agronomie et agronomes en France au XVIIIe siècle* 3 vols (Paris: SEVPEN 1967)

77 Michel, 'Un marchand rural en Nouvelle-France' 237–58; Michel, 'Le livre de compte de Gaspard Massue,' 89–96; Pilon-Lê, 'L'endettement des cultivateurs québécois'

78 Jacobs Papers, 63: 339, inventory of debts to the Sorel store of Samuel Jacobs and company, 4 July 1770; ibid. 63: 287, 'Etat des Ballances du Grand Livre de l'année 1767 et 1768 due à Samuel Jacobs et compagnie,' St Ours, 25 April 1768; ibid. 64: 360, 'A List of the Outstanding Debts of the Magazin à St Charles,' 30 July 1773

79 Ibid., vol. 156, account book, Jacobs Estate, 1787–92

80 An example from the list of debts in Jacobs' estate inventory: 'Augustin Allard fils de Simon ... une somme qu'il est à présumer avoir été entierement payé vu que le dit augustin allard a vendu sa terre au dit deffunt Samuel Jacobs.' Ibid., vol. 149, Samuel Jacobs estate inventory

81 Ibid.; ibid., vol. 154, accounts of Jacobs estate, list of farms, 1788. A passage from a letter from one of the executors of the Jacobs estate underlines the insecurity of tenure for tenant-farmers: 'The bearer Eustache Boiverd comes to take possession of the land at St. Ours as a farmer. Please to deliver him all the Catles fourages and every else [sic] belonging to the said farm. Augustin Fortier must quit it and make shift for himself in the best manner he can.' Ibid. 5: 64, M. Cornud to Peter Burn, 14 March 1792

82 ANQM, gr. Jehanne, lease by Samuel Jacobs to Pierre Audet dit Lapoint, 19 June 1778. Cf. ibid., lease by Samuel Jacobs to François Fontaine, 13 January 1784; ibid., lease by Samuel Jacobs to Antoine Charon dit Chabanac, 10 April 1786; ANQM, gr. Michaud, lease by Michel Cornud to Louis Bouvier fils, 9 February 1789

83 Joseph A. Schumpeter, *The Theory of Economic Development: An Inquiry into Profits, Capital, Credit, Interest and the Business Cycle* (Cambridge, MA: Harvard University Press 1934)
84 Marx, *Capital*, vol. 3, p 327

CHAPTER SEVEN: HABITANT-VOYAGEURS

1 An earlier version of this chapter appeared in my article, 'Fur Trade Labour and Lower Canadian Agrarian Structures,' Canadian Historical Association, *Historical Papers* (1981) 197–214
2 ACESH, XVII, C66, Martel to bishop, 30 October 1790
3 PAC, Jacobs Papers, 10: 756, 'Etat de ceux qui ont donné leur obligation pour le bois d'écarisage,' 29 December 1770
4 Dechêne, *Habitants et marchands de Montréal au XVIIe siècle* (Paris and Montreal: Plon 1974) 171–83
5 Ibid. 181–2
6 Ibid. 220–1. Data collected by Jean Laflamme on 146 engagés who signed on for the upper Ottawa trade between 1739 and 1752 shows an even stronger concentration on the Montreal area. The sample breaks down by parish of origin as follows:

City of Montreal	10	(7%)
Rest of island of Montreal	81	(55%)
Surrounding parishes	25	(17%)
Elsewhere	10	(7%)
Unknown	20	(14%)
Total	146	(100%)

Source of statistics: Jean Laflamme, 'La traite des fourrures dans l'outaouais supérieure (1718–1760)' (MA thesis, Université de Montréal 1975) appendice II
7 Fernand Ouellet, 'Dualité économique et changement technologique au Québec (1760–1790),' *HS-SH* 9 (November 1976) 269–70
8 George Simpson to James Keith, London, 18 November 1840. Cited in Carol M. Judd, ' "Mixt Bands of Many Nations": 1821–70,' in *Old Trails and New Directions: Papers of the Third North American Fur Trade Conference*, ed. Carol M. Judd and Arthur J. Ray (Toronto: University of Toronto Press 1980) 145n
9 Jesse Lemish, 'Jack Tar in the Streets: Merchant Seamen in the Politics of Revolutionary America,' *William and Mary Quarterly* 3rd series, 25 (July 1968) 371–407; Judith Fingard, *Jack in Port: Sailortowns of Eastern Canada* (Toronto: University of Toronto Press 1982) 126–39
10 AJS, files of Henry Crebassa, 1797, passim

11 ACESH, XVII, c66, J-Bte Kelly to Mgr Plessis, 13 April 1822
12 Louise Dechêne's study of engagement contracts signed between 1708 and 1717 suggests that only about 5 per cent of men in the Sorel area were involved in the fur trade then (*Habitants et marchands* 514–15). These notarized documents may not mention every man paddling a canoe to the northwest, but there is no reason to assume that they do not constitute a reasonable sample and the basis for a portrait of the fur-trade labour force. Regardless of the accuracy of the absolute numbers presented, Dechêne's figures, when viewed comparatively, indicate a striking inequality in the extent of involvement among the regions of New France. The Sorel region had one of the lowest rates of participation: only 5 per cent of the adult males here signed engagements, compared with 39 per cent in the nearby Boucherville area. For a slightly later period, a list of 146 engagements for the Ottawa (1739–52) includes no men from Sorel and only one engagé for the entire Richelieu valley. (Laflamme, 'La traite des fourrures dans l'outaouais supérieure,' app. II)

For the period between the Conquest and the American Revolution, a glance through the official Trade Licences, which give names and residences of canoe crew members, shows Sorel names to be quite rare. In one bundle of licences from the 1760s, only five local men were found out of a total of 322 engagés. Men from the city and island of Montreal and from nearby parishes such as Laprairie, Vaudreuil, Les Cèdres, and Ile Perrot seem to have been most numerous. An additional rough indication is furnished by the parish registers of Detroit which list the birth-places of 52 Canadian men married between 1760 and 1781. Among these grooms, who presumably came to Detroit because of the fur trade, there was not one man from Sorel. PAC, RG 4, B28, vol. 110, Trade Licences, 1763–8; Ernest J. Lajeunesse, ed., *The Windsor Border Region. Canada's Southernmost Frontier: A Collection of Documents* (Toronto: Champlain Society 1960) 343–55
13 AJS, gr. Antoine Robin, 1790–5; gr. Henry Crebassa, 1795–9; ANQM, gr. Louis Bonnet, 1791–6; E.Z. Massicotte, 'Répertoire des Engagements pour l'ouest conservés dans les archives judiciaires de Montréal,' *RAPQ*, 1942–3, pp 261–397; 1943–4, pp 335–444
14 Ouellet, 'Dualité économique' 294–6; Gratien Allaire, 'Les engagements pour la traite des fourrures: évaluation de la documentation,' *RHAF* 34 (June 1980) 3–26
15 At least it was in the seventeenth century. Hubert Charbonneau, Bertrand Desjardins, and Pierre Beauchamp, 'Le comportement démographique des voyageurs sous le régime français,' *HS-SH* 9 (May 1978) 127
16 AJS, gr. H. Crebassa and M.L. Duplessis, passim. These engagements in the 1830s were all for winterers serving terms of at least three years.
17 Carol M. Judd, 'The Ethnicity of Hudson's Bay Company Servants in the

Nineteenth Century,' paper presented to the Fur Trade Conference, Winnipeg, May 1978, Table 2

18 Simpson to Keith, London, 18 November 1840. Cited in Judd, 'Mixt Bands' 145n. Another document from the same period refers to 'the old voyageur parishes of Sorel, Maskinongé, and Yamaska.' A. Simpson, *The Life and Travels of Thomas Simpson, the Arctic Discoverer*, quoted in Philip Goldring, *Papers on the Labour System of the Hudson's Bay Company, 1821–1900*. Parks Canada Manuscript Report (Ottawa 1979) 1: 176. Cf. Marcel Giraud, *Le Métis canadien, son role dans l'histoire des provinces de l'Ouest* (Paris: Institut d'ethnologie 1945) 969.

19 Dechêne, *Habitants et marchands* 219–24; Charbonneau et al., 'Le comportement démographique' 126

20 Sorel parish archives, vestry accounts, 1730–1868

21 For evidence that Sorel habitants signed on as porkeaters to acquit seigneurial dues, see PAC, RG8, C, 634A: 20, Robert Jones to Col. Green, 2 August 1804

22 Of 187 engagements invoving men from St Ours and St Denis, as well as from Sorel, signed 1790–9, the breakdown by month is as follows: January – 70, Feburary – 55, March – 19, April – 13, May – 14, June – 0, July – 2, August – 2, September – 3, October – 2, November – 2, December – 5. In other words, 67 per cent of the contracts were concluded in the first two months of the year.

23 AJS, gr. A. Robin, 25 October 1795

24 Scottish Records Office, Dalhousie Papers, sec. III, no. 543, Lord Dalhousie's diary, 15 July 1820

25 John Lambert, *Travels through Canada and the United States of America, in the years 1806, 1807, & 1808*, 2 vols. 2nd ed. (London: C. Cradock and W. Joy 1814) 2: 509–10

26 For example, W.T. Easterbrook and Hugh G.J. Aitken, *Canadian Economic History* (Toronto: Macmillan 1956) 62

27 Normand Séguin, *La conquête du sol au 19e siècle* (Sillery: Boréal Express 1977) 166. The 1880 census, using English units, gives a figure of 24 cleared acres per farm, equivalent to 30 arpents.

28 Mathematically astute readers will notice that there is a discrepancy in the number of farms counted in Tables 24 and 25. This results from a deficiency in the 1831 census; the latter gives figures on both land and production for farms worked by their possessors, but provides no data on farm size or cultivated area for rented lands. This means that, for the 73 tenant-farmers of Sorel and St Denis, information can be found on crops (Tables 24 and 30) but not on land (Tables 25 and 26). These last two tables then apply to land-holding peasants only, although everything we know about tenant-farming suggests that the sizes of rented lands would have followed much the same pattern.

29 An earlier version of this table which appeared in my 'Fur-Trade Labour and Lower Canadian Agrarian Structures' (p 210), was based on an excessively broad definition of 'habitant.' In order to be consistent with other tables in this book that rely on the 1765 census, I have reduced the number of households covered, to include only those listed as having planted some quantity of grain. As a result, only 130 families from Sorel are counted instead of the 141 considered in the article. This alteration does not change the essential message of the table.

30 Dechêne, *Habitants et marchands* 284–8; Pauline Desjardins, 'La Coutume de Paris et la transmission des terres: le rang de la Beauce à Calixa-Lavallée de 1730 à 1975,' *RHAF* 34 (December 1980) 339

31 Allan Greer, 'Habitants of the Lower Richelieu: Rural Society in Three Quebec Parishes, 1740–1840' (PH D thesis, York University 1980) 201

32 Corrected census figures indicate 1790 populations of 1208 for Sorel and 1694 for St Denis and 1831 populations of 5063 for Sorel and 3074 for St Denis (see Appendix 1). Henripin's and Péron's revised estimates for Lower Canada are 141,900 for the 1786–90 period and 401,200 for 1826–30. 'The Demographic Transition of the Province of Quebec,' in *Population and Social Change*, ed. D.V. Glass and Roger Revelle (London: Edward Arnold 1972) 213–31

Note that the formula for calculating the the annual rate of population growth is $r = \dfrac{\log e\ (P_2/P_1)}{n}$ x 100%, where P_1 is initial population, P_2 is end population, and n is the number of intervening years.

33 Only Catholic population is considered here, first because the local Protestant population was generally 'urban' and second because there are no reliable registers of Protestant baptisms and burials to tell us about 'natural increase.' Moreover, except for the enumeration of 1831, the censuses do not provide separate figures for Catholic and Protestant populations. This is of little importance where St Denis is concerned for there was never more than a handful of Protestants there; the same can be said for Sorel before 1780.

For 1784 and 1822 however, the Catholic element in Sorel's population had to be estimated. The first of these censuses was taken in the middle of the (Protestant) Loyalist migration to Sorel. According to one estimate, there were 132 Loyalists in the parish in December 1783; another source indicates the number had risen to 316 by the following October (Azarie Couillard-Desprès, *Histoire de Sorel de ses origines à nos jours* (Montreal: Imprimerie des sourds-muets 1926) 128; Ivanoe Caron, *La colonisation de la province de Québec*, 2 vols (Quebec: L'Action Sociale 1923–7) 1: 126. The average of the two figures is 224; subtracted from the total population given by the census (1158), this suggests a Catholic population of 934. The Catholic population in 1822, on the other hand, was estimated on the assumption that it accounted for the same proportion of the total population at that date that it did in 1831. Thus the 1822 population (3711) was multiplied by the 1831 ratio of Catholic to total population (4804/5063).

34 Among males aged 18 to 24 years, 40 per cent in Sorel were married, while only 19 per cent in St Denis were married. *JHALC*, 1826, app. Q, census of Lower Canada, 1825

35 Richard A. Easterlin, 'Does Human Fertility Adjust to the Environment?,' in *Studies in American Historical Demography*, ed. Maris A. Vinovskis (New York: Academic Press 1979) 389–97; Helena Temkin-Greener and A.C. Swedlund, 'Fertility Transition in the Connecticut Valley: 1740–1850,' *Population Studies* 32 (March 1978) 27–41.

36 Franklin Mendels, 'Proto-Industrialization: The First Phase of Industrialization,' *Journal of Economic History* 32 (March 1972) 241–61; Franklin Mendels, 'Agriculture and Peasant Industry in Eighteenth Century Flanders,' in *European Peasants and Their Markets* 179–204, ed. William N. Parker and Eric L. Jones (Princeton: Princeton University Press 1975); David Levine, *Family Formation in an Age of Nascent Capitalism* (New York: Academic Press 1977); Wally Seccombe, 'Marxism and Demography,' *New Left Review* 137 (January–February 1983) 22–47

37 Eric Wolf, *Peasants* (Englewood Cliffs: Prentice-Hall 1966) 76–7

38 Normand Séguin's study of Hébertville in the Saguenay region in the late nineteenth century describes the formation of a semi-proletariat of poor subsistence farmers dependent on seasonal work in the woods. Séguin is at present involved in a group research project on the history of the St Maurice region in the second half of the nineteenth century; preliminary findings indicate a similar process of semi-proletarization and dependence on forestry wages. Séguin, *La conquête du sol au 19e siècle* (Sillery: Boréal Express 1977); Séguin, 'Problèmes théoriques et orientation de la recherche,' in N. Séguin, ed., *Agriculture et colonisation au Québec: aspects historiques* (Montreal: Boréal 1980) 181–97. Normand Séguin, 'L'agriculture de la Mauricie et du Québec 1850–1950,' *RHAF* 35 (March 1982) 537–62

On the liquidation of the peasant-worker system in the mid-twentieth century, see Gérald Fortin, 'Socio-Cultural Changes in an Agricultural Parish,' in Marcel Rioux and Yves Martin, eds, *French-Canadian Society* (Toronto: McClelland and Stewart 1964) 86–106. Fortin, along with with Léon Gérin and other sociologists, might be criticized for calling this semi-proletariat 'traditional,' and for stressing the continuity of French-Canadian rural society from the seventeenth century to the twentieth when, in fact, the social and economic structures of Quebec's peasant-woodsman communities had been shaped through the effects of the capitalist labour market.

CHAPTER EIGHT: TURNING THE NINETEENTH CENTURY

1 Joseph Bouchette, *A Topographical Description of the Province of Lower Canada, with remarks upon Upper Canada, and on the Relative Connexion of both Provinces with the United States of America* (London: W. Faden 1815) 211–12

2 Ibid. 205

3 Michel Gaumond and Paul-Louis Martin, *Les maîtres-potiers du bourg Saint-Denis, 1785–1888* (Quebec: Ministère des affaires culturelles 1978), 21–2

4 Gaumond and Martin, *Les maîtres-potiers* 23; Allaire, *Histoire de Saint-Denis* 291–2

5 Pierre Deffontaines, 'The *Rang*-Pattern of Rural Settlement in French Canada,' in Rioux and Martin, eds, *French Canadian Society* 16

6 Gaumond and Martin, *Les maîtres-potiers*

7 Censuses of 1831 and 1844; J.B.A. Allaire, *Histoire de Saint-Denis* 345–8; Azarie Couillard-Desprès, *Histoire de Sorel de ses origines à nos jours* (Montreal: Imprimerie des sourds-muets 1926) 308–19.

8 PAC, MG8, A6, 10: 358–9, ordinance of Gilles Hocquart, 30 September 1730; ibid. 12: 196–7, ordinance of Gilles Hocquart, 5 February 1734; A.J.E. Lunn, 'Economic Development in New France, 1713–1760' (PH D thesis, McGill University 1942) 475

9 Isaac Weld, *Travels through the States of North America, and the Provinces of Upper and Lower Canada, during the Years 1795, 1796, and 1797* 4th ed., 2 vols (London: John Stockdale 1807), 1: 333–4

10 AJS, gr. H. Crebassa, 1796–9, passim

11 PAC, MG 21, B, 54: 221–3, Haldimand to Germaine, 24 October 1779

12 PAC, Sorel seigneurie, vol. 1, Christopher Carter to ?, 15 March 1798. Cf. Weld, *Travels through the States* 1: 333

13 PAC, Sorel seigneurie, 7: 3972–5, Petition to Lord Dorchester by James Sawyer and 23 others, residents of William Henry, 1796

14 Scottish Records Office, Dalhousie Diary, 4 June 1826. Cf. ibid., 7 October 1822; Harold A. Innis and A.R.M. Lower, eds, *Select Documents in Canadian Economic History, 1783–1885* (Toronto: University of Toronto Press 1933) 34

15 Ronald Rudin, 'Local Initiative and Urban Growth: The Development of Four Quebec Towns, 1840–1914' (unpublished manuscript) 60–71

16 Adam Smith, *An Inquiry into the Nature and Causes of the Wealth of Nations*, ed. Edwin Cannon (New York: Modern Library 1937) 22. Cf. ibid., Book 1, chapters 1–4, Book 3, chapters 1 and 4

17 Robert Brenner, 'The Origins of Capitalist Development: A Critique of Neo-Smithian Marxism,' *New Left Review* 104 (July-August 1977) 33–6

18 Gilles Paquet and Jean-Pierre Wallot have made this point repeatedly in a series of articles: 'Le Bas-Canada au début du xixe siècle: une hypothèse,'

RHAF 25 (June 1971) 41–4; 'Crise agricole et tensions socio-éthniques dans le Bas-Canada, 1802–1812: éléments pour une réinterprétation,' ibid. 26 (September 1972) 187; 'Sur quelques discontinuités dans l'expérience socio-économique du Québec: une hypothèse,' ibid. 35 (March 1982) 483–521.

19 Fernand Ouellet, *Le Bas-Canada 1791–1840: Changements structuraux et crise* (Ottawa: Editions de l'université d'Ottawa 1976) 18

20 T.J.A. LeGoff, 'The Agricultural Crisis in Lower Canada, 1802–12: A Review of a Controversy,' *CHR* 55 (March 1974) 1–31; Gilles Paquet and Jean-Pierre Wallot, 'The Agricultural Crisis in Lower Canada, 1802–1812: mise au point. A Response to T.J.A. LeGoff,' ibid. 56 (June 1975) 133–61; Fernand Ouellet, 'Le mythe de "l'habitant sensible au marché": commentaires sur la contro-verse LeGoff-Wallot et Paquet,' *Recherches sociographiques* 17 (January-April 1976) 115–32; John McCallum, *Unequal Beginnings: Agriculture and Economic Development in Quebec and Ontario until 1870* (Toronto: University of Toronto Press 1980) 25–44; R.M. McInnis, 'A Reconsideration of the State of Agri-culture in Lower Canada in the First Half of the Nineteenth Century,' in *Canadian Papers in Rural History*, ed. Donald H. Akenson, vol. 3 (1982) 9–49; Serge Courville, 'La crise agricole du Bas-Canada: éléments d'une réflexion géographique,' *Cahiers de géographie du Québec* 24 (September 1980) 193–224; 24 (December 1980) 385–428

21 Daniel Thorner, 'Peasant Economy as a Category in Economic History,' in *Peasants and Peasant Societies*, ed. Teodor Shanin (Harmondsworth: Penguin Books 1971) 206–7

22 Paquet and Wallot, 'Crise agricole' 203

23 Karl Polanyi, *The Great Transformation* (Boston: Beacon Press 1957) 54

24 Paquet and Wallot, 'Crise agricole' 203

25 Polanyi, *The Great Transformation* 54

26 Gaetan Cloutier, 'La Crise Agricole au Bas-Canada (1815–1830): mythe ou réalité pour les gens de l'époque?' (Mémoire de maîtrise, Université de Mon-tréal 1977) 19–20

27 ANQM, gr. Migneault, donation par Paul Paquin père à François et Jean-Baptiste Paquin, 21 February 1837. Cf. ibid., donation par Marguerite Terrien à Jean Arpain, 6 July 1835; donation par Pierre Garant à Louis Garant, 25 January 1837; donation par Pierre Royer père et uxor à Louis Turcot fils, 2 September 1837; donation par Hélène Gendron à Charles Maranda et uxor, 14 March 1838; donation par Joseph Auger à Joseph Auger fils et uxor, 22 June 1838; donation par Joseph Bonier et uxor à Augustin Bonier, 29 Sep-tember 1838; donation par Louis-Eustache Charron et uxor à Eustache et Pierre Charron, 28 September 1839; ANQM, gr. L. Bourdages, donation par Louis Lefebvre et uxor à André Dupré et Marie Magdelaine Lefebvre, 8

October 1830; donation par Françoise Joubert à Jean-Baptiste Kimmeneur dit Laflamme son fils, 30 November 1830; testament d'Augustin Desmarais, 15 April 1831; donation par Jean-Baptiste Beaudro dit Graveline et uxor à Charles Beaudro dit Graveline leur fils, 20 August 1831; donation par Sr Jean-Baptiste Lussier et uxor à Jean-Baptiste Lussier fils, 15 September 1831; AJS, gr. N-D. Crebassa, donation par Jacques Potvin père et uxor à Jacques Potvin leur fils, 26 June 1832

28 See, for example, ANQM, gr. Migneault, donation par Pierre Royer père et uxor à Louis Turcot fils, 2 September 1837

29 ANQM, gr. C. LeNoblet Duplessis, répertoire

30 Wolf, *Peasants* 15–17

31 Lambert, *Travels through Canada and the United States*, 1: 131; Robert L. Jones, 'Agriculture in Lower Canada, 1792–1815,' *CHR* (March 1946) 33–51; Fernand Ouellet and Jean Hamelin, 'La crise agricole dans le Bas-Canada (1802–1837),' *Etudes Rurales* 7 (October–December 1962) 45–7

32 ANQM, gr. Jehanne, bail à ferme par René Guertin à Jacques Emery Codère, 29 April 1791

33 ANQM, gr. Migneault, bail à ferme par Frse. Meunier veuve Jos. Bernais à Jos. Delande dit Champigny, 28 January 1830

34 ANQM, gr. Jehanne, bail à ferme par Jean-Baptiste Corbeille à Pierre Corbeil, 19 September 1778

35 Ouellet and Hamelin, 'La crise agricole'; Fernand Ouellet, *Economic and Social History of Quebec 1760–1850; Structures and Conjonctures* (Toronto: Gage 1980) 186–95; Ouellet, *Le Bas-Canada* 177–96. For a critique of the concept of 'soil exhaustion,' see McInnis, 'A Reconsideration' 15–19.

36 Ivanhoe Caron, *La colonisation de la Province de Québec*, vol. 1: *Débuts du régime anglais 1760–1791* (Quebec: L'Action Sociale 1923) 275–80; Joseph Bouchette, *A Topographical Dictionary of the Province of Lower Canada* (London: Longman, Rees, Orme, Brown, Green, and Longman 1832), [unpaginated] 'St Denis'; census of Canada, 1844

37 Raw data are from the censuses of 1765 and 1831. The earlier census gives figures for all grains together and only for amounts planted. The 1831 census, on the other hand, distinguishes the various varieties of grain and provides figures, not on sowing, but on amounts harvested.

Harvest figures were estimated for 1765 on the assumption that seed-yield ratios were 1: 5.8 as suggested by R.C. Harris (*The Seigneurial System in Early Canada: A Geographical Study* (Madison: University of Wisconsin Press 1966) 153). It was further assumed, on the basis of information examined earlier, that two-thirds of the aggregate grain harvest at that time would have been wheat. On the basis of these assumptions, the figures on grain sown in 1765 were converted into harvest figures, for wheat and for all grains, consistent with the information provided by the census of 1831.

38 Ouellet, *Economic and Social History* 160, 259–60
39 *JHALC*, 1816, App. E
40 *JHALC*, 1823, App. T
41 Dechêne, *Habitants et marchands* 327
42 Fernand Ouellet, 'L'agriculture bas-canadienne vue à travers les dîmes et la rente en nature,' in *Eléments d'histoire sociale du Bas-Canada* (Montreal: Hurtubise 1972) 37–88
43 R.L. Jones, 'French-Canadian Agriculture in the St Lawrence Valley, 1815–1850,' in *Approaches to Canadian Economic History*, ed. W.T. Easterbrook and M.H. Watkins (Toronto: McClelland and Stewart 1967) 116; W.H. Parker, 'A New Look at Unrest in Lower Canada in the 1830's,' *CHR* 40 (September 1959) 209–17
44 ANQM, gr. Migneault, déclaration des sieurs Joseph Bousquet et Charles Lebau, 12 June 1839
45 Ibid., guardian's account book, 1831–7, enclosed with estate inventory of Jean-Baptiste Bourgeois and Agathe Leblanc. Note that these rental payments do not represent the total produce of the farm, but only the portion (probably one-half or one-third) turned over to the owner. Note also that grain was normally sold in the calendar year after it was harvested. The figures for 1831 therefore represent the produce of 1830, and so on. Cf. ibid., account book enclosed with estate inventory of Michel Dufault, 1 March 1830.
46 PAC, MG 29, C37, Sir Hugh Allan, 'Some Sketches of Events in an Active Life' 5–6 (I would like to thank Jean-Claude Robert for bringing this document to may attention). Cf. Bouchette, *A Topographical Dictionary*, 'St Denis,' 'St Ours.'
47 The samples involved are admittedly quite small and therefore the difference between the 1790s mean and that of the 1830s is not statistically significant. The figures are nevertheless suggestive and they certainly give no hint of any impoverishment. A study of 92 habitant estate inventories from the larger region of western Lower Canada shows a similar upward tendency in average fortunes. Mean net worth was 1587 livres in the period 1760–90; 1724 livres, 1791–1823; and 4609 livres, 1824–54. Pilon-Lê, 'L'endettement des cultivateurs québécois' 382
48 The contrast should not be overdrawn, however. See Michel Morineau's unflattering evaluations of the productivity of small holdings in England and France before 1840. *Les faux-semblants d'un démarrage économique: agriculture et démographie en France au XVIIIe siècle* (Paris: Armand Colin 1971) 24–6, 80–2
49 *JHALC*, 1816, app. E, testimony of David Anderson

50 Scottish Records Office, Dalhousie Diary, 14 July 1822, 22 May 1823
51 Robert Brenner, 'Agrarian Class Structure and Economic Development in Pre-Industrial Europe: The Agrarian Origins of European Capitalism,' *Past and Present* 97 (November 1982) 16–113.
52 ANQM, gr. Migneault, 1832–9, passim
53 Ibid., inventaire de Pierre Fortier et Marie Mercure, 29 April 1839. See also, 1831 census; ANQM, gr. Dutalmé, conventions des enfants de Pierre Noel Fortier à Marie-Angélique Charrette, 2 November 1808; ANQM, gr. Bourdages, contrat de mariage de Pre. Fortier et Marie-Elizabeth Mercure, 18 September 1811; ANQM, gr. Migneault, vente par Louis Robichaud à Pre. Fortier, 27 July 1831; ibid., obligation de Pierre Fortier à Sr Joseph Bousquet, 27 July 1831; Pierre Loiselle, *Mariages de St-Denis-sur-Richelieu (comté de Verchères) (1740–1964)* (Quebec: B. Pontbriand 1965) 102–3.
54 ANQM, gr. Bourdages, donation par Christophe Lussier et sa femme à Jean-Baptiste Lussier, 28 December 1811
55 Ibid., vente par Amable Brodeur à J-Bte. Lussier, 22 May 1817; ibid., vente par J-Bte Lussier et sa femme au Sr Antoine Gazaille dit St Germain, 23 June 1821; ibid., transport par Louis Gautron dit LaRochelle à J-Bte Lussier, 11 February 1822; ibid., vente par J-Bte Lussier et uxor à François Gaudet dit LeBlanc, 19 July 1824
56 ANQM, gr. Migneault, donation par J-Bte Lussier à Florentin Lussier et Marie Ledoux, son fils et bru, 28 June 1825; ibid., donation par J-Bte Lussier à Pierre Lussier, 28 June 1825; ANQM, gr. Bourdages, donation par Sr J-Bte Lussier et uxor à J-Bte Lussier fils, 15 September 1831
57 ANQM, gr. Bourdages, testament de Jean-Baptiste Lussier, écuier, 18 September 1831; ibid., testament de Marie-Josephte Gaudet, 18 September 1831
58 V.I. Lenin, *The Development of Capitalism in Russia* (Moscow: Progress Publishers 1967) 37–9, 41–2, 129–43, 175–90, 315–22
59 Teodor Shanin, *The Awkward Class: Political Sociology of Peasantry in a Developing Society: Russia 1910–1925* (Oxford: Clarendon Press 1972). Cf. Lutz Berkner, 'The Stem family and the Development Cycle of the Peasant Household: An Austrian Example,' *American Historical Review* 77 (April 1972) 398–418; A.V. Chayanov, 'Peasant Farm Organization,' in Daniel Thorner, Basile Kerblay, and R.E.F. Smith, eds, *A.V. Chayanov on the Theory of Peasant Economy* (Homewood, IL: American Economic Association 1966) 53–69.
60 C.P. Lucas, ed., *Lord Durham's Report on the Affairs of British North America* 3 vols (Oxford: Clarendon Press 1912) 2: 31
61 See, for example, R. Cole Harris and John Warkentin, *Canada before Confederation: A Study in Historical Geography* (New York: Oxford University Press 1974) 65–108.

62 Ouellet, *Le Bas-Canada* 175

APPENDICES

1 For a more detailed critique of the Lower Richelieu censuses, see Greer, 'Habitants' 21–6.
2 See Table 6.
3 For a more complete discussion of this source, see Dechêne, *Habitants et marchands de Montréal au XVIIe siècle* (Paris and Montreal: Plon 1974) 378–80 and Gilles Paquet and Jean-Pierre Wallot, 'Les inventaires après décès à Montréal au tournant du XIXe siècle,' *RHAF* 30 (September 1976) 163–221. On similar sources in other countries, see Ad Van de Woude and Anton Scheurman, eds, *Probate Inventories: A New Source for the Historical Study of Wealth, Material Culture and Agricultural Development* (Wageningen, The Netherlands: Afdeling Agrarishe Geschiedenis Landbouwhogeschool 1980).
4 Ouellet, *Economic and Social History* 65

Index